The Great Transformation of China

China's Economic Transformation, Innovation and Development

Series Editor
Fulin Chi
China Institute for Reform and Development
Haikou, Hainan, China

China is facing unprecedented challenges in its continued modernization process. This series brings together government insiders, academics, and policymakers in articulating specific social and political issues that China is trying to resolve, offering scholars around the world insights into what China's leadership see as the biggest challenges facing the nation and how best to resolve them. The series publishes monographs and edited volumes with contributions on a global basis dedicated to ground-breaking research on the Chinese modernization process.

More information about this series at
http://www.palgrave.com/gp/series/15346

Fulin Chi

Winning at the Turning Point

The Great Trend of China's Economic Transformation

ZHEJIANG UNIVERSITY PRESS
浙江大学出版社

palgrave macmillan

Fulin Chi
China Institute for Reform
and Development
Haikou, Hainan, China

Translated by
George G. Chen
Beijing, China

ISSN 2509-6001 ISSN 2509-601X (electronic)
The Great Transformation of China
ISBN 978-981-32-9478-3 ISBN 978-981-32-9479-0 (eBook)
https://doi.org/10.1007/978-981-32-9479-0

Jointly published with Zhejiang University Press, Hangzhou, China
The print edition is not for sale in Mainland of China. Customers from Mainland of China please order the print book from: Zhejiang University Press.

This Palgrave Macmillan imprint is published by the registered company Springer Nature Singapore Pte Ltd.
The registered company address is: 152 Beach Road, #21-01/04 Gateway East, Singapore 189721, Singapore

Preface

The Year 2020: A Historic Choice of Economic Transformation and Upgrading

A great nation with 13 billion people is facing a changing situation it has never faced for a thousand years. Change, transformation, and innovation feature the main melody of the era. In this era of high integration of growth, transformation, and reform, "great transformation" is exactly what decides the destiny of China. In other words, not only will "toxic assets" left in the traditional system have to be eliminated completely but also the new way for further growth needs to be paved quickly while letting loose the new motive force of development.

The major transformation in China's "13th Five-Year Plan" (FYP) is historically decisive. With the economic transformation as the focal point, both social transformation and government transformation are in the crucial period of transition in which innumerable thorny problems have to be tackled. Our general judgment is that the year 2020 is like a "gorge" we have to jump over. Specifically, by the end of 2020 we will have eliminated the pressure on short-term growth and changed the way for economic development while achieving a comparatively prosperous society in an all-round way and becoming one of the high-income countries in the world. If we plan well enough to make the best use of 2020, a mid-term period in the 13th FYP, we can lay a solid foundation for the medium-to-long-term peaceful and sustainable growth. If we fail to grasp the historical opportunity of 2020, we will lose the initiative of "great transformation", thus resulting in multiple systemic economic risks.

The significant breakthrough for achieving the economic transformation and upgrading in the 13th FYP period is how to cope with "four threes". Firstly, three major trends: one for industrial transformation and upgrading from "made in China" to "intellectually made in China"; one for urbanized transformation and upgrading from scale to population; and one for consumption pattern upgrading from material to service. Secondly, three major challenges: one for achieving a major breakthrough in structural reform by enhancing the structural adjustment despite the economic downturn; one for "corner overtaking" by responding to the global new round of scientific and technological revolution and increasing the ability to innovate; and one for a real and down-to-earth reform. At present, the transformation depends more on the all-round breakthrough in reform. It couldn't move forward at all without the change in systematic structure. And the growth would suffer big pressures. Thirdly, three major goals: one for industry, namely forming the service-dominated industrial structure by accelerating the process of service in manufacture; one for a major motive force, namely forming a consumption-oriented new pattern of economic growth, in which consumption guides investment and domestic consumption becomes a main force that spurs economic growth; and one for opening-up, namely forming a new open pattern dominated by service trade so as to redouble service trade in scale. Finally, three major relationships to be handled properly: one between the short term and the medium-to-long term in which the best job should be done for 2020 (the mid-term period) while resolving contradictions in the short term, basing ourselves on the mid-term and keeping our eyes on the long term; one between speed and structure which requires accelerating the structural adjustment while maintaining an increase by 7% or so; and one between policy and system in which the key is to gain a policy advantage in achieving institutional innovation under the economic pressure.

The past 40 years of reform and opening-up have left us numerable valuable assets. The most valuable one is that the more complex the situation may be and the more fundamental the change in environment, the more determined we will be in carrying out the reform and pushing through the transformation. All these require that the "great transformation" need overall arrangement and ambitious planning, need a significant breakthrough in the reform of industrial structure, urban-rural structure, regional structure, ownership pattern, open structure and administrative power structure, and need prospective planning in green sustainable development and "internet plus" development trends.

By judging the transformational reform in the 13th FYP period, China (Hainan) Institute for Reform and Development (CIRD) and Zhejiang University Press have jointly designed and published this set of series entitled *The Great Nation in Great Transformation—Economic Transformation and Innovative Development in China*. The book series has paid attention to readability based on being strategic, prospective and academic. It is our expectation that the series will offer enlightenment to readers who are closely watching the transformational reform in China while playing an active role in promoting the transformational reform in the 13th FYP period.

The authors of the series are mostly well-known scholars in their own subject areas, who wrote their respective books in their spare-time. As the director of the editorial board of the series, I wish, first and foremost, to extend my sincere thanks to the consultants, editorial board members, authors, and the leadership and editors of the press.

Last but not least, this set of series covers a wide range of subject areas, each volume representing its author's own research conclusions and academic opinions. The set does not require consistency in terms of viewpoints. Any criticism and correction from readers are truly welcome.

Haikou, China
September 2015

Fulin Chi

Contents

List of Charts

Chapter 2

Chapter 3

Chapter 4

Chapter 5

Chapter 6

List of Tables

Chapter 4

Chapter 5

Chapter 6

Chapter 7

Chapter 8

Chapter 9

CHAPTER 1

General Introduction: The 13th Five-Year Plan—Economic Transformation and Structural Reform

Practical cases show that for a business or a region, it is typical to win at the turning point rather than at the starting point. How to win at the turning point is a major challenge for both businesses and the government. Firstly, the 13th Five-Year Plan period marks the key historical link for China's economic transformation and upgrading, which will laid a secure foundation for the country's sustainable growth in the next ten or twenty years. Secondly, the transformation and development in the 13th FYP period features the high integration of increase, transformation, and reform with transformational reform promoting the growth as a general trend. Thirdly, economic transformation and upgrading have enormous growth potential and market spaces, whereas we are confronted with an increase of multiple contradictions, risks and hidden dangers. To adapt to the general trend of economic transformation and upgrading, structural reform is needed to solve the structural contradiction for the major objective of economic transformation and upgrading in the 13th FYP period.

1 The 13th Five-Year Plan Period: A Basic Trend for Economic Transformation

Economic development owes its dynamics to structural change and institutional innovation. Economic transformation and upgrading represent the greatest potential and the focus of attention in the 13th FYP

F. Chi, *Winning at the Turning Point*, The Great Transformation of China, https://doi.org/10.1007/978-981-32-9479-0_1

development. Despite the current economic downturn and increasing pressure of structural adjustment, the trend of economic transformation and upgrading has begun to emerge.

1.1 Industrial Structure Is Transforming from Industry Orientation to Service Orientation

(1) The general trend towards a service-oriented industry is reflected in five respects. One, since the year of 2000, China's service industry has been growing rapidly with its value-added being doubled every five years. Two, the proportion of the value-added in the country's GDP has increased apparently from 41.3% in 2001 to 50.5% in 2015. Three, the service industry has become the leading force boosting the GDP growth. In 2014, the tertiary industry contributed 3.5% to the GDP increase, 0.1% higher than the secondary industry. Four, the service industry has turned to be a major sector for making innovation and undertaking business. In 2015, there were 358 million newly registered service enterprises in China, an increase by 24.5% as compared with the previous year, constituting 80.6% of the total number of newly registered enterprises. Five, the service industry has become a major source for employment. By the end of 2015, employees in the service sector have made up 42.4 of the total number.

(2) It is an economic law that service-oriented industrial structure is formed in Late Industrialization, in which the development of the modern service sector whose value-added is higher than industry and agriculture indicates the general orientation in which industrial structure evolves. In this particular period of time, the value-added of the service sector makes up more than 60% of the GDP. Generally, China's industrialization has undergone three stages since the reform and opening-up in 1978: the first stage is the initial stage of industrialization in which processed products and light industrial products took the leading position. The second stage is the mid-industrialization in which heavy industry and chemical industry constituted the major components of the industry. The third stage is the mid-and-late industrialization in which the service industry starts to become a leading industry. During the 13th FYP period (2016–2020), therefore, China has begun to enter Late Industrialization in which a service-oriented industrial structure is basically formed in terms of economic law.

(3) The 13th FYP period will witness the forming of a modern service-oriented industrial structure. Currently, there is still a big gap in comparing the process of China's service industry with the corresponding stage of industrialization. In 2015, for example, the value-added of China's service industry accounted for 50.5% of its GDP, 8–10 percentage points lower than the figure of the other countries of BRICS, and over 20 percentage points lower than that of the developed countries. The 13th FYP has set 56% as the expected target for the growth of service industry. Judging from the real situation, it is likely to reach 58% by 2020.

First, in the 13th FYP period or an even longer period, the conditions are favorable for the proportion of the service sector's value-added in the GDP to increase by 1.2 percentage points. It is projected that it will rise to about 58% by 2020 from the present 50.5%, or likely approach 60%. Thus, a service-oriented industrial structure will basically be formed.

Second, the service industry is expected to maintain an average annual rate of increase by 8–9%. And its value-added is likely to reach over 50 trillion yuan (US$8.33 trillion) by 2020 from the present 30 trillion yuan (US$5 trillion).

Third, the internal structure of service industry has been optimized to a large degree. Currently in China, the producer-service sector, focusing on research and development, finance, and logistics, only accounts for about 15% of the GDP, 40% or so of the service industry, while in terms of the manufacturing power of Germany, the corresponding proportion is about 40% and over 70% respectively. China's low proportion of the modern producer-service sector in the GDP represents an outstanding weakest link for the transformation and upgrading of its manufacturing industry. It is expected that China's innovation-driven strategy will enable the proportion to reach about 25% by 2020, which will become a powerful driving force for the transformation and upgrading of the country's manufacturing industry.

(4) The major conditions for the development of service industry will be dealt with in two aspects. In one aspect, the new round of technological revolution and the global trend of manufacturing transformation are facilitating the development of producer-service industry. In this context, global manufacturing in the future 5–10 years will be in the critical period transforming from production-oriented service industries to service-oriented industries. By now, among the 51 industries covered by the

Global 500 companies, 28 belong to the service industry, namely, 56% of the total number of the companies are engaged in the service industry.[1] At present, China's industrial transformation and the new round of global technological revolution have been joined. This will effectively facilitate the transformation and upgrading of China's manufacturing industry from production-oriented industries to service- oriented industries, creating essential external conditions for promoting the development of modern service industry, especially of producer-service industry.

In the other aspect, changes in residents' consumption pattern have promoted the rapid development of living services industry. These changes are an important internal driving force for the transformation of a country's industrial structure. Currently, demands for service consumption such as education, medicine, health, and tourism are rising rapidly and comprehensively, thus becoming an important driving force for the transformation of industrial structure and the development of modern service industry.

1.2 Urbanization Structure Is Transforming from Scale Urbanization to Population Urbanization

(1) Urbanization is still in the stage of rapid development. China's scale urbanization reached 54.7% in 2014, and rose to 56.1% in 2015. Generally, the urbanization process still lags far behind the industrialization process. Practically, in Late Industrialization, the urbanization rate of permanent population should be about 65%. At present, this rate in China is just a little above 55%, which is nearly 10% lower and still has room for development. In addition, the development of China's small and medium-sized cities is relatively slow. The regional distribution of new urbanization is not reasonable enough. And there is still a long way to go before urbanization arrives in Central and Western China.

(2) A new pattern of the urbanization of registered population will basically be formed during the 13th FYP period. Whether to coordinate urbanization with industrialization or to look at the practical needs of the overall construction of a moderately prosperous society, population urbanization ought to reach the following targets in the 13th FYP period:

[1] Chi Fulin: *Restructuring and Breaking the Blockade: Historical Challenges from Structural Transformation*, China Workers Press, 2016.

One, the urbanization rate of permanent population will not be lower than 60%. By deepening the reform of household register system and speeding up the equalization of basic public services both in urban and rural areas, the urbanization rate of permanent population in the future five years will possibly increase at an annual rate of no lower than 2%. By 2020, the urbanization rate of permanent population in China will have possibly reached 65% or so.

Two, the urbanization rate of registered household population will reach 50% or so. Although the urbanization rate of China's registered household population has surpassed 55%, that of its registered household population is rather low, only 39.9% in 2015, 16% lower than that of the permanent population. The low urbanization rate of the registered household population is an outstanding contradiction for China's new urbanization process, which is not fit for the goal of building a moderately prosperous society in an all-round way. The 13th FYP sets 45% as the expected target for the urbanization rate of the registered household population, and this target is likely to reach about 50% if the household registration system reform is quick enough.

(3) The historical conditions for urbanization have undergone fundamental changes. In the beginnings of the founding of the People's Republic of China there was no urban-rural binary household registration system in China. To accelerate its industrialization, China began to implement this system in the late 1950s. With industrialization growing till now, the historical conditions for the household registration system have changed fundamentally:

First, the urban-rural integration process has been accelerated notably. With the implementation of scale operation and acceleration of modernization in agriculture, there will be a growing trend for rural population to flow to cities.

Second, the structure of migrant workers from rural areas has undergone significant changes. As the post-'80s and post-'90s have become the main body of the migrant workers, most of them have settled in cities, and it would be difficult for them to return to the rural areas. One important objective of the household registration system reform during the 13th FYP period is to make the identity of "migrant workers" a past history.

Third, historical conditions have emerged to replace the urban-rural binary household registration system with residence permits. This practice will be a breakthrough for the comprehensive and further reform of the household registration system. To carry out the residence permit system in an all-round way, migrant workers should be given access to the same basic public services as urban residents. With regard to the design for residence permits, some people worried about the "basin effect" that might occur in large and medium-sized cities. In practice, however, the standard can be set higher for large cities, while for small and medium-sized cities it can be reasonably less strict. It is under such a condition that free population movement has begun to be allowed gradually. On the whole, with the prerequisite of accelerating the construction of public finance system and achieving the equalization of basic public services in urban and rural population, it is very likely for China to implement residence permits in an all-round way by 2020.

1.3 Consumption Pattern Is Transforming from Material Consumption to Service Consumption

(1) A historical key link for the change of China's consumption pattern. Since 2008, China has generally entered a new development stage in which people's development is an important goal. Urban and rural residents have spent more and more on the development of their own, which fully reflects a fundamental change in the stage of social development. In this new stage, urban and rural residents' consumption keeps growing. For instance, China's retail sales of consumer commodities increased to 30.09 trillion yuan (US$5.09 trillion) in 2015 from 18.39 trillion yuan (US$3.07 trillion) in 2011, with an average annual increase of 13.4%, 6.5% higher than the growth rate of the GDP.

(2) Consumption pattern that is upgrading rapidly. First, it is upgrading from subsistence consumption to developmental consumption. Urban residents' consumption priorities have changed from industrial consumer goods to services such as education, medical treatment, health, and tourism. Rural residents' consumption priorities have changed from living necessities to industrial consumer goods.

Second, it is upgrading from traditional consumption to new consumption. Chinese people's demands for such new consumption as green consumption, information consumption, and convenience consumption keep rising. For example, in the past ten years, urban and rural residents' information consumption has kept an annual increase rate of about 20%.

Third, it is upgrading from material consumption to service consumption. From 2000 to 2014, China's urban residents' service consumption per capita rose from 1960.92 yuan (US$326.82) to 7563.44 yuan (US$1260.57), an annual increase of 10.1%. And in terms of 2014, service consumption made up as high as 45.32% of the total consumption. It is expected that by the end of the 13th FYP period, this rate will increase to more than 50%, and even around 60% in some developed regions. This will be a powerful driving force for accelerating the development of modern service industry.

(3) The 13th FYP objectives for the upgrading of consumption pattern. The 13th FYP period will be a new stage in which urban and rural residents' service consumption will grow in a rapid and comprehensive way; thus the contribution rate of consumption to economic growth will obviously be increased.

First, the increase rate of social consumer goods' retail sales in 2015 was 10.6%, so it is possible for an average annual increase by 9–10% during the 13th FYP period.

Second, the overall consumption will rise to 50 trillion yuan (US$8.33 trillion) by 2020 from 30 trillion yuan (US$5 trillion) in 2015.

Third, the contribution rate of consumption to economic growth during the period of 2013 to 2015 increased from 48.2 to 66.4%. Considering that the increase was achieved despite the rapid decrease in contribution rate of investment, so the contribution rate of consumption to economic growth will remain steady at about 65% during the 13th FYP period.

2 The 13th Five-Year Plan Period: Economic Transformation and Upgrading and Economic Growth Potential

China's economy will grow at an intermediate speed in the 13th FYP period. The growth will take on an "L" shape, while a new driving force for growth will begin to emerge, and economic structure will change notably. On the whole, during the 13th FYP period, the average annual economic growth rate will remain 6–7%, and the average growth rate is expected to reach 6.5%. It implies that China will not only cross the middle-income trap successfully, but also make steady contributions to the world economic growth in the new stage.

2.1 The Outstanding Features of Transformational Growth

(1) It is obvious that economic growth is relying more on economic transformation. During the 13th FYP period, economic transformation has great potential for economic growth. A breakthrough in economic transformation will not only ease the pressure on short-term economic growth, but also form an important foundation for the medium-to-long-term sustainable growth.

(2) The successful transformation or otherwise of a region is subject to its economic growth. For instance, the "new Northeast phenomenon" is mainly caused by being both less adequate and less open in transformational development in Northeast China.

(3) Economic transformation and upgrading will release growth potential. Thanks to economic transformation and upgrading, the potential economic growth rate will remain 6–7%, which is an essential foundation for China's economic growth at an intermediate speed. As a new driving force is gradually formed, China is likely to achieve an annual economic growth by 6.5% during the 13th FYP period.

2.2 The Leading Role of Modern Service Industry for Economic Growth

(1) The effects of service industry on economic growth. The forming of the service-oriented industrial structure and the acceleration of tertiarization will bring fresh impetus to economic growth.

First, an initial calculation shows that by 2020 the value added of China's service industry will make up about 58% of its GDP, and the contribution rate of service industry to economic growth will increase to 72.5–79.6% from 62.8% in 2014.

Second, during 1978–2014 when China's industrialization was in the stage of rapid development, the contribution rate of every 1% rise of the secondary industry represented 0.62% of economic growth, and that of every 1% rise of the tertiary industry represented 0.33%.

Third, according to initial estimates, during the 13th FYP period, the contribution rate of every 1% rise of the service industry will go up to 0.49% in economic growth, bringing along 3.8–4.3% of economic growth.

(2) The impact of modern service industry on innovation. Take regional innovation for example. Every 1% rise of service industry will contribute a 10.4% growth of regional innovation, and every 1% rise of

regional innovation will contribute a 4.3% increase in service industry's proportion to the GDP.

(3) Promoting the transformation and upgrading of manufacturing industry by way of modern service industry. The key to making China's manufacturing industry bigger and stronger lies in accelerating the development of producer-service industry, which will lead the manufacturing industry to a medium-to-high level. As high-end manufacturing is a global trend, it is necessary to take hold of this trend and extend manufacturing to the service link and shift pricing power to the service link as well, hence facilitating the transformation of manufacturing industry from production orientation to service orientation. At present, it is imperative to reform the irrational incentive system in scientific research, and create an environment which is conducive to scientific research and development with the policy featuring result-oriented evaluation and favoring scientific and technical personnel.

(4) Service-oriented industrial structure leading the economic new normal. First, 6.5% will be the new normal of economic growth rate. The value added of service industry will increase by around 9% annually, laying a significant foundation for China to keep its economic growth rate around 6.5%.

Second, a steady and gradual increase in employment will be a new normal. According to statistics, in 2008, every 1% rise of China's GDP only created 700,000–800,000 new jobs; and in 2013, every 1% rise of China's GDP created 1.5 million new jobs.[2] It means that employment is not only related to economic growth but also to the transformation of industrial structure, and that the service sector has become a major source for increasing employment.

Third, it will be a new normal of mass entrepreneurship and innovation. Modern service industry is a sunrise industry, a most promising area for the broad masses of people to make innovation and undertaking business.

Fourth, gradual improvement in benefit structure will be a new normal. The increase in the number of employees in the service sector, especially in the producer services industry will effectively change the benefit structure and rapidly expand the middle-income group.

[2] Li Keqiang: Every 1% Rise of GDP Creates 1.5 Million New Jobs. *Workers' Daily*, November 5, 2013.

Fifth, green growth and green transformation will be a new normal. An initial calculation shows that if the proportion of the tertiary industry as to China's GDP of 2012 increased to 55% from 46.1%, China's national energy consumption would be expected to decrease by 14.16%, and sulfur dioxide emissions be expected to reduce by 18.23%.[3]

2.3 *Consumption's Role in Driving Economic Growth*

(1) Consumption is an indispensable driving force for economic growth. With the help of service consumption, consumption has become an important engine for promoting economic growth. A rapid growth of service consumption will bring historical changes to the role of investment and consumption in fuelling economic growth, and gradually establish consumption's leading role in fuelling economic growth. In 2011, the contribution rate of consumption to economic growth was 62.83%, surpassing that of investment (45.35%) for the first time. In 2015, the contribution rate of final consumption to the GDP growth was 66.4%, 14.8% higher than the previous year. Consumption has thus gradually established its No. 1 role in driving economic growth.

(2) Over 1.3 billion people's comprehensive and rapid consumption growth is not only the greatest highlight of China's economic growth, but also an outstanding advantage for its economic transformation. Despite the slight decline of China's economic growth in 2015, consumption in practice has facilitated industrial transformation and played a role in stabilizing economic growth. It has been proved by practice that consumption is both the goal for production and the driving force of production.

(3) Service consumption guides the rapid development of new forms of business operation. Transformation of consumption pattern drives economic transformation, while service consumption facilitates the increase of service economy's proportion and level, becoming a driving force for economic transformation and upgrading. Take health service for example. In recent years global health service accounts for about 15.6% of the total expenditure, whereas it is only about 1.5% in China. At present, the role of consumption in facilitating economic

[3]Chi Fulin: Forming the Service-Led Industrial Structure. *People's Daily*, August 26, 2015.

transformation and upgrading has not been given enough attention in China. Therefore, it is through the supply-side structural reform and release of 1.3 billion people's consumption demands that would become an essential internal productive power for China's economic growth.

2.4 The Significant Impact of New Urbanization on Economic Growth

(1) Population urbanization still remains an important driving force facilitating economic growth. To speed up population urbanization process in the 13th FYP period will release tremendous dividends for development: it not only promotes consumption but also helps to expand investment space, creating favorable conditions for cutting overcapacity and destocking. Research shows that every 1% rise of urbanization level will lead to 1.5–2% rise of GDP. It is expected that by 2030, small and medium-sized cities will become the most powerful driving force for China's economic growth, contributing 40% of urban GDP growth.[4]

(2) Population urbanization will spur investment effectively. A calculation shows that in recent years every one new urban resident will bring about 100,000 yuan (US$16,667) of investment, and that if 270 million migrant workers from rural areas become urban residents, it will bring 27 trillion yuan (US$4.5 trillion) of government investment. It is expected that China's permanent population will reach 60% or more in 2020, bringing about 42 trillion yuan (US$7 trillion) of investment.[5]

(3) Population urbanization will boost consumption considerably. Research shows that every 1% rise of urbanization rate will lead to 2% rise in urban population's annual consumption expenditure.[6] Currently, China's urban population's consumption is 3.6 times the amount of rural population's. In the coming 5–10 years, population urbanization will bring immense consumption potential.

[4]Zhou Zixun: New Urbanization May Become a New Driving Force for China's Economic Growth. *China Economic Times*, December 22, 2014.

[5]Chen Qingsong: A Rigorous Financial Test for New Urbanization. *China Enterprises News*, April 1, 2014.

[6]Zhu Min: How to Give Better Play to Urbanization's Role to Boost Consumption. *China Economic Times*, May 13, 2013.

2.5 *Five Major Relationships Needing to Be Well Handled for the Transformational Development in the 13th FYP*

(1) Speed and structure. During the 13th FYP period, China's economic transformation faces both numerous problems resulting from short-term economic downturn pressures and important opportunities for medium-to-long-term development potential released by economic transformation and upgrading. In this particular context, therefore, it is essential to plan well and follow closely the development path to economic transformation and growth, allowing transformational development to release enormous potential of economic growth. So attention should be paid to the adjustment of economic structure and the improvement of economic quality while economic growth is maintained at the rate of 6.5%.

(2) The short term and the medium-to-long term. The short-term plan cannot be made separate from the medium-to-long-term plan. Contradictions and hidden troubles in the short term cannot be left for the medium-to-long term, nor can the adjustment of economic structure in particular be delayed for the sake of short-term economic acceleration. To solve short-term problems, the first step should be taken for economic transformation and upgrading, and then short-term contradictions be resolved by taking the long view of 2020 (the mid-term). In a nutshell, both temporary and permanent solutions to economic problems ought to be sought.

(3) Policy and system. In the current economic situation, short-term policy stimulation can support keeping economic slowdown no worse at all. To ease off economic downturn pressures, however, policy stimulation is not the major resort. The key solution to the problems is to adapt to the development trend and bring about the amplification effect of policies in making institutional innovation. Furthermore, policies should match institutional innovation so as to promote the systemic innovation.

(4) The government and market. Numerous structural contradictions in economic life stem from a distorted government-market relationship caused by too much administrative intervention which is, however, unconsciously adopted often by the government in cutting overcapacity, destocking, and deleveraging. To implement structural reform, it is imperative to prevent both the government from replacing the market and the return of economic growth in the government-dominated mode.

(5) Overarching design and infrastructural innovation. Overarching design is important for structural reform, but infrastructural innovation is even more so. China is a major country in transformation, and regional

situations differ tremendously. Many reforms cannot be carried out in the same way. Reforms need to take full advantage of both overarching design and infrastructural innovation are a must. In other words, overall planning has to be coordinated and promoted with a greater determination and courage to break though vested interests. Meanwhile, pilot reforms should be arranged to meet the demand of economic transformation and upgrading, and local governments should explore innovation based on the local situations so as to give full play to innovation at the grassroots. Local governments are also encouraged to go ahead with pilot reforms based on the local reality by following the Central Government's unified arrangement. An incentive mechanism should be instituted to encourage reform, and more decision-making power should be given to local governments, thus creating a favorable environment for comprehensive social reform.

3 Structural Reform with Economic Transformation and Upgrading as the Main Line

The important objective of structural reform is to promote economic transformation and upgrading. One of the highlights of the 13th FYP is to adapt to the trend for economic transformation and upgrading and promote economic transformation and upgrading. To resolve structural contradictions in economic transformation by way of structural reform depends on how much structural reform is effectual by adapting to the need of and the trend for economic transformation, and on how quickly measures will be advanced to play a pulling role for supply-side structural reform so as to achieve the dynamic equivalence between supply and demand. Economic transformation and upgrading raise internal requirements for structural reform, and its dependability on structural reform is obvious enough. For structural reform is the most essential condition for promoting economic transformation and upgrading.

3.1 Marketized Reform with the Opening of Service Industry Market as a Focal Point

(1) It is a main trend from industrial market to service market. Whether it is upgrading from industry orientation to service orientation, upgrading from material consumption to service consumption, and upgrading

from scale urbanization to population urbanization all raise new requirements for the opening of service market. During the 13th FYP period, the key to marketized reform is whether market can adapt to the main trend for industrial transformation, consumption transformation and urbanization transformation, allowing market to play a decisive role in resource allocation in the service sector.

Since the reform and opening-up that started in 1978, the market opening in the industrial field has stimulated market vitality greatly, playing an essential role in pushing forward the country's quick industrialization. During the 13th FYP period, to realize the opening of industrial market to service market will bring about powerful driving force for the development of the country's service industry, thus releasing generous dividends for the new round of marketized reform.

(2) The opening of service market that lags behind is a weakest link of marketized reform. First, low marketization of service industry. According to statistics, more than 80% of China's industrial sector is the manufacturing industry, which belongs to the department of high marketization, whereas more than 50% of the service sector, which belongs to the department of monopolistic competition, has still been monopolized by the administrative power.[7] At present, such service markets as education, healthcare, and civil aviation have been open to social capital. The problem is that marketized reform in these fields is lagging behind; State-owned enterprises (SOEs) have still monopolized the market, whereas private enterprises are always in a weak position.

Second, low openness of service industry. For example, the four Pilot Free Trade Zones (PFTZ) in Shanghai, Guangdong, Tianjin and Fujian have played an important role in promoting the openness of service market. Judging from the negative list of the four PFTZs, however, there are still quite a few restrictions on the service industry. For example, the negative list contains 122 Special Administrative Measures, 80-odd items of which are targeted for the service industry. This is well above common international standards.

Third, low level of service. As phenomena of monopoly are available in many services, service quality is generally not high. Recent years have witnessed constantly increased complaints from consumers for service

[7] Zhang Bin: Logic of the Downturn Trend of China's Economy, *21st Century Business Herald*, October 14, 2013.

quality. During the period of 2010–2014, for example, the number of complaints about service from every ten thousand consumers registered by the consumers' associations in China went up to 2.08 from 1.49, an increase by 39.6%.[8]

Four, high service price. In the situation of price control and no effective competition, prices have stayed high in many services. In 2015, for example, China's broadband internet access average speed ranked No. 91 in the world, whereas one megabit per second internet access fees were 3–5 times higher in China than in developed countries.[9]

(3) The opening of service market is the "largest dividends" of marketized reform. At present, as far as the increase in social capital investment is concerned, the service sector has surpassed the industrial sector. The proportion of social capital in fixed asset investment is more than half of the total amount. The opening of service markets can reverse the rapid decline in investment. The gradual opening of educational, medical and telecommunications markets will make enormous room for social capital in investment, thereby speeding up social capital's access into service sector. Take healthcare industry for example. It is expected that by 2020 the country's total consumption will be higher than the total medical consumption and market potential of healthcare industry will rise to 8 trillion yuan (US$1.33).[10]

(4) The important tasks of opening service market. First, attention is to be paid to handle well both the interest of the industry and that of the department, while breaking up the administrative monopoly and market monopoly of service market.

Second, the facilitation reform of service market needs to be promoted so that social capital becomes the main force motivating the development of modern service industry.

Third, all prices should be liberalized in service market so as to form a unified, open and fair market system.

Four, adjusting the policies of land appropriation for the service sector and industrial sector have to be sped up to achieve the policy equality for

[8] Quality Is the Key for the Service Industry to Reach the Medium-to-High Level. *China Quality News*, December 9, 2015.

[9] Chi Fulin: *Restructuring and Breaking the Blockade: Historical Challenges from Structural Transformation*, China Workers Press, 2016.

[10] Wang Changlin: The New Force Propelling the Growth of 7% Industry. *Guangming Daily*, August 7, 2015.

both sectors. But prices of land use for service industry have been 4–5 times higher than those of industrial land on average, the prices for service industry being even as high as 9 times.

Five, business tax are to be replaced with value-added tax in the whole service industry. To speed up the adjustment of tax policy should be guided by the promotion of the opening of service market. Also, a favorable policy environment should be created for service growth by structural tax cuts.

(5) The opening of public service market ought to be accelerated with the focus on the government's purchase of public services. In the opening of service market, the role of the government is of vital importance, but too much administrative intervention by the government ought to be reduced. In terms of government procurement, the objective is high efficiency and low cost with a view to increasing the supply efficiency of public service and reducing the supply cost of public service effectively.

3.2 Structural Policy Adjustment and Structural Reform with Optimizing the Environment of Enterprise Development as a Focal Point

(1) It is of urgency to optimize the environment of enterprise development in the period of economic transformation. In the context of economic transformation and upgrading, real economy faces tough challenges, and therefore space should be created by relying on market for the transformation and development of enterprises. In the process of economic transformation and upgrading, the government should create a market environment and market space for the development of State-owned enterprises. Meanwhile, State-owned enterprises (SOEs) should create opportunities to achieve the transformation of product structure, organizational structure, and institution, promoting mergers and the reorganization of enterprises actively and steadily.

At present, resolving overcapacity has become an important task of supply-side structural reform. During the economic transformation, some overcapacity industries will gradually get out of the difficult position. At the same time, the government should offer appropriate policy support to zombie enterprises that still have space for further development.

(2) There should be a new breakthrough for enterprise decentralization. In these two years decentralization has made important progress in

reducing the number of approvals. The next important step is to reduce the institutional cost of enterprises.

First, the national business name registration system will be implemented by drawing on the international trade system. At present, the trade system reform has made substantial progress but there is still some room for improvement.

Second, the management system of general investment projects will be abandoned at an appropriate time. In the conditions in which the development of real economy goes at a rather slow speed, the said management system needs to be abandoned ASAP, thus being conducive to the grand environment of innovative market development.

Third, industrial policy will be replaced by fair competition policy. In the stage of industrial take-off, industrial policy is able to play an extremely important supporting role for industrial growth. When the market economy system is basically formed, however, government functions should be transformed and market regulation be enhanced while replacing industrial policy with fair competition policy.

(3) Entrepreneurship is to be encouraged to protect the property rights and innovation income of entrepreneurs. As the main roles in supply-side structural reform are enterprises and entrepreneurs, attention should be paid to entrepreneurship in industrial transformation and the policy environment, legal environment, market environment and social environment be constructed.

(4) Some breakthrough should be made in mixed ownership. State-owned enterprises need to cut overcapacity through reform. In the current situation in which financial revenue grows slowly, if SOEs need to get out of the difficult situation, they have to make a new breakthrough in developing mixed economy and, through various means, enable social capital to be involved in SOEs' reform, vitalizing the enterprises.

3.3 The Second Round of Opening-up with Service Trade as a Focal Point

(1) The dependability of economic transformation and upgrading on service trade increases markedly. Unlike 2001 when China joined the WTO, the manifest challenge in foreign trade during the 13th FYP period is the market opening of service trade in two directions.

First, upgrading of domestic consumption pattern calls for the acceleration of the opening process with service trade as a focal point, which is to develop the service-oriented manufacturing industry while establishing service standards, consumption standards and environmental standards. Therefore, the opening of service trade should be sped up so as to adapt to the upgrading need of domestic consumption pattern.

Second, the focus of the new global round of trade liberalization lies in service trade. After joining the WTO, the country's foreign trade policy is supposed to focus on the market opening of goods trade. At present, service trade is not only the focus of bilateral free trade agreements and regional free trade agreements but also the focus of multilateral free trade agreements. In this background, opening to the rest of the world needs to focus more on the service trade-centered market opening.

Third, opening of service trade has become a basic trend for China's further opening-up. In the initial stage of industrialization, China grasped the historical opportunities of increasing the needs of global trade in goods and of transfer of developed countries' manufacturing industry while promoting the direct global integration of manufacturing industry. As a result, the country has become the second largest economy and the first largest goods trading nation, thus making enormous contributions to the growth of global economy and trade. In the future five years, the process of service trade-centered global free trade will be accelerated markedly, whereas the dependability of the country's economic transformation and upgrading on the internal and external opening of service trade and service market will increase apparently. In this context, therefore, the characteristics and focal points of the country's opening will make a marked change.

(2) The lag in service trade growth has been the "short board" for the country's supply-side economy. Although China has been the largest goods trading nation in the world, service trade takes up a rather low percentage. In 2014, global service trade made up about 20% of the total foreign trade, while China only accounted for 12.3%. In 2014, China's service trade volume numbered US$604.3 billion, constituting less than one sevenths of the goods trade volume, which accounted for more than 10% of the world's total goods trade volume whereas the service trade volume only for 6.2% of the world's total. Among the top ten service trading nations of the world, China's service trade volume averaged US$448 per capita, which made up 12% of the U.S's, 6% of Germany's and 16% of Japan's respectively. This requires taking rapidly increasing

the service trade level as the key point to optimize the trade structure and expand effective supply.

(3) Service trade is to be taken as a focal point to speed up the "second round of opening-up". In comparison with the "first round of opening-up" featured by opening industrial market in order to make China's manufacturing industry globalized, the second round of opening-up's historical mission is to comprehensively implement free trade strategy with service trade as a focal point, to orderly propel the internal and external opening of service market. Meanwhile, the process of global free trade will thus be pushed on, and an important role will be performed during the new round of global free trade.

(4) The development of service trade needs to attach importance to the establishing of China-Europe Free Trade Area. On June 30, 2015, European Union, for the first time, expressed support for the feasibility study of China-Europe FTA. To establish China-Europe FTA is importantly significant. Firstly, it will play an important role in improving governance structure globally and stabilizing economic growth. Secondly, it will be a win-win situation in which Europe opens up China's market while China transforms and upgrades its consumption pattern. If the joint percentage of China's and Europe's service trade rises to 20%, the total service trade volume will be somewhere between €200 billion and €2200. This will be a big boost to China's economic transformation and upgrading, especially in environmental protection and service- oriented technical transfer of manufacturing industry. In this connection, therefore, an opportunity has to be grasped to conduct the feasibility study of China-Europe FTA and negotiations on investment and trade with service trade as a key.

3.4 Decentralization with Regulatory Transformation as a Main Point

(1) Regulatory changes are a key to decentralization developing in depth. In economic transformation and upgrading, to play a better government role is a key to regulatory transformation. In reality, however, being hard to achieve a breakthrough in reform in economic and social transformation has a lot to do with being out of place in regulatory transformation. At the same time, the root cause why "once decentralization it would lead to disorder" is being backward in market regulation transformation. Therefore, such backwardness has been

the biggest "short board" as well as the biggest obstacle for decentralization. The key to decentralization development in depth is regulatory transformation.

(2) New measures are required for regulatory system transformation. At present, no clear separation of powers between approval and regulation represents the most manifest contradiction. Take securities market regulation. In reality, the above-mentioned power combination tends to make the related authority pay more attention to approval while neglecting the independence, professionalism, authority and standardization of regulation/supervision. The key to resolving the contradiction between both powers is to separate them. Besides, separation is to be achieved between decision-making power, executive power, and supervision power in regulatory transformation.

(3) The independence, authority and professionalism of the market regulatory agencies should be protected. The administrative power structure of optimized market regulation should be adjusted. Unified comprehensive market regulatory agencies be established ASAP in the financial field, consumption field and anti-monopoly field, thus forming a new situation of market governance collaboratively by the government and society. At the same time the leading role of the government's market regulation is stressed, the autonomy of various types of market players should be guided actively to increase the enterprise's social credibility, enhance the self-discipline of market players, and do business honestly, while giving full play to the self-disciplinary role of trade organizations and to the supervisory role of public opinions and the general public. By doing so can the ecological system of unified, open, and fair markets gradually be formed and the market governance system adaptable to the market economy soon be established.

(4) Regulatory changes are a profound government revolution. Regulatory changes involve a series of revolution about the idea, interest and power structure of the government. This revolution is both profound and complicated, calling for further common understanding and ever greater determination and resolution to break the vested interest.

CHAPTER 2

Industrial Change as a Turning Point from Industry Orientation to Service Orientation

The core of China's economic transformation and upgrading during the 13th FYP period is industrial structural change. For one thing, industrialization has entered the late stage in which a general trend is marked by the accelerated development of service industry. For another, contradictions caused by irrational industrial structure have become ever manifest. In terms of service-oriented industry structure formed in 2020, the key is to propel the opening of market by breaking the monopoly as an essential point while making an effort to resolve the contradictions between policy and system during the opening of service industry.

Forming the structure of service-oriented industry represents the objective law of evolution of industrial structure in China's Late Industrialization. The problem is that owing to the opening of service market that lags far behind, the institutional structure has not yet been formed to release the development potential of service industry. A transfer from industrial market opening to service market opening has become a primary task to complete structural reform during the 13th FYP period.

1 A Main Trend Towards Service Orientation

During the 13th FYP period, as industrialization enters the late stage, whether industrial transformation and upgrading or urbanized structural changes will raise a new requirement for accelerating the development of modern service industry. It will be a main trend from industry orientation to service orientation.

F. Chi, *Winning at the Turning Point*, The Great Transformation of China, https://doi.org/10.1007/978-981-32-9479-0_2

1.1 The New Global Round of Industrial Revolution Will Clearly Show the Importance of Developing the Producer Services Industry

The 13th FYP period is the crucial time for China's transformation of industrial structure. The new global round of industrial revolution and China's Late Industrialization will converge historically, and the dependability of industrial transformation and upgrading on the development of producer services industry will be enhanced in an all-round way.

(1) The arrival of Industrial Revolution 3.0 and Industrial Revolution 4.0

If the history since the Industrial Revolution is divided into four periods, Industrial Revolution 1.0 (1760–1860) was the period of steam engine; Industrial Revolution 2.0 was the period of electrification. Driven by the Internet, big data technology and more, Industrial Revolution 3.0 and Industrial Revolution 4.0 are arriving almost at the same time. Industrial Revolution 3.0 features "the Internet + new energy", thereby propelling the human society to say good-bye to the petrochemical energy gradually. Industrial Revolution 4.0 is marked by "the Internet + the manufacturing industry", thus introducing the manufacturing industry into the Digital Age. While the new global round of revolution has brought a new opportunity for industrial development, it has been undermining and eroding the foundation of traditional heavy industry and chemical industry. Since 2015 the prices of petroleum, coal, and nonferrous metal have dropped sharply, causing energy-depending countries to get into hot water. For example, in the beginning of 2016, the oil price fell below the lowest point since the international financial crisis in 2008. Generally speaking, in the new industrial age, the factors of production are characterized by softening of the industrial structure, which is distinctly different from the traditional industrial age. An industrial power would be subject to its powerful industrial service capacity but not to its powerful production capacity.

(2) Industrial Revolution 3.0 that depends on the producer services industry

At present, it is urgently necessary for China to fight off challenges from increasingly serious environmental pollution, ecological destruction, and shortage of energy resources via Industrial Revolution 3.0. It is by replying on new energy that haze problems in particular could be solved. In other words, systemic restructuring should be done to traditional industries like power, automobile, and iron and steel. Take photovoltaic solar energy to be introduced extensively into millions of families. The point for the example is not the making link of solar PV but the service link. The core problem waiting to be solved is whether it is in line with the growth of modern service industry with new and high technology as an important point. Furthermore, research and development as well as sales have to be enhanced while reducing the transaction cost, so that surplus electric power of the families will be sold timely.

(3) Industrial Revolution 4.0 that relies more on the producer services industry

With Germany's intelligent manufacturing as a representative, industrial powers have been trying to capture the height of Industrial Revolution 4.0. The return of manufacturing to the U.S. is not based on traditional Industrial Revolution 2.0 but on Industrial Revolution 4.0. In this context, China's manufacturing industry is facing the rise of the cost of such factors as labor force and land and the challenge of gradually losing traditional competitive edge. How to build the foundation of its Industrial Revolution 4.0 and how to regain its international competitive edge of manufacturing industry have become an unavoidable big problem for its industrial transformation and upgrading in the 13th FYP period. For example, in the manufacturing process, all related data for design, research ad development, and production are gathered and analyzed through the sensor, forming an automatic intelligent production system. In this way, information technology can be infiltrated into the production links and traditional processing equipment be transformed with intelligent equipment and advanced technology, thus promoting the change in production mode from large-scale, homogenous and extensive production to intelligent, digital, intensive and flexible production.

1.2 New Requirements Raised for the Development of Living Services Industry by New-Type Urbanization

During the 13th FYP period, China has been transforming from scale urbanization to population urbanization. With the process of population urbanization speeding up, demand for the development of modern service industry is pressing on a daily basis.

(1) Population urbanization that propels the change from industry orientation to service orientation

After nearly 38 years of reform and opening-up, China's urbanization has been growing from industry-oriented urbanization to service-oriented urbanization. As social groups of new generation like the post-'80s and the post-'90s have become the mainstream group, they have raised very high their requirements for urban service quality has risen rapidly while they tend to choose jobs in the service sector rather than in the traditional industrial sector. Cities built up by heavy and chemical industries in the past will see their citizens flow out if there is a lack of service quality in these cities. But people will flow into Cities whose economy is propped up by modern service industry will gradually become a vast agglomeration of population and form a motive force for sustainable economic growth. According to the report prepared by OECD (Organization of Economic Cooperation and Development) concerning China's urban policy review in 2015, big Chinese cities with a population surpassing 10 million have reached fifteen. In addition to Beijing, Shanghai, Guangzhou and Shenzhen, the first four such cities, there are Wuhan, Chengdu and Chongqing in Central China and Southwest China, followed by Tianjin, Hangzhou, Xi'an, Changzhou, Shantou, Nanjing, Ji'nan, and Harbin in the new list. The reason these cities are able to attract population inflow boils down to more developed service industry, higher city life quality, and more competitive job offering. On the contrary, however, according to the 6th national population census in 2010, the total population of Northeast China's three provinces was 109.95 million, which means net population outflow of 1.8 million in the past ten years based on the 5th population census in 2010.[1] This phenomenon reflects to a large degree the difficult situation faced by the traditional industry-oriented cities.

(2) Population urbanization whose dependence on the development of living services industry is fully enhanced

[1] Net Population Outflow of 1.8 Million from Northeast China Within the 10 Years: An Investigation to be Conducted by the National Health and Family Planning Commission. *Beijing News*, November 12, 2015.

Judging by international experience, Late Industrialization along with the rapid growth of population urbanization will enable a country to promote urbanization quickly. However, as the development of education, healthcare, culture, care service for senior citizens, and entertainment lags behind, as there is a big gap between the urban and rural areas in basic public services, the contradiction that the urbanization process is behind the industrialization process is still very glaring. The rate of China's present registered population urbanization is not yet 40%, well below the global average level of 60% in population urbanization in Late Industrialization. If further reforms in the household registration system are carried out during the 13th FYP period, the registered population urbanization rate is expected to rise to 50% or so.

1.3 Consumption Pattern Upgrading and Moving Towards a Service Power

China has entered the new age of consumption at present. Only by following the general trend for upgrading consumption upgrading and speeding up the development of modern service industry can a new opportunity for the new stage of development be grasped to release the new motive force so as to gain the initiative in stabilizing the growth, promoting the reform, adjusting the structure, benefiting people's livelihood and preventing risks.

(1) Consumption pattern upgrading is an essential prerequisite for forming the service-oriented pattern

① Consumption upgrading brings an enormous demand for service upgrading. Along with the constant increase in economic growth, changes in consumer demand of the general public chiefly reflect an increase in factors they pursue for service quality. In other words, consumption upgrading can't do without service upgrading. Take software development for example. It is past the age in which software is developed to match hardware, although the production of some new hardware is still in considerable need of software development, the greatest demand of which is actually to meet the most direct service needs of consumers. Therefore, to expand domestic demand and promote consumption in the 13th FYP period has to place service upgrading as a top priority.

② Release on service-oriented consumption demand spurs the development of service industry. For example, these years with big data and more new IT revolution developing, the living services industry has kept upgrading. Such services as mobile learning, mobile medical care and mobile health have been growing fast, promoting the transformation and upgrading from traditional living services industry to modern living services industry. Big data-driven industrial transformation and upgrading should be sufficiently oriented to the service of new consumer demands and of ever higher, more convenient education, health and fitness.

③ Service-oriented consumer demand release promotes the transformation and upgrading of traditional industries. For example, urban and rural residents in the survival stage take food and clothing as their main objective. After solving the problem of food and clothing, they raise the high requirements for the environment, safety and service of food, which promotes the constant innovation and development of catering service and the transformation from traditional agriculture to green agriculture. In the situation in which more and more attention is paid to green food consumption, therefore, there will be more and more pressure and impetus of transformation and upgrading from traditional agriculture and green agriculture.

(2) Expanding the market space of service industry growth by upgrading consumption pattern

① Consumption pattern upgrading provides enormous market space for the innovation and development of service industry. Take e-commerce for example. Although the development of Alibaba.com and Jingdong.com, Inc. can be ascribed to constant innovation in their own service, technology, marketing and management, the core cause is to manage to grasp the historical opportunities brought by the upgrading of Chinese residents' consumption pattern and release on consumer demand. What's more, both e-companies have succeeded in combining modern IT, adapting to the change of consumption pattern of modern urban residents, and further developing an effective approach to release on consumer demand. Tmall's total trading volume of "November 11" in 2015 reached 912.17 trillion yuan (US$152.03), an increase by 59.72% as compared with the previous year. With the upgrading of consumption pattern and the acceleration of release on consumer demand, the market space for innovation and development of service industry will be larger and larger.

② The growth of consumer demand promotes the forming of a trend for rapidly growing service industry. Consumption upgrading along with rapid expansion of consumption scale has generated the prime power for becoming a service power, driving the service industry to be a leading industry in national economy. Since the international financial crisis in 2008, China has begun to go from a big producer to a big consumer. Some worried about the possibility that being a big consumer would reduce the competitiveness of the country's economy, making the rest of the world hard to bear. From a realistic point of view, however, consumption pattern upgrading will provide a motive force for becoming both a big consumer and a service power. Growing into a big consumer will bring modern service enterprises like Alibaba and Apple Inc. enormous market space. Release from China's consumption potential will be a contribution to China itself and to the world as a whole.

(3) Providing the constant power for the innovation and development of service industry by upgrading consumption pattern

The basic point of departure for innovation is to satisfy the needs of human beings. Only by meeting the market demand of service innovation can market returns be achieved. In the years of sellers' market, commodities could be sold once they were produced by enterprises, which seldom cared about consumer service and experience. With buyers' market being formed, consumers would have more choices for commodities. The competitiveness of enterprises is not merely subject to the quality of commodities but more and more to service quality. No matter whether it is a retailer, manufacturer, or a consulting firm, enterprises that is able to adapt to consumers' needs and make innovation in service will decide their own competitiveness. For example, the reason why Apple Inc. is a powerful enterprise is thanks to the core of Apple mobile phones. It is a new software development model, which turns service into software, an innovative model for consumer service. Consumers can thus use more powerful phones in a more convenient and comfortable way. Take another example from the Haier Group Corporation. Its household electrical appliances are of good quality, but its after-sales service has become much better known as the Haier Model. Consumers have not only bought quality products but enduring quality service.

Release on demand of over 13 billion consumers is promoting the innovation and development of China's service industry, while providing market opportunities for numerous international modern service giants. To grasp the major trend for consumption pattern upgrading and plan the overall arrangement and development of modern service industry actively will become the important task for economic transformation and upgrading in the 13th FYP period.

2 Forming Service-Oriented Industrial Structure Basically

Compared with the previous situation, China's present basic situation is changing fundamentally. Its main reflection is that the service industry will be the clear highlight of economic growth, becoming both the main engine powering economic growth and the driving force propelling the upgrading of the whole industrial structure. By 2020, forming the industrial structure with the service industry as a leading role will have become the essential condition for achieving China's industrial transformation and upgrading.

2.1 *Modern Service Industry Growth Is an Important Prerequisite for Ranking Among the World's High-Income Countries*

The basic trend for global economy is marked by the full growth of modern service industry, which is a distinctive feature of high-income countries. Being a middle-income country and developing modern service industry constitute an important prerequisite for becoming a high-income country.

(1) The full growth of service industry is a basic trend for global economy

According to the development law of the world's industrial structure, as the world's industrialization process advances constantly, the full growth of service industry will a basic trend for global economy. Since the mid twentieth century, global economy has been undergoing a profound structural change, which features the transformation of global economy to service economy especially in developed European and American countries. For example, during the period of 1980 to 2004, the value added of global service industry increased from 56 to 68% (even to 72% in high-income countries, 53% in middle-income countries, and 49% in low-income countries) in proportion to the GDP. In terms of employment rate by service industry, in 2009, high-income countries made up 68.5%; upper-middle-income countries made up 56%; and lower-middle-income countries made up 47.3%.[2]

(2) Developing service economy is a distinctive feature of the industrial structure of developed countries

The rapid growth of modern service industry with higher value-added than traditional industry and agriculture is the only way to a high-income country. Since the 1950–1960s, no developed countries have failed to undergo the structural change of service-oriented economic transformation. In other words, the value added of service industry and employment contribution account for a leading position in economic social development (see Table 1). In terms of the proportion in 2004, the U.S. made up 77%; France 76%; the U.K. 73%; Japan, Singapore and South Korea 68, 65 and 56% respectively. In terms of employment rate by service industry, in 2009, high-income countries reached 68%.[3]

2.2 *Forming Service-Oriented Industrial Structure Basically*

Forming service-oriented industrial structure basically will not only have decisive influence over China's economic transformation and upgrading but also lead the new normal of economy, upgrading the economic structure to a new stage.

(1) Service industry will clearly show its position and role in national economy

① Service industry will expand in scale constantly. During the 2000 to 2015, the value added of China's service industry rose from about 3.97 trillion yuan (US$0.66 trillion) to about 34.16 trillion yuan (US$5.69), an increase by 7.6 times. Basically, the value added of service industry doubled every five years (see Chart 1). The year of 2012 was a turning point and its value added of service industry reached 24.3 trillion yuan

[2] Chen Xian et al.: *China's Service Economy Report of 2009*, Shanghai University Publishing House, 2010.

[3] Please refer to the same-title book mentioned above.

Table 1 The value-added of countries' service industry in proportion to employment by service industry (unit: %)

	Low-income countries		*Lower-middle-income countries*		*Upper-middle-income countries*		*High-income countries*	
	Service	*Employment by service*	*Service*	*Employment by service*	*Service*	*Employment by service*	*Service*	*Employment by service*
Average	44.1	27.3	53.5	44.5	60.4	58.3	68	69.8
Median	44.9	25.5	55	41.8	62.5	59.9	71.1	71.3
Max.	63.4	44.3	79	61.9	78.3	75.2	98	85.8
Min.	21.3	8.6	19.6	24.7	20	28.4	4.7	54.4
SD	11	12.9	13.8	10.1	13.1	9.3	16.9	8.2
Sample	33	8	49	20	45	31	44	51

Note Countries are categorized as per World Bank standards. The countries are divided into four categories according to GNI per capita: low-income countries, lower-middle-income countries, upper-middle-income countries, and high-income countries. The division standards are specified as below: lower than US$995; US$996–3945; US$3946–12,195; US$12,196 to up; Sampling is based on the following data: the proportion of the value-added of service industry is mainly from the data of 2009 that contain 171 valid samples. The data for a few countries are from 2008 or earlier for lack of data needed. The data about employment rate by service industry are mainly from 2007 that contain 110 valid samples for serious lack of data of 2008 and 2009; and Reference: Jiang Xiaojuan: "Service Industry Growth: Real implications, Multiple Effects, and Development Trends", *Economic Research*, Issue 4, 2011

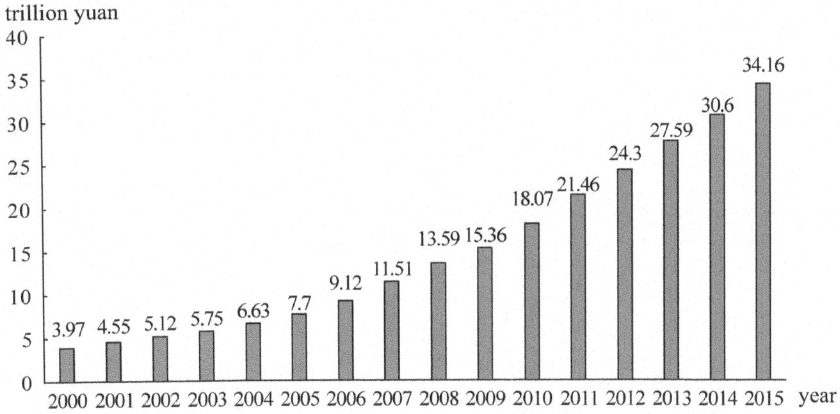

Chart 1 Increase in value added of service industry in 2000–2015 (*Source* National Bureau of Statistics: *China Statistical Yearbook 2015*, China Statistics Press, 2015; *Statistical Bulletin of 2015s National Economy and Social Development*. http://www.stats.gov.cn, February 29, 2016)

(US$4.05 trillion), which for the first time surpassed the value added of the industry (24.02 trillion yuan or US$4 trillion). In 2015, the value added of the secondary industry was 27.4 trillion yuan (US$4.57 trillion), whereas that of the tertiary industry was 34.16 trillion yuan (US$5.69), a figure being 6.76 trillion yuan (US$1.13 trillion) larger than that of the secondary industry. It is a prevailing trend that the service sector surpasses the industrial sector in scale.

② Service industry will grow faster than other industries. Since the beginning of the twenty-first century, the increase in value added of China's service sector has surpassed that of the industrial sector most of the time. From 2001 on, when the proportion of the secondary industry in the GDP was surpassed by that of the tertiary industry for the first time, the tertiary industry grew faster than the secondary industry in 11 years out of the total 15. In 2015, the secondary industry grew at the rate of 6.0%, whereas the tertiary industry at the rate of 8.3%, which is an increase by 2.3 percentage points over the secondary industry (see Chart 2).[4] It is clear that in the circumstances of overcapacity reduction

[4]National Bureau of Statistics: *Statistical Bulletin of 2015s National Economy and Social Development*. http://www.stats.gov.cn/, February 29, 2016.

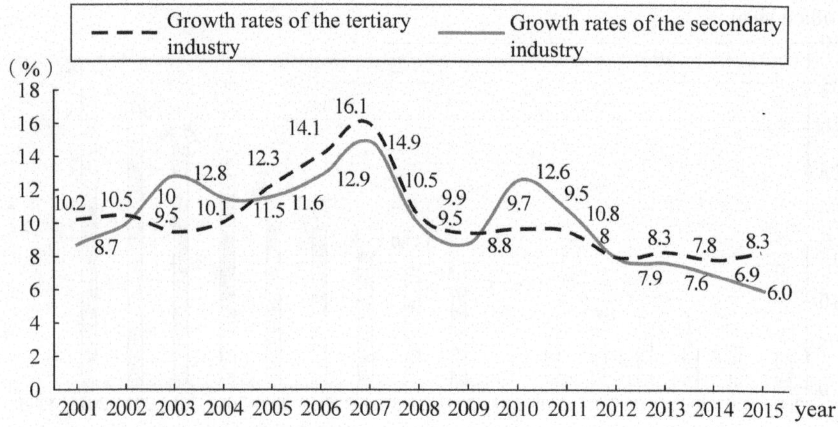

Chart 2 A comparison of growth rates of China's tertiary industry and the secondary industry in 2001–2015 (*Source* National Bureau of Statistics: *China Statistical Yearbook 2015*, China Statistics Press, 2015; National Bureau of Statistics: *Statistical Bulletin of 2015s National Economy and Social Development.* http://www.stats.gov.cn/, February 29, 2016)

the service industry can serve as an important factor for stabilizing economic growth and as a main engine for promoting economic growth.

③ Service industry begins to become a leading force spurring the GDP's growth. In 2013, China's tertiary industry promoted the domestic GDP's increase by 3.7 percentage points, which is balanced with that promoted by the secondary industry. In 2014, China's tertiary industry promoted the domestic GDP's increase by 3.5 percentage points, which is 0.1 percentage points higher than that of the secondary industry (see Chart 3).

(2) There is still tremendous room for improvement in terms of the proportion of service industry in the GDP

In 2015, the value added of China's service industry in the GDP reached 50.5%, a figure much lower than that of developed countries registered in 2000 on average (70.1%), and lower than that of Russia, Brazil, and South Africa of BRICS respectively. Generally, compared with these three countries, the value added of China's service industry in the GDP is at least 10 percentage points lower. Compared with developed

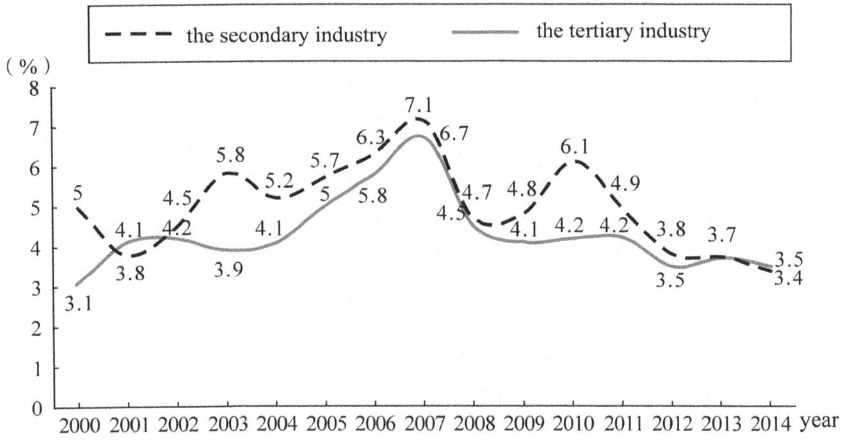

Chart 3 Promoted increase of GDP by the secondary industry and the tertiary industry in 2000–2014 (*Note* "Promoted increase" refers to the growth rates of GDP multiplied by the contribution rates of three industry types. *Source* National Bureau of Statistics: *Statistical Bulletin of 2015*, China Statistics Press, 2015)

countries, it is at least 20 percentage points lower (see Chart 4). Compared with the real demands of Late Industrialization, it is at least 6 percentage points lower. All these show there is enormous room for the market development of China's service industry.

(3) Towards service industry-oriented strategic objectives

① The proportion of service industry in the GDP will have reached 58% or so by 2020. From the observation of the 12th FYP period, China's 12th FYP points out, "By 2015, the value added of the country's service industry in the GDP will have increased by 4 percentage points as compared with 2010", namely, an increase from 43 to 47%. Actually, however, the said value added went up by 3.5 percentage points over the target set by the 12th FYP. In this case, in the 13th FYP period or even longer period of time, it is possible that the value added will increase by 1.2 percentage points. It is estimated that by 2020 the value added of China's service industry in the GDP will grow from 50.5 to 58% and likely close to 60%. Thus, the service-oriented industrial structure will basically be formed in China.

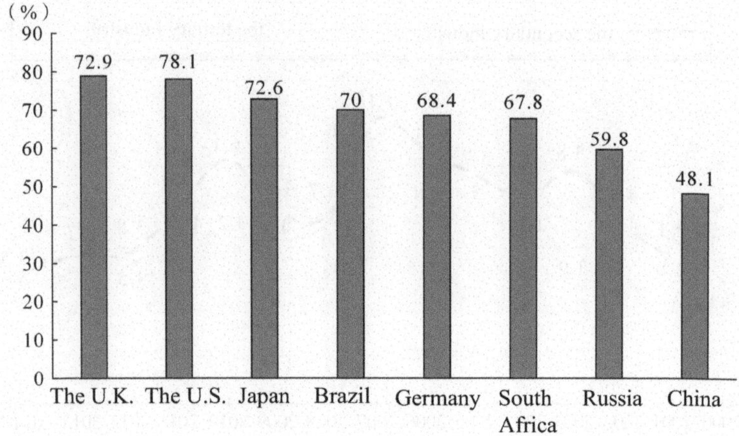

Chart 4 Proportions of China's and some other countries' service industry in 2013s GDP (*Note* The data for China is that of 2014. *Source* National Bureau of Statistics: *Statistical Bulletin of 2015*, China Statistics Press, 2015)

② Service industry will maintain an increase by 8%. By initial calculation, if the proportion of service industry is to increase by 58% or so during the 13th FYP period, the value added of service industry is required to increase annually by about 8% on average. Considering that the value added of 2015s service industry reached 34.2 trillion yuan (US$5.7 trillion), an increase by 8.3% as compared with the previous year, it is suggested that an average increase by 8% in the value added of service industry should be set as the important binding target for the 13th FYP period.

③ The scale of service industry will surpass 50 trillion yuan (US$8.33 trillion). Since the international financial crisis in 2008, in the context where the domestic and foreign economic situation has undergone a profound and complicated change, the value added of China's service industry has risen form 13.6 trillion yuan (US$2.67 trillion) in 2008 to 34.2 trillion yuan (US5.7 trillion) in 2015, achieving the two-fold increase in scale. If this growth rate or an increase by 8–9%, is to be maintained in the 13th FYP period, the value added of the country's service industry is expected to rise from 34.2 trillion yuan (US$5.7 trillion) in 2015 to 50.2 trillion yuan (US$8.37 trillion)—50.6 trillion yuan (US$8.43 trillion) in 2020 (see Table 2).

Table 2 An estimated increase in the 13th FYP's service industry

Year	*Value added of service industry (100 million yuan) (the growth rate: 8%)*	*Value added of service industry (100 million yuan) (the growth rate: 9%)*
2016	368,892.4	372,308.0
2017	398,403.8	405,815.7
2018	430,276.1	442,339.1
2019	464,698.2	482,149.7
2020	501,874.0	525,543.1

Source These figures are based on changes of value added of service industry in the future five years, which is calculated roughly by taking the value added of 2015s service industry as the base and according to the annual growth rate of 8 and 9%

2.3 *Service Industry Orientation Leads the New Normal of Economy*

During the 13th FYP period, forming service industry-oriented industrial structure is the strategic choice for adapting to and leading the new normal of economy. To achieve this important objective, it can bring about the new normal of economy growing at a medium and high speed on the basis of transformation and upgrading, and guide the new normal of development in expanding employment, making innovation and undertaking business, harmonizing the different interests, and promoting green environmental protection.

(1) Forming the new normal of economy growing at an intermediate speed

During the 13th FYP period, if service industry can maintain the double-digit growth or a bit lower growth rate (8–9%), the value added of China's service industry is expected to increase twofold to 50.2–52.6 trillion yuan (US$8.37–US$8.77 trillion), which will lay a sound foundation for the new normal of maintained moderate growth of the country's economy at a rate of 6–7%. In this way, therefore, China's total GDP by 2020 will have reached 85.5–91.34 trillion yuan (US$14.25–US$15.22 trillion), with GDP per capita being over US$11,000. China is thus expected to enter the rank of high-income countries from the upper-middle-income countries.[5]

[5] Chi Fulin: *The Choice of Transformation for 2020—Trend and Challenge for China's Economic Transformation and Upgrading*, China Economic Publishing House, 2015.

(2) Forming the new normal of constantly increasing new employment opportunities

Data shows that in 2008 with each one percentage point increase in the country's GDP it would create new employment for 700,000–800,000 people. In 2013 with each one percentage point increase in the country's GDP it would absorb 1.5 million people for new employment in cities and towns.[6] In other words, the employment problem has to do with the speed and industrial structure. As economic transformation and upgrading speeds up, the service-oriented industrial structure will serve as the main carrier to expand employment. In the next five years, China will have to solve the employment problem for 6–7 million college graduates every year while a considerable part of the agricultural employment population of 240 million will transfer to urban areas. In such a grave situation, to ease the medium-to-long-term pressure on employment effectively, it is necessary to rely on the vigorous development of service industry, forming a new situation in which the service industry will create new jobs.

If the service industry is able to create as many jobs during the 13th FYP period as the present GDP (for 1.5–1.7 million people), if the value added of the industry grows at an average annual rate of 9%, at least 13.5–15.3 million jobs will be created every year.[7] This will effectively cope with employment for agricultural transfer population, labor force released from the transformation and upgrading of manufacturing industry, and new labor force increased every year.

(3) Forming the new normal of green development

Service-oriented economic transformation has a distinctive feature of guiding industrial structure upgrading, which will apparently reduce the dependence of economic growth on the resource environment forming a service-oriented industrial structure means the change of economic growth mode. In other words, the growth mode to be gradually realized

[6] Li Keqiang: One Percentage Point Increase in GDP Creates 1.5 Million Jobs. *Workers' Daily*, November 5, 2013.

[7] Chi Fulin: *The Choice of Transformation for 2020—Trend and Challenge for China's Economic Transformation and Upgrading*, China Economic Publishing House, 2015.

is from one that relies on resource factor input and at the cost of high environmental cost to another in which attention is paid to increase resource efficiency and environment-friendliness. From the viewpoint of green development, it is important to strengthen environmental protection, but it is more important to make a change in industrial structure. According to initial calculation, if the proportion of service industry increases from 50 to 55% in the next five years, China's total energy consumption will decrease about 14% while carbon dioxide emissions will decrease by 18%.[8] Therefore, to make a new service-oriented way by which to achieve industrialization and urbanization with the lower cost of resource environment will be to create an active condition for reaching the objective of China's and global carbon emission reduction, and an important support for realizing China's green development.

(4) Forming the new normal of mass entrepreneurship and innovation

① Developing more space for doing business with service industry. As service industry requires much less capital, its threshold and difficulty for starting business are lower than the manufacturing industry. Transnational corporations that grew rapidly are chiefly part of the service industry, like Amazon, Google, Facebook and other international service giants. Take Zhongguancun, China's first new and hi-tech industrial development zone in Beijing. In 2013 the total income of Zhongguancun modern service industry exceeded 2 trillion yuan (US$0.33 trillion), an increase by 53.8% as compared with 1.3 trillion yuan (US$0.22 trillion) in 2011. This record-high figure made up 66.7% of the total income of Zhongguancun's enterprises, a nearly five-percentage-point increase over 61.8% in 2011.[9] In light of the law of industrial development, service industry, featuring various divisions with high individualization and diversification, can offer enormous space for doing business. One thing worth noticing particularly is the rapid development of China's big data and Internet industry has brought the traditional industries opportunities for mode remaking. Many such industries

[8]Chi Fulin: Transformation and Reform Towards a Service Power—The Megatrend for China's Economic Transformation and Upgrading in 2020. *Journal of Shan ghai University (Social Science Edition)*, Issue 1, 2015.

[9]An Investigation Shows the Lowest Confidence for the Development of Innovative Service Industry, accessible at http://www.eeo.com.cn/, June 19, 2014.

can achieve large-scale disintermediation through online customization, bringing about the new round of business launching.

② Guiding the innovation wave with service industry. With the opening of service market and under the guidance of enormous consumer demand, China is expecting great waves of entrepreneurship and innovation. Take DiDi and KuaiDi for example.[10] These two taxi-hailing APPs companies of less than three years of age have made a tremendous impact on the traditional taxi service area. In addition, corresponding APP emerged in traditional housekeeping service, whose O2O mode has begun to be marketized. It can be expected, therefore, that with improved informatization, the service mode as of DiDi and KuaiDi will be adopted in traditional service industry.

(5) The new normal that guides the gradual optimization of interest structure

① The proportion of compensation of employees (CE) should be increased in a service industry-oriented way. As the service industry is a human capital intensive industry, whether in traditional service industry or modern service industry, service quality is directly related with human beings but loosely related with capital factors. Since the service industry depends highly on the development of people with lower requirement for constant capital but higher requirement for variable capital, the proportion of CE in the service sector is generally higher than that of CE in the industrial sector. Judging by the situation of other countries, CE has a direct relation with the proportion of service industry. Generally, the higher proportion of service industry those countries may have, the higher probability there will be the higher proportion of their CE (see Table 3). Judging by the Chinese situation, according to the calculation of the research group of China (Hainan) Institute for Reform and Development, during the period of 2005–2012, the correlation coefficient between the proportion of service industry in all provinces and the proportion of CE reached 0.97. As the proportion of service industry increased by one percentage point, the proportion of CE would increase by 0.38 percentage point. During the 13th FYP period, if the proportion

[10] **[The Translator's Notes]** Didi Dache and Kuaidi Dache, China's Two Largest Taxi-Hailing APPs, Merged in 2015 to Become the Largest APP Company in China.

Table 3 The proportion of service industry in economies and the proportion of compensation of employees (unit: %)

Countries	*The proportion of service industry*	*The proportion of CE*
Mexico	62.2	28.21
Poland	84.8	36.81
Czech Republic	60	42.09
Italy	72.9	42.29
South Korea	58.2	44.86
South Africa	67	45.16
Australia	77.9	47.53
Spain	71.3	48.77
Russia	59.3	50.14
Japan	71.5	50.6
The Netherlands	64.8	51.06
Germany	71	51.25
Canada	66.1	52.3
France	79.2	53.31
The U.K.	77.6	54.41
The U.S.	78.8	55.32

Note CE (compensation of employees) is calculated in home currency based on 2010; In terms of data for the proportion of service industry, data for Canada is based on 2008; those for France on 2009; and those for South Africa and Mexico on 2011; and The proportion of CE is arranged in ascending order
Source The data are prepared based on ***International Statistical Yearbook 2013***

of China's service industry could increase by about 10 percentage points, the proportion of CE would increase by 3.8 percentage points, namely, an increase from 45.6% in 2013 to 49.4% in 2020, which is close to 50%.[11] This will, therefore, reverse the constant decline of CE in China while optimizing the distribution pattern of national income sustainably.

② The middle-income group size should be expanded in a service industry-oriented way. Judging from the international experience, the rapid growth of service industry will facilitate the steady development of middle class greatly. Take the U.S. for example. During the period of the 1940s–1970s, thanks to the forming of service industry-oriented setup, the size of the U.S.'s white-collar class increased fivefold. Judging from the Chinese situation, although China's middle class has only about 25%

[11] Chi Fulin: *The Choice of Transformation for 2020—Trend and Challenge for China's Economic Transformation and Upgrading*, China Economic Publishing House, 2015.

of the national population, its proportion will probably have reached 35–40% by 2020, with the service industry growing sustainably and being able to create employment ceaselessly. It is thus estimated that the proportion of middle class will have reached 35–40% by 2020. During the 13th FYP period, if the proportion of employment in service industry reaches more than 50%, the employment population in service industry will be no less than 400 million. Both in producer services industry like finance, modern logistics and research & development and in living services industry like education and medical care, there will be enormous potential for nurturing and forming the middle class nationwide.

3 Service Sector as a Weakest Link in Marketized Reform

Since China's reform and opening-up in 1978, its market has opened mainly in the industrial sector, whereas the service market has lagged seriously and the service sector has become the weakest link in national marketized reform. To speed up the market opening from the industrial sector to the service sector is an important way for forming the service-oriented industrial structure.

3.1 The Service Sector Has Become the Weakest Link in Marketized Reform

Since China's reform and opening-up, with the industrial sector as the focus, the serious backwardness of service market boils down to "three low's and one high": low marketization of service industry, low openness to the outside world, low service level, and high service price.

(1) Low marketization of service industry

Data show that over 80% of China's industrial sector is the manufacturing industry, which belongs to a highly marketized department.[12] When social capital enters the service market, it will not only face being excluded by the national monopolistic industry but have to go

[12] Zhang Bin: The Logic of China's Economic Downward Trend. *21st Century Business Herald*, October 14, 2013.

through miles of red tape for administrative approval. At present, service markets such as education, medical care, and aviation have been open to social capital. The problem with these domains, however, is that their marketized reform has lagged behind: SOEs have still been in a monopolistic position, whereas non-State-owned enterprises have been in a weak position. For instance, the total number of China's privately run hospitals at present are close to half of the total number of State-owned hospitals, but the former have only made up about 10% of the market of medical care industry.[13]

(2) Low openness of service market to the outside world

Since 2013, China has chosen Shanghai, Guangdong, Tianjin and Fujian as Pilot Free Trade Zones (PFTZs). Generally speaking, the opening of service market is an important content for the four PFTZs, especially in financial, educational, cultural, and medical markets which have opened much greater to foreign capital. Based on international experience, in free trade agreements between countries, developed countries generally have fewer restrictions than developing countries. The former have less than 30 items for restrictions, whereas the latter have less than 40 items (see Table 4). Although the four PFTZs have made considerable progress in the opening of service industry at present, the negative list used by the PFTZs imposes somewhat tough restriction on the service industry. For the list contains 80-odd items out of the 122 special governing measures targeted on the service industry, well above general international standards, which in turn restricts the service trade growth.

(3) Low service level in service industry

Compared with developed countries, the value added of China's service industry in the GDP is relatively lower. This is only a superficial phenomenon. The crux of the matter, however, is that the service level in the sector is generally not high. For example, in telecommunications, the Internet speed is slow and service complaints are too many to count. In tourism, customer satisfaction has been on the decline for years straight.

[13] Private Hospitals Equal Public Hospitals in Number but Only Make Up 10% of the Market. *Qingdao Daily*, April 10, 2014.

Table 4 Categorized industries in which the negative list of restrictive measures for international investment is available (unit: item)

Party (A/B)	*Date of contract*	*Classification standard*	*Primary industry*	*Secondary industry*	*Tertiary industry*
The U.S.	05/06/2003	CPC	0	2	29
Singapore			0	7	68
The U.S.	06/06/2003	HS	0	2	28
Chile			3	3	57
The U.S.	01/01/2005	HS	0	2	30
Australia			1	0	27
Australia	07/30/2008	CPC	2	1	37
Chile			3	3	40
Canada	12/05/1996	CPC	3	7	29
Chile			3	5	33
Japan	03/29/2007	CPC, JSIC	2	7	47
Chile			3	2	26
Japan	02/20/2011	ISIC, NIC	3	7	19
India			12	14	7

Source Fan Zhenglan and Zhang Baoming: International Comparison and Empirical Study on the "Negative Listings". *Shanghai Journal of Economics*, Issue 12, 2014

According to statistics from China Tourism Academy, the index of national tourists' satisfaction went from 80.66 in 2012 down to 74.1 in 2014. Complaints lodged by consumers because of service quality problem kept increasing. By the end of 2014, the country's consumers' association had received 2.08 out of ten thousand complaints about service, which is an increase by 39.6% based on 1.49 complaints out of ten thousand service complaints in 2010.[14]

(4) Higher market price in service industry

It is reasonable to some extent that the government takes price control of basic public service. But the development of quite a few services in China needs to be promoted by making use of price mechanism and competitive mechanism. Although in recent years it has lifted price control in a large number of services, the government has still exercised too

[14] Quality Is the Key for the Service Industry to Reach the Medium-to-High Level. *China Quality News*, December 9, 2015.

general, too much price control. According to *the Central Government Pricing Catalogue* promulgated by the National Development and Reform Commission in October 2015, the Central Government has reduced the pricing range to 7 categories with 20 items, a reduction by about 80%.[15] But the prices for water, electricity and gas, for postal charges, and banking service have still been in control. Price control gives rise to service market price distortion. For example, the telecommunications industry is one of the domains of whose capital the state holds the highest percentage. Despite the introduction of social capital in sales link these years, competition still remains inadequate. The service price is high and the improvement of service quality is slow. According to statistics from Akamai, China ranked No. 91 worldwide in broadband average Internet access speed in 2015, which is only 18% of South Korea's Internet access speed. But the cost of average one megabit per second broadband Internet connection in China is 3–5 times as much as in developed countries.[16]

3.2 The Market Opening from the Industrial Sector to the Service Sector

Since the reform and opening-up in 1978, the market opening of the industrial sector has stimulated the vitality of the market greatly, playing an important role in promoting the rapid industrialization process of the country. The implementation of opening from the industrial market to the service market during the 13th FYP period will add considerable momentum to the development of China's service industry, releasing generous dividends of the new round of marketized reform.

(1) The market opening of the industrial sector will enable China to become the number one manufacturing economy in the world

① The market opening of the industrial sector will propel the fast industrialization of China. According to the practice of reform and

[15] Li Hongpeng and Wen Rujun: The Central Government Reduces the Pricing Range to 7 Categories with 20 Items. *Legal Evening News*, October 21, 2015.

[16] Chi Fulin: The Reform in the 13th Five-Year-Plan Period Should Take the Opening of Service Industry as the Focal Point. *Economic Information Daily*, October 29, 2015.

opening-up since 1978, the industrial sector has been the forward position for opening the country's market. It is by grasping the historical opportunity of globalization and accelerating the pace of market opening in the industrial sector that China can be able to make full use of the bases of both international and domestic markets and promote the rapid development of industrialization. During the period of 1978–2014, the value added of China's industry increased by 11.2% on average annually. The industrialization process has sped up markedly especially after China's entry into the WTO. During the period of 2003–2011, the value added of above-scale industries increased 15.4% on average annually, with an annual average increase by 17% between 2003 and 2007 inclusive.[17] The proportion of value added of industry in the GDP and the contribution rate of economic growth have remained about 40% for a long time, becoming the important force promoting economic growth (see Chart 5).

② China has become the number one manufacturing nation in the world. The fast industrial growth has enabled the global influence of China's manufacturing industry to grow continuously. According to data from Global Insight, the proportion of the output of China's manufacturing industry in the world reached 19.8%, displacing the U.S. in total manufacturing value-added as the largest global manufacturer. In the world's 500 industrial goods, the production of China's 220 goods ranks first worldwide.[18] Although there is some overcapacity in some manufacturing activity, the global competitiveness of China's manufacturing industry is still fairly high. According to *2013 Global Manufacturing Competitiveness Index* prepared by Deloitte and US Council on Competitiveness, China's manufacturing competitiveness index will still be on top (see Table 5).

③ The international competitiveness of industrial enterprises will increase substantially. The opening of the industrial sector has developed the breadth and depth of domestic industrial enterprises' participation in

[17] National Bureau of Statistics: *The Substantial Increase of Industrial and Economic Strength and the Constant Improvement of Economic Structure—A Series of Report on the Achievement of Economic and Social Development from the 16th National Congress of the CPC to the 18th National Congress of the CPC (8)*. http://www.stats.gov.cn/, September 4, 2012.

[18] National Bureau of Statistics: *The Substantial Increase of Industrial and Economic Strength and the Constant Improvement of Economic Structure—A Series of Report on the Achievement of Economic and Social Development from the 16th National Congress of the CPC to the 18th National Congress of the CPC (8)*. http://www.stats.gov.cn/, September 4, 2012.

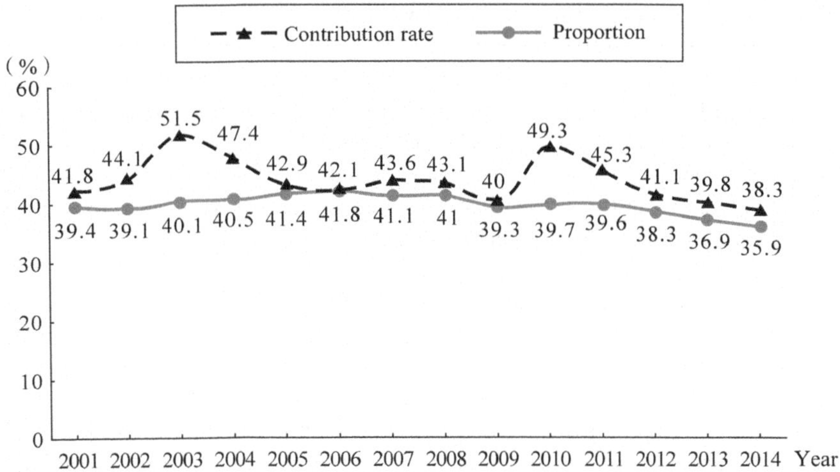

Chart 5 The proportion of China's industry's value-added in the GDP and contribution rate to economic growth in 2001–2014 (*Source* National Bureau of Statistics: *China Statistical Yearbook 2015*, China Statistics Press, 2015)

Table 5 Major countries or regions manufacturing competitiveness index rankings and projection

Rank	*2012*		*2018*	
	Countries/regions	*Index score*	*Countries/regions*	*Index score*
1	China	10	China	10
2	Germany	7.98	India	8.49
3	The U.S.	7.84	Brazil	7.89
4	India	7.65	Germany	7.82
5	South Korea	7.59	The U.S.	7.69
6	Taiwan (China)	7.57	South Korea	7.63
7	Canada	7.24	Taiwan (China)	7.18
8	Brazil	7.13	Canada	6.99
9	Singapore	6.64	Singapore	6.64
10	Japan	6.6	Vietnam	6.5
11	Thailand	6.21	Indonesia	6.49
12	Mexico	6.17	Japan	6.46
13	Malaysia	5.94	Mexico	6.38
14	Poland	5.87	Malaysia	6.31
15	The U.K.	5.81	Thailand	6.24

Source Deloitte and US Council on Competitiveness: *2013 Global Manufacturing Competitiveness Index*, 2013

international competition, thus increasing the international competitiveness of industrial enterprises substantially. In 1992 there were only two Chinese enterprises on the *Fortune* Global 500 list. Nine were placed on the list in 2000. It was not until 2015 that Chinese enterprises went up to 94, of which industrial enterprises made up two thirds.[19]

(2) The focal point of market resource allocation will shift from the industrial sector to the service sector

① As it is in Late Industrialization, the focal point of market resource allocation will shift from the industrial sector to the service sector. During the 13th FYP period, to adapt to the new trend and new structure for economic transformation and upgrading, it is necessary to call for a shift of growth power. Judging by the international experience, it is an objective law of industrial structure evolvement to replace the traditional industry of low value-added with the modern service industry of high value-added; it is also an objective trend for a country to grow from mid-Industrialization to Late Industrialization. Currently, when China is entering the particular historical stage of Late Industrialization, to allow the market to play a decisive role in resource allocation, there is a prominent contradiction in the service sector and the key to resolving the contradiction is to open the service market.

② The policy for opening the service market is from liberalizing market access to "except no admission". Since the reform and opening-up, China's service sector was first under governmental administration and then its market access was liberalized. When it comes to the late twentieth century, the service market involving general competitive fields was basically open to social capital, whereas such services as education, medical care and finance have been strictly under control. Since the beginning of the twenty-first century with China entering the WTO, to break the "glass windows" through which social capital can go into the service market like education, medical care, aviation, and finance, the State Council publicized "old 36 policies for non-public economic development" in 2005 and "new 36 policies for non-public economic development" in 2010 respectively, with a view to encouraging and guiding social capital into the fields to which no law or regulations denied access

[19] *Fortune* Global 500 List of 2015 Published and China's 94 Firms on the List. *Zhejiang Daily*, July 29, 2015.

categorically. In practice, these "old and new policies" played an important role in promoting the development of China's service industry. Given this, however, social capital's access to the service market still has been prevented both by administrative monopoly and market monopoly under the influence of the traditional system.

3.3 The Opening of Service Market that Will Release Enormous Dividends of Reform

Despite the decline in the investment in the industrial sector, a substantial increase of private investment in service industry has played a considerable role in stabilizing the economic growth. During the 13th FYP period, with the acceleration of opening of service market, impressive results will be achieved in promoting the initiative of social capital and making "the cake" of service industry bigger.

(1) The growth rate of social capital investment in service industry surpasses that of the industrial sector

Since the 12th FYP period (2011–2015), while expanding the market of the industrial sector, the service industry has further opened its market to social capital. Currently, a substantial increase of private investment in service industry has played a considerable role in stabilizing the economic growth, although investment has declined in the industrial sector. In 2013, for instance, private investment in fixed assets of service industry grew at the rate of 25.4%, an increase by 4.7 percentage points over the industrial sector. Under the influence of macroscopic economic downturn these two years, the growth rate of private investment in fixed assets of the industrial and the service sector all dropped heavily. According to statistics, China's private investment in fixed assets of service industry went up by 9.4% as compared with the previous figure, which corresponds to the industrial sector (see Chart 6).

(2) Social capital makes up more than half of the total investment in fixed assets of service industry

Since the 12th FYP period, in changing the mode and adjusting the structure, the amount of investment in service industry has increased constantly, while the percentage of social capital in the investment to the

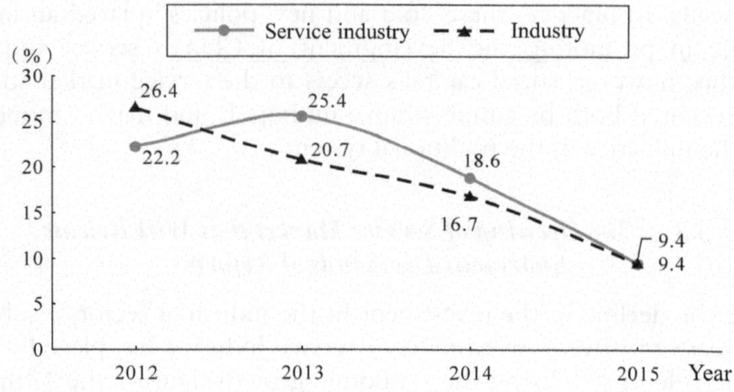

Chart 6 The growth rate of private investment in fixed assets of the service sector and the industrial sector in 2012–2015 (*Source* Date are prepared according to the statistics provided by China's National Bureau of Statistics concerning private investment in fixed assets over the years)

service industry has risen markedly. According to statistics, the amount of private investment in fixed assets of service industry grew from 10.1 trillion yuan (US$1.68 trillion) in 2012 to 16.4 trillion yuan (US$2.73 trillion) in 2015, while private investment in fixed assets of service industry went from 51.3% of the 2012s total investment in fixed assets in social service industry up to 52.7% of the 2015s total investment (see Chart 7).

(3) The opening of service market will bring social capital enormous space for investment

With the gradual opening of educational, medical and other services markets, social capital has found quicker access into the service sector, playing an important role in satisfying social diversified public demand. In terms of the educational field, by the end of 2014 there were various kinds of 155,200 non-government schools (educational institutions), which numbered about 43.02 million students in total.[20] According to

[20] Ministry of Education: *Statistical Bulletin on the Development of National Education in 2014*. http://www.moe.gov.cn, July 30, 2015.

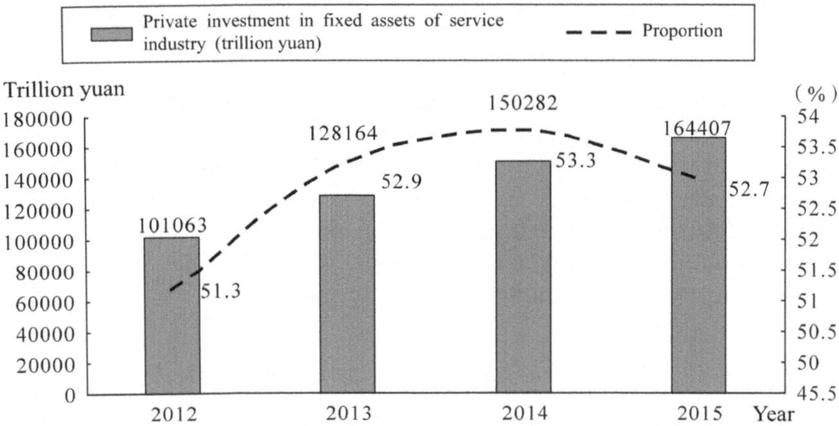

Chart 7 Private investment in fixed assets of China's service industry (*Source* Data were prepared according to the statistics provided by China's National Bureau of Statistics concerning investment in fixed assets of the social services industry and private investment in fixed assets in 2012–2015)

the projection by one institution, China's market size of non-governmental education in 2018 would exceed one trillion yuan (US$0.17 trillion).[21] In terms of the medical and health field, there were 12,546 private hospitals nationwide in 2014, which accounts for 48.5% of the total number.[22] According to the estimate by another institution, during the 13th FYP period, the total market consumption of China's health service industry will exceed the total medical consumption, with the market potential of health service industry being as high as 8 trillion yuan (US$1.33 trillion).[23] This will bring social capital enormous space for investment.

[21]Zero Power Intelligence Group: *Report on China's Non-government College-Industry Market Dynamics and Development: An Outlook and Projection for 2013–2018*, 2013.

[22]National Health and Family Planning Commission: *Statistical Bulletin on the National Development of Health and Family Planning in 2014*. http://www.moh.gov.cn, November 5, 2015.

[23]Wang Changlin: New Impetus to Support 7% of Industrial Development. *Guangming Daily*, August 7, 2015.

4 Promoting the Opening of Service Industry Market with Breaking the Monopoly as the Focus

During the 13th FYP period, the key to resource allocation by market lies in the service sector. To allow the market to play a role in resource allocation in the service sector needs to break the administrative monopoly and market monopoly in service market ASAP and to completely lift price control in competitive service market to form a unified, open, fair and competitive market environment, so as to make social capital become a main force for modern service development.

4.1 Service Market Is to Be Open to Social Capital

Forming the service-oriented industrial structure has to speed up the opening of service market, lift control on social capital's access to the service sector while encouraging social capital to enter the sector.

(1) The potential of China's social capital is enormous

Very different from the initial stage of reform and opening-up in which the industrial development was lacking in capital, China at present has no lack of capital to develop its service industry. It has an untold number of residents' savings. According to statistics, the bank deposit of urban and rural residents rose from 10.36 trillion yuan (US$1.73 trillion) to 48.53 trillion yuan (US$8.09 trillion) during the period of 2003–2014, a quadruple increase within eleven years (see Chart 8). In addition, a huge number of high-net-worth individuals (HNWI) have become an important force for social capital investment.

Statistics show that by the end of 2014 HNWIs with the investable capital of more than 10 million yuan (US$1.67 million) exceeded 1 million in number, an increase by 330,000 persons over 2012. The combined investable capital of HNWIs reached 32 trillion yuan (US$5.33 trillion) while these HNWIs showed relatively concentrated interest in innovative industries and consumer services (see Chart 9). However, China's service market has not adapted to the new situation and suffered from the "glass door" of policy or mechanism to varying degrees. Whether to be able to achieve decisive results in economic transformation and upgrading and mobilize all social forces to make the "cake" of service industry bigger depends largely on the opening process of service market.

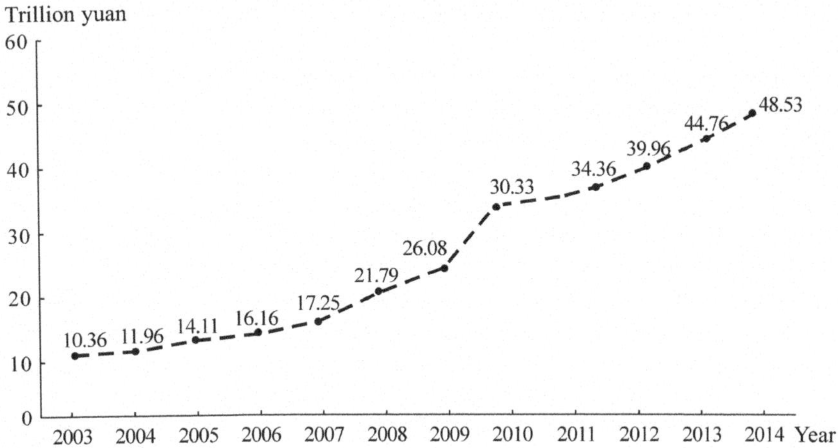

Chart 8 Bank deposit of China's urban and rural residents in 2003–2014 (*Source* National Bureau of Statistics: *China Statistical Yearbook 2015*, China Statistics Press, 2015)

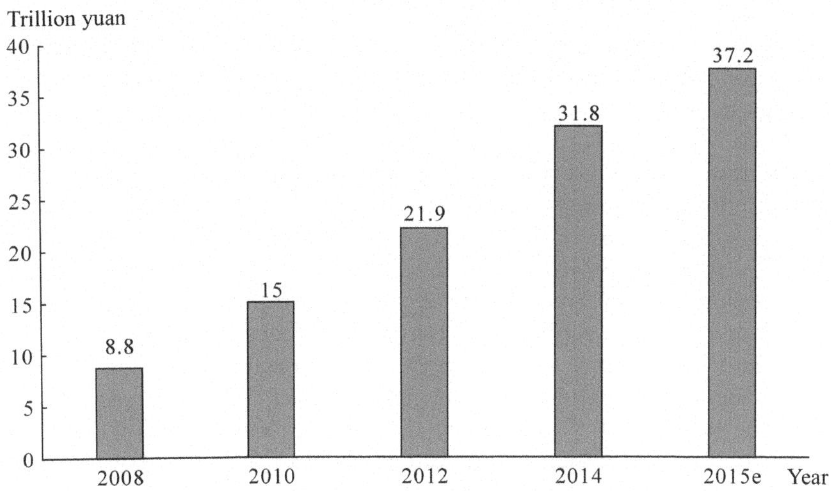

Chart 9 The investable asset size of Chinese HNWIs in 2008–2015 (*Source* China Merchants Bank: *China Private Wealth Report*, May 2015)

(2) The opening of service market has to be facilitated to social capital

Market access is to be further liberalized in banking, securities, insurance, telecommunications and express mail service industries while removing some unreasonable restrictions on business scope. By following the principle of "except no admission", unreasonable preset approval items have to be sorted out and eliminated completely and administrative supervision be shifted to legal supervision. Moreover, restrictions on social capital have to be broken effectively while encouraging social capital to enter the educational, medical, health and cultural fields. Taking the development of the government purchase of social services as the focal point, public welfare social organizations should be supported for their special role in public services. Marketization shall be sped up in public resource allocation. At the same time, the overall competitive mechanism should be introduced in selling the franchise rights in urban and rural public services, whereas the government purchase should be standardized and perfected in administrative service resource allocation.

4.2 *Administrative Monopoly and Market Monopoly Are to Be Broken in Service Industry*

The root cause that the opening of service market lags behind lies in both administrative monopoly and market monopoly in service market. During the 13th FYP period, the opening of service market should be facilitated while breaking completely the administrative monopoly and market monopoly in service market and guiding more social capital's access to the service sector.

(1) It is necessary to promote the strategic adjustment of State-owned capital in the service sector, withdraw the State-owned capital in the service sector from the general competitive fields, and make more room for domestic social capital and foreign capital. Meanwhile, State-owned capital in the service sector is to be allocated in public services so that State-owned capital will be used to satisfy the growing public needs of the whole society, thus making greater contribution in public services.
(2) It is necessary to open the competitive links in monopolistic industries to social capital in an all-round way.

All forms of administrative monopoly should be further broken in electric power, telecommunications, petroleum, aviation and postal service industries. Reduction of State-owned shares in the capital market should be promoted, while part of the State-owned capital be withdrawn from unnatural monopoly links to make room for social capital. Complete separation of natural monopoly from competitive links shall be achieved. State-owned capital can be stressed as the capital dominance in the natural monopoly, whereas competitive links be opened to social capital. Furthermore, the market access system shall be perfected in infrastructural fields; control on monopolistic industries be relaxed or lifted gradually; a market competition mechanism be introduced extensively to encourage social capital to involve in fair competition in infrastructural fields.

(3) It is necessary for the natural monopoly of the monopolistic industry to attract social capital to involve fully

According to different characteristics of different industries, the railway network (infrastructural facilities which belong to the natural monopolistic industry and is operated in the State-owned-capital-controlled company) will be separated from the railway passenger and freight transportation (which features market competitiveness), with a view to liberalizing competitive business. Through BOT (build-operate-transfer) and TOT (transfer-operate-transfer) social capital can be encouraged to involve in investment. Such industries as banking, insurance and aviation that have a lot to do with people's livelihood can be completely opened to social capital. As for those fully marketized natural monopolistic industries and enterprises, it is advisable for them to withdraw completely from the monopolistic system if possible while exploring the reform in mixed ownership if not possible or not yet ready conditionally.

(4) It is necessary to improve the franchise system in urban public service while actively guiding social capital to involve

For urban public service, it is necessary to improve the franchise system and establish the reasonable price mechanism. Separation of powers has to be achieved between government administration and public institutions, between government administration and enterprise management, and between public institutions and enterprises in urban public service, so as to establish a sound market competitive mechanism, an enterprise operative mechanism, and governmental supervision mechanism. Monopolistic operation has to be broken up while introducing a market competitive mechanism and enhancing the operational efficiency of urban construction. Full use of capital market ought to be made in order to change fundamentally the single mode of government investment for urban public service while allowing social capital to invest in urban public service. Besides, it is better to make use of the existing operating assets of public service and actively guide social capital to invest by way of franchise mode, thus easing up the fund shortage in public service construction effectively.

4.3 Forming a Fair Service Market Environment

To speed up the opening of service market, it is necessary to get rid of various outdated administrative rules and regulations, eradicate market barriers and form a unified, open and fair market environment.

(1) Removing service market barriers

Unlike the manufacturing industry, the service market is mainly local. The entry of service enterprises from other places will impact on and replace local enterprises to some degree in the short period of time. To protect local economy, therefore, many local governments will protect their local service enterprises more or less. During the 13th FYP period, to break up the market separation and regional blockade in the service sector, all service domains shall be open to non-local social capital unless otherwise stipulated legally, while establishing a unified, open and fair service market system nationwide. Service enterprises and service products will be allowed to have free access to all local markets. Those service domains open to local enterprises should be all open to non-local enterprises, with a view to promoting the free flow of various production factors nationwide and improving the efficiency and fairness of resource allocation

(2) Establishing open and transparent market rules

① Criteria for equal, standard, open and transparent market access have to be established. It is necessary to relax access criteria for investment in service industry, to maximally reduce restrictions on the business services, general investment projects and qualifications of service enterprises. On the basis of preparing the negative list, service domains beyond the negative listings should be legally open to various kinds of capital on an equal footing.

② Internal and external capital should be treated equally. Service domains which no State laws or regulations prohibit access to should be opened to both external capital and internal capital at the same pace. During the 13th FYP period, therefore, effort has to be made for private enterprises, foreign enterprises and SOEs to acquire equal treatment that includes market access, the post-access stage and business process.

③ An incentive and punishment mechanism needs to be established for trustworthy enterprises and dishonest enterprises. So it is necessary to set up and perfect the management system of service enterprises for credit information collection and inquiry and credit investigation. Credit information sources for various parts of the country are to be integrated so as to speed up the forming of a national unified system for public joint credit reporting and of a notification system for market players' credit information. Through the systems, therefore, credit information of service enterprises is to be issued regularly while establishing the joint punishment mechanism for dishonest enterprises and creating an honest and trustworthy business environment.

(3) Accelerating the elimination of administrative regulations that restrict the opening of service market

① The relevant provisions and practices that hinder the national unified market and fair competition have to be eliminated and rescinded. In line with the "except no admission" principle, it is required to eliminate the provisions and procedures that conflict with the laws and regulations and restrict various market players' access to the service industry while prohibiting and punishing various acts that implement favorable policies illegally.

② The establishment of a mechanism whereby competition policies and industrial and investment policies are coordinated has to be accelerated. It is required to eliminate various discriminatory policies and provisions while treating all types of market players equally in investment approval, equity ratio, financing service and financial and taxation policies, thereby promoting the construction of a unified, open, and fair market system.

③ Charges involving service industry has to be straightened out. Administrative fees involving enterprises ought to be straightened out while actively exploring the "zero charges" system and strengthening the burden reduction of service enterprises. In various parts of the country, charging standards for service enterprises need to be set according to the actual situation while reducing the administrative fees for small and medium-sized service enterprises according to the prescribed power.

4.4 *Lifting Price Control of Service Market*

To form a new situation of open service market, it is necessary to deepen the price reform in the service sector, allow the market to play a decisive role, improve the pricing mechanism of the government and strengthen the government's market regulation of service prices.

(1) Deepening the overall price reform in the service sector

① Service prices in competitive domains have to be liberalized completely. Practice shows that to liberalize the service prices in competitive domains is conducive to making full use of market competition to expand the supply of service industry and improve the quality of service industry development. The Fifth Plenary Session of the 18th Central Committee of the Communist Party of China (CPC) put forward a special statement, "Commodity prices and service prices in competitive domains have to be liberalized completely." During the 13th FYP period, according to the spirit of the Fifth Plenary Session of the 18th CPC Central Committee, service prices in competitive domains should be lifted soonest. In principle, the government won't make a price invention in the competitive domains of service industry. Basic liberalization of prices in competitive domains and links will have been achieved by 2017.

② The price formation mechanism in monopolistic industries has to be improved. Monopolistic industries need a certain price regulation, but a control over prices can be lifted in competitive links. Therefore, it is necessary to differentiate competitive links from natural monopolistic links and establish different types of price formation mechanism. Nevertheless, government pricing is still to be implemented for the natural monopolistic links in service industry, whereas for the competitive links in service industry the government will lift price control completely while introducing a competitive mechanism and implementing enterprises' independent pricing. Besides, price reform should be accelerated in water, petroleum, natural gas, electric power and transportation, liberalizing prices in competitive links.

③ The price formation mechanism in public service has to be improved. It is necessary to distinguish between basic public services and non-basic public services, to which different price mechanisms should be applied respectively. Basic public services are all that the government must be responsible for and service prices can be set lower through the government's control. But deregulation should be practiced in non-basic public services. On the basis of the "bottom-line standard", it is required to accelerate the forming of a price formation mechanism chiefly decided by the market in non-basic public service. The government's pricing range should be mainly confined to important public utility, public welfare services, and network-type natural monopolistic links. In basic public service, the government still reserves the pricing power to safeguard necessary public welfare. For non-basic public service like non-governmental education, and social capital-run care service for senior citizens, price control must be lifted, allowing prices to be decided completely by the supply and demand relation in the market.

(2) Improving the government's pricing mechanism

① It is necessary to improve the list of the government pricing items constantly. For commodities and services included in *the Central Government Pricing Catalogue*, the regular assessment of the effectiveness of price reform and the degree of market competition needs to be made while adjusting specific pricing items timely during the 13th FYP period. At the same time, government pricing information must be made known to the public so as to improve price transparency and receive social supervision, making the pricing power be exercised in the open and transparent condition.

② It is necessary to standardize the government's pricing procedures. According to *the Central Government Pricing Catalogue*, specific management methods need to be formulated; pricing procedures be standardized; social participation in the government's pricing process be improved; experts' demonstration meetings and social hearings be promoted, all with a view to ensuring standardized, open, transparent pricing procedures and restricting the government's pricing action effectively.

(3) Enhancing the price supervision of service market

① It is necessary to enhance the administrative supervision of the pricing department. This department should enhance dynamic monitoring and analysis of related service prices and timely make market prices known. In the meantime, it should make a tour of price inspection and intensify the investigation of illegal practice like price fraud and price forcing while giving due punishment to those involved so that consumers' rights and interests are protected practically. In addition, broadband network speed has to be increased while reducing the broadband fees. Last but not least, it is of primary importance to establish and amplify the legal system of service price supervision, thus supervising the service market according to law.

② It is necessary to improve the social supervisory system of price. During the 13th FYP period, the information disclosure system of service industry should be established and perfected and public supervision be strengthened. Full use of the national four-level networking (networking at national, provincial, municipal and county levels) should be made as a price reporting management information system[24] to encourage consumers and business operators to participate in price supervision. Also, the social credit system should be relied on to promote the establishment of price system, build business operators' price credit files.

③ It is necessary to improve the price hearing system. Consumers should be encouraged to attend the price hearings, for which the ratio between service providers and consumers is to be fixed reasonably. Social intermediary organizations should also be encouraged to attend the price hearings, whose entire procedures are open and standard and completely under social supervision.

4.5 *Promoting the Government Purchase of Public Service*

In the new stage which witnesses the overall rapid growth of public demand, the promotion of the government purchase of public service

[24] **[The Translator's Notes]** The system is operational via the hotline telephone (12358) for price supervision.

is not only an objective requirement for the supply mode of innovative public service but also an important measure for raising public service quality and supply efficiency.

(1) A main trend for the government purchase of public service

① The socialization and marketization of public service are a trend of the times. When in the new stage of development, especially in the background of overall deepening reform, the major purpose of the government purchase of public service is to make public service open, fair and beneficial to the maximum. Although China started the government purchase of public services in 2003, its development has been rather slow in the traditional institution system with the institutional innovation of public service lagging behind. For example, the national government procurement volume in 2014 made up 11.4% of the nation's financial expenditure, of which the service procurement accounts for 11.2%.[25] In developed countries in Europe and America, their government procurement volume makes up 30–40% of their respective financial expenditure, of which the service procurement makes up more than 50%.[26]

② The new system has to be established for the government purchase of public services. During the 13th FYP period, how to make full use of social capital in expanding the supply and demand of public service depends on the purchase volume of the government. The Fifth Plenary Session of the 18th CPC Central Committee pointed out, "The government will no longer directly undertake innovative ways of providing public services that can be provided by the government purchase of services. What can be provided by the cooperation of the government and social capital can attract the participation of social capital extensively." Therefore, it is imperative to adapt to the main trend for the changed demand of public service for over 13 billion people, take the forming of multiple suppliers and multiple competitors as the basic objective of developing and improving the government purchase of public services while accelerating the cancellation of some discriminatory policies on market organizations and social organizations in the process of the

[25]The Department of the State Treasury Under the Ministry of Finance: *Brief Information of National Government Procurement in 2014*. www.mof.gov.cn/Jul.30, 2015.

[26]Chi Fulin: The Government Purchase of Public Services Calls for Being Open and Competitive. *Economic Information Daily*, April 30, 2014.

government purchase of public services. Efforts are required to make, by 2020, the institutional arrangement in the legalized, standardized and transparent mechanism for the government purchase of public service. This will enable the purchase volume of the government to reach 15–20% of the nation's financial expenditure and the service procurement to reach 30–40% of the government procurement.

(2) Accelerating the market opening of public service industry

① It is necessary to differentiate the open market of basic public services from that of non-basic public services. The market of non-basic public services should be fully opened. In service for senior citizens, nurseries and kindergartens, professional training, health care, and family service, for example, the market is to be fully open while introducing competition and letting the market play a decisive role in resource allocation. The competitive mechanism is to be introduced into basic public services like compulsory education, basic medical and health care, basic housing security, basic social insurance, employment service, and public culture. The government will increase its efforts to purchase public services from society while encouraging enterprises and public welfare organizations to take part.

② It is necessary to improve the institutional mechanism for opening up the market for public services. All areas where laws and regulations are not legally prohibited should be opened to social capital in an orderly manner. Using the experience of developed countries, all public services must invite public bidding in accordance with the law while introducing the market competition mechanism and promoting the marketization of public service by exploring various means like contract outsourcing, public-private partnership (PPP), and a voucher system.

(3) Formulating institutional arrangements for the government to purchase public services ASAP

① It is necessary to specify the government's guide to purchasing public services. On January 4, 2015, the Ministry of Finance, the Ministry of Civil Affairs and State Administration for Industry and Commerce jointly promulgated *Administrative Measures on the Government's Purchase of Services (Provisional)*, which stipulates the basic principles, buying subjects and undertaking subjects, purchasing catalogues and guidance catalogues concerning the government purchase of services. It is suggested that the guidance catalogues concerning the government purchase of services be further specified and then more operational.

② It is necessary to develop public welfare organizations. To promote the government purchase of public services needs to emancipate the mind and treat the institutions within the system and the public welfare organizations outside the system equally, while following the same rules of the game to take the social organizations as the main body to undertake the government purchase of public services. For this, it is suggested to establish the public welfare legal person system ASAP and grant social organizations like a public welfare organization the status of public welfare legal person.

③ It is necessary to establish a fair competition mechanism. Except some special domains, a competition mechanism should in principle be introduced into most public services. Meanwhile, the notification system should be established for the government purchase of public services, while purchasing public services from social organizations by means of contracts and entrustments and avoiding under-the-table operations to the maximum extent, so as to ensure the fair competition of various undertaking subjects. Fair competition must be achieved between institutions in the system and public welfare organizations outside the system. At the same cost, therefore, the government will purchase public services from those that can provide more public welfare.

④ It is necessary to include the government purchase of public services in the Government Procurement Law. So, the government purchase shall be based on the law, which stipulates the scope and procedures for the said purchase. This is how to make the purchase standardized and institutionalized.

5 Solving the Contradiction Between Policy and System in the Opening up of Service Market

Over the years the development of China's service industry lags behind, which is largely due to the structural contradiction between policy and system in the growth of the country's service industry. At the same time, the current fiscal, taxation and the financial system have hindered the growth of service industry.

5.1 *The Opening up of Service Industry Market Is Confronted with the Structural Contradiction Between Policy and System*

The growth of China's service industry is confronted with various unreasonable policies, which has seriously affected the healthy development of the said industry. During the 13th FYP period when the service-oriented industrial structure needs to be formed, it is necessary to make an effort to solve the various contradictions between policy and system in the opening up of service industry market.

(1) The growth of service industry is confronted with the contradictions between policy and system

At present, the lack of supply in the service market reflects the prominent structural contradictions on the supply side. Take the land policy for example. In the fourth quarter of 2015, the prices of commercial services and industrial land in the major monitoring cities across the country were 6729 yuan (US$1121.50) per square meter and 760 yuan (US$126.67) per square meter, the former price being 7.85 times higher than the latter.[27] The main reason is that the current macro-policy and macro-system structure are partially characteristic of encouraging industrial development and restraining the development of service industry. Specifically, one of the causes is that the reform of the investment system lags behind, which makes it difficult for private capital to invest in the service sector and reverse the imbalance between supply and demand. The second cause is that due to the unfinished reform of replacing business tax with value-added tax in the development of service industry and slow progress in the reform of consumption tax, it is difficult for local governments to change their behavior pattern of "emphasizing investment over consumption". The third one is that the financial structure is not rational, and the development of inclusive finance is relatively backward, which makes it difficult for small and medium-sized enterprises to alleviate the financing difficulties effectively. The fourth is that the structure of education is not rational, leading to a serious shortage of practical and technical talents badly needed for economic transformation. Given all these, therefore, the development of the service industry is confronted

[27] The Urban Land Price Dynamic Monitoring Group of China Land Survey and Planning Institute: *Summary of Land Price Monitoring Report of Major Cities in China in the Fourth Quarter of 2015*, China Urban Land Price Network, January 15, 2016.

with a series of contradictions between policy and institutional structure, and failure to resolve these contradictions will make it difficult to create a favorable environment in which the opening of service market is established.

(2) The transformation of investment structure is to be promoted with the opening of service market

Judging from the current situation, steady growth requires investment. The key is to make investment marketable and efficient. Therefore, it is necessary to highlight the guiding role of consumption in promoting investment transformation, expand the proportion of investment in service industry with real demand, and realize the interaction and integration between investment and consumption. For this, the suggestion is ① to adapt to the trend towards the rapid growth of the service consumption demand, and increase investment in education training, housekeeping service, health service, pension service, tourism service and sports service; ② starting from the actual needs of industrial transformation and upgrading, to increase the investment in information, research and development, design, logistics and other producer services; ③ to adapt to the basic trend of the comprehensive and rapid growth of the demand for public goods in China, with the focus of investment being shifted to education, medical care, social security and other basic public services; and ④ to launch another batch of major projects to open up to social capital in the areas of telecommunications, education, health care and finance ASAP.

(3) Policies concerning service industry and industrial land use are to be adjusted

① In land supply, preference should be given to modern service industry and the proportion of land used in the said industry be increased. In the general planning and urban and rural planning of land use, an overall arrangement needs to be made of development land for service industry in scale, layout and sequence while adjusting the structure of urban land use and applying more land to the modern service sector.

② In terms of new land for construction, particular stress should be laid on new services. Priority should be given to the land use for emerging service projects involving high-tech, high-value-added, low-consumption and low-emission, of which the State encourages the development. Industrial enterprise should be encouraged to start the self-operated producer services industry that promotes the transformation and upgrading of enterprises by using self-owned industrial land. For industrial enterprises that increase their own industrial land plot ratio for the sake of self-operated producer services industry, through obtaining approval according to the law, they will be entitled to conduct the related formalities in line with new uses.

③ The price gap between service industry and industrial land should be narrowed. Local pilot projects are encouraged with policy adjustment being intensified and all kinds of preferential policies given to service land, while substantially reducing the price for service land and trying to realize basically "the same price for the same land" regardless of service land or industrial land throughout the country by 2020.

(4) The use of water, electricity, gas and other resource factors are to be made by services and industry on an equally competitive basis

① The same price for water use by services and industry shall be achieved. During the 13th FYP period, the same price for water use by services and industry can be achieved ASAP in line with the actual situation in various places in various ways. One is to reduce the current water price of service industry directly to the level of industrial water price by means of financial subsidy or joint financial commitment with water supply enterprises. Two is to bring the current price of water for services into line with that for industry by raising the water price for industry and lowering that for services. Three is to simplify the urban water supply price, which falls into two major categories: price for domestic water and special industries like high water consumption industries (bath and car wash) and price for the rest, including industry, administrative institutions, infrastructure, commerce, catering, and services.

② The same price of electricity shall be realized for services and industry. The consolidation of electricity prices will be stepped up with a view to achieving the same price for commercial and general industrial electricity. First, the commercial electricity price and the general industrial electricity price are combined into the general industrial and commercial electricity price. Then, non-industrial and general industrial and commercial electricity will be combined into general industrial and commercial electricity and other electricity, including Party and government organs and public institutions.

③ The same price of gas shall be realized for services and industry. One is to simplify the classification of gas prices and implement the same price for industrial and commercial natural gas. In terms of gas prices for different uses, the current four categories of the residents' life, industrial production, commercial services, and other utilities will be adjusted to three categories of uses for the residents' life, non-residents' life and others. Two is to implement the policy of integrating industrial and commercial services. The gas use for "commercial service" and "industrial production" will be combined into that for "non-residents' life". Meanwhile, according to the actual situation of each district, the new price standard will be determined through the way of price adjustment, upward or downward.

5.2 *The Fiscal and Taxation Structure Is to Be Formed for the Benefit of Service Industrial Growth*

A rational tax system structure is conducive to enhancing the effective incentive of economic transformation and industrial structure adjustment, and is the basic condition for straightening out the relationship between government and market, government and enterprises, government and society. To form a service-oriented industrial structure during the 13th FYP period, it is necessary to speed up the reform of tax system structure, form a fair tax environment for the development of service industry and lighten the burden of enterprises, thereby forming the fiscal and taxation structure conducive to the development of service industry.

(1) A fair tax environment for the development of service industry should be basically formed

① The reform of "replacing business tax with value-added tax" (BT to VAT) will be completed. "BT to VAT" is a key measure for forming a fair tax environment for the manufacturing industry and service industry. Since the pilot reform was started in 2012, the reform of "BT to VAT" has sped up, and up to 2015 there were only the last four industries (building, real estate, finance and daily life service) still pending. These four industries involve nearly 10 million taxpayers, who double the number of taxpayers for the "BT to VAT reform". *The Report on the Work of the Government 2016* stated clearly that from May 1, 2016 on, the pilot reform of "BT to VAT" would extend to the building industry, real estate, finance, life services so as to ensure that all industry tax decrease instead of increase. But considering that these industries feature diversified departments and sections, a rich variety of business forms, and complex interest adjustment, it is highly necessary to work out the reasonable tax rates, tax calculation methods, deduction methods and other tax elements while arranging the transition policy properly.

② The reform in value added tax will be promoted. Firstly, the reduction of tax rates. Eighteen of the 21 APEC member countries and regions have introduced VAT and similar goods and services taxes (except Brunei, Hong Kong and the United States). In addition to China, the 17 members have the VAT average standard rate for 11.15%, which China's two VAT rates are higher than, being significantly higher than Japan (8%) and Thailand (10%), Vietnam (10%), Singapore (7%), South Korea (10%) and Australia (10%). China can consider simplifying current rates and lowering them on the basis of consolidated rates. For instance, the tax rate for transportation, food and other products for people's livelihood can be reduced to less than 10%, while implementing the practice of 1 basic tax rate plus 2 preferential tax rates, namely, 1 basic tax rate reduced to 13% with 2 preferential tax rates being 6% and zero tax rate respectively. In addition, a single VAT rate (around 8%) could even be considered for specific regions.

Secondly, the reduction of the collection rate of small-scale taxpayers. Reduction of tax rates from the current 3 to 1% means to substantially reduce the tax burden on small and micro businesses. For enterprises in industry-wide loss, the VAT preferential tax rate shall be implemented according to the tax rate collected from small-scale taxpayers to reduce the burden of enterprises, so as to avoid the bankruptcy of a large number of enterprises.

Thirdly, the expansion of the scope of VAT deduction. In consideration of encouraging the development of innovative enterprises, the total research & development expenditure involved in technological innovation shall be included in the deduction scope except for the fixed assets such as equipment involved in technological innovation.

③ A tax system environment must be created for the equitable development of manufacturing and service industries. One, increasing tax support for producer services industry. In August 2014, China's State Council issued *Guiding Opinions of the State Council on Accelerating Development of the Producer Services Industry to Promote Adjustment and Upgrading of the Industrial Structure*, which points out: "Scientific and technological type and innovative enterprises of producer services industry specialized in research and development design, test, inspection and certification, and energy conservation and environmental protection may apply for recognition as a high-tech enterprise, to enjoy a preferential tax rate of 15% on corporate income tax." On this basis, further preferential policies shall be formulated by drawing on the tax support of some developed countries for producer services.

Two, cleaning up tax preferential polices timely. Previously, regional preferential polices were good for industry and large enterprises but not good for the development of service industry. The State Council did propose speeding up the cleanup of regional tax preferential policies, but in May 2015 it suspended the cleanup due to increased downward pressure on the economy. From the perspective of the trend of transformation and upgrading, focus should be on forming a unified market and promoting fair competition. In the short term, a good job shall be done to find out the real situation and make an objective assessment of the possible impact after the suspension. Once the economic situation improves, the cleanup will be resumed in time, thus laying a solid foundation for the formation of a unified market and the development of service industry.

(2) The tax structure should be optimized

① The relatively low proportion of direct tax restricts economic transformation and upgrading. Generally speaking, the higher proportion of direct tax will be more conducive to the development of service industry, the release of consumption and the adjustment of income gap.[28] There are 18 categories of taxes in China,[29] of which 7 categories are indirect tax, including VAT, consumption tax, business tax, tariff, resource tax, urban maintenance and construction tax, and land value-added tax, and the remaining 11 are direct tax. In terms of tax revenue, direct tax accounts for about 40% whereas indirect tax accounts for about 60% (see Table 6). According to the Third Plenary Session of the 18th CPC Central Committee's overall planning

[28] Jia Kang: The Imbalance of the Proportion Between Direct Tax and Indirect Tax Will Hinder the Economic Transformation. *People's Daily*, October 10, 2012.

[29] The current 18 categories of taxes include VAT, consumption tax, vehicle purchase tax, business tax, tariff, enterprise income tax, individual income tax, land VAT, property tax, urban land use tax, cultivated land usage tax, deed tax, resource tax, vehicle and vessel tax, tonnage tax, stamp tax, urban maintenance and construction tax, and tobacco tax.

Table 6 China's total tax revenue and structure in 2014

Tax categories		*Tax take (¥100 million)*	*Proportion (%)*
Indirect tax	Domestic VAT	30,855.36	–
	Domestic consumption tax	8907.12	–
	VAT/consumption tax on imports	14,425.3	–
	VAT/consumption tax on exports	−11,356.5	–
	Business tax	17,781.73	–
	Resource tax	1083.82	–
	Urban maintenance & construction tax	3644.64	–
	Tariff	2843.41	–
	Land VAT	3914.68	–
	Subtotal	72,099.6	60.5
Direct tax	Enterprise income tax	24,642.19	–
	Individual income tax	7376.61	–
	Property tax	1851.64	–
	Stamp tax	1540	–
	Urban land use tax	1992.62	–
	Vehicle and vessel tax	541.06	–
	Tonnage tax	45.23	–
	Vehicle purchase tax	2885.11	–
	Cultivated land usage tax	2059.05	–
	Deed tax	0.45	–
	Tobacco tax	141.05	–
	Other taxes	0.45	–
	Subtotal	47,075.71	39.5
Grand total (¥100 million)		119,175.31	100

Source National Bureau of Statistics: *China Statistical Yearbook 2015*, China Statistics Press, 2015

of the reform in the fiscal and taxation system the basic orientation of tax reform goes from mainly indirect tax to mainly direct tax. In other words, the tax mainly from the production and business links will be mainly from income, property, and consumption, in order to meet the needs of economic transformation and upgrading. From an international point of view, direct tax in high-income countries accounts for an average of 63.56% or so.[30] By 2020, it is quite likely that China will

[30] Liu Guoyan et al.: The Direct Tax and Indirect Tax Ratio in China: An International Comparative Approach. *Public Finance Research*, Issue 4, 2015.

enter the rank of high-income countries. At present, the proportion of direct tax less than 40% is significantly lower. In order to adapt to the trend of China's economic transformation and upgrading, it is necessary to change the pattern of low direct tax rate.

② A breakthrough in individual income tax reform is to be achieved. In reforming individual income tax, it is good to have a new idea of "wide tax base, low tax rate and tax burden reduction", which is taking the reduction of tax burden level of taxpayers as the basic starting point.

Firstly, expanding the tax base. Individual income tax means to "pay taxes when you have income". The comprehensive and classified individual income tax should be implemented ASAP. Given the burden of family support, the tax shall be levied on the total income of the residents after deducting the reasonable tax allowance.

Secondly, reducing or even eliminating the tax exemption amount. This is good for low-income people. For every increase in the fixed income tax, the marginal income of high-income people is much higher than that of low-income people, which results in an even wider gap in income.

Thirdly, lowering tax rates. At present, the income tax rate of wages and salaries is 3–45%, which is divided into seven tax rates. It can be considered to further simplify the tax rates and reducing the marginal tax rate. If the idea of universal taxation is adopted, the tax rate can be designed to be 1–30%.

Fourthly, implementing the negative income tax system. For poor families or recipients of subsistence allowance, after they pay income tax, the income tax will be returned to them according to the local living standard, thus forming a negative income tax system. This can increase the protection of low-income people.

③ The property tax system is to be improved. One is to change the pattern in which the proportion of property tax income is too low. The current property tax in China is all local tax, mainly including such minor categories of tax as property tax, urban land use tax, land VAT, deed tax, and vehicle and vessel tax. In 2014, the sum of five categories of tax revenue only made up 3.72% of the total revenue, with the revenue of property tax accounting for only 1.56%.[31] The role of property tax in regulating income distribution is far from being fulfilled. This requires

[31]The figures are based on the calculation by the research group of China (Hainan) Institute for Reform and Development according to *China Statistical Yearbook 2015*.

speeding up the improvement of the property tax system and optimizing the property tax structure.

Two is to introduce new property taxes in due course. At present, the urban families each own close to 1.1 set of apartment on average. According to the data of China's household finance survey in 2013, the home ownership rate of urban residents was at 87%, whereas the said rate was 91.2% according to the sampling survey in 2015. Nearly 20% of urban and rural households own more than two apartments.[32] China's residential property ownership is out of keeping with property tax collection. In the past few years, China carried out a property tax pilot reform in Chongqing and Shanghai, but it has not been implemented or actually implemented. During the 13th FYP period, a new property tax should be introduced ASAP, which includes such key points as nationwide tax collection, deduction of per capita basic housing area, one of the main local taxes, combination of existing taxes, and combination of urban land use tax and cultivated land usage tax.

Three is to merge duplicate property taxes. Some researches point out that there is a problem of double taxation between deed tax and stamp tax.[33] In the current situation of increasing destocking pressure, the combination of deed tax and stamp tax can play a certain positive role. In 2014, for example, the deed tax for the whole year was about 400 billion yuan (US$66.67), the stamp tax was 154 billion yuan (US$25.67), and the national commercial housing sales area amounted to 1.21 billion square meters. Preliminary calculations showed that the cost of commercial housing could be reduced by 127 yuan (US$21.17) per square meter if stamp duty were incorporated into deed tax. If the deed tax were incorporated into the stamp duty, the cost per square meter could be reduced by 330 yuan (US$55).

(3) Efforts should be increased to reduce corporate burdens

① Structural tax cuts should be increased. China's current macro tax burden is on the high side, and there is still room for tax reduction. For example, judging from the proportion of the total government revenue

[32] *Social Blue Book: Nearly 20% of Urban and Rural Households Own More Than Two Sets of Apartments*. China News Network, December 24, 2015.

[33] Liu Zhicai: Problems of China's Property Tax System and Improvement Suggestions. *Modern Finance*, Issue 1, 2006.

in the GDP,[34] the macro tax burden level of enterprises measured 29.1%, given the total government revenue of 19.71 trillion yuan (US$3.29 trillion) in 2015. According to the World Bank, the optimal macro tax burden for China was about 25%,[35] which indicates that China still has at least 4 percentage points of tax reduction. According to the survey, the tax burden of small and micro enterprises in micro enterprises and industrial and commercial enterprises was generally higher than that of other types of enterprises. The tax burden of micro and small enterprises was 2.5 to 3.6 times respectively as much as that of large enterprises.[36] Therefore, it may be considered to heighten the standard of a small number of taxpayers in a moderate manner while forming an automatic tax reduction mechanism for small and micro enterprises, like significantly raising the threshold of VAT and business tax for small and micro enterprises.

② An all-round cleanup of unreasonable charges shall be carried out. Although the State government canceled the administrative fees or charges for the national annual inspection of enterprises, afforestation fees, etc. during the 12th FYP period, there were still more than 200 administrative fees and government-managed funds according to the Ministry of Finance's open list. To this end, it is necessary to further streamline administration and delegate more power and cut administrative fees and charges. In the early stage of the 13th FYP period, it is also necessary to comprehensively clean up, integrate, cut down and cancel the nationwide administrative fee collection items, such as preset approval service. By 2020, it will be the task ahead to reduce more than half of administrative fees and substantially reduce the administrative expenses borne by enterprises.

③ The social security burden of enterprises shall be reduced substantially. The vast majority of small and micro enterprises belong to

[34]The large part of the total government revenue, which is designated for the public sector, includes government fund revenue, operating budget revenue of SOEs, etc. in addition to the fiscal revenue. According to the data released by the Ministry of Finance, in 2015, the total revenue of Chinese government amounted to 19.71 trillion yuan (US$3.29 trillion), including 4.23 trillion yuan (US$0.71 trillion) from the government fund, 0.26 trillion yuan (US$0.043 trillion) from the State-owned capital management budget and 15.22 trillion yuan (US$2.54 trillion) from the financial budget.

[35]Zhu Jianfang: China's Macro Tax Burden. Securities Network, May 20, 2013.

[36]Xu Sheng: The Current Situation of Tax Burden of Enterprises: Investigation and Suggestions for Policy. *Study Times*, August 26, 2013.

labor-intensive enterprises, whose social insurance payment accounts for a large proportion of enterprise costs. By taking the characteristics of small and micro enterprises and of the service industry into account, the adjustment can be made as follows: one point is that the social average salary taken as reference for payment should reflect the actual situation of all employees' income, making it closer to their real paying ability. Another point is to increase the flexibility of policy for the payment. Considering the reality of labor-intensive small and micro enterprises, it is a good idea to formulate the multi-level payment standards and appropriately reduce the payment rate.

5.3 A Basic Pattern of Financial Support for the Real Economy Will Be Formed

The 13th FYP period is a key period for China to promote supply-side structural reform. Objectively speaking, China's current financial structure is not in line with the trend of economic transformation and upgrading, whereas the financial situation is being featured by money that are not basically involved in real production but used to make money instead. During the 13th FYP period, the financial reform ought to basically serve the real economy, increase the integration of finance and the real economy, effectively reduce the financing cost of the real economy, and create conditions for achieving the breakthrough of the supply-side structural reform.

(1) Integration of finance and the real economy will be promoted

① Within the current financial structure, financing is still difficult and costly to small and medium-sized enterprises. Although great importance has been attached to these problems and a series of policies and measures come out like "making good use of capital stock" and "making maximum use of excess reserves", the real economy has still suffered from serious "money hunger", especially micro, small, and medium-sized enterprises whose financing problem still remains truly outstanding. According to the survey on financing difficulty with banks, 41.8% of small and micro enterprises deemed it difficult; 31.03% deemed it rather difficult; and 27.79% deemed it very difficult.[37] In terms of the overall

[37]Wu Chu: We Are Not for the Support Policies That Appear Attractive but Not Practical to Micro, Small and Medium-Sized Enterprises. *China Youth Daily*, March 8, 2015.

financing cost, small and micro enterprises would actually have to pay additional hidden cost, namely, over 10% more than the original total cost. To be specific, financial institutions would charge small and micro enterprises loan rates that go up another 20–30% above the benchmark, plus the insurance cost, asset valuation fees, financial consulting fees and so on.[38]

② The allocation of financial resources should be increased to the real economy. More financial resource allocation to the real economy to improve the efficiency of financial service for the real economy needs to reduce the financing cost of the real economy, and further needs to accelerate product innovation in the financial market while vigorously developing financing instruments like bonds. According to the international experience, high-yield bonds can solve the financing difficulties of small and medium-sized enterprises. Through high-risk and high-yield bonds, investors with strong risk tolerance will be attracted to share the risks of small and medium-sized enterprises in the process of enterprise transformation, technological progress and innovation. This requires a financing way combining high-yield bonds and debt stocks. In addition, more work should be done to vigorously develop modern financing lease, directly importing foreign investment, providing such financing means as project financing, commercial paper and export credit, and constructing multi-level financial markets, so as to effectively solve the problem of financing difficulty for small and medium-sized enterprises.

③ The proportion of direct financing should be increased while reducing the financing cost of enterprises. In proposing the task of reducing costs, the Central Economic Work Conference held in 2015 required "lowering the financial cost of enterprises, and the financial sector to create a policy environment for the normalization of interest rates and offer favorable conditions to the real economy". At present, the high financing cost of enterprises is because in China's financial structure the proportion of direct financing is too low, and the proportion of indirect financing is too high. By measuring in the incremental method, the proportion of direct financing in China in 2014 was only 17.4% (see Table 7). Although the stock method is used in international institutions like the World Bank, there is still a significant gap between the

[38] Small and Micro Enterprises' Report on Financing Development: 40% of Them Have to Pay over 10% More Than the Financing Cost. *Economic Information Daily*, April 8, 2013.

Table 7 China's direct financing scale and proportion in 2002–2114

Year	*Increment of social financing scale (¥100 M)*	*Corporate bond (¥100 M)*	*Domestic stock financing by non-financial enterprises(¥100 M)*	*Direct financing scale (¥100 M)*	*Direct financing proportion (%)*
2002	20,112	367	628	995	4.95
2003	34,113	499	559	1058	3.10
2004	28,629	467	673	1140	3.98
2005	30,008	2010	339	2349	7.83
2006	42,696	2310	1536	3846	9.01
2007	59,663	2284	4333	6617	11.09
2008	69,802	5523	3324	8847	12.67
2009	139,104	12,367	3350	15,717	11.30
2010	140,191	11,063	5786	16,849	12.03
2011	128,286	13,658	4377	18,035	14.06
2012	157,631	22,551	2508	25,059	15.90
2013	173,169	18,111	2219	20,330	11.74
2014	164,773	24,329	4350	28,679	17.41

Source National Bureau of Statistics: *China Statistical Yearbook 2015*, China Statistics Press, 2015

proportion of China's direct financing and that of developed countries. To reduce the financing cost of enterprises, it is necessary to develop the direct financing system, improve the proportion of direct financing, and make the most of itself in risk-sharing, benefit sharing, market pricing and multi-level service, so as to better serve small and medium-sized enterprises and innovative enterprises.[39] A real effort will be made to increase the proportion of direct financing by non-financial enterprises in the social financing to 25% and the balance of the bond market in the GDP to 100% by 2020.[40]

During the 13th FYP period, to increase the proportion of direct financing has to foster an open and transparent capital market actively, propel the healthy development of the multi-level capital market, promote the reform in the system of stock and bond offerings, and focus

[39] Qi Bin and Zha Xiangyang: Direct Financing and Indirect Financing: An International Comparison. *China Finance Review/New Finance Review*, Issue 6, 2013.

[40] *Guidance Reader for the CPC Central Committee's Proposal on Formulating the Thirteenth Five-Year Plan (2016–2020) for National Economic and Social Development*, People's Publishing House, 2015.

on accelerating the development of the bond market. Therefore, more effort has to be made to energetically develop corporate bond financing, strengthen the market-oriented constraint mechanism of the bond market, promote bond market connectivity, actively develop the private bond market, and unify rules and regulations. Meanwhile, it is important to implement a proactive fiscal policy, expand the issuance of government bonds and explore the development of municipal bonds to replace loans from local government financing platforms.

(2) Financial innovation should be allowed to play a leading role in industrial transformation and upgrading

① The support of financial innovation for agriculture, rural areas and rural residents or farmers (hereinafter referred to as "three rural issues") should be strengthened. Starting from the prominent contradiction of solving the financial shortage in rural areas, it is urgent to increase the preference of financial resources to rural areas, agriculture and farmers. To rely on the traditional financial system to achieve full coverage of financial services in rural areas, the cost is huge and the financial institutions are not motivated enough. This needs to develop rural Internet finance vigorously to solve this problem effectively.

One is to speed up the development of "the Internet + agriculture". The Internet will be used to transform traditional agriculture, get the agriculture onto the Internet speedily, encourage e-commerce to enter the villages' households and farmers to involve in e-commerce actively, and accelerate the development of rural logistics.

Two is to improve rural financial services, accelerate the development of financial services focusing on small rural loans, actively develop financial services for farmers and increase their property incomes. By relying on the real transaction data of the Internet, effective credit enhancement is carried out for farmers and agricultural households. All these are to be done for accelerating the development of rural consumer finance.

Three is to develop new models like crowd-funding for agriculture. By attracting urban funds directly into areas urgently needed for the development of agriculture, rural areas and farmers, the outflow of funds from rural areas will be reversed effectively.

② The support of financial innovation for research and development should be strengthened. To adapt to the rapid development trend of big data, cloud computing, and mobile Internet and take the initiative to meet the challenges of the "industrial 4.0", the key is to increase the intensity of innovation and change the situation of our country's innovation that is relatively lagging behind. This requires the formation of an effective financial support system, especially the vigorous development of venture capital.

One is to encourage innovative service platforms to strengthen the cooperation with financial institutions. A role as a bridge of innovation and business undertaking service platform must be played to support the cooperation between the maker space, innovation works like new incubator and angel investors, venture investment, and Internet financial institutions, so as to make innovations in investment and financing services. Work also needs to be done to establish a database for enterprises engaged in scientific and technological innovation and support financial institutions in carrying out scientific and technological financial services and product innovation. Furthermore, the construction of a credit system for enterprises engaged in scientific and technological innovation shall be strengthened to address information asymmetry between enterprises engaged in the said innovation and financial institutions, and promote effective links between financial institutions and scientific and technological innovation enterprises.

Two is to make full use of capital market to support enterprise innovation. Effort will be taken to support the listing of start-up enterprises or their issuance of bills for financing while encouraging start-ups to raise funds through the bond market. Besides, an active study should be conducted to guide the unprofitable Internet and high-tech enterprises to the GEM (growth enterprises market) listing system and set up a strategic emerging industry board at the Shanghai stock exchange. What's more, a pilot study should be made to accelerate the trial of a national system for transferring shares of small and medium-sized enterprises to the GEM, while studying and removing the institutional barriers to the listing of special equity structure start-ups in China in order to improve the rules of the capital market. And the development of regional equity markets shall be standardized for small and medium-sized enterprises, supporting equity pledge financing.[41]

[41] State Council: *Opinions of the State Council on Several Polices and Measures for Vigorously Promoting Mass Entrepreneurship and Innovation*. http://www.gov.cn, June 11, 2015.

③ The support of financial innovation for entrepreneurship should be increased.

One is to encourage financial institutions to develop products and services that support entrepreneurship. For farmers' entrepreneurship, it is advisable to seize the right opportunities for the reform in the circulation system of rural land contracted management right and in the collective forest rights system, to expand the scope of the rural collateral effectively, explore the development of such new products as circulation mortgage of land contracted management right, the forest right mortgage, mortgage of right to use waters and tidal land. It is also advisable to energetically develop mutual insurance and co-insurance loans for college-graduate village officials, flexibly adopt such repayment methods as bullet repayment and amortization, expand the coverage of loans and increase the rate of loan satisfaction.

Two is to mobilize financial institutions to support entrepreneurship. Full play will be given to the guiding role of public finance, discount and subsidy guarantee fees, to provide credit risk compensation for financial institutions, and to arouse their enthusiasm to develop venture loan to support entrepreneurship. At the same time, a public welfare guarantee fund will be set up with financial funds to provide guarantee for young entrepreneurs, while actively exploring ways to build a risk prevention mechanism shared by the government, banks and young people.

Three is to increase support for entrepreneurship in the new financial operation. Support will also be given to developing Internet finance, guiding and encouraging the standardized development of crowd-funding platforms, carrying out trials of public and small-sized equity crowd-funding, and strengthening risk control and standardized management. Policies on guaranteed loans for business start-ups will be enriched and improved. Insurance funds will be supported to take part in entrepreneurship and innovation and develop new forms of business like mutual insurance. Further work will be done to perfect intellectual property valuation, pledge and circulation system, to promote the normal and large-scale development of such services as intellectual property pledge financing and usufruct securitization of patent licensing fees, and to support the financial development of intellectual property rights.[42]

[42] State Council: *Opinions of the State Council on Several Polices and Measures for Vigorously Promoting Mass Entrepreneurship and Innovation*. http://www.gov.cn, June 11, 2015.

(3) Financial openness to social capital should be increased

① There is a lot of room for social capital to take part in finance. In recent years, China has continuously strengthened the policy support for social capital entering the financial field and achieved obvious results. Observed from the results of the analysis of the ownership structure of listed companies, the shareholding level of State-owned capital in the financial companies listed in recent ten years has declined obviously, whereas social capital has gradually become important shareholders of listed financial companies. Although social capital has entered the financial field in large numbers, the potential of social capital to participate in finance is still considerable. According to data from the Survey and Research Center for China Household Finance (CHFS), China in 2013 still had 22.3% of households with private financial liabilities, and the private financial market scale of the country's households was 5.28 trillion yuan (US$0.88), which is an 18% increase in comparison with 4.47 trillion yuan (US$0.745 trillion) in 2011.[43] Nevertheless, there is still great potential for developing private finance.

② Access threshold should be defined reasonably. At the Third Plenary Session of the 18th CPC Central Committee, it was proposed to ensure the equal use of production factors in various ownership economies in accordance with the law, and to uphold the equality of rights, opportunities and rules in the non-public economy and the public economy. Private capital should be allowed to initiate the establishment of banks and be treated equally in terms of access standards. Observed from the specific access requirements, most countries have focused on such aspects as the amount of minimum capital, executive experience, internal control system and IT systems, and the requirements should be applied to for all applicants equally in these aspects. Judging from China's current situation, the development orientation and operation of private finance are very different from those of large State-owned financial institutions. For this reason, appropriate access threshold should be established for various kinds of private financial institutions in light of the actual situation. On the basis of strengthening supervision, the threshold

[43] Report on Private Financial Development: Households' Private Lending Exceeds 5 Trillion Yuan. *Yangtze Evening Post*, February 27, 2014.

can be reduced appropriately for private capital to access the financial sector, so as to facilitate the transfer of private financial organizations from "under the ground" to "above the ground" and to promote the standardization, legalization, and institutional transformation. At the same time, the access rules for all kinds of non-governmental financial institutions should be improved ASAP.

③ Fair competition between various financial institutions should be ensured. All types of financial institutions should be treated as equals. In terms of supervision and approval, the rule should be made not to place too many obstacles to private financial institutions, resulting in the phenomenon of "glass doors". In view of the weak position of private financial institutions in market competition, the government gives certain support and preferential policies to realize the fair competition of various financial institutions.

(4) Innovation of inclusive financial system should be promoted

① Funding should be ensured for inclusive finance. In order to achieve business sustainability, inclusive finance needs government policy support in addition to the efforts of inclusive financial institutions themselves. So it is important to further increase the Central Bank's targeted reduction of financial institutions' required reserve ratios, and adopt low-interest leverage tools to ensure the adequacy of financial loans.

② The fiscal interest discount for special groups should be increased. It is through fiscal discount interest that reduces the burden of small and micro enterprises, farmers and other special groups. An institutionalized discount interest policy shall be established to ensure that the real interest rate of inclusive financial loans is not higher than that of general commercial loans. Where financial resources permit, the full discount interest rate system for financial loans will be explored so that small and micro enterprises, farmers and other special groups can enjoy low-interest and interest-free loans. In addition, financial funds are encouraged to provide a partial discount on the inclusive financial loans of rural specialized cooperatives.

③ Financial rewards and compensation shall be made to financial institutions that develop the business of inclusive finance. For small loans under a specified amount, financial institutions shall be given certain rewards and risk compensation, so as to reduce the risk of financial institutions and mobilize their enthusiasm to develop inclusive financial services.

5.4 *The Transformation and Upgrading of State-Owned Enterprises Shall Be Promoted*

It is China's current industrial overcapacity and insufficient service supply that promote the transformation and upgrading of enterprises. This is to meet the requirements of cutting overcapacity, and to allow State-owned capital to play an important role in promoting the structural change of national industry while increasing service supply.

(1) Overcapacity reduction is an important task in the reform of State-owned enterprises

① The focus and difficulty of cutting overcapacity lie in State-owned enterprises. The excess capacity accumulated over the years is directly related to the distortion of market supply and demand and the difficulty of market clearing both caused by the lagging reform of State-owned enterprises. The first task of the 13th FYP is to reduce the downward pressure on the economy through supply-side reform.

At present, the main challenge for de-capacity is State-owned enterprises. Generally speaking, if private enterprises are in the state of overcapacity, they will naturally be eliminated from the market under the condition of insolvency. However, State-owned enterprises represent a different case. Due to the soft budget constraint and the support from the government and banks as well as the resettlement of employees, it is difficult for SOEs to quit the market even after years of losses. In recent years, eight major industries (steel, coal, cement, glass, petroleum, petrochemical, iron ore and non-ferrous metals) largely covered by SOEs are the "areas of industrial overcapacity", about 80% of which are loss-incurring enterprises. At present, these eight industries have contributed to the drop in PPI by 70–80%.[44] China Iron and Steel Association's latest statistics showed that in 2015 the main business of national large and medium-sized iron and steel enterprises suffered annual cumulative losses of more than 100 billion yuan (US$16.67), an increase in losses by 24 times as compared with the previous year. At the same time, however, the market showed no sign of a turnaround, resulting in industry-wide

[44] Li Jin: 2016 Will Be the Critical Year for Overcapacity SOEs. www.hexun.com, December 13, 2015.

losses for the period of January and February 2016 that total 11.4 billion yuan (US$1.9 billion).[45]

② State-owned enterprises should play an important role in reducing overcapacity.

Firstly, in the new situation, the focus of deepening the SOE reform is to reduce overcapacity. Overcapacity highlights the irrational allocation of State capital, especially in traditional industries, overcapacity industries and heavy chemical industries in which the proportion of allocation is too heavy. In order to optimize the allocation of State capital, top priority needs to be given to capacity reduction.

Secondly, to give full play to the important role of State-owned capital in industrial transformation, it is necessary for the reform of State-owned enterprises to make some progress in reducing production capacity. Only when excessive capacity is removed will State capital have the conditions to optimize its allocation and enhance its vitality, control and influence.

Thirdly, only by solving the problem of reducing production capacity in the reform of State-owned enterprises can a new pattern in which the market determines resource allocation be formed. To allow the supply and demand relationship of market to determine the entry or withdrawal of State-owned capital is to respect the market rule, to provide the effective ways to solve the "soft constraints" of State budget, to introduce a major measure for State-owned enterprises to better integrate in the modern market economy, and to meet the objective requirement for a new pattern in which the market determines resource allocation.

Finally, the allocation of State capital should be optimized with the emphasis on reducing production capacity. In order to meet the requirement of overcapacity reduction, it will create favorable conditions for the optimization and restructuring of State-owned capital and create important opportunities for new breakthroughs in developing mixed ownership.

(2) The reform of State-owned enterprises shall be promoted in a classified manner

① Large traditional State-owned enterprises shall be transformed into innovative ones. The key to industrial transformation and upgrading is

[45] China Iron and Steel Association: The Main Business of the Iron and Steel Industry Suffers over 100 Billion Yuan Last Years. www.cnstock.com, April 7, 2016.

the transformation of large enterprises into innovative enterprises. For one thing, large enterprises play an important role in the real economy. Statistics show that in 2015 China's top 500 enterprises' operating income reached 59.5 trillion yuan (US$9.92 trillion),[46] approximately 93.6% of the GDP (63.6 trillion yuan/US410.6 trillion) in 2014. The total tax paid by Top 500 was 3.98 trillion yuan (US$0.66 trillion), which accounts for the 33.4% of the country's total amount of tax.[47] It should be noted that without the transformation and upgrading of large enterprises, China's manufacturing territory would be difficult to change. For another, the profits of industrial enterprises above designated size have been on the decline, and the operation situation of large State-owned enterprises remains grave. According to statistics, the total profit of national industrial enterprises above designated size in 2015 was 6.36 trillion yuan (US$1.06 trillion), a 2.3% decrease as compared with the previous figure. Of the industrial enterprises above designated size, the State-owned holding companies yielded the total profit of 1.09 trillion yuan (US$0.18 trillion), a 21.9% decrease as compared with the previous year, which hit a new low in history.[48]

② Strengthening the producer services industry should be taken as an important task in developing mixed ownership.

One is to strengthen the producer services industry in State-owned enterprises. By following the tide of new technological revolution, international manufacturing giants like IBM and Apple have accelerated the divestment of manufacturing links and focused on product research & development and design, becoming world-class innovative enterprises. The key to the international competitive advantage of China's high-speed railway is to strengthen the producer services industry, which is led by research & development and design.

Two is to promote social capital participation in SOE reform with a focus on strengthening the producer services industry. Some large State-owned industrial enterprises will be pushed to take off their productive business, transfer it to social capital operations, and focus their main business on producer services. Some large State-owned industrial

[46] Hua Yedi and Xiang Zhiqiang: Sinopec Wins the Top 500 List of China's Enterprises for 11 Years Running. www.xinhuanet.com, August 22, 2015.

[47] Feng Liguo and Li Suyun: How Is the Profitability of China's Large Enterprises? www.caixin.com, September 28, 2015.

[48] National Bureau of Statistics: *Statistical Bulletin of 2015s National Economy and Social Development*. http://www.stats.gov.cn, February 29, 2016.

enterprises will be pushed to extend the industrial chain around the producer services industry, with part of the producer services industry being transferred to the social capital operation and the main business focusing on the high-end link of producer services industry.

Three is to foster a batch of high-end producer services industry groups. By developing mixed ownership will headquarters economy be fostered in State-owned enterprises, while making full use of modern information network technology and platforms and developing a batch of specialized R & D services with international competitiveness and a strong resource allocation ability both domestically and internationally.

③ A batch of State-owned enterprises will be reorganized and integrated in some production capacity sectors.

One is to promote the merger and reorganization of State-owned enterprises by focusing on improving industrial concentration. Improving industrial concentration is an important condition for the sustainable development of traditional industries. Take the iron and steel industry for example. The iron and steel industry of the United States, Japan and South Korea represents the highest level in the world. The said industry in these three countries is highly concentrated. In 2007, the first four steel companies in the United States had a market share of 68.7%. Japan's first four iron and steel enterprises took a 73.9% market share. And the market share of South Korea's first four steel companies was 88.87%. In other words, as for the market structure of the iron and steel industry, which is characterized by being maturity, effective competition and economies of scale, the market concentration of the first four companies should not generally be smaller than 60%, whereas the first four iron and steel enterprises in China only had a market share of 35%. Take another example about the coal industry. The current market concentration of China's top four enterprises is only 20%, and that of the top eight enterprises is no larger than 28%. The reasonable proportion should reach 40 and 60% respectively. The top 10 corporate market concentration in the United States, Australia, South Africa, India and Germany is 46, 50, 60, 90 and 100% respectively. The low concentration of coal industry in China has brought serious social problems such as resource waste, environmental pollution and occupational health and safety.[49] This needs to increase the industrial concentration as an

[49] Li Rongrong: The problem Is Not Monopoly But Too Low Industrial Concentration. www.sasac.gov.cn, March 25, 2014.

important means of State-owned enterprises to carry out the reform in cutting capacity and to promote cross-regional reorganization and acquisition of State-owned enterprises in the iron and steel, coal, nonferrous metals, and other fields, thus forming a more efficient market structure.

Two is to promote the merger and reorganization of "SOE + SOE". In the field of overcapacity, there are often multiple listed companies of State-owned enterprises in the same industry. Some of these companies are strong and profitable whereas others are weak and less profitable. These State-owned enterprises can, through the cross-regional merger and reorganization, realize the complementary advantages, improve economies of scale, and enhance profitability, thus forming a large-scale comprehensive industrial group with transnational operations, and becoming a global leader. Then the merged or reorganized group will formulate unified overseas market development strategy and through joint efforts obtain a more favorable position in the international competition.

Three is to encourage mergers and acquisitions in the form of "private enterprises + State-owned enterprises". Such encouragement with capacity reduction as an opportunity is not only beneficial to resolving the plight of the State-owned enterprises, but also to creating conditions for social capital to involve in the State-owned enterprises' reform, but also conducive to making a breakthrough in developing mixed ownership. *Guiding Opinions of the CPC Central Committee and the State Council on Deepening the Reform of State-Owned Enterprises*, issued in August 2015, states clearly, "In principle, all commercial SOEs whose core business belongs to industries and fields of sufficient competition shall implement corporate-style shareholding reform, actively attract other State-owned capital or various types of non-State-owned capital to diversify equity, adopt flexible approaches where State-owned capital may be the absolute or relative controlling shareholder, or be merely a shareholder, and focus efforts on promoting their listings as a whole." It is suggested that specific policies should come out to encourage private enterprises to acquire through capital market part of the controlling interest of the commercial State-owned enterprises, and merge and reorganize SOEs, realizing the win-win situation of SOEs and private enterprises.

④ A batch of "three-high industries" (high pollution, high consumption, high emission) and "sunset industries" have to be cleaned up and withdrawn.

Firstly, State-owned capital exits from the "three-high industry" in principle. As a national capital, State-owned capital needs to play a key role in promoting "green development". Therefore, a comprehensive assessment of SOEs in the "three-high industry" ought to be made. State-owned enterprises that have failed to meet the national standards of energy consumption, environmental protection, quality and safety and have run for a loss for years with overcapacity shall be closed down, suspended, merged, switched to other products, or divested and reorganized. It is imperative to formulate a comprehensive reform plan and strive for the complete withdrawal of State capital from the "three high industry" by 2018.

Secondly, the proportion of State capital in the "sunset industry" shall be reduced. The "sunset industry" doesn't mean an industry that society doesn't need. Instead, any country needs a "sunset industry". The problem is that excessive allocation of State capital in the "sunset industry" is not conducive to the development of the leading role of State capital in industrial transformation, and to the preservation and appreciation of State capital. It is suggested that State-owned enterprises be divided into commercial SOEs and SOEs in public welfare nature and the related regulations be formulated, which restrict the proportion of commercial SOEs in the "sunset industry", making the most of them withdraw. Only by doing so can State capital be promoted to concentrate in the fields of public service and people's livelihood and in strategic emerging industries. It is expected that by 2020 the new pattern of the rational allocation of State-owned capital will be formed.

Thirdly, some "zombie enterprises" should be eliminated. The "zombie enterprise" mainly refers to indebted companies that have no hope of recovering but have been saved from failure by lenders or governments. The existence of "zombie" enterprises does hamper the market clearing, and take up a lot of economic resources that should otherwise be used for innovation, leading to long-term mismatch and low efficiency of resource allocation while becoming a heavy burden to the government and financial institutions. The existence of "zombie enterprises" is also a long-term problem, which is quite difficult to solve. But a positive and sound policy is required. It is necessary to properly handle the relationship between the interests of all parties concerned, to be specific, both to focus on resolving the trouble back at home, and to make full use of marketing tools such as bankruptcy, reorganization, and acquisition, with a view to realizing the optimal allocation of State-owned capital and the preservation and appreciation of its value.

(3) People's problems shall be solved

It will be difficult to push forward the reform of State-owned enterprises without solving the human problems. At present, some enterprises take no accident as the precondition. In this situation, many things cannot be done and reform cannot be implemented either. To solve the problems of people, the key is "marketization of hiring managers" and "professional manager system", which were put forward by the government work report of 2016. By taking this as the breakthrough point, the selection mechanism, the governance structure, the system of wages, and the anti-corruption mechanism are to be set up. Importantly, concrete measures must be taken in these aspects so that reform measures can be implemented ASAP and the current passive situation can be reversed ASAP, too. At present, for State-owned enterprises, the use and management of human resources are the most critical and urgent problem that hinders the implementation of SOE reform. The government work report of 2016 proposed the "incentive mechanism and fault tolerance and error correction mechanism to support reform innovators", which is suggested to first implement in State-owned enterprises.

CHAPTER 3

Urbanization as a Turning Point from Scale to Population

In the 13th FYP period, China has entered a new stage of population urbanization. New-type urbanization is still the greatest potential for China's development. Based on this, new ideas are needed to deepen the reform of the household registration system in the 13th FYP period. The first idea is a change from population control to service and management of population. The second is a change from the dual household registration system in urban and rural areas to the comprehensive implementation of the residence permit system. The third is a change in the population management from the public security department to the population service department. By 2020, it will be a historic breakthrough to replace the dual household registration system in urban and rural areas with the residence permit system.

Joseph Eugene Stiglitze, an American economist and a recipient of the Nobel Memorial Prize in Economic Sciences (2001) said, "China's urbanization and the new technology of the United States are the two engines of driving the development of the world economy in the 21st century." If China has achieved the rapid growth of economy with urbanization as a carrier in the past 30 years, it will also depend on the transformation and development of urbanization to achieve the fair and sustainable development in the next five years. It can be said that the 13th FYP period is the key five-year period from scale urbanization to population urbanization. Population urbanization will affect the overall transformation and development while becoming the "biggest dividend" of China's transformation and development.

F. Chi, *Winning at the Turning Point*, The Great Transformation of China, https://doi.org/10.1007/978-981-32-9479-0_3

1 Population Urbanization as the Core of New-Type Urbanization

During the 13th FYP period, in the background of economic downward pressure, accelerating the process of population urbanization will release a new development dividend, which can not only effectively boost consumption but broaden the space for investment, creating favorable conditions for de-capacity and de-stocking.

1.1 The 13th FYP Period: China's Urbanization Is Still in the Stage of Rapid Development

During the 13th FYP period, China's urbanization will still be in the stage of rapid development. Urbanization faces opportunities and challenges of transformation and upgrading. Population urbanization will provide important historical opportunities for urbanization transformation and upgrading.

(1) Urbanization is advancing rapidly

Observed from the international experience, the urbanization rate ranging between 30 and 70% represents the stage of rapid urbanization development. Judging from the situation in China, the 1978–2015 witnessed an increase in urbanization rate from 17.9 to 56.1%, the average annual growth of almost 1%. It means that China has taken over 30 years to cover the urbanization some Western countries underwent in about a hundred years or even several hundred years. For example, Latin America took 210 years; Europe took 150 years; North America 105 years.[1] In 2015, China's nominal rate of urbanization was 56.1%, which indicates the stage of rapid development of urbanization. In the next five years, China's urbanization will not only have a large space for development, but also enjoy the high speed of development.

(2) Most provinces, autonomous regions and cities are in the "accelerating period" of rapid urbanization

[1] Ren Zongren: Public Governance in the Process of New-Type Urbanization. www.people.com, May 19, 2013.

Observed from the urbanization rate of permanent population in China's 31 provinces, autonomous regions and cities in 2014, besides the nominal urbanization rate of Shanghai (89.6%), Beijing (86.3%), Tianjin (82.2%) and other 19 provinces, autonomous regions and cities, which all exceeded 50%, that of the rest 12 provinces, autonomous regions and cities all fell below 50%, which indicates the "accelerating period" of rapid urbanization (see Chart 1). For those provinces, autonomous regions and cities whose nominal urbanization rate is above 50%, however, their actual urbanization rate were mostly below 50% if factors like non-native population were excluded. In this context, therefore, no matter whether the nominal urbanization rate or the actual population urbanization rate, most provinces, autonomous regions and cities in China are in the "accelerating period" of rapid urbanization.

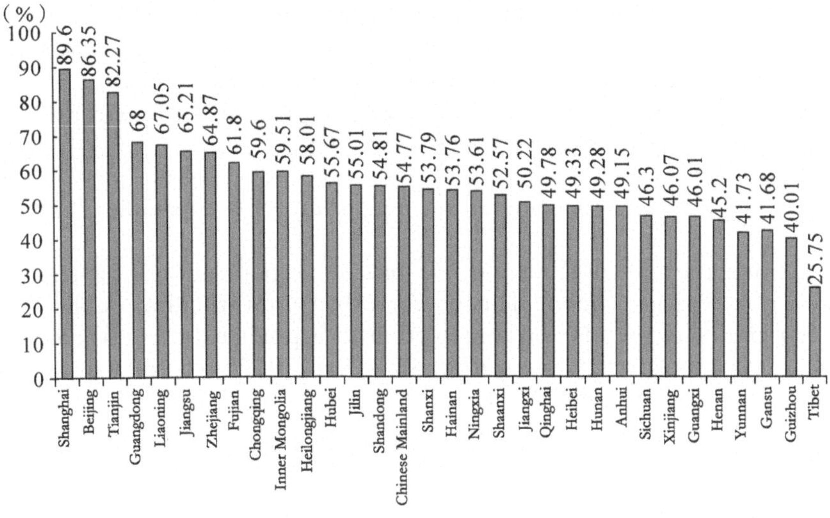

Chart 1 The urbanization rate of permanent population in China's 31 provinces, autonomous regions and cities in 2014 (*Source* National Bureau of Statistics: *China Statistical Yearbook 2015*, China Statistics Press, 2015)

(3) There is enormous room for the development of population urbanization

Data show that China's population urbanization rate in 2014 was only about 36%. Based on the development prospect in 2020, the reasonable range of population urbanization rate should not be lower than 50%. In other words, if the population urbanization rate grew at an average rate of no less than 2.5% during the 13th FYP period, it would reach 52%, the average rate of the world's population urbanization. From a realistic point of view, as long as relevant reforms focusing on the citizenization of migrant workers are in place, it is possible that the urbanization rate will reach more than 50% in 2020.[2]

1.2 Population Urbanization Is the Biggest Advantage of Expanding Domestic Demand

From the perspective of development trend, China's population urbanization will release great demand for investment and consumption. The main potential of expanding domestic demand and promoting consumption lies in the people-oriented, new-type urbanization. That is to say, population urbanization in the 13th FTP period bears the important historical mission of expanding domestic demand.

(1) Population urbanization is the biggest carrier to expand investment

During the 13th FYP period, the process of population urbanization will bring big investment demand for urban infrastructure, public service facilities and residential construction. It is predicted that if the nominal rate of urbanization goes from 53.73% in 2013 up to 60% in 2020, the investment demand will reach 42 trillion yuan (US$7 trillion).[3] For example, there is a lack of more than 50 million parking spaces in cities, which alone could lead to about 3 trillion yuan (US$0.5 trillion) of investment.[4]

[2]Chi Fulin: A Fair and Sustainable Path Should Be Taken for Urbanization. *People's Daily*, January 23, 2013.

[3]MOF Promotes PPP to Boost Urbanization: Investment Demand Reaches 42 Trillion Yuan. *21st Century Business Herald*, September 26, 2014.

[4]The Task List of New-Type Urbanization Will Bring About Huge Investment Potential. www.cnr.cn, May 14, 2015.

(2) Population urbanization will boost the consumption demand of more than 1.3 billion people

The transfer of rural population to urban areas will bring about a huge "cumulative effect" of consumption, which is conducive to expanding urban consumer groups and promoting the upgrading of consumption pattern and the release of consumption potential.

In 2014, China's urban and rural residents' consumption level was 2.9:1. Based on this calculation, the urbanization rate of registered household population will rise to 50% by 2020 when there will be an increase in agricultural population resettlement by nearly 200 million, which will bring new consumption totaling 3.3 trillion yuan (US$0.55 trillion).[5]

1.3 Population Urbanization Will Release Reform Dividends in a Variety of Way

Under the influence of the acceleration of China's aging population and other factors, accelerating population urbanization will release new dividends in a variety of way.

(1) Population urbanization is a new dividend of economic and social development

Improving the quality of workers through population urbanization is conducive to increasing total-factor productivity (TFP) and reducing the decline of potential growth rate. Studies show that in the average annual GDP growth at around 10% in 1982–2009 the contribution rate of TFP accounted for 1%, nearly half of which comes from the increased efficiency of re-allocation of resources brought by labor force from agriculture to non-agricultural industries.[6] With the development of economic society, however, demographic dividend has decreased by degrees with the number of migrant workers falling from the average growth of 5.5% in 2010 to that of 1.3% in 2014 (see Chart 2). The difficulty of migrant

[5] The figure is based on the calculation of relevant data from *China Statistical Yearbook 2015*.

[6] Cai Fang: A Few Viewpoints on Demographic Dividend. *Economic Daily*, June 18, 2015.

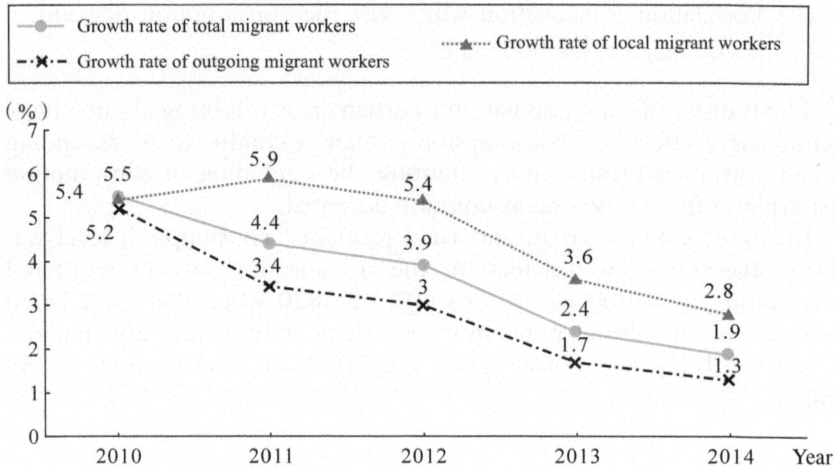

Chart 2 The growth rate of the total number of migrant workers in 2010–2014 (*Source* National Bureau of Statistics: *Monitoring and Investigation Report on Rural Migrant Workers in 2014*. http://www.stats.gov.cn/, April 29, 2015)

workers in resettling in cities will lead to a decline in the momentum of urban development due to labor shortage. During the 13th FYP period, by deepening the reform in household registration system and the basic public service system, to promote the citizenization of agricultural transfer population and optimize the distribution of labor factors will significantly increase the urban labor supply, thus extending the period of demographic dividend.

(2) Population urbanization will increase total-factor productivity

The 13th FYP period is a key stage for China's economic structure to move towards the middle and high end. International experience shows that the higher stage of development a country may be in, the higher TFP, brought about by the improved quality of workers, will be depended on by economic growth. Migrant workers are an important source of urban labor supply in the future, which is closely related to the improvement of China's TFP. In general, the level of education migrant workers receive is related to the quality of China's economic development and the transformation and upgrading of industrial structure. According to *Monitoring and Investigation Report on Rural Migrant*

Table 1 The educational level of China's rural migrant workers in 2014 (unit: %)

Educational level	*Rural workers (total)*	*Migrant workers*	*Local workers*
No schooling	1.1	0.9	1.6
Primary school	14.8	11.6	18.1
Junior high school	60.3	61.6	58.9
Senior high school	16.5	16.7	16.2
Postsecondary	7.3	9.3	5.2

Source National Bureau of Statistics: *Monitoring and Investigation Report on Rural Migrant Workers in 2014*. http://www.stats.gov.cn/, April 29, 2015

Workers in 2014 issued by National Bureau of Statistics, migrant workers aged between 21 and 40 accounted for 53% of the total number and were in the best period of employment. Observed from the level of education, however, those with high school education and above only made up 23.8% (see Table 1), whereas those who received skills training for only 34.8%. In the next five years, it is necessary to speed up the breaking down of the urban and rural household registration system, to increase the educational level and skills of migrant workers, especially those born in the 1980s, the 1990s and the 2000s, and to transform and upgrade demographic dividend to human resource dividend, thus promoting the improvement of TFP.

2 Forming a New Pattern of Urbanization of Registered Household Population Basically

The transformation of scale urbanization should be promoted into population urbanization with registered household population as a major carrier. By focusing on policy and institutional innovation and effectively releasing the potential of internal demand of urbanization, the new pattern of registered household population urbanization will be basically formed by 2020.

2.1 China Has Entered a New Stage of Urbanization of Registered Household Population

Since the reform and opening up in 1978, the dynamic mechanism of China's urbanization has changed profoundly. In the next five years, the population urbanization driven by industrial transformation and consumption upgrading will speed up.

(1) Urbanization driven by industrialization and industrial development tends to slow down gradually

The rapid development of urbanization in China in the last 38 years is mainly driven by industrialization and industrial development. The most typical is that cities are formed around factories. The phenomenon of "one factory, one city" is quite common. When industrialization has reached a certain level in general and there is even excess production capacity, industry-led urbanization will begin to inhibit consumption and repel population urbanization. In recent years, "ghost cities" appear in some places, which represent a typical phenomenon caused by industrial urbanization. "Industrial towns", which are formed by being highly dependent on resource exploitation and heavy chemical industry, and the development mode of "factory towns" will inevitably lead to the decline of the towns, if they can't transform themselves ASAP due to failure to meet the requirement of consumption upgrading and adapt to the change in demand during population urbanization, and if the pillar industry in cities and towns decline.

(2) The upgrading of the consumption pattern has accelerated the development of population urbanization

When entering the new developmental stage, urban and rural residents' demand in basic survivability will decrease, while their developmental consumer demand increases fully, which is especially represented by a rapid increase in the service consumption demand of rural residents and agricultural transfer population as in education, health care, pension and culture and in consumer durables. The upgrading of the residents' consumer pattern has provided an important impetus to the development of population urbanization.

① Observed from the rural areas themselves, with the improvement of economic development and rural residents' life quality, rural population including professional contractors, private business owners and those who become rich first, is gradually migrating to the town, especially the county seat, for the pursuit of quality of life and better prospects for development.

② In terms of agricultural transfer population in cities, a number of migrant workers gradually have stable employment and also higher income after long-term hard work. Their life style and consumption mode have been urbanized, despite their rural household register.

③ Migrant workers with stable jobs, living conditions and stable income (their overall income being not high) will gradually get their children and parents living together, thanks to the constant development of basic public services such as the urban social security system, housing system and education. This has given impetus to population urbanization.

④ Quite a number of migrant workers (older ones included) who have no stable job or are unlikely to have one for a short term and living conditions will choose to buy houses in the small and medium-sized towns of their origin so as to become citizenized.

(3) Innovation in urban and rural integration system will accelerate the process of population urbanization

① The integration of urban and rural basic public service systems will promote the citizenization of migrant workers into a stage of acceleration. For a long time, rural migrant workers have not been entitled to enjoy urban education, medical care, old-age care, housing and other basic public services equally, which has seriously hindered the citizenization of migrant workers. In 2006, the State Council issued *Several Opinions on Solving the Problems of Migrant Workers*, which made comprehensive provisions on the construction of the social security system for migrant workers. Especially in recent five years, the social security system has gradually been improved. The migrant workers have begun to be introduced into the urban housing security system. The children of migrant workers have gradually enjoyed basic equal compulsory education with those of urban residents. This series of policies and measures that promote the equalization of basic public services which both agricultural transfer population and urban residents enjoy have pushed migrant workers and their families into the urbanization process.

② The reform of the household registration system will accelerate population urbanization. Since 2011, the State Council has issued *Notice on Actively and Steadily Promoting the Reform of the Household Registration System* and *the National New Urbanization Plan* (2014–2020) and other policy documents and plans, which take the acceleration of household registration system reform as an important measure to promote new urbanization. The purpose is to phase out the discrepancy of basic public services caused by the different household registration systems of urban residents and rural residents, and to protect the equal sharing of fruits by urban and rural residents. In general, the acceleration of the reform of the household registration system in the 13th FYP period will further promote the process of population urbanization.

Special Citations [2-1]

Major Planning for the Reform of the Household Registration System Since the 3th Plenary Session of the 18th Central Committee of CPC

The National New Urbanization Plan (2014–2020) issued by the State Council on March 16, 2014 states that it is necessary to establish a new residence permit system and fully implement the floating population residence permit system while, with the residence permit as a carrier, establishing and improving the basic public service providing mechanism linked with the length of residence, which is to be taken as the important basis of applying for the registered permanent residence at the place of residence.

Opinions on Further Promotion of the Reform of Household Registration System issued by the State Council on July 24, 2014 proposes establishing "human-centered, scientific and efficient, standardized and orderly new household registration system" and further adjusting the transfer policy of registered household, unifying the urban and rural household registration system, and fully attaining the development goals of residence permit system.

Opinions on Further Improvement of Service for Migrant Workers issued by the State Council on September 12, 2014 put forward that migrant workers and their families who have not yet settled at the city/town of import can apply for residence permit in accordance with the law, thereby enjoying basic public services. In cities/towns with the relative concentration of migrant workers, it is mainly for them to rely on available resources like comprehensive community service facilities and platforms for labor, employment and social security services, while establishing integrated service platforms for migrant workers and integrating public service resources of various departments, with a view to providing convenient, efficient, high-quality comprehensive one-stop service for migrant workers.

The Central Urban Work Conference held on December 20–21, 2015 defined the task of promoting the reform in planning, construction, management, and household registration reform, improving the management level, and striving to build smart cities, in order to promote the equalization in basic public services for urban permanent population with the implementation of the residence permit system as a focus, strengthen urban public management and heighten the quality of citizens.

On January 1, 2016, the *Provisional Regulations on Residence Permit* (issued by the State Council), became effective. The residence permit system shall be set up across the country to promote the urban basic public services and facilities to complete coverage of permanent population, while actively creating conditions to gradually raise the level of public services that residence permit holders are entitled to.

Source China (Hainan) Institute for Reform and Development.

2.2 The Urbanization Rate of the Registered Household Population Will Reach 50%

By 2020, a new pattern of urbanization of the registered household population will basically be formed, with the emphasis on achieving a population urbanization rate of about 50%, which will be one of the important indicators of the new-type urbanization in the 13th FYP period.

(1) 2020: the urbanization rate of China's registered household population will reach about 50%

In 2011, the urbanization rate of permanent population exceeded 50%, whereas the urban permanent population surpassed the rural permanent population for the first time. This is a historic change in China's economic and social structure, marking its entry into the era of urbanization in general. In 2015, China's urbanization rate of permanent population reached 56.1%, but the urbanization rate of registered household population was only 39.9%.[7] During the 13th FYP period,

[7] There Is Still a Difference of 16.2% Between the Urbanization Rate of Permanent Population and That of Registered Population in China. *Economic Daily*, April 27, 2016.

according to the goal set by the Fifth Plenary Session of the 18th CPC Central Committee, which is to speed up the urbanization rate of registered household population, it is imperative to deepen the reform in the household registration system and accelerate the equalization of basic public services between urban and rural areas, so that the urbanization rate of registered household population in the next five years is likely to increase at an annual rate of not less than 2%. It is estimated that by 2020 the urbanization rate of China's permanent residents will probably exceed 60%, and the urbanization rate of the registered household population will increase to about 50%. From a realistic point of view, as long as relevant reforms focusing on the urbanization of migrant workers are in place, the urbanization rate of more than 50% of the registered household population will be conditional and possible by 2020.

(2) The gap between the urbanization rates of permanent population and registered population will be narrowed down to about 10%

① To keep the gap between the above-mentioned two rates at about 10% is taken as the expected indicator of urbanization development in the 13th FYP period. According to statistical calculation, in 2000–2015, the gap between the urbanization rates of permanent population and registered (household) population grew from 10.5% up to nearly 16.2%. At present, although 270 million migrant workers work in cities, it is hard for them to enjoy the same basic public services in education, employment, social security as urban residents do, and therefore they are still in a state of "semi-urbanization".

Observed from the reality, the problem of migrant workers has become the focus of the contradiction between the urban and rural dual system structure. By 2020, the gap between the urbanization rates of permanent population and registered population should be narrowed down to about 10% as the anticipated objective of the development of national urbanization transformation. In other words, the urbanization rate of permanent population will reach 60%, and that of registered population will reach 50%. The rest population will be left to the management of floating population.

② The gap between the urbanization rates of permanent population and registered population can be narrowed down to 5–10% in some areas. For such provinces and autonomous regions as Shandong, Jiangsu, Jilin, Heilongjiang, Qinghai, and Ningxia, the gap between the urbanization rates of permanent population and registered population

Table 2 2013 comparison between the urbanization rates of permanent population and registered population in China (unit: %)

Area	*Urbanization rate of permanent population*	*Urbanization rate of registered population*	*Gap*
The whole country	53.73	35.93	17.8
Beijing	86.3	80.92	5.38
Tianjin	82.01	62.8	19.21
Shandong	53.75	42.97	10.78
Shanghai	89.6	90.03	−0.43
Jiangsu	64.11	57.43	6.68
Zhejiang	64	32.02	31.98
Fujian	60.77	34.2	26.57
Guangdong	67.76	53.69	14.07
Hainan	52.74	37.83	14.91
Hebei	48.12	32.37	15.75
Liaoning	66.45	51.67	14.78
Jilin	54.2	46.98	7.22
Heilongjiang	57.4	48.92	8.48
Shanxi	52.56	33.74	18.82
Henan	43.8	22.6	21.2
Anhui	47.86	22.92	24.94
Hubei	54.51	34.64	19.87
Hunan	47.96	22.26	25.7
Jiangxi	48.87	26.59	22.28
Inner Mongolia	58.71	41.27	17.44
Guangxi	44.81	19.43	25.38
Chongqing	58.34	40.02	18.32
Sichuan	44.9	28.82	16.08
Guizhou	37.83	16.38	21.45
Yunnan	40.48	27.24	13.24
Tibet	23.71	17.34	6.37
Shaanxi	51.31	38.01	13.3
Gansu	40.13	27.55	12.58
Qinghai	48.51	42.22	6.29
Ningxia	52.01	39.81	12.2
Xinjiang	44.47	42.59	1.88

Source National Bureau of Statistics: *China Statistical Yearbook 2014*, China Statistics Press, 2014; Department of Population and Employment Statistics, National Bureau of Statistics: *China Population and Employment Statistics Yearbook 2014*, China Statistics Press, 2014

have already been about 10%, and so it is appropriate to speed up the urbanization of registered population (see Table 2). For example, in 2012, the gap between the urbanization rates of permanent population and registered population was 7 percentage points. According to the *Plan for the New-Type Urbanization of Jiangsu Province and the Integration of Urban and Rural Development (2014–2020)*, which takes the "orderly promotion of agricultural transfer population urbanization as the primary task of promoting new-type urbanization and integration of urban and rural development", it is required to reduce the gap between the urbanization rates of permanent population and registered population to 5%.

③ For areas with a larger gap between the said two rates, the buffer time can be set and transitional measures can be adopted. The eastern coastal areas and developed cities like Beijing and Shanghai are the main areas for agricultural population transfer, making it difficult to narrow the gap between the urbanization rates of permanent population and registered population. Firstly, however, public services can be expanded from registered population to permanent population. Secondly, it is preferable to give those migrant workers priority to citizenization, who have enjoyed stable employment, stable housing, the considerable length of residence and the local social security. But highly mobile agricultural transfer population will be subject to the management of floating population.

3 Letting "Migrant Workers" Become History

The citizenization of migrant workers is both the core and focus of promoting the urbanization of registered population. With the acceleration of the reform of the household registration system in both urban and rural areas and the progress in equalization of basic public services, it will be possible for "migrant workers" to step down from the historical stage by 2020.

3.1 The Conditions "for Migrant Workers to Become History" Have Been Met

At present, China has already entered the important period for accelerating the transformation and development of urbanization. Whether in terms of practical demand or of the development trend, the citizenization of migrant workers should be accelerated during the 13th FYP period. It is high time to "let migrant workers become history".

(1) The citizenization of migrant workers has reached a critical point

For one thing, migrant workers have tended to live in cities for a long time. Even if *hukou* or registered permanent residence is not accessible to them, about 80% of them will remain in cities. In other words, there is a strong realistic demand for migrant workers to become citizenized. For another, a lot of social contradictions and risks have accumulated because migrant workers have not been integrated into urban society for long, nor have they been able to enjoy their due rights. Faced with the imbalance of interest relations and the prominent social contradictions, the time and space constraints to solve the citizenization of migrant workers have been significantly strengthened. To promote the urbanization of rural migrant workers and let the migrant workers settle down in cities while enjoying the same rights and obligations as urban residents do will not only benefit China's economic and social stability but also win the initiative for on-going transformation and development.

(2) Urbanization of rural migrant workers can turn the potential consumption demand of a large group of 270 million people into realistic demand

Citizenization of migrant workers is not only the process of transforming rural consumption into urban consumption but the process of narrowing the gap between urban and rural consumption. According to the calculation based on survey data from the National Bureau of Statistics, the income of migrant workers in 2015 was about 36,000 yuan (US$6000) per person. If there is an income of 10,000 yuan (US$1667) to be spent in rural areas, then the migrant workers will annually bring about rural consumption at 2.7 trillion yuan (US$0.45 trillion). With migrant workers living and working in cities, there will be improvement for them in consumption environment and their ability to consume as well as changes in their willingness to consume. This will inevitably promote consumption upgrading in such aspects as food, clothing, shelter and transportation. Among all migrant workers, the new generation's consumption potential is particularly enormous. According to the survey, the new generation of migrant workers has higher spiritual and cultural needs than their parents.

(3) The citizenization of migrant workers contains great demand for investment

The citizenization of migrant workers will lead to a great demand for investment in infrastructure and basic housing. In the case of housing, only 1% of migrant workers bought houses in 2014, according to the National Bureau of Statistics, whereas 20% of them most expect help with housing from the government. Counting by 270 million migrant workers, there are 54 million in total who are eager to solve the housing problems, which will involve nearly 150 million people's urban settlement when these migrant workers' families are counted in. Suppose that the migrant workers and their families have 20 square meters of living space per person with the cost of 1000 yuan (US$167) per square meter, it will lead to the housing needs worth 3 trillion yuan (US$0.5 trillion), which will boost an upstream and downstream investment of about 6 trillion yuan (US$1 trillion). Different from the current real estate, the housing demand of migrant workers and their families is a kind of rigid demand, which is conducive to the adjustment of China's economic structure.

3.2 *The Development of Supporting Services and Facilities for the Citizenization of Rural Migrant Workers Needs to Be Accelerated*

Citizenization of migrant workers is an important condition for forming a new pattern of urbanization of registered population, and accelerating the construction and improvement of relevant supporting services and facilities is an important measure to speed up the citizenization of migrant workers.

(1) Full coverage of basic public services for permanent residents shall be achieved

According to *Monitoring and Investigation Report on Rural Migrant Workers in 2014*, the coverage rates of migrant workers' work injury insurance, medical insurance, pension insurance, unemployment insurance and maternity insurance in 2014 were 29.7, 18.2, 16.4, 9.8 and 7.1% respectively. Although their "five-insurance" coverage rates increased by the percentage points of 5.6, 5.1, 6.6, 6.1 and 5.1% respectively (see Table 3) as compared with 2008, migrant workers' insurance rates still remain obviously lower than those of urban workers. The 13th FYP period should be the period in which the focal point is to increase

Table 3 The proportion of migrant workers covered by social security (unit: %)

	2008	*2009*	*2010*	*2011*	*2012*	*2013*	*2014*
Pension insurance	9.8	7.6	9.5	13.9	14.3	15.7	16.4
Work injury insurance	24.1	21.8	24.1	23.6	24	28.5	29.7
Medical insurance	13.1	12.2	14.3	16.7	16.9	17.6	18.2
Unemployment insurance	3.7	3.9	4.9	8	8.4	9.1	9.8
Maternity insurance	2	2.4	2.9	5.6	6.1	6.6	7.1

Source The proportion of this table is based on the ***Monitoring and Investigation Report on China's Rural Migrant Workers in 2012–2014*** issued by the National Bureau of Statistics

the social security coverage rate of migrant workers while making it possible for agricultural transfer population to enjoy equal education, employment, social security, health care, housing and other aspects of basic public services, in order to achieve a complete coverage of the permanent population in basic public service.

(2) Migrant workers who have settled in cities should be brought into line with the urban housing security system

Housing is the biggest problem that migrant workers face when they want to resettle in the city, and it is also an essential part for them to live a stable life in the city. In 2014, migrant workers who bought houses in where he is working only made up 1% of the total number; those who enjoy the housing provident fund accounted for only 5.5%.[8] As the income of migrant workers is significantly lower than the housing price, it is very difficult for a large number of migrant workers to buy houses in the first- and second-tier cities within a short period of time, and their basic housing demand will have to be met through various ways. For example, while bringing migrant workers into line with the scope of public rental housing security under the governments at all levels, the governments can come out with support policies for enterprises that have employed more migrant workers and, under the conditions where the future planning is to be followed, encourage them to construct dormitories for migrant workers on the land purchased in accordance with the

[8] National Bureau of Statistics: *Monitoring and Investigation Report on Rural Migrant Workers in 2014*. http://www.stats.gov.cn, April 29, 2015.

law. In order to promote the development of the housing rental market, the comprehensive tax rate of 5% can be implemented according to the practice of Shanghai to reduce the tax burden of the house lessors.

(3) "Four integrations" shall basically be achieved

Citizenization of migrant workers is both for migrant workers to gradually acquire the same identity, same rights, and equal status as urban residents enjoy and for migrant workers and their family to achieve the urbanization of life style and consumption patterns, finally becoming the new citizens after making the migrant workers integrated into the cities. By drawing practical experience of Guangzhou and Zhuhai, training for a full range of professional, personalized, optimized integration projects is to be carried out through designing and arrangement, to speed up the integration of migrant workers into the local society in the fields of culture, economy, politics, life and more. In other words, migrant workers have pre-job training and work under the contract; their children are entitled to school education, and their life has improved; they can participate in politics; they can safeguard their legal rights and interests; they can live with dignity.[9] Those are effective ways to promote the "four integrations" for migrant workers and their family: "the integration of individuals into enterprises, children into schools, families into communities, and groups into society".

3.3 The Time Is Ripe for the Citizenization of Migrant Workers

At present, the timing and the conditions are ripe for comprehensively solving the problem of urbanization of migrant workers. "Let migrant workers become history" ASAP is not money problem on the whole; the key is subject to the determination the Central Government is supposed to make and a breakthrough to be achieved in policy and system.

(1) The main structure of migrant workers has undergone a profound change

[9] Feelings Can't Replace the Way for Solutions. *Nanfang Metropolis Daily*, January 7, 2016.

Table 4 Changes in the age structure of migrant workers in 2010–2014 (unit: %)

	2010	*2011*	*2012*	*2013*	*2014*
16–20 years of age	6.5	6.3	4.9	4.7	3.5
21–30 years of age	35.9	32.7	31.9	30.8	30.2
31–40 years of age	23.5	22.7	22.5	22.9	22.8
41–50 years of age	21.2	24	24	26.4	26.4
Above 50	12.9	14.3	14.3	15.2	17.1

Source *Monitoring and Investigation Report on China's Rural Migrant Workers in 2014*. http://www.stats.gov.cn, April 29, 2015

The new generation of migrant workers has a strong desire to integrate into the city, and they have tried to turn into "non-agricultural full-timers". At present, the post-'80 migrant workers constitute nearly 60% of the total number (see Table 4). Some surveys show that 85% of the new generation of migrant workers has not engaged in agricultural work.[10] As many as 61% of migrant workers under 20 are willing to stay in cities.[11] Their level of education, their desire for urban life, and their industry all determine that most of them will not return to the rural areas. Both the change of the main body of migrant workers and the progress of economic and social development have made it difficult to postpone the citizenization of migrant workers for another ten years.

(2) The timetable for the citizenization of migrant workers has to be set out clearly

Firstly, qualified migrant workers will be citizenized in the first two to three years of the 13th FYP period. That is to make the citizenization of migrant workers with relatively stable jobs, relatively fixed residences and the willingness to stay in cities an important binding target of the 13th FYP. Migrant workers eligible for the above three criteria account for 60–80%, whereas the remaining population is left to the management

[10] A Survey Shows: 85% of the New Generation of Migrant Workers Have Not Engaged in Agricultural Production. Xinhuanet, April 24, 2012.

[11] How Do the Rural Areas with Gradually Decreased Resident Population Feed China? *People's Daily*, March 20, 2012.

Table 5 The requirements and standards for citizenization and the proportion of migrant workers

Basic conditions for the citizenization of migrant workers	*Reference standards*	*The proportion of migrant workers that meet the standards*
Having relatively stable jobs	1 year and above	Above 70%
Having relatively fixed residences	Rented rooms; employer-arranged dormitories; purchased flats	Above 80%
Willingness to stay in cities	Cities/towns where they work; cities of one's origin small towns near one's ancestral homes	ca. 60%; above 80% of the new generation of migrant workers
The proportion and number of migrant workers that meet the requirements of citizenization	Of 270 million migrant workers, 60–80% in line with the basic conditions of urbanization number 160–200 million people; more than 80% of the new generation of migrant workers meets the basic conditions of citizenization	

Source The table is prepared by the research group of China (Hainan) Institute for Reform and Development (CIRD)

of floating population (see Table 5). Conditions for such citizenization in big cities like Beijing, Shanghai, Guangzhou and Shenzhen can be higher than those in small and medium-sized cities. Secondly, it will take another three to five years to basically solve the citizenization of the existing migrant workers by deepening the reform of the household registration system and making the institutional arrangement of equalization of urban and rural basic public services.

(3) The deepening reform of the household registration system will be carried out

① It is necessary to make a shift from limiting population mobility to guiding and serving population mobility. The population interflow in urban and rural areas and other regions is an important manifestation of the vitality of economic and social development, and the re-allocation of labor resources can effectively improve total factor productivity. *The National Plan for New-Type Urbanization (2014–2020)* proposes "promoting orderly population mobility, reasonable distribution and social integration". To deepen the reform of the household registration system, the primary task is to promote the transformation from "restriction" to "guidance and service" for the floating population, so as to achieve the fine management of the floating population.

One is to establish a policy system conducive to population mobility. For example, institutional guarantee has to be provided for the transfer of employment of floating population between urban and rural areas and between regions, by speeding up the transfer and continuation of various social security systems.

Two is to give priority to the settlement of people who have already obtained employment, residence and insurance coverage in cities for a certain number of years. Farmers' rights and interests in rural areas must be ensured to reduce their family worries in the ancestral homes, while creating capital accumulation for farmers to live or resettle in cities and enhancing the attraction of urban resettlement.

Three is to guide rural migrant workers to find jobs and live in small and medium-sized cities, bringing about urbanization in the nearby city. Accelerating the development of small and medium-sized cities should be taken as the main direction to optimize the size and structure of cities, and strengthen the guidance about the distribution of industrial and public service resources while improve their quality and increasing their quantity.

② It is necessary to make a transition from population control to population service. From the very start the household registration system is the system featured by the purpose of population control and strong administrative characteristics. Maintaining social order and stability is the main target of the system, which stresses control rather than service, emphasizes the short-term function rather than the long-term one, and is responsible for emergency management rather than service-conscious management. Since the reform and opening up, with the acceleration of population urbanization and the increase in the size of floating population, the malpractice of population management model with the main purpose of preventing and controlling has become increasingly prominent. In recent years, for example, social problems and labor disputes concerning migrant workers caused by a large number of left-behind elderly, left-behind children, and left-behind women have posed severe challenges to the traditional prevention-oriented and control-oriented management model.

Firstly, a change should be made from emergency management to guidance management. Practically speaking, it is more and more difficult for the population management model, which mainly focuses on public security management, to adapt to the profound change in social structure and the trend for diversification of interest subjects brought about by population urbanization. For example, the long-term effective mechanism for the effective protection of the legitimate rights and interests of migrant workers has not been established yet, and the prominent problem is that there is no buffer mechanism for contradictions between the employers and employees. Pushing forward population urbanization in an orderly manner, it is important to build an effective platform for negotiation and expression of opinions under the principle of fairness and through such means as law and policy. Especially for the weak party whose interest is damaged, it is just through institutionalized forms and channels that his or her interest can be expressed effectively, his or her legal rights and interests can be protected, or his or her corresponding administrative, judicial relief can be obtained.

Secondly, a transition should be made from population control to population service. The key is to speed up the reform in social security system by establishing a multi-level social security system. Therefore, it will adapt to the diversified social security demands of floating population, and achieve complete coverage of permanent population in public service.

③ It is necessary to make a transformation from "the management of people by certificates" to "big data" management service.

"The management of people by certificates" is the main means of population management in China. Specifically, population information is grasped through temporary residence permit, employment permit for foreign population, marriage certificate, child-bearing certificate, rental permit, and other certifications. Practice has proved that due to informal employment and no fixed residence on the part of a large number of floating population, the said population management method, namely, "the management of people by certificates", will not only be difficult to accurately grasp the information of floating population and provide accurate service, but also bring permanent population a lot of trouble that they have to prove themselves with certification frequently and they are even often required to prove their mothers are none other than their mother with certification. With the wide application of modern information technology like "big data", it is necessary and mature to build a modern social governance system through establishing the large database network of citizens' information.

4 Replacing the Urban-Rural Binary Household Registration System with Residence Permit

For a long time, population urbanization lags behind the scale urbanization in China. The root cause is the urban-rural dual household registration system. Only by breaking the dual household registration system and replacing the urban-rural dual household registration system with residence permit can a new pattern of population urbanization be formed.

4.1 Conditions Are Ripe for the Comprehensive Implementation of the Residence Permit System

Generally, the household registration system reform after years of exploration has achieved important results. Conditions are ripe for implementing the residence permit system comprehensively. But the key is to achieve a substantial breakthrough in deepening the reform of household registration system by breaking the pattern of interests.

(1) The residence permit system includes some functions of household registration

In the last ten years, the pace of reform in the household registration system has been accelerated. The system of residence permit is being explored constantly in various places, and the policy effect is being shown continuously. In making a comparison between the residence permit system being implemented in various places and the current household registration system, it is found that urban registered residents (or urban residents with *hukou*) can enjoy comprehensive social security and welfare benefits, whereas people with residence permits (not including temporary residence permits) can only enjoy part of the same service and treatment as registered residents who live with those with residence permits in the same locality. Although there is difference between the *hukou* system and the residence permit system, the gap is narrowing.

The conditions in which the *hukou* system emphasizes gaining the welfare benefits and rights on the basis of one's identity is becoming ever less important, whereas the consciousness of the residence permit system that emphasizes gaining the welfare benefits and rights on the standardized basis of one's residence, employment and payment of social insurance is ever increasing. This has laid a sound foundation for establishing the uniform residence permit system by 2020 nationwide (see Table 6).

(2) The equalization in basic public services needs to be accelerated

In recent years, the State Council issued *Several Opinions on Solving the Problems of Rural Migrant Workers*, and a series of policies and measures of promoting the urbanization of floating population with emphasis on migrant workers whose children's education, vocational training, the level of public health and social security have continued to improve. In October 2015, the fifth Plenary Session of the 18th CPC Central Committee put forward reform measures "to fully implement the major disease insurance system of urban and rural residents", "integrate the urban and rural residents health policy and management", and "implement the basic national pension system", which have created favorable policy conditions for promoting the equalization of urban permanent population in basic public services with the implementation of the residence permit system as the goal during the 13th FYP period.

(3) Floating population has a strong desire to integrate into the city

According to *Report on the Development of China's Float Population 2015*, in 2014, 55% of the floating population lived in their current residences for three years or more, and 56% intended to live in the same locality for another five years or more.[12] With the increase in the residence period of floating population in the place of current residence and the increase in their willingness to live on, the social demand for the comprehensive implementation of the residence permit system is becoming ever increasing.

[12] Department of Float Population of National Health and Family Planning Commission: *Report on the Development of China's Float Population*, China Population Publishing House, 2015.

Table 6 Comparison between the rights and interests of people in different social strata or groups: a Shanghai case

Demographic categories and policy measures	*Registered permanent residents*	*Residence permit (more accumulated points)*	*Residence permit (standard accumulated points)*	*Floating population for short-term residence or with no residence permit*
Education	Being entitled to education resources and enjoying the right to participate in the Shanghai college entrance examinations	Children can apply for acceptance of compulsory education and participate in the local senior high school entrance examinations and college entrance examinations	Children can apply for compulsory education and participate in local full-time regular secondary vocational school independent recruitment exams and higher vocational school independent recruitment exams	Being uncertain of applying for acceptance of compulsory education; not allowed to participate in local college entrance exams
Social insurance	Shall take out basic medical care and pension insurance and unemployment insurance for urban employees, or social insurance for small towns; enjoy minimum living guarantee	I, my spouse and the children living with me may take out social insurance in accordance with the relevant provisions of the city and enjoy relevant treatment	Those who take out the city's social insurance shall enjoy relevant treatment	No social security benefits
Housing security	Shall enjoy the right to take out housing provident fund and housing subsidy; enjoy policy treatment for affordable housing and low-rent housing	May apply for public rental housing according to the city's relevant regulations; may pay and use housing provident fund in the city according to the State and the city's relevant regulations		No housing security arrangement

(continued)

Table 6 (continued)

Demographic categories and policy measures	*Registered permanent residents*	*Residence permit (more accumulated points)*	*Residence permit (standard accumulated points)*	*Floating population for short-term residence or with no residence permit*
Other welfare systems	Shall enjoys special rights and interests such as compensation for accidental disability and compensation for housing demolition and relocation in addition to the treatment enjoyed by the residence permit holder	In accordance with the relevant provisions of the State and the city, free to enjoy basic family planning technical services in the city; in accordance with the relevant provisions of the State and the city, children who live with their parent(s) can enjoy basic public health services like vaccination of the national immunization planning project, and license processing rights involving passport and motor vehicle driving license in the city		Family planning technical services for basic projects stipulated by the State

Source The Interim Provisions on Shanghai Residence Permit; Rules for Implementation of Interim Provisions on Shanghai Residence Permit; Proposed Regulations on Point Management of Shanghai Residence Permit and Rules for its Implementation; and Management Methods for Shanghai Residence Permit

(4) Information technology provides technical support for the implementation of residence permit system

In the era of big data, the rapid development of information science and technology not only provides a solid technical guarantee for the implementation of residence permit system, but also opens up a wide space for the expansion of residence permit function. At present, the ID card can be managed on the Internet, and the localization management of citizens and other residents and cross-locality management have basically been realized. Drawing on the experience of the United States and other countries and regions, and using modern information technology like big data, a new residence permit system with the personal ID number as the core information will be formed, so as to record, manage and serve the resident's life through his/her residence permit.

4.2 A Unified National Residence Permit System Shall Be Established in a Classified and Step-by-Step Way

On January 1, 2016, the Interim Regulations on Residence Permits came into effect, which marks not only the end of the era of temporary residence permits in China, but also a new stage of reform in the household registration system. To establish a nationwide unified residence permit system in a classified and step-by-step way is an important way to promote population urbanization in China.

(1) It is a major historical breakthrough to replace the dual household registration system in urban and rural areas with the residence permit system

① The residence permit system breaks through the classification of the status defined by the household registration system and achieves identity equality. The household registration system bears a deep identity mark, and there are class differences between the urban and rural *hukou*. There are more than 60 different kinds of unequal social welfare in urban and rural areas. To implement the residence permit system is to no longer distinguish between urban and rural household registration. To live in the city means you are an urban resident, whereas to live in the countryside means you are a rural resident. Farmers and citizens differ only in their occupations, not in their identities or rights.

② The residence permit system breaks through the simple population control function of the household registration system, emphasizing both service and management. With the expansion of population flow, the household registration system with population control as its main function has become more and more restrictive to the optimal allocation of labor resources. The core idea of the residence permit system is to highlight the residential concept and service concept. For one thing, it can play the role of registration and management of floating population instead of temporary residence certificate. For another, by relying on the residence permit system, basic public services can be extended to the floating population.

③ The residence permit system is a goal, not a transition. The reform of the household registration system has not stopped in the last nearly ten years, but the overall reform has lagged far behind and the old system has tended to be even strengthened in some respects. For example, the household registration system is combined with the restriction on house purchase and car purchase, which strengthens the necessity of the household registration. Deepening the reform of the household registration system in the 13th FYP period is not a common reform or innovation, but to create conditions for the traditional dual household registration system to exit the historical stage and fully implement the residence permit system.

(2) A nationwide unified residence permit system will basically be established by 2020

① The coverage of residence permit system needs to be increased. At present, many areas have the problem of low coverage of residence permits. A variety of means can be explored in various places to increase the coverage of residence permits and play an active role of residence permits. Take the following measures for example. One of the measures is to bring float population that are in informal employment and living in illegal buildings for a long time into the residence permit system. Another measure is to allow non-native population to gain residence permits free of charge with their temporary residence permits as continuous residence certification. And yet another is to require enterprises to handle the residence permits for employees, thus increasing the rate of processing residence permits. By the end of 2016, full coverage of the residence permit system for floating population will have basically been achieved.

② The threshold for float population to apply for residence permits should be lowered. Observed from the practical situation, the application conditions in some areas are too high, which is not conducive to mastering the information of floating population. This situation is also easy to make the residence permit become the second household registration, losing the fairness. According to *Report on the Development of China's Floating Population 2013*, the main job of floating population is in the private sector or in self-employment. The considerable proportion of the said population have neither social insurance coverage nor house/room rental certification, which makes it difficult to reach the residence permit application conditions (see Table 7). In this context, therefore, the residence permit application conditions should be made as low as possible. By following the path of reform, namely, the "low threshold, ladder-orientation, the progressive type", the relevant rules should be specified to try to enlarge the coverage of policy. On the basis of keeping the basic requirements unchanged, the corresponding services should be provided for floating population with different conditions.

③ Service levels should be improved. Conditions will actively be created to gradually expand the provision of public services and facilities for residence permit holders and raise service standards. On the basis of keeping the basic requirements unchanged, public services covered by residence permit, such as education, employment, social security, health care, family planning, housing security, culture and sports, and certification, will be increased. Residence will be pegged to welfare. Based on the residence permit holders' residence duration, paid social insurance and contributions to the local economy, a "progressive" welfare model will be established so that they can enjoy different levels of public service and different rights and interests. At the same time, the residence permit system should be set up reasonably to prevent the generation of new social differentiation inside the city and avoid the formation of "social welfare concentration" (see Table 8).

④ Technical means should be improved. Accurate population information data is the basic condition for the comprehensive implementation of residence permit system. To do this, it is necessary to establish a dynamic, nationwide networking, inter-department-linked system of national population basic information database and management, a unified social credit code system and a relevant real-name registration system, thus improving the social credit system. Besides, department database project docking will be implemented so as to integrate the data

Table 7 Comparison of different application conditions for residence permits and policies and arrangements for those who have not met the application conditions in 1 province and 4 cities

Areas	*Residence requirements*	*Requirements for employment and paying social insurance*	*Application requirements*	*Policies and arrangements for those who fail to meet the application requirements*
Shenzhen	Living legally and stably for 12 full months	Lawful and stable employment; Taken out social insurance for 12 full months running or for 18 full months within 2 years before the date of applying for the residence permit, counting from the day of handling the residence registration to the day of claiming the residence permit	All the requirements should be satisfied at the same time	Apply for residence registration
Shanghai	Living in the city legally and stably	Lawful and stable employment; Paid the 6-month social insurance; Or lived in the city for 6 months for refuge with one's relatives/friends of Shanghai resident register, or for studies/training	All the requirements should be satisfied at the same time	Handle residence registration
Zhengzhou	Planning to live for 30 full days and available residence certificate	Available employment certification	All the requirements should be satisfied at the same time	Apply for temporary residence registration

(continued)

Table 7 (continued)

Areas	*Residence requirements*	*Requirements for employment and paying social insurance*	*Application requirements*	*Policies and arrangements for those who fail to meet the application requirements*
Chengdu	A flat purchased or record for lease on the flat or room(s) + paid the 6-month social insurance	Signed labor contract and paid the 6-month social insurance	Plan to live for more than one year and satisfy one of the two sets of requirements	For one planning to stay more than 7 days, apply for residence registration; For one planning to stay more than one month, apply for "Temporary Residence Permit in Chengdu"
Jiangsu	Planning to live for 6 full months and available residence certificate	No clear requirements	Residence certification only	Apply for residence registration

Source The table is prepared based on the paper entitled "Residence Permit System Reform and New Policies" (Lu Jiehua and Li Yue: *Journal of China National School of Administration*, Issue 5, 2015), *Regulations on Residence Permits of Shenzhen Special Economic Zone*, *Management Methods for Shanghai Residence Permits*, *Interim Management Measures for Zhengzhou Residence Permits*, *Management Regulations on Chengdu Residence Permits*, and *Management Measures for Residence of Floating Population in Jiangsu Province*

Table 8 Comparison of some welfare benefits of residence permit holders in 1 province and 4 cities

Areas	*Education*	*Employment*	*Housing*	*Others*
Shenzhen	When meeting certain conditions, holders can enjoy basic public education in accordance with the relevant regulations	Holders can apply for vocational skill training subsidy and professional skill appraisal subsidy	No clear rules	When meeting certain conditions, holders can enjoy corresponding rights and interests in public culture, employment support, social assistance and housing security in accordance with the relevant rules
Shanghai	Holders' children can receive compulsory education, attend the exams of full-time secondary vocational school/independent recruitment exams of full-time high vocational schools; When meeting certain conditions, they can attend high school recruitment of students and regular high school entrance exams	Holders can take part in vocational skills training; being eligible for model worker and vocational qualifications assessment and test	Holders can apply for Shanghai public rental housing; pay and use the housing provident fund in Shanghai	Holders' spouses and cohabiting children may take out the city's social insurance and enjoy relevant treatment in line with the relevant provisions of the city
Zhengzhou	Holders' children can enjoy the same school admission policy as children of migrant workers	Holders enjoy vocational skills training and public employment services	When meeting certain conditions, holders can buy restricted commercial housing and apply for public rental housing	Holders can enjoy certain rights and interests and public services after confirmation by the municipal government

(continued)

Table 8 (continued)

Areas	*Education*	*Employment*	*Housing*	*Others*
Chengdu	When meeting certain conditions, holders may arrange compulsory education for their children Children of "temporary residence permit" holders shall go through the relevant procedures in accordance with the admission policy of the year	Holders enjoy public employment services	No clear rules	Holders enjoy social insurance and other public services provided by the local people's government as prescribed
Jiangsu	Holders enjoy the same basic public education as the local registered population; Holders' children enjoy gradually the qualifications to take part in the secondary school and college entrance examinations in the local district, in view of their continuous schooling years therein, etc	Holders enjoy job services	No clear rules	When meeting certain conditions, they can gradually enjoy the same rights as the local household registration population, in education subsidy, employment support, housing security, pension service, social welfare and social assistance

Source The table is prepared based on the paper entitled "Residence Permit System Reform and New Policies" (Lu Jiehua and Li Yue: *Journal of China National School of Administration*, Issue 5, 2015), *Regulations on Residence Permits of Shenzhen Special Economic Zone*, *Management Methods for Shanghai Residence Permits*, *Interim Management Measures for Zhengzhou Residence Permits*, *Management Regulations on Chengdu Residence Permits*, and *Management Measures for Residence of Floating Population in Jiangsu Province*

resources and data acquisition system mastered by such departments as public security, human resources and social security, family planning, civil affairs, housing and urban-rural development, and industry and commerce (all to be stored in the population database), and make the automatic comparison and update of data possible.

⑤ Institutional integration should be integrated. One is to promote the integration of the residence permit system with the household registration system and unify the main functions of population registration and service management of residence permit system. Two is to promote the integration of interprovincial residence permit system. Three is to basically establish a nationwide unified residence permit system with the only identification number by 2020.

(3) A unified national residence permit system will be established in a classified and step-by-step way

① Within two to three years, the function of welfare housing allocation of the household registration system shall be removed, the household registration system be totally terminated in small and medium-sized cities, and the residence permit system established in one step. In addition to the big cities, small and medium-sized cities and organic towns will terminate the household registration system. Anyone who has a stable and legal residence or has leased a house/room, and his/her cohabiting spouse and minor children, parents, etc., can apply for the permanent residence registration in the locality. In megacities or big cities where the household registration system and the residence permit system are both implemented, the public service level should gradually be improved for residence permit holders while gradually liberalizing the settlement policy for agricultural transfer population that has regular jobs according to local financial conditions.

② Within three to four years, except for some megacities and large cities, the household registration system of other medium-sized cities shall basically be liberalized and the residence permit system fully be implemented. Taking the residence permit as a carrier, the basic public service provision mechanism which is related to the residence duration and other conditions should be established and improved. Residence permit holders will enjoy the same rights of employment, basic public education, basic medical and health services, family planning services, public cultural services, and certificate processing services as the local registered population. In view of their continuous schooling years in the local area, children accompanying their migrant parents should gradually enjoy the qualification to participate in the local secondary and college entrance examinations. What's more, the conditions for rural residents to settle down in cities include withdrawal of the right to the contracted management of land, the right to the use of house sites and the right to the distribution of collective income.

③ By 2020, the national system of residence permit with the ID card code as the only mark shall fully be implemented. Residence permit holders shall enjoy the same basic public services as local permanent residents. Urban and rural residents shall exercise all the basic rights of citizens, including the right to vote and the right to be elected, in accordance with local standards in their permanent residence. The population with the short residence duration shall be included in the management system of floating population.

4.3 *The Reform of Relevant Support Systems Should Be Accelerated*

Observed from the exploring practice of the household registration system reform across the country in recent years, due to the lagging reform in the supporting system, a lack of unified national policy guidance, the residence permit system differs considerably from place to place, affecting the implementing effect of the system. The overall implementation of the nationwide unified residence permit system by 2020 requires the Central Government to introduce supporting reform measures ASAP.

(1) The all-level governments' responsibilities for basic public service should be clarified

① The responsibilities of the Central Government should be strengthened in basic social security services. It is imperative that the Central Government only provide the unified standards while changing the situation that the policies are not unified and mainly provided by local governments.

② The responsibilities of the Central Government and provincial governments should be standardized in basic education, public health and basic medical services. It is necessary to further specify the scope of services provided by the Central Government and provincial governments, the proportion of expenditures and the limit of their administrative authority, and determine the proportion of responsibility for expenditures in accordance with the scope of benefits. To solve the problem of difficulty in making a direct connection between the funds of compulsory education in both the immigrant places and the emigrant places, the compulsory education voucher system of compulsory education throughout the country shall be implemented. And the scheme for the unified national college matriculation examination for migrant children shall be made public ASAP.

③ The responsibilities of local governments in public employment services should be strengthened. Since the benefits of public employment services are largely local, and the spillover effect is limited, local governments should bear the primary responsibility for expenditure.

(2) Based on the change of floating population, a fiscal and tax system with dynamic matching between financial resources and administrative rights should be established

① The Central transfer payment system shall be improved and the financial resources of the inflow place be ensured. Also, the proportion of general transfer payments should be increased through multiple channels. In terms of annual increment, the share of general transfer payment should be increased while gradually increasing its proportion. The special transfer payment fund to be cleaned up and canceled will be turned to general transfer payment fund. It is to implement the Central Government's rewards and compensation mechanism for basic public services in the inflow place of float population.

② A fiscal responsibility mechanism for the area under jurisdiction should be established so as to achieve the full coverage of urban residents in basic public services. In calculating the per capita population, it is required for the local government and finance of the immigrant place to calculate the total population, rather than the population supported by finance, in order to achieve the full coverage of basic public services. Focusing on adjusting the fiscal expenditure structure, a certain proportion of fiscal revenue created by the floating population is to be taken as an input to basic public services for floating population so as to solve the supply problem of basic public services for floating population.

(3) The establishment of a unified urban and rural social security system shall be accelerated

① To work towards the goal of 2020, it is a first step completed by 2017, namely, to bring all kinds of qualified people into the social security system, giving priority to migrant workers, employees of non-public economic organizations and people with flexible employment to take out insurance. At the same time, the level of security will be raised, the gap in benefits be narrowed and the goal of ensuring basic security be reached for key groups. By 2020, the integration of urban and rural residents' basic medical insurance system and of the urban and rural minimum living security system will be achieved with the systems unified, barrier-free insurance transfer and continuation, thus building a fair and sustainable social security system and achieving the equalization in basic public services basically.

② The integration of urban and rural social security systems shall be promoted. The framework of a social insurance system designed on the basis of one's identity shall be broken to set up a shared social security system as the goal and promote the overall development of urban and rural social security systems. It is, therefore, necessary to promote the timely integration of medical insurance for urban residents with the same system structure, similar financing mechanisms and similar treatment levels. At the same time, all kinds of social insurance systems in urban and rural areas will be developed as a whole unified financing channel, unified fund management, unified institutional management, and clear rights and interests.

③ The transfer and continuation of social security and the medical treatment mechanism in other places shall be improved. Learning from the computational method of the EU multinational endowment insurance rights and interests, a new mechanism for Chinese employees' basic pension insurance treatment will be established, and it is "section-based calculation and total-sum provision", making their pension rights and interests not lose at all due to their stay at different places. *Measures for Linkage of Urban and Rural Pension Insurance Systems* will further be improved, so as to protect the legitimate rights and interests of floating population while exploring ways for the transfer and continuation of unemployment and maternity insurance.

(4) Let the agricultural transfer population enter the city with "land property rights"

① Household land contracting should be brought into the legal protection of property right. Here are a few suggestions for the *Land Management Law*. The first suggestion is to add in Section 2 an article that "a rural land user who shall be endowed with land usufructuary right is entitled to enjoy, possess, utilize, and profit from the land use right in accordance with the law". The second suggestion is to change in Section 14 the article that "the duration of land contract operation is 30 years" to the one of "establishing stable and permanent rural land contract relations". The law defines it as "farmers' property right" and places it under the legal protection of property.

② Farmers shall be granted the complete property right of housing legally. To end ASAP the current law restricting farmers' homestead to "one household, one residence" and confining the transfer to the semi-commercialization of the village, and to grant farmers' homesteads and their owners complete property rights, it is necessary to issue uniform and lawful homestead certificates, giving farmers the right to use homesteads from the legal nature of usufructuary right and the complete right to possess, utilize, profit from, transfer, and mortgage.

③ Rural construction land should be given equal access to the market. It is suggested to add an article in Section 9 of *Land Management Law* that "a unified land market shall be established by the people's governments at and above the county level and it is mainly through the market that land resources are allocated". This is to provide the legal basis and institutional guarantee for the circulation of farmers' land use right. Therefore, it is suggested that the implementation scheme come out soonest for establishing a unified urban and rural construction land market and that, under the conditions of strict planning and use control, an open, just, fair unified trading platform and trading rules be established to break the exclusive monopoly pattern of the current local government and activate the secondary market of land, thereby promoting the development and perfection of market for land mortgage, lease and transfer.

5 Promoting the Balanced Allocation of Urban and Rural Public Resources

The lagging development of small and medium-sized cities has become a formidable obstacle to the formation of a new pattern of population urbanization in the 13th FYP period. Whether focusing on strengthening the infrastructure construction of central cities or on increasing the allocation of public resources in small and medium-sized cities in the 13th FYP period will be a remarkable judgment about the direction of investment strategy. The 13th FYP clearly put forward "promoting the balanced allocation of urban and rural public resources" and suggested focusing on the balanced allocation of public resources in the small and medium-sized cities, while increasing investment to make the small and medium-sized cities become an important carrier of agricultural transfer of population.

5.1 The Lagging Development of Small and Medium-Sized Cities Restricts Population Urbanization

Over the years, China has repeatedly stressed the coordinated development of small, medium-sized and large cities, producing little effect. As the public resource allocation has favored large and medium-sized cities, which still has not been changed fundamentally, the development of small and medium-sized cities remain relatively backward, becoming an "obvious weakest link" in the process of population urbanization.

(1) The development of small and medium-sized cities lags behind seriously

① The rate of urbanization radiated by small and medium-sized cities remains low. According to relevant statistics, at present, the urbanization rate of China's small and medium-sized cities and the areas directly influenced and radiated by these cities is only about 35%, far lower than the national average of 55%.[13]

② The quality of development of small and medium-sized towns is not high. Take Beijing, Tianjin and Hebei for example. The backward development of small and medium-sized towns in the highly developed central cities has become a weak link in the integration of Beijing, Tianjin and Hebei. Due to the lagging development of production and living infrastructure in small and medium-sized towns around Beijing, Tianjin and Hebei, many new towns under construction have become "sleeping towns", which are far from giving full play to the function of evacuating people.

[13]China's Urbanization Rate in Small and Medium-Sized Cities Is Only 35.1%: Next 20 Years Will Be a Main Battlefield for Urbanization. www.xinhuanet.com, October 21, 2013.

③ Small and medium-sized towns are shrinking. Related studies show that during the period of 1990–2012, the proportion of China's big cities increased from 12.8% in 1990 to 13.8% in 2000, and then rose rapidly to 24.4% in 2012. The proportion of China's medium-sized cities went from 25.8% in 1990 up to 38.2% in 2012. The proportion of China's small cities reduced significantly, decreasing from 61.4 in 1990 to 53.1% in 2000 and further to 37.4% in 2012.[14] According to the calculation based on the data published by National Bureau of Statistics, of China's cities at and above the prefectural level in 2014, the proportion of large cities, medium-sized cities and small cities were 48.97, 33.56 and 17.47% respectively.[15] It is clear that small cities were seriously underdeveloped.

(2) The space for the development of small and medium-sized towns is enormous

① Small and medium-sized cities have a growing tendency for absorbing agricultural transfer population. From the realistic perspective, the capacity of large cities to absorb a large number of rural migrant population has gradually been weakened, while the role of small and medium-sized cities in absorbing employment and promoting the equalization of urban and rural basic public services has gradually been becoming clear. Among the rural labor force that has been transferred across the country, more than 50% is absorbed by small and medium-sized township and village enterprises in counties, and more than 90% of the rural labor force in China's eastern economically developed areas is transferred in small and medium-sized towns of the same areas.[16]

② The reform of residence permit system is combined with destocking in real estate so as to stabilize the real estate market. Combining the reduction of real estate inventory with the reform of the urban residence permit system and accelerating the settlement of rural migrant population in small and medium-sized cities will bring about more benefits.

[14] Wei Houkai et al.: *The Way of China's Urbanization to Harmony and Prosperity*, China Social Sciences Academic Press, 2014.

[15] National Bureau of Statistics: *China Statistical Yearbook 2015*, China Statistics Press, 2015.

[16] Chi Fulin: The Development of Small and Medium-Sized Towns with the Emphasis on Equalization of Public Resources Allocation. *China Economic Times*, January 6, 2014.

The housing prices in the first-tier cities across the country have basically exceeded 10,000 yuan (US$1667) per square meter. Housing prices in the second-tier cities have also reached a certain high level, making it difficult for rural migrant workers to afford housing. Those in most small and medium-sized towns in counties are largely around 3000 yuan (US$500) per square meter, and the cost of house purchase is far lower than that of first- and second-tier cities. Data from the National Bureau of Statistics show that by the end of February 2016, the area of commercial housing for sale was 739.31 million square meters.[17] These stocks are mainly distributed in third-tier and fourth-tier cities.

③ It is less difficult to carry out the reform of the household registration system in small and medium-sized cities. In recent years, household registration has basically been liberalized in small and medium-sized towns. According to data from *Monitoring and Investigation Report on National Rural Migrant Workers in 2014*, among the migrant workers from small towns, those who move within the province and out of the townships make up 46.1%. During the 13th FYP period, therefore, it is good to take the lead in implementing the residence permit system in small and medium-sized cities and towns and establishing the institutional mechanism of urban-rural integrated system, which is more qualified as well as more realistic to promote the local urbanization of agricultural transfer population.

(3) County urbanization will become an important carrier of population urbanization in China's 13th FYP period

① Small and medium-sized towns with county regions as the focus will become an important force driving the medium-speed growth of China's economy. As a relatively independent economic unit, county regions have played an important role in economic and social development over the years. For example, 95% of the land area of China's counties and 75% of its population contribute 60% of the country's GDP and 25% of its fiscal revenue. According to statistics, in 2013, the national county regional GDP reached 31.9 trillion yuan (US$5.32 trillion), accounting for 56.1% of the nation's GDP. In the 13th FYP period, important attention will be focused on institutional innovation to release the potential of domestic

[17] National Bureau of Statistics: The National Real Estate: Development, Investment, and Sales in January–February 2016. www.stats.gov.cn, March 12, 2016.

demand in small and medium-sized towns. More than 2000 small and medium-sized towns in counties across the country will become the main driving force for China's medium-speed growth.

② Small and medium-sized towns have huge consumption potential. County population urbanization will promote the overall consumption level of small and medium-sized towns. Statistics show that in 2015, urban and rural residents' consumption level differs by 12,169 yuan (US$2028).[18] If 50% of 160 million migrant workers who flow to small towns can settle there, they will bring new consumption worth about 1 trillion yuan (US$0.17 trillion). If 60% of 270 million migrant workers settle down in small and medium-sized towns, they will bring new consumption of 2 trillion yuan (US$0.33 trillion).

③ Small and medium-sized towns have the great potential for investment. Take infrastructure for example. Statistics show that at present the level of investment in infrastructure in small towns is only about 13% of large cities. To complete the infrastructure construction for county population urbanization will release the huge investment potential. According to the related plan, investment in the sewage treatment plants, supporting pipe network and the reconstruction of sewage treatment plants only in county-level cities and county towns during the 13th FYP period will exceed one hundred billion yuan (US$16.67 trillion), whereas investment in nationwide network construction with an emphasis on small and medium-sized towns is expected to exceed 1 trillion yuan (US$0.17 trillion).[19]

④ It is necessary to turn the county towns into an important platform for the accumulation of population. In reality, not all small and medium-sized towns have the potential to make it big. If investment is made blindly in small and medium-sized towns without the potential to make it big, new problems will occur. So it should be noted that county town is the political, economic, cultural and education center of the county. Compared with large and medium-sized cities, the outstanding characteristic of county towns is the close relationship between agriculture, rural areas and rural residents. Compared with small towns in remote

[18] National Bureau of Statistics: *Statistical Bulletin of 2015s National Economy and Social Development*. www.stats.gov.cn, February 29, 2016.

[19] Yao Xuanjie: Spillover-Effect Investment in Broadband Infrastructure to Be Launched: Big Potential in Small and Medium-Sized Towns. *China Securities Journal*, August 8, 2013.

areas, county towns have such advantages as relatively perfect infrastructure, relatively high level of public service and strong industrial support capability. Taking the county seat as the important carrier of population urbanization, it is a good idea to lead such factors as industry, capital and population to the county town and propel the integration and development of the industry and city under a certain condition, which is conducive to helping to improve the efficiency of resource utilization, reduce transaction costs and promote the economic growth driven by a shift from production factors to innovation, upgrading the quality of economic development.

5.2 The Balanced Allocation of Public Resources Shall Be Promoted in Large and Medium-Sized Cities with Emphasis on County-Level Urbanization

China has repeatedly emphasized the coordinated development of big, medium-sized and small cities and small towns, but in reality there has emerged, instead of the realization of the reasonable layout of urbanization, a tendency towards "polarization"—the rapid expansion of big cities and the relative shrinkage of small and medium-sized cities and small towns. The core factor is the unbalanced allocation of public resources in large and medium-sized cities and small towns, which have given rise to many problems such as lagging industrial development and weakened population agglomeration. The important role of small and medium-sized cities and small towns in the 13th FYP period is to promote the equal allocation of public resources of urban and rural areas.

(1) Investment in public resources in small and medium-sized towns shall be increased

① "Public welfare concentration" formed by the household registration system shall be broken. The experience about the development of urbanization in cities and towns in developed Euro-American countries shows that the reasonable distribution of urbanization is mainly about the balanced allocation of public resources. For example, Harvard University is located in Cambridge, Massachusetts. Small towns with some thousands of people in Germany also have equal regional transportation, communications, electricity, water and other infrastructure networks. In Norway, 20,000 small towns also have universities, education, health care, and culture, which are much the same as cities. The balanced allocation of public resources has created good conditions for the balanced development of cities and towns. In addition, the convenient living supporting conditions make small towns enjoy advantages that big cities cannot match. To increase the "popularity" of small towns in China and to solve the problem that "the town is visible but few townspeople are", the key is to enhance the ability of absorbing employment, upgrading the convenient degree of life and increase the availability of high quality public services.

② Public welfare concentration formed by the administrative hierarchy shall be broken. At present, a large number of migrant workers who don't have access to the same public welfare as urban residents have rushed or even flocked to big cities rather than settle in small towns, the main cause of which lies in the serious imbalance of public resource allocation between cities and towns of different sizes and at different levels. For example, megacities and big cities are far superior to small and medium-sized cities and towns in a wide variety of public facilities such as road area per person, public buses, libraries, cinemas and theaters per ten thousand people, Tertiary A hospitals, and the number of key universities. For this, agricultural population transfer shall be guided to small and medium-sized towns in an orderly way during the 13th FYP period. Its importance is to obtain the divorce of resource allocation of government public services from administrative levels, to delegate more power for development to grass-roots small and medium-sized towns, increase investment in public resources for small and medium-sized towns, and make agricultural transfer population in small towns willing to live, able to live, gain full employment, and afford to buy houses.

(2) The balanced allocation of public resources shall be taken as the focus of the reform of Central and local fiscal and taxation systems

In the next three to five years, China needs to take county urbanization as an important channel through which to realize the nearby urbanization of migrant workers, so as to reduce the pressure on large cities. County finance will play a decisive role in county urbanization. From the perspective of reform practice, the county revenue cannot always be earned by selling land, and county finance cannot only be "payroll finance". In another new round of reform in the fiscal and taxation system, it is necessary to take strengthening the county finance as an important goal, to incorporate newly added local tax into the county finance with no reservation, to raise the dividing proportion of value added tax on the part of the people's governments at the county level, to implement the sharing policy of consumption tax, to increase the transfer payment of the governments at various levels for small and medium-sized towns, to ensure the application of new financial fund for urban construction mainly to small and medium-sized towns, and to improve the population agglomeration function of small and medium-sized towns substantially.[20]

(3) Reform in the land use system shall be conducted

Ensuring the land resources needed for the development of small and medium-sized towns is an important condition for the development of small and medium-sized towns. Not all small and medium-sized towns are in a condition to absorb migrant workers. While emphasizing the role of county-level cities, the quota of urban construction land should be inclined to small and medium-sized towns with relatively larger population, guiding the industrial layout to transfer to small and medium-sized towns. At the same time, the quota of land use planning should be tilted to government-subsidized housing, medical and health care, education and social security, so as to improve the carrying capacity of population in small and medium-sized towns. The policy of "the same land price" for land used both for services and for industrial use should be implemented ASAP, so as to promote the development of the service sector in small and medium-sized towns and the transformation and upgrading of township industries while increasing their capacity to absorb employment.

(4) Attention shall be focused on improving public infrastructure in small and medium-sized towns

Infrastructure in megacities like traffic and water supply extended to small and medium-sized cities and small towns will promote the diffusion of public service function of the central areas of megacities to surrounding small and medium-sized cities and small towns and the connection between big, medium-sized and small cities and small towns with the comprehensive transportation network and information network. Special funds will be earmarked to strengthen the infrastructure

[20] Chi Fulin: *The Choice of Transformation for 2020—Trend and Challenge for China's Economic Transformation and Upgrading*, China Economic Publishing House, 2015.

construction in small and medium-sized cities and small towns and improve public service facilities. Full play will be given to the advantage of policy-based finance while increasing financial support to public welfare areas such as public facilities, public services and people's livelihood in small cities and towns.

5.3 *The System in Which Public Resource Allocation Is Based on the Administrative Level Should Be Broken*

The lagging development of small and medium-sized towns is directly related to the system in which public resource allocation is based on the administrative level. To acquire the inclination of public resource allocation towards small and medium-sized towns has become an important guarantee for speeding up the process of population urbanization.

(1) The uneven allocation of public resources has become a prominent factor in the unbalanced development of large, medium-sized and small cities and towns

① The allocation of basic public goods is seriously uneven. Take medical resource allocation for example. According to *China Statistical Yearbook 2015*, in 2014, for hospital beds per 1000 people in medical and health institutions, the city enjoyed 7.84 beds per 1000 people, whereas the countryside only 3.54 beds, with the former being 1.21 times higher than the latter. In addition, the city has 9.70 health technicians per 1000 people, whereas the countryside has only 3.77, with the former being 1.57 times higher than the latter. Eighty percent of China's quality medical resources is concentrated in large cities while 80% of the resources in large hospitals. The top 50 hospitals in China are mainly situated in Beijing, Shanghai and Guangzhou.[21]

② The development of infrastructure in small and medium-sized cities is lagging behind. In 2014, the Chinese urban water penetration rate, gas penetration rate, sewage treatment rate and hazard-free treatment rate of domestic garbage reached 97.64, 94.56, 85.94 and 91.77% respectively. However, in small and medium-sized towns that constitute

[21] Chi Fulin: The Development of Small and Medium-Sized Towns with Emphasis on the Equalization of Public Resource Allocation. *China Economic Times*, January 6, 2014.

the main body of county towns, the above four indicators were 88.89, 73.23, 80.19 and 71.58% respectively.[22]

(2) The root cause lies in the administrative hierarchical urban management system

① The allocation of public resources according to the administrative level has formed the public welfare concentration effect. To allocate public resources in accordance with the hierarchical system, the largest share of allocated public resources is for provincial cities, followed by sub-provincial cities, prefectural cities and county-level cities in descending order. Small and medium-sized towns only have the smallest share. The administrative hierarchical mechanism for public resource allocation has not only caused a serious shortage of allocated public resources in small and medium-sized towns, holding no attraction for floating population, but also given rise to important institutional factors due to the rapid expansion and blind expansion of big cities.

② Land quota is concentrated in cities with high administrative levels, whereas land quota for small and medium-sized cities and towns is in short supply. At present, the quota of land use for construction is mostly concentrated in large and medium-sized cities, and the proportion of quota shared by towns at county and below-county levels is rather small. Take Henan Province for example. By 2020, land use in industrial agglomeration areas above the county level and at the provincial level will have accounted for 96% of the land quota, while land use in small towns only for 4%.[23] Due to the lack of new land quota for construction in small and medium-sized towns, a lot of capital construction and public service facilities like residents' housing, schools, and hospitals there have failed to improve at all for many years. In some central towns the population density is about 10,000 people per square kilometer, giving rise to a series of problems such as high housing prices, large class size in schools and difficulty in getting medical treatment in grass-roots hospitals.

[22] Ministry of Housing and Urban-Rural Development: Statistical Bulletin on Urban and Rural Construction in 2014. www.mohurd.gov.cn, July 3, 2015.

[23] Li Song: The Investigation Shows the Impulsive Grabbing of Land by Small Towns, Highlighting Illegal Problems. *China Comment*, Issue 13, 2013.

③ Public financial resources have been continuously concentrated in cities with high administrative levels. Firstly, cities with high administrative levels can use administrative means to concentrate the financial resources of other towns under their jurisdiction. According to *China Urban Statistical Yearbook 2014*, the per capita public financial revenue in the districts under the jurisdiction of the municipalities directly under the Central Government was nearly six times that of counties and county-level cities in 2013. In terms of fiscal expenditure per capita, the former was nearly four times that of the latter (see Table 9). Secondly, the proportion of financial retention in small and medium-sized towns was bit too low. For the proportion for county financial retention, the existing dividing proportion of value added tax is relatively small. In addition, the more economically developed towns, the smaller proportion of financial revenue. What is retained for the local town's financial resources is not much, far from satisfying the basic needs of town construction and town urban public service.

Table 9 Comparison of per capita financial revenue and expenditure of cities at various levels in 2013

	Counties and county-level cities	*Districts under the jurisdiction of prefectural cities*	*Districts under the jurisdiction of provincial cities*	*Districts under the jurisdiction of municipalities directly under the Central Government*
Per capita financial expenditure (*yuan*)	5329.6	9984.1	12,537.3	21,317.7
Per capita financial revenue (*yuan*)	3324.2	7224.2	11,752.5	18,592.5
Financial expenditure ratio	1	1.0	2.4	4
Financial expenditure ratio	1	2.2	3.5	5.6

Source The calculation is based on *China Urban Statistical Yearbook 2014*

(3) "Relieving the traffic congestion" and "revitalizing the city" can be done by the "evacuation" of public resources

Under the administrative hierarchical urban management system, the "double favorable feature" characterizes the tendency that public resource allocation is favorable to the administrative centers and to the large cities, which leads to the imbalance of urban scale structure. Megacities like Beijing and Shanghai as well as provincial capital cities and central cities will relieve the traffic congestion and other "big city diseases" by constantly relying on administrative-level advantages and increasing infrastructural facilities and the input of public goods through administrative means, in order to improve the population carrying capacity or restrict the inflow of population through other administrative means like household register and housing purchasing limitations. On the contrary, however, "big city diseases" have become increasingly serious. Beijing, for example, implemented the most restrictive household registration policy, but its total population reached 21.15 million in 2013. From 2000 to 2013, Beijing's permanent population grew by an average of nearly 600,000, resulting in a total population of 7.52 million.[24]

And in marked contrast to the big cities, small and medium-sized towns are rather weak in comprehensive function like population bearing, short of public service, and generally lacking in industrial support and "popularity" due to their low administrative levels and small-scale, poor infrastructure. For example, some new towns around Beijing do have industries but can't make a real city in any case, thus becoming known as "sleeping towns". They are difficult to play a carrier role. This shows that the lagging development of small and medium-sized towns is not an industrial problem, but mainly the allocation of public resources such as education, medical care, and culture, which cannot meet the needs of the transfer of labor force.

[24]The Report Says Beijing Should Reduce the Household Registration Benefits While Clarifying the Qualifications for Non-native Population. *Guangming Daily*, May 27, 2014.

CHAPTER 4

Consumption Pattern as a Turning Point from Material Consumption to Service Consumption

As China enters the Late Industrialization, the 13th FYP period will see a major trend towards the overall and rapid growth of over 1.3 billion people's service consumption, while the consumption pattern is upgrading from material consumption to service consumption. However, the problem is that the imbalance of investment and consumption has become a prominent structural contradiction in the current economic operation. By 2020, a new pattern of consumption-oriented economic growth will basically be formed. The key is to promote investment transformation and achieve a dynamic balance between investment and consumption.

During the 13th FYP period, along with China entering the Late Industrialization, the consumption pattern is turning from material consumption to service consumption. It can be said that the rapid growth of service consumption is not only the biggest bright spot and the biggest advantage in China's economic transformation map, but also an important driving force of economic transformation. By grasping the major trend for the upgrading of China's consumption, the historical opportunity of economic transformation can be seized, winning the initiative of structural reform.

F. Chi, *Winning at the Turning Point*, The Great Transformation of China, https://doi.org/10.1007/978-981-32-9479-0_4

1 A Main Trend Towards the Overall and Rapid Growth of Service Consumption

China has entered a new stage of development, which is characterized by the overall and rapid growth of service consumption. To keep abreast of the major trend for consumption upgrading, release over 1.3 billion people's new demand for service consumption and lead the new supply of service consumption has become the strategic focus of deepening structural reform in the 13th FYP period.

1.1 The 13th FYP Period Will Witness the Transformation from Material Consumption to Service Consumption

As China enters the middle and high income stage, the consumption subject has undergone historic changes, and the whole society has begun to enter the new era of mass consumption. Compared with the past, the trend and characteristics of the transformation of the consumption pattern of urban and rural residents from material consumption to service consumption are more and more obvious.

(1) Consumers have become classified

① The middle-income group has become important consumers. The general judgment is that in the 13th FYP period China will enter the middle and high income stage, bringing about a middle-income group of some 300 million.[1] Middle-income people are more likely to receive better education, pay more attention to the quality of life, and are willing to pay higher prices for higher quality and safer services and products. The trading-up of the middle-income group has become an important force to promote the transformation of the consumption pattern from material consumption to service consumption.

② The new generation of consumers, such as the "post-'80s", "post-'90s" and "post-'00s", is on the rising path. At present, the "post-'80s" make up a total population of 228 million, the "post-'90s" constitute a total population of 174 million, and the "post-'00" account for a total

[1] Miao Shubin and Fang Shuanxi: It Is a Big Strategy to Expand the Middle-Income Group. *Guangming Daily*, April 23, 2013.

population of 126 million.[2] The combined population totals 528 million, which have become the main force of service consumption, fashion consumption, and Internet consumption. Their consumption ideas, consumers' rights, consumption consciousness and consumption discourse are deeply influencing the whole business environment. In recent years, many brands, including world famous brands, have identified China's "post-'80s" and "post-'90s" as the biggest target customers.

③ Aging population and the elderly consumer group are expanding. By the end of 2015, China's population over the age of 60 accounted for 16.1% of the total population, amounting to 222 million.[3] According to the relevant prediction by the Ministry of Human Resources and Social Security, by 2020, China's population aged above 60 will make up 19.3% of the total population.[4] The expansion of the elderly consumer group is driving the rapid development of health services, pension services and other services.

(2) The material consumption ratio continues to decline

① The growth of material consumption demand is slowing down. Over the last ten years, the growth of China's urban residents' material consumption demand has slowed down markedly. The average annual growth rate (1.54%) in the term of 2011–2014 only accounted for less than one fifths of the average annual growth rate (8.67%) during the term of 2000–2010. Besides, the growth of rural residents' material consumption demand has taken a downward turn. The annual growth rate from 2011 to 2014 was about 5 percentage points lower than that from 2000 to 2010.[5]

② The proportion of material consumption demand has decreased. In recent years, the popularization of durable consumer goods has been

[2]What do You Mean by the Population Panic: The Population of "the Post-'90s" Become Smaller Than That of the "Post-'80s" by 30%, and the "Post-'00s" Even Smaller? www.bjzq.com.cn, May 31, 2015.

[3]National Bureau of Statistics: *Statistical Bulletin on National Economic and Social Development 2015*. www.statis.gov.cn, February 29, 2016.

[4]Zhou Di: Aging Population Is Troubling China. *Democracy and Law Times*, November 24, 2015.

[5]The data come from *China Statistical Yearbook 2015*, in which material consumption chiefly includes three categories of food, tobacco and alcohol, clothing, and residence. To keep the consistency of data, cash consumption expenditure per capita is adopted.

increasing in both urban and rural areas. For example, although urban and rural residents spend more on food and clothing, their share of total consumption is declining. Judging from the urban and rural residents' consumption pattern, per capita consumption of food and clothing in urban residents' consumption expenditure during the term of 1990–2014 increased from 864.7 yuan (US$144.1) to 7501.5 yuan (US$1250.3). But their spending proportion went from 67.61% down to 44.94%. In rural residents' consumption expenditure, per capita consumption of food and clothing rose from 199.9 yuan (US$33.3) to 2811.0 yuan (US$468.5), but their spending proportion declined from 53.34 to 41.85%.[6]

③ The supply capacity of material consumption has shifted from insufficient to excessive. With the acceleration of industrialization, China, as the world's largest manufacturing country, has generally shifted from shortage of material consumption products to oversupply, and the supply of general material consumption products tends to be saturated. After the expansion of blowout consumption, color TV sets, refrigerators, air conditioners, computers, automobiles and other big ticket consumer durables have been available in Chinese ordinary families. From then on, therefore, it is hard to find an industry with no surplus products in the area of material consumption.

(3) Service consumption demand grows in a comprehensive and rapid way

① The proportion of service consumption has constantly increased. According to statistics, from 2000 to 2014, per capita service consumption expenditure of China's urban residents rose from 1960.92 yuan (US$326.82) to 7563.44 yuan (US$1260.57), which registers an average annual increase by 9.4%. Take per capita urban residents' medical and health care, transportation and communication, and education and entertainment for example. If service consumption increases as at an average annual growth rate as in 1985–2014, the proportion of the said three major types of service consumption expenditure will be close to 39% by 2020. If the annual average proportion increases by 0.8–1 percentage point, the proportion of the above three major types of service

[6]The data were taken from *China Statistical Yearbook 2015*. To keep the consistency of data, cash consumption expenditure per capita is adopted.

consumption expenditure will exceed 40% by 2020. At the same time, with the constant release of service consumption demand, the proportion of urban residents' service consumption is expected to increase annually on average by 0.5–0.6 percentage point, and will reach 50% or so by 2020 when the service consumption constitutes the major part of consumption expenditure.[7]

② Service consumption has increased rapidly. Even in the current context of macro-economic recession, consumption growth in education, tourism, entertainment and culture still remaines strong. In 2015, per capita consumer spending on education, culture, and entertainment nationwide was 1723 yuan (US$287.17), which are 23.3% higher than in 2013, the average annual growth of 11% and 2 more percentage points than the nation's residents' average consumption expenditure in terms of average annual growth rate.[8] Take movie consumption for example. In 2015, the moviegoers in all cities across the country were 1.26 billion, an increase by 51.8% as compared with the previous year. The national total box office receipts were 44.069 billion yuan (US$7.345 billion), an increase by 48.7% as compared with the previous year. The single film box office record rose from 1 billion yuan (US$0.17 billion) directly to 2.439 billion yuan (US$0.407 billion).[9]

(4) There is an apparent trend for material consumption service

① Material consumption has become service-oriented. Take the upgrading of food consumption for example. In addition to good and safe food, consumption calls for good service. In reality, catering enterprises that can better meet the needs of consumers enjoy greater popularity in the market, while consumers are willing to accept slightly higher prices. For example, it was by virtue of high-quality service that *Haidilao*, a Sichuan-style hotpot small company, grew into a large

[7] Chi Fulin: *The Choice of Transformation for 2020: The Trend and Challenge for China's Economic Transformation and Upgrading*. China Economic Publishing House, 2015.

[8] National Bureau of Statistics: *The Rapid Growth of China's Residents' Income and the Overall Improvement of People's Living Standards Since 18th National Congress of CPC*. www.statis.cn, March 8, 2016.

[9] Qiu Yue: Farewell to 2015: The Sustainable Growth of Cultural Consumption. *Guangming Daily*, January 14, 2016.

catering enterprise. However, some of the traditional-brand restaurants have declined day by day just because of poor service.

② Service elements are integrated into material products. It is necessary to integrate service elements into even traditional material consumption, so as to meet customer needs. A lot of value-added service integrated into material products has become a prominent feature of upgrading from traditional consumption to new consumption. The introduction of more service elements is also rapidly changing the application structure of traditional products. For example, the mobile phone is no longer a simple communication tool, but one introduced into with various value-added services of the Internet. Various online and offline services have far exceeded the value of the phone itself. In general, therefore, if the traditional material products are not close to customers by featuring integrated service elements, it is difficult to find a market again.

(5) Service consumption has enormous growth potential

In the next five to ten years, the growth of service consumption will not only be rapid, but also show the outstanding characteristics of large potential and scale. Especially eight major domains of service consumption like information consumption, health consumption, tourism and leisure consumption, education consumption, culture consumption, pension consumption, sports consumption, and green consumption are growing rapidly with any consumption being able to bring a one-trillion-yuan(US$0.17 trillion)-level market space.

Special Citations [3-1]

Eight Major Domains of Service Consumption That Enjoys Enormous Growth Potential

1. **Information consumption**. According to *Several Opinions of the State Council on Promoting Information Consumption and Expanding Domestic Demands* issued in 2013, China's information consumption will exceed 3.2 trillion yuan by 2015, the average annual growth by over 20%, which will cause related industries to produce new output valued at more than 1.2 trillion yuan. Among the new output value, the Internet-based new-type information consumption will reach 2.4 trillion yuan, the average annual growth by over 30%. E-commerce transactions will exceed

18 trillion yuan; and online retail transactions will exceed 3 trillion yuan.

2. **Health consumption**. On October 14, 2013, *Several Opinions of the State Council on Promoting the Development of Health Service Industry* proposed that China's health industry should produce more than 8 trillion yuan by 2020. China will still remain one of the most attractive markets in the world and the fastest growing market then.
3. **Tourism and leisure consumption**. In 1994–2013, the number of tourists among China's urban and rural residents and their total tour cost increased on average by 10.10 and 18.63% respectively over the same period of economic growth and urban and rural residents' income growth. It is worth noting that the total cost of rural residents' tourism and travel expenses per capita increased annually on average by more 1.6 percentage points and 8.11% than urban residents respectively. This shows that rural residents' travel demand was getting released.
4. **Education consumption**. *Report on the Development of China's Education Market in 2014* shows that more than half of China's households spent more than 5000 yuan on education training annually, of which nearly 30% of the households spent more than 10,000 yuan. By the end of 2013, China's total household savings had reached 45 trillion yuan, of which education consumption spending had reached 2 trillion yuan. This would provide a broad space for developing the education market in China. It was estimated conservatively that China's training market would reach one trillion yuan in the next few years.
5. **Cultural consumption**. At the same time, the rapid rise of demand in the cultural domain led to the rapid growth of cultural industry. According to statistics, the proportion of China's urban residents' spending on culture accounted for an increase by 6.6% in 2004 to by 7.3% in 2012. It is expected that China's total cultural consumption demand will reach 16.65 trillion yuan by 2020.
6. **Pension consumption**. According to *China Report of the Development on the Aging Industry 2014*, China's elderly market consumption potential in 2014 was 4 trillion yuan, and is expected to increase to 8 trillion yuan by 2020. China's aging industry is entering a rapid growth period.

7. **Sports consumption**. The value added of China's sports industry reached 400 billion yuan in 2015. According to the goal set in *Several Opinions of the State Council on Accelerating the Development of Sports Industry and Promoting Sports Consumption*, it is to reach 3 trillion yuan by 2020, namely, an annual growth of 50%, and 5 trillion yuan, an annual growth by nearly 30%.
8. **Green consumption**. China's green demand and green consumption started late, but is growing rapidly with the continuous strengthening of people's green consumption concept. According to one survey, 94% of urban consumers are willing to pay 45% more for "green" products and services. For example, green buildings have become a consumption focus in recent years. In 2011, China's urban energy-saving buildings only accounted for 23% of the total floor space of existing buildings. By 2020, the proportion of China's green buildings in the new buildings will exceed 30%, which will bring enormous space for green consumption.

Source The citations are prepared by the research group of China Institute for Reform and Development.

1.2 *Upgrading of Consumption Pattern Is a Profound Economic and Social Change*

As China enters a new era of consumption, service consumption is bringing about changes in economic and social life and more. The full release of service consumption of over 1.3 billion people means the modernization of the way of life, mode of production, business model, and social structure and the formation of the basic pattern of shared social development, triggering a profound change in policy and institutional structure.

(1) Service consumption leads to profound changes in lifestyle

① The quality of life is being further pursued. As the new generation of social groups, such as the "post-'80s", the "post-'90s" and the "post-'00s", gradually grows into the backbone of the society, people are pursuing ever higher quality of life, thus forming a new driving force for industrial reform.

First, they pursue change. The new generation of social groups is more in pursuit of differentiation, and personalized and diversified consumption has gradually become the mainstream. Therefore, the era of imitative, wave-style and total quantitative consumption in the great industrialization is basically over.

Second, they pursue quality. The quantitative consumption demand gradually gives way to the quality consumption demand. Commodities with more service connotation and high service content are more likely to be sought after by consumers.

Third, they pursue the trend. Leisure and entertainment have become fashionable, as people seek more functional, higher-quality real estate.

Fourth, they pursue convenience. People pursue more convenient life. For example, Internet shopping is replacing physical store shopping, which has become the trend of the times. In 2015, China's total retail sales of social consumer goods grew by 10.7%, as compared with the previous year, while national online retail sales rose by 33.3%.[10]

② Green and health are being further pursued. As China enters the stage of high income, people are more in pursuit of a green and healthy lifestyle, thus forming a new driving force for the whole society to promote green transformation and green growth.

First, people pay more attention to the ecological environment. For example, in the face of increasingly severe smog, there has been a phenomenon of purchasing fresh air in recent years, and environmental protection has become a major social concern.

Second, the pursuit of green food has become a new trend. According to the survey, 94% of urban consumers are willing to pay 45% more for green products and services.[11]

Third, demand for health services has skyrocketed. As medical devices enter consumers' homes, wearable smart devices in the field of big data health become popular.

Fourth, body-building has become a national fashion. Going to the gym for fitness has become popular and fashionable among the people, thus promoting the sports industry to a rapidly growing sunrise industry.

③ Education and culture are being further pursued. The demand for high quality education and cultural products has increased dramatically.

[10]National Bureau of Statistics: *The National Economy Progresses Well and Performs Well in Its Steady Operation*. www.statis.gov.cn, January 19, 2016.

[11]Shan Jinggang: Promoting the Green Rise of Hainan with Green Development: A Special Interview with Xia Feng, Assistant to the Dean of China (Hainan) Institute for Reform and Development. *Hainan Daily*, November 13, 2015.

Nowadays, it is more and more common for families with better economic conditions to send their children to all kinds of interest-oriented classes and send them to study abroad. According to statistics from the U.S. Department of Homeland Security, in the 2005–2006 academic year, only 65 Chinese secondary school students with private passports attended high school in the United States. It was not until the 2012–2013 academic year that 23,795 Chinese students went to private high school in the U.S. The number of students increased by 365 times in a short span of seven years.[12]

(2) Service consumption leads to profound changes in production mode

① There will be a shift from production-oriented mode to service-oriented mode. When in the new era of service consumption, the mode of production will shift from production-oriented one to service-oriented one in the era of big industry. The general trend is that although society still needs simple processing and manufacturing, the role of processing and manufacturing in economy is getting smaller and smaller, while service is playing an outstanding role in the whole socialized mass production, and economy is becoming tertiarized. The essence of production is service, and manufacturers are increasingly inclined to provide overall service solutions. Value creation is more and more inclined to the service link, while the profit of simple processing and manufacturing link is poorer and poorer.

② The era of mass customization has arrived. The growth of consumer demand for personalized and differentiated products has caused to the transformation of traditional mass standardization and assembly line production to mass customization. The general trend is that many consumers choose customized products in the fields of clothing, accessories, household articles, home decoration, automobile, etc., which will be produced by enterprises in line with customers' choices and requirements. Under the condition that the profit of traditional industries is poor, the adoption of mass customization production can enable enterprises to obtain differentiated competitiveness and maintain relatively high profit margins. Consumers participate in product research and development and design, and the interaction between consumers and

[12]The Number of Chinese Children Going to US High School Increased by 365 Times in 7 Years. *Shenzhen Economic Daily*, March 11, 2014.

producers has increasingly become an important means for manufacturing to form differentiated products and services and reduce market risks.

③ "Internet plus" has already started the creative subversion and reconstruction of traditional industries. In the new era of service consumption, consumption and production are more and more inseparable from the Internet value-added services, resulting in "Internet plus" subversion and reconstruction of traditional industries by in the subversion and reconstruction of traditional industries by "Internet plus". "Expanding the space of network economy" has been written in the national "13th FYP".

First, Internet companies have subverted traditional industries creatively. For example, e-commerce is a creative subversion of physical stores. Big data means a creative subversion of education and health in terms of process reengineering, and also a creative subversion to traditional schools and hospitals.

Second, more and more traditional manufacturing industries complete their own transformation by relying on "Internet plus". More and more Internet enterprises, relying on the advantages of grasping customer terminals and intervening in traditional industries such as finance, have become competitive new enterprises.

Third, even Internet companies need creative subversion of their own to win new space for further development. Tencent's mobile QQ, for example, is the arrival of a traditional Internet business on the mobile side, which later has upended itself and upgraded itself through WeChat.

(3) Service consumption has evoked profound changes in business model

① Enterprise development is more dependent on creativity. Forming new ideas to meet consumers' differentiated and diversified demands has become a key factor for enterprises to be invincible, thus promoting the advent of the era of creative economy. Creative intensive industries have replaced land and labor intensive industries as a general trend, and creativity determines the life and death of enterprises. More and more new businesses are being created by ideas, such as the iPhone, which represents a typical example of an idea that makes a great enterprise. The creative industry is based on consumer experience. What people value is not the brand only, but the experience of the brand. The core of such an exclusive experience is high-quality service and differentiated service.

"Starbucks is not selling coffee," said Starbucks President Howard Schultz once. "It's the experience to coffee."

② Enterprises will be more of service solution providers. Unlike traditional enterprises producing a product or service, enterprises in the new era, especially innovative enterprises, are becoming service solution providers increasingly.

First, attention should be paid to discover new consumer needs. It has become an important feature of innovative enterprises to provide overall solutions to meet customers' new demands. For example, Huawei, Alibaba and the like get new markets mainly by offering solutions.

Second, attention should be paid to provide solutions. Even the traditional manufacturing industry needs to extend the value chain by providing overall solutions. For example, the booming of 4S stores in the automobile industry which, by providing full service to automobile consumers, have become an important way for enterprises to expand their profit sources.

Third, attention should be paid to innovate service modes. As more and more manufacturing products are sold, there will be subsequent service profits. For example, smart wearable devices are products that become the carrier of follow-up service, while service becomes measures to extend the product life cycle.

③ Enterprises are increasingly dependent on professional core competitiveness. Due to consumers' demanding pursuit of service quality, a service solution often requires several professional enterprises to work out jointly. In this case, therefore, enterprises are more and more dependent on the core competitiveness of specialization. Without specialization, enterprises are more and more difficult to survive. Specialization becomes the core condition for enterprises to generate profits. Even very competitive large enterprises also need to strengthen the professional core business, while taking away the basic, common non-core business they provide and allowing the business to be outsourced by external professional service providers. It is an important means to reduce the cost and improve the quality to reorganize the value chain and optimize resource allocation by service outsourcing.

(4) Service Consumption Has Evoked Profound Changes in Social Structure

① Service consumption promotes the rise of the middle class. Consumption shapes people's social role. Observed from the experience of developed countries, service consumption has shaped the new middle class. Generally speaking, the middle class as a social role is prominently featured by its trading-up. They not only satisfy the traditional material consumption but pursue the quality of life and service consumption. Income is only one of the indicators by which to define the middle class. People who have money dare not to spend, who have money are not well educated or highly cultured, or who have money do not pursue service consumption can hardly be ranked among the middle class in the real sense.

The service industry-oriented structure can effectively increase payment for labor, pushing more workers into the middle class. In general, the higher proportion the service sector has in the country, the higher proportion the payment may be for workers. According to the calculation by China (Hainan) Institute for Reform and Development, during the period of 2006–2012, the correlation coefficient between the provincial proportion of service industries in the whole country and that of payment for workers reached 0.97. For every 1 percentage point increase in the proportion of service industries, the proportion of workers' payment increased by 0.38 percentage point.

② The service industry has become the main channel to expand employment. The expansion of the middle class has been accompanied by the substitution of white-collar jobs for blue-collar ones. Service consumption promotes the expansion of the middle class. It also leads to the increase of jobs in the service sector, along with the increase of white-collar workers. In America, for example, with the transformation of economic structure dominated by industry into services, the size of the white-collar class went from about 10 million in the 1940s up to 50 million in the 1970s, which registers an increase by four times within the 30 years. As a result, white-collar workers made up more than 50% of the total workforce in 1980.[13]

At present, the proportion of employment in the service industry in the developed countries mostly accounts for 70–80% of the total employment, whereas the proportion in China was only 40.6% in 2014. The development of service industry will bring about enormous potential for employment. According to data released by the National Bureau of Statistics, the proportion of service industry in the national GDP reached

[13]Wang Huimian: A Big Strategy to Expand the Middle-Income Group. *Shenzhen Economic Daily*, March 11, 2014.

the record level of 50.5% in 2015. In the next five years, if the value added of the service sector will presumably achieve an annual growth by an average of 8%, the number of new jobs will reach about 12 million each year.[14] In other words, only by forming an industrial structure with service industry as the main body can a new normal of increasing employment be formed.

③ Service consumption promotes urban-rural integration. The gap between urban and rural residents is largely reflected in consumption gap. In 2014, the proportion of China's urban and rural residents' per capita consumption was 2.9:1, which is about three rural residents' consumption equivalent to one urban resident's consumption. From the perspective of a trend for future development, the general material consumption like color TV sets, refrigerators and computers has begun to be popularized in rural areas, and the consumption gap between urban and rural residents will be mainly reflected in service consumption. If rural residents' basic public service consumption in education, health care and pension and non-basic public service consumption in culture, entertainment and health care are both satisfied effectively, the gap between urban and rural areas will greatly be narrowed, thus speeding up the urban and rural integration quickly. Observed from the actual situation of China's provinces, autonomous regions and cities in 2014, the higher the proportion of service industry in the province, the smaller the income gap between urban and rural areas, which shows significant negative correlation between the two (see Table 1). According to the calculation by China (Hainan) Institute for Reform and Development, for every increase of 1 percentage point in the proportion of tertiary industry, the income gap between urban and rural areas will be narrowed by 0.014%. During the 13th FYP period, if the proportion of service industry increases 10 percentage points, the income gap between urban and rural areas will be expected to narrow by 0.14 percentage point.

④ Service consumption is conducive to adjusting the interest structure. In recent years, as the national income distribution structure is not rational, wealth is concentrated in the government and monopolistic industries, the residents' income gap widens while the gap between the poor and the rich increases, affecting the effective release of the national

[14] Hu Jian: Premier Li's Interpretation of GDP Data: 1 Percentage Point Leads to 1.3 Million Jobs. *National Business Daily*, November 7, 2013.

Table 1 The proportion of tertiary industry in various provinces, autonomous regions, and municipalities (directly under the Central Government) and the income gap between the urban and rural areas in 2014

Provinces, autonomous regions, and municipalities	*The proportion of tertiary industry (%)*	*The gap between the urban and rural areas (times)*	*Provinces, autonomous regions, and municipalities*	*The proportion of tertiary industry (%)*	*The gap between the urban and rural areas (times)*
Beijing	77.9	2.57	Hubei	41.5	2.29
Tianjin	49.6	1.85	Hunan	42.2	2.64
Hebei	37.3	2.37	Guangdong	49	2.63
Shanxi	44.5	2.73	Guangxi	37.9	2.84
Inner Mongolia	39.5	2.84	Hainan	51.9	2.47
Liaoning	41.8	2.6	Chongqing	46.8	2.65
Jilin	36.2	2.15	Sichuan	38.7	2.59
Heilongjiang	45.8	2.16	Guizhou	44.6	3.38
Shanghai	64.8	2.3	Yunnan	43.3	3.26
Jiangsu	47	2.3	Tibet	53.5	2.99
Zhejiang	47.8	2.08	Shaanxi	37	3.07
Anhui	35.4	2.5	Gansu	44	3.47
Fujian	39.6	2.43	Qinghai	37	3.06
Jiangxi	36.8	2.4	Ningxia	43.4	2.77
Shandong	43.5	2.46	Xinjiang	40.8	2.66
Henan	37.1	2.38	The whole country	48.1	2.75

Source National Bureau of Statistics. ***China Statistical Yearbook 2015***, China Statistical Publishing House, 2015

consumer demand seriously. From the perspective of a trend towards the upgrading of consumption structure, it is beneficial to adjust the interest structure by releasing the service consumption demand and increasing the proportion of service consumption. For example, to release the demand of service consumption in education and medical care both needs to increase the government expenditure on public services such as education and health care and constantly improve the level of equal basic public services, and needs to expand the effective service supply through opening the markets. This process will make a profound impact on the initial distribution pattern and redistribution pattern. It will help to narrow the income gap between the urban and rural areas, between the regions, and between the groups of people. It will help to break the pattern of service industry monopoly, reducing the inequality in income distribution caused by monopoly. And it will help to optimize the structure of government expenditure, thus forming a more reasonable distribution pattern of government, enterprises and residents.

2 Service Consumption as a New Engine of Industrial Change

The enormous potential of service consumption in the 13th FYP period is not only a prominent advantage in economic growth, but also a new driving force for economic transformation and upgrading.

2.1 A New Pattern of Consumption-Oriented Economic Growth Will Basically Be Formed

In 2015, the contribution rate of final consumption expenditure to the GDP growth was 66.4%, and the forming of a new pattern of consumption-oriented economic growth is becoming a major trend.

(1) There is an obvious trend towards the upgrading of consumption structure

① There is still considerable room for improvement in the consumption rate. According to statistics, China's final consumption rate in 2014 was 51.2%, about 30 percentage points lower than the average in developed countries. This shows that in the next few years there is still large room for improvement in terms of China's final consumption rate.

② The era of personalized and diversified consumption has arrived. With the change of consumption concept, consumption level and consumption pattern, new consumption focuses will keep emerging.

③ Aging population and population urbanization can boost consumption effectively. For example, as China's population aging intensifies, its elderly consumer groups continue to expand, thus promoting the rapid improvement of health and old-age consumption.

(2) The consumption will gain the momentum of rapid growth

① Consumption growth is remarkably faster than the GDP growth. According to statistics, in 2015, the total retail sales of social consumer goods in China showed a real growth by 10.6%, as compared with the GDP growth by only 6.9% in the same period. It is estimated that the growth rate of China's social retail consumer goods will remain around 10% in the next five years, 2–3 percentage points higher than the GDP.

② Consumption will increase substantially.

It is estimated that China's total retail sales of consumer goods will increase from 30 trillion yuan (US$5 trillion) in 2015 to about 50 trillion yuan (US$8.33) in 2020.

③ The consumption rate will increase significantly. The final consumption rate in China is expected to rise from 51.2% in 2014 to about 60% in 2020. Residents' consumption rate will go from 37.7% in 2014 up to 42% or so in 2020.[15]

(2) Consumption will be the main driver of economic growth

Some domestic scholars believe that consumption is only the purpose of production and cannot be the driving force for growth. In real life, however, consumption has become an important driving force for economic growth. It can be judged that the final contribution of consumer spending to the GDP growth during the 13th FYP period will be stable at around 65%.

[15] Chi Fulin: New Trends and New Drivers of Economic Transformation. *China Finance*, Issue No. 1, 2016.

2.2 *Service Consumption Will Become an Important Driving Force for Economic Transformation and Upgrading*

Under the particular circumstances in which downward pressure on investment and cutting overcapacity in traditional industries is mounting, and export meets complicated and varied situations, service consumption is growing in a comprehensive and rapidly way. These represent real highlights and real advantages in economic transformation and upgrading during the 13th FYP period. To grasp the historical opportunity in the new era of service consumption and release the new demand of service consumption is an effective way for China to achieve industrial transformation and upgrading and cut the overcapacity in traditional industries.

(1) Service consumption promotes tertiarization of economy

The rapid and comprehensive growth of service consumption has greatly accelerated China's tertiarization. From 2001 to 2008, the proportion of China's service industry in GDP stayed around 40%. From 2012 on, however, the proportion of service industry increased significantly, and the year of 2012 saw the rise of the proportion by more than 1.2%. By the end of 2015, the value added of service industry had maintained the growth at a higher rate than both the GDP and the secondary industry for 12 quarters running, reaching a 50.5% share of GDP. Since the outbreak of the international financial crisis in 2008, the economic situation at home and abroad underwent profound and complex changes. Despite that, however, the value added of China's service industry rose from 13.1 trillion yuan (US$2.18 trillion) in 2008 to 26.2 trillion yuan (US$4.37 trillion) in 2013, achieving the scale multiplication. The value added of service industry in 2015 even went to as high as 34.16 trillion yuan (US$5.69 trillion).

(2) Service consumption promotes the rise of high-end manufacturing

"Service consumption + high-end manufacturing" is shaping a new model of "intellectually made in China". Although intelligent manufacturing originated in the West, the biggest consumer market is in China. Wearable smart devices and household robots have become a new focus of service consumption and key areas that high-end manufacturing enterprises in China compete for. Intelligent manufacturing has thus been the new engine for innovation in the country. In 2015, new, intelligent, automation equipment and high-end electronic information products became the new growth points; new energy automobile production rose by 161.2% over last year; industrial robots grew by 21.7%; smart TV sets grew by 14.9%; and smart phones grew by 11.3%.[16] According to the *Research Report on Wearable Devices*, the Chinese intelligent wearable devices in 2015 held a share of market worth 12.58 billion yuan (US$2.10 billion), the growth rate being as high as 471.8%.[17] In 2014, with the rapid development of intelligent information technology, the research and application of domestic intelligent robots in China were booming. The year 2015 became known as the "first year" of domestic robot promotion and popularization in China. For example, *Haier* for the first time launch eight series of 39 smart wireless products that would soon enter the market of smart home robots.[18]

(3) Service consumption spurs on technological upgrading

Whether in the service industry or in the manufacturing industry, technological upgrading and service demand present a trend towards integration. Take software development. Although some new hardware production still has a large demand for software development, the priority of software development is to adapt to the most direct service needs of consumers. For example, the core of the Apple mobile phone is to adopt a new software development mode, which turns service into software, an innovative consumer service mode, thus making consumers more convenient and more comfortable, and the use functions of cell phones more powerful. In the manufacturing industry, technological upgrading and consumer demand for service are more and more closely combined with each other. One more example. For 3D printing

[16] National Bureau of Statistics: Industry Maintains the Medium and High Speed Growth While Emerging Industries Continue to Grow: China's Industrial Development Since the 18th National Congress of CPC. www.statis.gov.cn, March 3, 2016.

[17] China's Wearable Market in 2015 Worth 12.5 Billion Yuan: A Growth by 471.8%. www.cnstock.com, December 24, 2015.

[18] Zhang Tingting and Wang Jian: Haier and Jiashida Signed the Agreement on Strategic Cooperation. www.people.com.cn, November 25, 2015.

technology that is expected to undergo a major technological breakthrough, the important feature is connecting the production link with the consumption link seamlessly. The future 3D technology will widely be used in the field of medical and automobile services.

(4) Service consumption promotes the rise of new pillar industries

Based on the international experience, from the middle-income stage to the upper- middle-income stage, the rapid growth of service consumption will cause a batch of living services to become a pillar industry, forming a new sunrise industry. This is the objective trend towards tertiarization of a country. For example, health industries in developed countries now account for 15% of the GDP.[19] In the next five years, as the real estate industry and heavy chemical industry play a less important role in promoting economic growth, China needs to develop pillar industries in the service sector.

According to international standards, industries whose value added accounts for about 5% of the GDP can reach the standards of pillar industries. China has the conditions to develop several key pillar industries in the living services industry. For example, the big health industry will account for nearly 5% of the GDP, and it is expected to become one of the pillar industries in the first two to three years of the 13th FYP. It is estimated that the consumption potential of China's elderly population will increase from about 8% to about 33% of the GDP in 2014–2050, and the pension industry is expected to become one of the most promising pillar industries.[20]

2.3 Service Consumption Will Become a New Engine Driving Economic Growth

The overall rapid growth of service consumption is changing the pattern of China's economic growth. In recent years, the rate of industrial development in service consumption is much higher than the GDP growth rate, which has become an important factor to ease the downward

[19] The Development and Enlightenment of the American Health Industry. www.maydeal.com, October 18, 2012.

[20] Chen Yu: The Consumption Potential of China's Elderly Population Reaches About 106 Trillion Yuan by 2050. *Economic Daily*, December 3, 2014.

pressure of China's economy. Driven by service consumption, the characteristics of the stage at which consumption becomes an important driving force of economic growth have gradually been strengthened.

(1) The rate of industrial development in service consumption is far higher than the GDP growth rate

The rate of industrial development in service consumption is not only much higher than that of traditional industrial development but much higher than the GDP growth rate. According to preliminary accounting data of the National Bureau of Statistics, in 2015, China's GDP growth rate was 6.9%; the growth rate of secondary industry was 6%; whereas related industries in the field of service consumption mostly maintained a double-digit growth. Take tourism for example. From 2013 to 2015, the average annual growth of domestic tourists exceeded 10%, and the average annual growth of domestic tourism revenue exceeded 15%. Also, information consumption achieved a blowout growth. At the end of 2015 the number of the Internet users was 690 million people, 22% higher than that at the end of 2012.[21] The online retail sales in 2015 grew by 31.6%, far more than the rate of increase in total retail sales of social consumer goods.[22]

(2) Service consumption has become the main driving force of economic growth

Driven by service consumption, consumption has become an important engine driving economic growth. The rapid growth of service consumption has brought about a historic change in the role of investment and consumption in driving economic growth, while the leading role of consumption in driving economic growth has gradually been established. In 2011, the contribution rate of consumption to economic growth reached 62.83%, higher than that of investment for the first

[21] National Bureau of Statistics: Service Industry Continues to Expand While Emerging Industries Grow Rapidly: The Development of China's Service Industry Since the 18th National Congress of the CPC. www.statis.gov.cn, March 7, 2016.

[22] National Bureau of Statistics: *Statistical Bulletin on National Economy and Social Development*. www.statis.gov.cn, February 29, 2016.

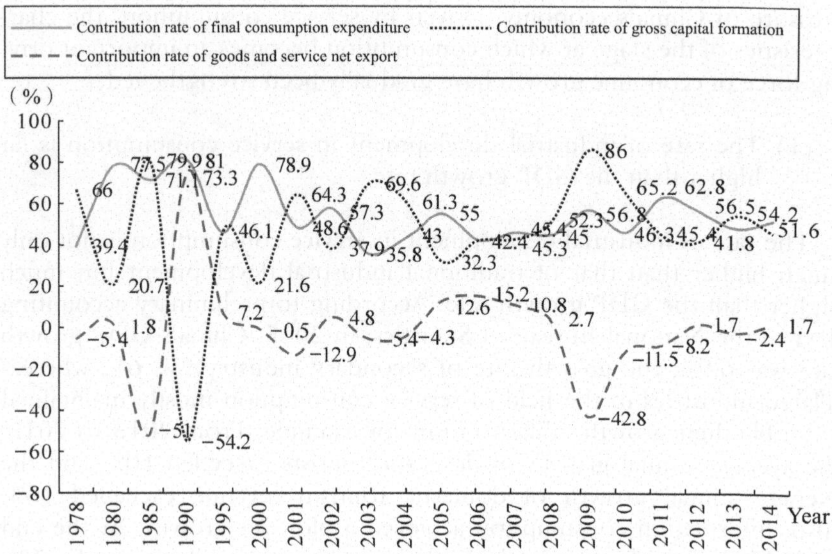

Chart 1 The contribution rate of three major demands in 1978–2014 to economic growth (*Source* National Bureau of Statistics. *China Statistical Yearbook 2015*, China Statistical Publishing House, 2015)

time (45.35%). The contribution rate of investment and consumption to economic growth (see Chart 1) showed a turning point for the first time. In 2014, the contribution rate of China's final consumption expenditure accounted for 51.6%. In 2015, the contribution rate of the final consumption to GDP growth made up 66.4, 14.8% higher than last year. In this context, therefore, the position of consumption as the "first driving force" in stimulating economic growth has been secured step by step.

(3) Service consumption brings great investment demand

Take health consumption for example. It will promote the rapid growth of investment demand in medical and healthcare industries. With the rapid release of medical and health needs of urban and rural residents, China will become the fastest growing and largest medical market. According to the forecast report prepared by McKinsey & Company, China's health care market will exceed one trillion US dollars by 2020.

According to the forecast based on the research of China Academy of Science and Technology for Development, by 2020, China's biomedical industry alone will form a pillar industry worth about 8 trillion yuan (US$1.33 trillion).[23]

(4) Service consumption has become an important carrier of innovation and entrepreneurship

According to *Entrepreneurs' Report 2014*, the most promising industries for entrepreneurs are service industries. For example, directly employed by online stores nationwide by the end of 2014 were more than 10 million people, of whom 6.18 million people were employed by online stores founded by college students, contributing 60% of the total employees.[24] Many college students apply new technologies such as cloud computing and intelligent terminals to the service consumption field. In Qingyanliu Village of Yiwu, Zhejiang Province, otherwise known as "the first village of *Taobao*", with the advantage of the "global distribution center of small commodities", e-commerce has mushroomed everywhere and even around Yiwu. The village, originally home to just 1486 villagers, now has more than 8000 people, with more than 2000 *Taobao* stores and the annual turnover of one billion yuan (US$0.17billion).[25]

3 Achieving the Dynamic Balance Between Investment and Consumption

China's current overcapacity is mainly a structural problem. It is not the overall overcapacity of Three Industries, but the overcapacity in some industrial domains and the shortage in most service consumption supply. In particular, the glaring contradiction is that the living services industry is in short supply.

[23]Zhang Bin: Health Industry Would Reach 10 Trillion Yuan by 2020 While CSE Actively Distributes the Health Industry. *Economic Information Daily*, April 12, 2013.

[24]Chen Xujia: College Students' Online Stores Employing 6.18 Million. www.gov.cn, July 28, 2015.

[25]Yu Shihang: Let Folk Masters Display Their Talents. www.gov.cn, March 16, 2015.

3.1 *The Imbalance Between Investment and Consumption Is a Prominent Structural Contradiction*

When China is in the new era of service consumption, the supply side faces prominent structural contradictions, as in some excess supply of material consumption and most of the service consumer supply contradictions.

The key question is to reach the consensus ASAP about accelerated transformation from investment orientation to consumption orientation, so as to adapt to the trend for service consumption and speed up the change of investment structure chiefly in the traditional heavy chemical industrial projects, finally achieving the substantial expansion of investment in service of investment.

(1) Material consumption is in excessive supply

Material consumption in excessive supply is not only reflected in the traditional manufacturing industry, but also in the emerging manufacturing industry that has also begun to suffer overcapacity. Surprisingly, no sooner are some projects launched than the market supply is already in excess. In 2010, China surpassed the United States to become the world's largest manufacturing country. According to the general standards of global manufacturing, overcapacity is inevitable when the utilization rate of enterprise capacity is below 90% and continues to decline. Statistics show that at present the average capacity utilization rate in China's manufacturing industry is about 60%, not only lower than the current industrial utilization rate of 78.9% in the United States and other developed countries but also lower than the average level of 71.6% in the global manufacturing industry.[26] According to the latest statistics released by the Ministry of Industry and Information Technology, 22 of China's 24 industries now have severe overcapacity.[27] According to the Chinese enterprise managers' follow-up questionnaire survey in 2013, China had 19 manufacturing industries whose capacity utilization rate was below 79%, 7 manufacturing industries whose capacity utilization rate was below 70%, and only 2 whose utilization rate was close

[26] Zhou Yanwu: China's Urbanization Is Over Already. www.hexun.com, December 8, 2012.

[27] Zhang Rui: Overcapacity Weighs Down All China's Manufacturing. *China Economic Herald*, September 27, 2012.

to 79%.[28] At the same time, such strategic emerging industries as wind power equipment, polycrystalline silicon and photovoltaic suffered overcapacity. According to the data, the capacity utilization rate of China's photovoltaic equipment was less than 60% in 2012, and that of wind power equipment was less than 70%.[29]

(2) Service consumption supply is seriously insufficient

① Service consumption has demand but lacks supply. As a growing economy, China has witnessed the constant emergence of focuses of service consumption, but there is a prominent contradiction in the supply shortage in education, old-age care, health, culture and more.

② Education service supply is seriously insufficient. For example, the current mobile education demand is growing, but the supplies run relatively low. Research shows that over the next five years China's mobile education market will reach 150 billion yuan (US$25 billion), but it can provide educational service for only a share of 1.6%.[30]

③ The supply of pension service is seriously insufficient. China has been an aging society, and the demands for the elderly health management service industry, the elderly rehabilitation and nursing industry, and the elderly household service industry have all grown rapidly, with a total demand of about 1 trillion yuan (US$0.17 trillion). However, there are currently less than 100 billion yuan (US$16.67 billion) of products and services for the elderly each year. In some megacities, if one begins to wait to be accepted into a public nursing home at the age of 50, it takes him/her 30 years, or even 40 years, to be accepted. For there is a serious shortage of pension service. In addition, the development of China's health service industry lags behind seriously. The proportion of the said industry makes up less than 5% of GDP, which is far below the 17.6% for the U.S. health service industry and about 10% for other OECD countries.[31]

[28]Lin Huocan: Establishing a Long-Term Mechanism to Reduce the Overcapacity. *Economic Daily*, November 18, 2014.

[29]Photovoltaic Capacity Utilization Rate Less Than 60% and Wind Power Equipments Are Less Than 70%. www.xinhuanet.com, March 6, 2013.

[30]Zhao Zheng: Mobile Education: Subversion of Traditional K12 Auxiliary Market. *China Business Journal*, July 19, 2014.

[31]Kuang Xianming: From Material Consumption to Service Consumption. *China Business Journal*, April 4, 2015.

④ The supply of cultural consumption demand is insufficient. The value added of China's cultural industry constituted 3.76% of GDP in 2014 and over 5% in 2015.[32] It is a huge gap as compared with the United States. At present, China's cultural industry accounts for less than 5% of the world's cultural market, whereas the United States accounts for 42%.[33]

⑤ The development of sports industry lags behind seriously. In countries with relatively developed global sports industry, the value added of their sports industry accounts for about 1–3% of GDP. For example, the value added of U.S. sports industry accounts for 3% of GDP. In 2014, the value added of the sports industry in China took a 0.63% share of GDP.[34]

(3) Insufficient effective supply leads to a large outflow of service consumption

There is insufficient supply of service consumption, including the insufficient effective supply due to quality problem. With the rapid growth of the middle and high income groups in China, people are more willing to pursue high-quality service consumption and spend money on these aspects. Generally, however, due to the slow transformation of related industries, the contradiction of low quality of service consumption supply is increasingly prominent. A large amount of service consumption goes abroad, instead of driving the development of China's own emerging industries, which has become a painful experience for China's industrial transformation and upgrading.

Take education for example. People's demand for high-quality education increases rapidly, but the quality of education in China has improved slowly over the years. The number of Chinese people going abroad for studies at their own expenses rose from 314,800 in 2011 to

[32] National Bureau of Statistics: The Value Added of Cultural Industry in 2014 Constitutes 3.76% of GDP. www.ce.cn, November 26, 2015.

[33] Let the "Internet+" Open a New World for the Cultural Market. www.cq.wenming.cn, November 2, 2015.

[34] Zuo Yi: The Value Added of Sports Industry Makes Up About 1–3% of GDP, While That of the US Sports Industry About 3%. www.sports.qq.com, December 23, 2015.

423,000 in 2014.[35] If per capita expenditure is estimated at 100,000 yuan (US$16,667), it will cost more than 40 billion yuan (US$6.67 billion). It is important to note that there is a tendency to study abroad at a younger age among Chinese students. Take tours for example. The demand of high-income groups for high-quality tours has been increasing, but the domestic tourism industry has been characterized by high prices, poor service quality and cheating on tourists. In recent years, the number of Chinese citizens traveling abroad has increased considerably, and their overseas shopping, hairdressing and medical care are quite common. The Ministry of Commerce data shows that in 2015 China's outbound tourists numbered 120 million person-times, and their consumption abroad (shopping and hotel expenses) totaled 1.5 trillion yuan (US$0.25 trillion).[36]

3.2 The Key Is to Promote Investment Transformation

Investment is the key, just because with the upgrading of China's consumption demand structure, there is enormous investment demand and investment space in service consumption.

The problem is that the government-led and industrial investment-led traditional model has led to the imbalance of consumption structure. As a result, there are prominent structural contradictions in the investment field, which include both problems with excessive heavy industry investment and overcapacity, and prominent contradictions about insufficient investment in the service sector and shortage in supply.

(1) The root cause of the imbalance between supply and demand is the imbalance in the structure of investment and consumption

Overcapacity in some material consumption fields coexists with a serious shortage of supply in most service consumption fields. The important

[35] In 2014 Chinese Students Studying Abroad Number 460,000 While Returned Students Over 360,000. *Xinmin Evening News*, March 10, 2015.

[36] Ministry of Commerce: Minister Gao Hucheng Introduces the Development of Commerce in 2015 at the Press Conference of State Council Information Office. www.mofcom.gov.cn, February 23, 2016.

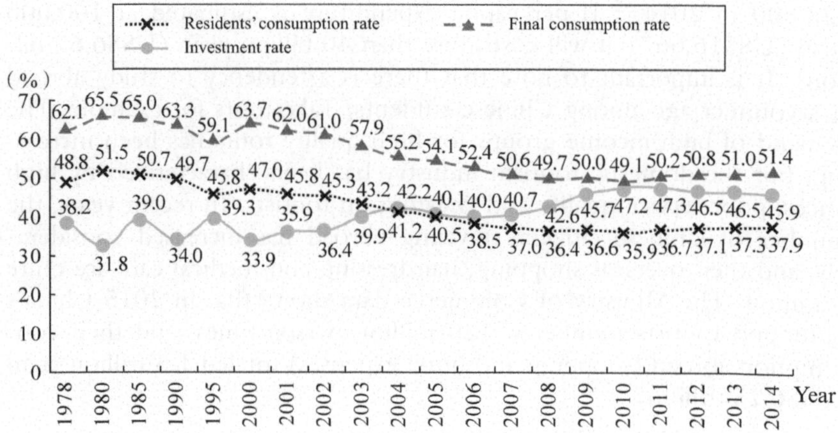

Chart 2 The change trend of China's final consumption, residents' consumption rate and investment rate in 1978–2014 (*Source* National Bureau of Statistics. *China Statistical Yearbook 2015*, China Statistical Publishing House, 2015)

reason about that lies in the long-term imbalance in investment consumption structure in China and the ill-matched relations between investment structure and consumption structure. From the perspective of the change trend of investment rate and consumption rate, the overall investment rate in China showed an upward trend from 1978 to 2014. It was only 31.8% at the historical lowest point in 1983, whereas it rose to 47.3% at the historical highest point in 2011. By 2014, the investment rate remained at 45.9% (see Chart 2). According to the IMF's conservative estimate, China's overinvestment could reach 12% of GDP.[37]

Compared with the constant increase of investment rate, China's final consumption rate shows a downward trend. It rose to 65.5% in 1981 at the historical highest point. It went down to 49.1% in 2010 at the historical lowest point. Residents' consumption rate decreased from 48.8% in 1978 to a record low of 2010 at 35.9%. It was not until 2011 that appeared 0.8 percentage points' recovery. In 2014, China's final consumption rate and residents' consumption rate registered 51.4 and 37.9% respectively, which only recovered to the 2006 levels.

[37] Martin Wolf: China Should No Longer Delay Reform and Adjustment. *Financial Times*, April 12, 2014.

Table 2 The consumption rates and investment rates of different countries in the stage of per capita GDP being US$5000–US$6000

Countries	*Years*	*Per capita GDP (US$)*	*Per capita GDP (US$)*	*Per capita GDP (US$)*
China	2011	5445	49.1	48.3
	2012	6100	49.2	48.1
The world	2002	5323	–	20.6
	2003	5918	–	20.7
Japan	1976	5111	67.58	31.7
	1977	6230	67.74	30.7
South Korea	1989	5438	67.74	30.7
	1990	6153	64.01	33.9
Singapore	1981	5579	58.67	44.8
	1982	6051	55.6	46.2
The U.S.	1971	5360	80.86	19.1
	1973	6461	78.98	20.7
Germany	1974	5457	75.73	24.68
	1975	6035	78.93	22.78
Russia	2005	5337	66.23	20.08
	2006	6947	66.1	21.17
Brazil	2006	5793	80.34	16.76
	2007	7197	80.15	18.33

Source The calculation is based on World Bank database

In the stage of per capita GDP being US$5000–US$6000, China's investment rate is higher than that of the United States by nearly 30 percentage points, and higher than that of Singapore by 3.5 percentage points. But China's consumption rate is lower than that of the United States by 31.8 percentage points, that of South Korea by 14.9 percentage points, that of Russia by 17.1 percentage points, and that of Singapore by 9.6 percentage points respectively (see Table 2).

(2) Investment transformation is guided by the upgrading of consumption pattern

① The investment structure should be adjusted. In the process of cutting overcapacity, it is imperative to reduce the investment in heavy chemical industry with overcapacity and in infrastructure, and transfer the investment focus to education, health care, social security, and other areas of public consumption, so as to optimize the investment structure. This will not only heighten domestic consumption expectations, but also effectively narrow the gap between urban and rural areas and resolve social contradictions.

② The sources of investment should be optimized. In reality, the government-led investment model is increasingly unsustainable. For example, it has caused the problems of increasing overcapacity, diminishing marginal returns on investment, and increasing financial risks. Furthermore, the government-led investment will exert a certain "crowding-out effect" on social investment, resulting in insufficient participation of social forces. Therefore, government investment cannot be used as the main channel to expand investment. Instead, it should be focused on areas with basic security and high returns on social benefits. More competitive areas should yield to social investment, while government investment should not necessarily be in quantity or in all areas, but its role must be dominant. One focal point is, by adjusting the stock of government investment, to adjust the strategic allocation of State capital and increase the investment in the social sector in the direction of public welfare. Another focal point is to release the vitality of social capital and expand private capital investment.

③ Diversified investors should be formed. In reality, China has a higher degree of marketization in the industrial sector and a serious shortage of competition in the service sector. In recent years, people have complained more about the monopoly of education, healthcare, telecommunications and other service industries and the resulting high price and low quality services. In the service sector the administrative monopoly should be broken, especially by introducing government procurement and the PPP mode and forming diversified investment subjects in the field of services, so as, through the competition, to improve quality, reduce prices, and form the effective supply.

3.3 It Is Important to Expand Investment in the Living Services Industry

In November 2015, the State Council issued *Guiding Opinions on Accelerating the Development of Living Services Industry and the Promotion of Consumer Pattern Upgrading*. Its focal point is to develop the living services industry which is close to people's life, great in demand potential, and strong in driving role. Therefore, it is necessary to start from the overall economic transformation and the real needs of social residents to increase investment in life services.

(1) It is urgent to increase investment in the living services industry with the most pressing social demand

Residential and family services, health services, pension services, tourism services, sports services and cultural services are the key areas in which social demand is high and effective supply is insufficient. In these areas, the market can be liberalized, prices can be liberalized, and the market can play a decisive role in regulating supply and demand. It is suggested, in these areas, to promote the comprehensive negative list management ASAP, open up the market threshold, widely mobilize multiple ownership enterprises (including social capital enterprises and foreign capital enterprises) to make a bigger "cake", effectively raise the quality of service and form a group of well-known brands, and make a real breakthrough in releasing service-oriented consumer demands.

(2) It is fundamental to increase investment in the living services industry related to population urbanization

Investment in the living services industry related to population urbanization will be the most potential investment area in the 13th FYP period. In the next five years, by accelerating the promotion of equalization of basic public services, of the balanced allocation of public resources in big and medium-sized and small cities and small towns, and of investment in the living services industry that speeds up population urbanization, will multiple bonuses from the transformation be earned. First, it is conducive to easing the pressure of the economic downturn, seeking potential economic growth. Second, it is conducive to raising the level of population urbanization, achieving shared development. Third, it is conducive to releasing the consumption potential of the large rural market, forming a new pattern of urban-rural integration. According to estimates, for every additional citizen in China, it needs a minimum of a new integrated investment of 100,000 yuan (US$16,667) in such domains as education, health, culture, and infrastructure. For any additional increase in population urbanization rate by 1–1.55%, it needs additional increase in 15–20 million people, with an integrated investment of about 1.5–2 trillion yuan (US$0.25–0.33 trillion). For any additional increase in population urbanization rate by one percentage point, it will promote the final consumption growth by 1.6 percentage points or so.[38]

(3) It is necessary to develop and expand pillar industries of living services industry

① The health industry should be taken as an important pillar industry for development. Specifically, it is to increase investment in health industry, to encourage social capital into such fields as healthy check-up, health consultation, health culture, health tourism, and fitness, and to promote the health care industry to extend to the large health industry, which will increase its proportion in the GDP from the current 4–5% to about 10% by 2020.

② The cultural industry should be taken as an important pillar industry for development. Specifically, it is to increase investment to promote the development of new-type service industries like cultural creativity and design service, to promote the digitalization and networking process of the production, dissemination and consumption of cultural service products, to promote the optimization and upgrading of animation, cartoon and game industry, to promote the growth of new media and new business such as mobile multimedia broadcasting and television and network broadcast television, to promote the integration and development of traditional media and new media, so as to form a number of stronger culture enterprise groups by 2020, which will increase the proportion of the value added of cultural industry in the GDP from the current 6–8%.

③ The pension industry should be taken as an important pillar industry for development. Specifically, it is to encourage social capital to go into the basic life care, rehabilitation and nursing, mental comfort, cultural service, emergency rescue, and hospice care, to achieve the upgrading of pension industry through the use of network information technology, so as to form a group of professional elderly care services with high social reputation and service quality, which will increase its proportion in the GDP from the current 3–6% or so by 2020.

[38]Liang Da: Enormous Domestic Demand Potential Can Be Released Via Population Urbanization. *Shanghai Securities News*, January 9, 2013.

4 Adapting to Consumption Upgrading and Pushing Forward the Reduction of Housing Inventory

Real estate is an important pillar industry in China. In the context of structural surplus, it has become the focus of social attention. In the new era of service consumption, real estate is no longer simply to meet basic housing needs, but to meet a large number of service needs. During the 13th FYP period, while reducing housing inventory, it has become an important direction for the sustainable development of real estate industry to promote the transformation of real estate industry from scale orientation to service orientation.

4.1 It Is Important to Promote the Transformation of Real Estate from Scale Orientation to Service Orientation

Over the years, China has developed a real estate development model that aims to meet basic housing needs and features large-scale expansion, and has promoted the real estate industry to become an important pillar industry. Today, with the change in real estate consumption demand, the traditional road is getting narrower with market pressure growing ever greater.

(1) Scale-oriented real estate development is not sustainable

① There is mounting pressure from real estate destocking. Since the second half of 2014, China's inventory of newly-built commercial housing increased significantly. According to data released from the National Bureau of Statistics, by the end of 2015, the area of commercial housing for sale amounted to 718.53 million square meters, an increase by 15.6% as compared with the previous year. It shows that the area of China's commercial housing for sale hit an all-time high.[39] According to data from *China Report on Housing Development 2015–2016* prepared by the Chinese Academy of Social Sciences, based on the calculation of the total inventory of commercial housing in 2015, the total inventory for 2016 was expected to reach 39.96 billion square meters, of which the forward housing inventory would be 35.700 billion square meters, with the sales

[39] WorldUnion: *Annual Report on Real Estate Market 2016*, January 2016.

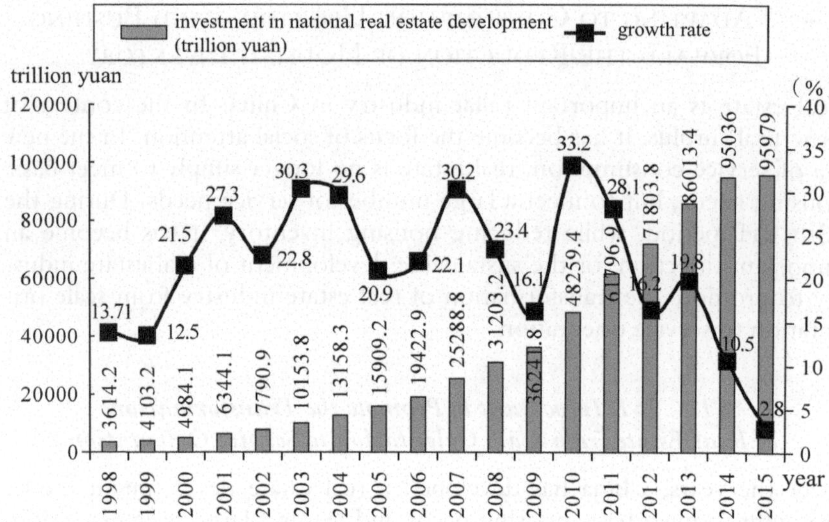

Chart 3 The lowest level of growth rate of real estate investment reached in 2015 within nearly 17 years (*Source* National Bureau of Statistics. *China Statistical Yearbook 2015*, China Statistical Publishing House, 2015; National Bureau of Statistics. *The National Economy in 2015 Progresses Well and Performs Well in Its Steady Operation*. www.statis.gov.cn, January 19, 2016)

cycle being 4.5 years. In terms of the area of ready homes for sale, the inventory would be 426 million square meters, with the sales cycle being 23 months.

② The growth rate of real estate investment declines rapidly. In 2010, the growth rate of China's real estate investment was 33.2%, reaching the highest point in history. Five years after that it went down all the way. In 2015, the growth rate of national real estate investment fell to 2.8%, 7.7 percentage points lower than 2014, which became its lowest level since 1998 (see Chart 3).

③ "De-stocking" should be focused on third-tier and fourth-tier cities. Since 2016, housing prices in first-tier cities like Beijing, Shanghai and Shenzhen have risen rapidly with a series of national policies on de-stocking. According to statistics, in January and February 2016, the pure commodity housing sales prices in Shanghai were 35,911 yuan (US$5985) per square meter and 36,381 yuan (US$6064) per square meter respectively, which showed an increase by 25.6 and 24.2%

respectively as compared with the previous corresponding months. While the housing prices rose rapidly, the housing stock in Shanghai fell rapidly. By the end of February, Shanghai's new pure commodity housing stock was 9.37 million square meters, a decline by 26.9% as compared with the previous corresponding month.[40] By contrast, however, real estate inventories in third-tier and fourth-tier cities rose again, with 739.31 million square meters of unsold residential space nationwide at the end of February, an increase of 20.77 million square meters over the same period of the previous year. According to the relevant data, in February, the cumulative stock-to-sales ratio of commercial housing in the third- and fourth-tier cities was 32.07 months. Although it dropped by 14% as compared with last February, the ratio still far exceeded the reasonable range of 15 months.[41]

(2) The demand for service-oriented real estate increases gradually

Currently, important changes have begun to happen to the relationship between supply and demand of residential housing. Firstly, as the aging of population speeds up, the rigid demand for housing became weaker than ever before and the peak of scale development is over. Secondly, the post-'80s and post-'90s gradually become the main group buying houses that pursue more individualized service, so simple residential property is not their cup of tea. Thirdly, with the accelerated urbanization, working couples and families are quite common and the rhythm of their life and work is much faster. For them, therefore, the residential function is not enough and the expected functions and demands have to be service oriented, as in terms of health, medical care and house keeping. Fourthly, with the expansion of the high-income group in the society, people's demand for the service function of real estate has significantly increased, and the old-age real estate, tourist real estate and cultural real estate have been much sought after.

(3) Some real estate enterprises begin to be service oriented

[40] E-house China R&D Institute: *Analysis and Prediction of Shanghai Real Estate Market Trend in the First Two Months of 2016*. www.askci.com, March 30, 2016.

[41] Housing Inventories in 3rd–tier and 4th–tier Cities Are Enough to Sell for Another 30-odd Years. *Beijing Times*, April 15, 2016.

In recent years, due to structural surplus in the real estate industry, how to direct attention to customers' individualized needs and integrate special service elements into housing construction has become the key to the model of real estate developers to create new profits. For example, because of the rapidly rising demands of aging population and other people for health service, it is important for the real estate industry and the medical health industry to cooperate for innovation, so as to promote the transformation and upgrading of the real estate industry, to change the real estate supply system that mainly serves the single residential function, and raise the value of the real estate industry while bringing something fresh to real estate investment. Take Vanke for example. Since 2014, the project called "*Vanke Yi*" has been on the way nationwide. It is a project special for college graduates and those who are new comers in Shenzhen Special Economic Zone. The project aims to provide a comfortable living environment and a communication platform. It has been launched or officially implemented in such cities as Chongqing, Xiamen, Guangzhou, Dongguan and Xian, with the occupancy rate ranging from 80 to 90%.[42]

4.2 *De-Stocking Shall Be Completed in the Course of Transformation and Development*

In the short run, it is very important for the real estate industry to remove the housing stock. But it is more important to find a way out for the transformation and development of traditional real estate. From the perspective of medium- and long-term sustainable development of real estate industry, the important way out is to be service oriented. During the 13th FYP period, the housing stock should be removed in the process of accelerating the real estate transformation.

(1) Organic combination of de-stocking and population urbanization should be attained

"De-stocking" should focus on accelerating the process of population urbanization. *National New Urbanization Planning 2014–2020* put forward the target of "three hundred-million-people's", which

[42] Chen Shu and Lu Yun: Service Orientation Is Expected to Become a New Growth Point in China's Real Estate Market. www.xinhuanet.com, October 30, 2015.

includes "efforts to achieve the agricultural transfer of a population of one hundred million and other permanent population to cities and towns". If this batch of rural residents becomes urban residents brought into the urban housing system by 2020, as per the housing standard of 30 square meters per capita (cf. the standard of per capita 32.9 square meters for urban residents in 2012), it will bring the new demand for 3 billion square meters of housing area. Therefore, it is suggested that the "efforts to achieve the agricultural transfer of a population of one hundred million and other permanent population to cities and towns" should be taken as an important means to de-stock, while the package deal should be adopted to reduce the proportion of down payment on housing, to allow migrant workers to move with their "land property rights" into the city, and to oblige the governments to purchase low-rent houses in order to solve the housing problems of 100 million people. It is particularly important to combine the vigorous development of small and medium-sized towns with the solution of the real estate inventory in third- and fourth-tier cities, so as to achieve the dual goals of local urbanization and "living and working in peace and contentment" for the rural migrant population.

(2) The transformation from real estate to service will reduce the risk of economic operation

In the situation where China's economy is highly dependent on real estate, it will bring great downward pressure to the economy if the real estate inventory is not removed timely. In 2015, the country's real estate investment in fixed assets reached 9.5979 trillion yuan (US$1.6 trillion), constituting 17.4% of the total fixed-asset investment.[43] Many provinces are highly dependent on real estate investment. Hu Zhigang, Vice President of China Real Estate Association thinks that the investment in real estate development cannot exceed 25% of the total investment in fixed assets. According to the statistics released by *China Real Estate Weekly*, however, seven of the 31 provinces and municipalities (directly under the Central Government) in China have exceeded the proportion of 25%, that is Shanghai (57.18%), Beijing (56.17%), Hainan (53.02%), Guangxi (30.77%), Guangdong (30.77%), Zhejiang (28.33%), and

[43]National Bureau of Statistics: *Statistical Bulletin on the National Economy and Social Development 2015*. www.statis.gov.cn, February 29, 2016.

Chongqing (25.66%) respectively.[44] However, it should also be noted that without changing the structural de-stocking, only short-term problems could be solved, so could temporary oversupply. From a medium- and long-term perspective, if the transformation to service-oriented real estate is too slow, the economy will continue to maintain its habitual dependence on scale-oriented real estate, which is not conducive to the sustainable development of the industry.

(3) The transformation to service-oriented real estate will reverse the decline in corporate performance

Under the traditional scale-oriented real estate model, China's overall real estate market is depressed, the overall profit space of real estate is shrinking, and the performance of real estate enterprises is seriously differentiated. According to statistics, in 1998–2014, China's real estate development investment grew from 3614.2 million yuan (US$602.37 million) to 9.5036 trillion yuan (US$1.58 trillion), an average annual growth rate of more than 20%. But the corporate profits fell quickly. In 2014, the operating profit showed a negative growth by nearly 36% as compared with the previous year (see Chart 4). In the first half of 2015, 67 of the 144 real estate listed companies saw the decline of their revenue compared with the same period last year, and 74 others saw the decline of their profits and even the increase in losses.[45]

Despite the depression of overall real estate market, Vanke, Poly, and Evergrande, leading enterprises in service-oriented transformation bucked the market trend, achieving relatively good performance. According to the report prepared by Vanke in the mid-2015, the company's net profit in the first half of the year reached 679 million yuan (US$113 million), an increase by 23.6% as compared with the same period of last year. The net profit of Poly's real estate in the first half of 2015 grew by over

[44] Ranking of 31 Provinces, Autonomous Regions and Municipalities Directly Under the Central Government by Dependence on Real Estate Investment: Increasing the Risks of Domestic Real Estate Investment in the Next Five Years. www.chinafcdc.com, December 26, 2015.

[45] Luo Zheng: Listed Housing Enterprises Seek Transformation Due to Corporate Debt Differentiation. *Economic Information Daily*, September 10, 2015.

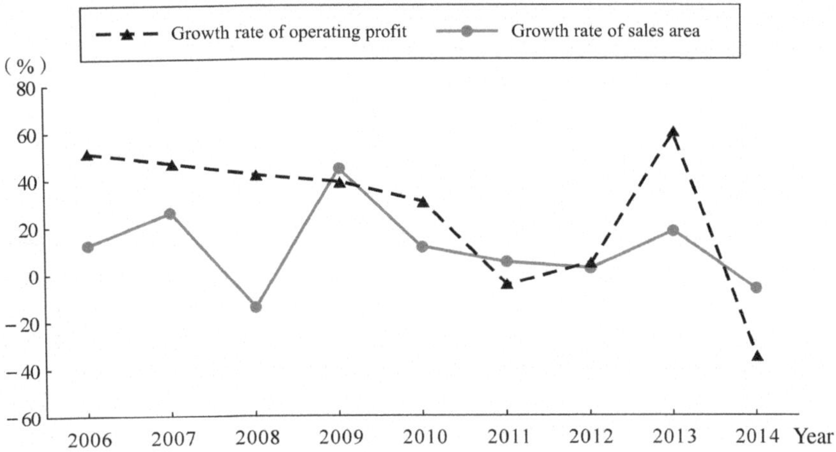

Chart 4 China's real estate sales area and the change of the operating profit in 2006–2014 (*Source* National Bureau of Statistics. *China Statistical Yearbook 2015*, China Statistical Publishing House, 2015)

40%.[46] For the first eleven months of 2015, Vanke, Evergrande, China Overseas Property, and Country Garden combined to achieve the sales exceeding one hundred billion yuan, of which Vanke grew by 20.06% and Evergrande by 42.8% as compared with the same period of last year.[47]

4.3 *The New Model of Service-Oriented Real Estate Needs to Be Explored*

Judging from the experience of developed countries, real estate can well be maintained as the pillar industry in the national economy through service. In the United States, for example, real estate still remains an important pillar industry, since the service-oriented process of real estate has been completed with the industry being able to win by quality. In China,

[46] Luo Zheng: Housing Enterprises' Debt Differentiation in the First Half of the Year Leads Some Listed Companies to Seek Transformation. *Economic Information Daily*, September 10, 2015.

[47] Ji Xuejiao: 25 Housing Enterprises' Sales in November Increase by a Big Margin. *Finance and Investment*, December 25, 2015.

while de-stocking, the new pattern of real estate service will initially be formed during the 13th FYP period, and the country's real estate industry will gain new development space.

(1) The new business model of service-oriented real estate needs to be explored

It is an important way for the real estate industry to keep "sunrise industry" by adapting to the changes in real estate demands and form a new type of service-oriented business of real estate. If new focal points of housing consumption can be grasped, a considerable number of real estate enterprises can still gain new development space. For example, in the elderly care industry, the needs of the elderly in life care, medical and health care, rehabilitation care and other aspects are increasing. According to estimates by the Research Center for Senium Science under the Chinese Academy of Social Sciences, the business opportunity of China's elderly care market is about 4 trillion yuan (US$0.67 trillion), which is expected to increase to 13 trillion yuan (US$2.17 trillion) by 2030.[48] This enormous demand for elderly care service can be met mainly through community nursing service and home-based care service, while service-oriented real estate is exactly the carrier of release of elderly care service consumption. During the 13th FYP period, it is necessary to strive to promote the development of the real estate market segmentation, to form specialized segmented markets out of commercial real estate, elderly care real estate, tourism real estate, industrial real estate, and cultural real estate with good market potential and development prospects, and to produce a group of real estate developers with professional brands and high quality, thus promoting real estate to form a new industrial chain, through which to substantially increase the value added of real estate industry and change the situation of declining industrial profits.

(2) The new model of service-oriented real estate needs to be developed

The profit model under which the real estate industry achieved asset appreciation through land acquisition with high investment and rapid

[48]The Chinese Academy of Social Sciences Estimates China's Elderly Care Market Will Reach 13 Trillion Yuan by 2030. *International Financial News*, November 30, 2015.

housing construction in the past is unable to adapt to the new situation. In the future, real estate developers will not sell houses only, but provide comprehensive, high-grade value-added services. In addition to providing customers with high cost performance products and housing-type design, it is highly necessary to provide quality life service, property management, property service, rental service, real estate service, business comprehensive supporting services, etc.

To adapt to the changes in housing demands of different groups, it is essential during the 13th FYP period to go beyond the original model of residential development and turn to service-oriented business-innovation model. This needs to implement the service mode of mass customization in the field of real estate, and enable a considerable number of real estate developers to do the design, research and development as the core business up to the standards of specialization and perfection, forming a new development model for tailoring to customers' needs and providing the overall solution.

(3) "Internet + real estate" needs to be developed

To improve the traditional real estate industry with the Internet thinking is creating new business opportunities and new business models, and are changing the ecology of real estate industry in a profound way. The development and planning, sales and post-sales services of real estate industry, and all other related links are inseparable from the Internet. During the 13th FYP period, it will become the top priority of real estate transformation and upgrading to support real estate enterprises' use of big data, cloud computing, mobile Internet and other new technology to improve the service level, and develop customer participation in designing new products, new models and new platforms.

CHAPTER 5

Opening-Up as the Turning Point Is Shifting from Goods Trade to Service Trade

In the 13th FYP period, China's further opening-up and the new round of global free trade have formed a historical intersection, which provides an important opportunity for China's "second opening-up" focusing on service trade.

For this, it is necessary to fully implement the strategy of free trade, accelerate the construction of "the Belt and Road Initiative", create external conditions favorable to economic transformation and upgrading in the internal and external opening of service industry market, promote the process of global free trade in the opening-up, and enhance the institutional right to speak in China's participation in global economic governance in the opening-up.

Therefore, what is known as the "second opening-up" with emphasis on service trade in China's modernization process is featured by adapting to the new trend of global free trade, forming a new pattern of opening-up that focuses on service trade, creating good external conditions for China's economic transformation and upgrading, and effectively enhancing the institutional right to speak in China's participation in global economic governance.

F. Chi, *Winning at the Turning Point*, The Great Transformation of China, https://doi.org/10.1007/978-981-32-9479-0_5

1 Developing Goods Trade—A Main Trend for the New Round of Globalization

The rise of global service trade has become the new trend for global free trade in the post-WTO era. It is mainly characterized by the fact that service trade has become the new engine of global free trade, the focus of bilateral and multilateral free trade talks, and an important area for the construction of the rules of global economic governance.

1.1 Service Trade Has Become a New Engine of Global Free Trade

With the development of world trade, the trade structure changes constantly, and service trade grows faster than goods trade, becoming the main growth point of global trade development, and the driving force of world economic growth.

(1) Service trade grows faster than goods trade

According to the statistics by WTO, the global service trade volume (not including government services) amounted to US$1.44 trillion in 2000 but to US$9.8 trillion in 2014, almost reaching the mark of US$10 trillion. Between 2001 and 2014, global service trade grew faster than GDP and goods trade in most of the years. Since 2012, global service trade has grown by 3–5 times faster than goods trade. For 2014, the growth rate of global service trade was 4.2%, whereas that of global goods trade was only 0.6% (see Chart 1). The rapid growth of service trade has given new impetus to global trade.

(2) Service trade has become a new growth point of global trade

It mainly features ① the rapid growth of goods trade promotes the rapid growth of such service trade as logistics, sales, information and financial service, while a new pattern promoted mutually by goods trade and service trade is forming; ② the division of labor between developed countries deepens constantly, and the upgrading of emerging economies' manufacturing industry becomes more dependent on developed countries' producer services industry with emphasis on the design, research and development, which form a huge market of service trade; ③ exchanges of people between different countries have led to the rapid growth of transnational tourism, overseas education, and transportation.

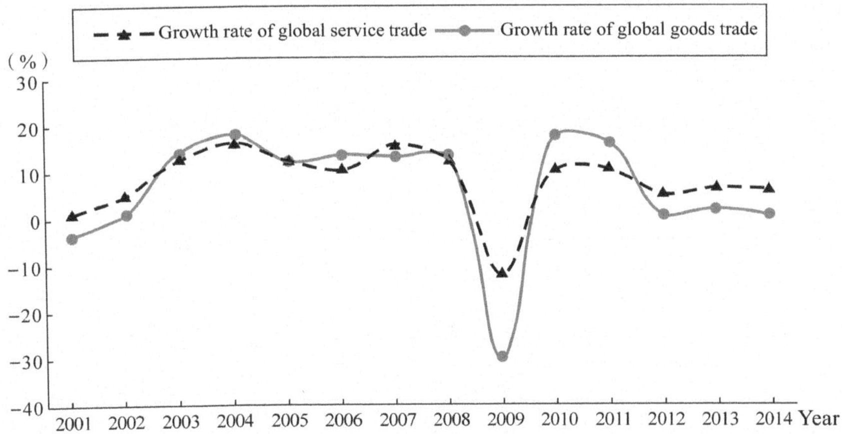

Chart 1 The growth rate of global service trade and goods trade in 2001–2014 (*Source* Data preparation is based on WTO annual world trade reports and statistics on international trade)

(3) Service trade has become a new driving force for world economic growth

① Emerging services are becoming a new growth point of service trade. In 2014, the global service trade grew by 4.2% whereas the global GDP by only 2.5%. With the advent of the era of big data, emerging service trade like computer and information service and communications service has grown rapidly, serving as a driving force for global economic growth.

② Service trade drives the optimal allocation of global resources. The producer services industry in developed countries dominates the global allocation of manufacturing industry, causing the manufacturing industry to flow to lower-cost regions and becoming a driving force for optimal allocation of global resources.

③ Emerging economies are beginning to become a new force for service trade export. Since 2000, the average annual growth rate of service trade of China, India, Russia, and Brazil has remained higher than that of North America and Western Europe. At present, the emerging economies have reached the proportion of over 30% in global service export and of 40% or so in five major services like tourism, construction, transportation services, other commercial services, and computer and information services.[1] China and India have ranked among the world's top 10 exporters of service trade.[2]

1.2 *Service Trade Is the Most Important Area for the Reconstruction of Global Trade Rules*

With the rapid development of service trade, service trade has become the main content of global free trade negotiations, while inter-regional service trade agreements have increased rapidly.

(1) Service trade has become the focus of the new stage of free trade negotiations

The importance of service trade negotiations has increased. When the Doha round of service trade talk stalled, 23 WTO member countries whose service trade accounted for 70% of the global service trade started negotiations on the *Trade in Services Agreement* (TISA).[3] Under this agreement, negotiations have expanded from traditional services to emerging services such as e-commerce, information service, environmental service and energy service. The role of TISA has been strengthened increasingly in promoting the liberalization of global service trade.

(2) Service trade agreements have grown rapidly.

According to data on the WTO's official website, as of January 18, 2016, 417 regional free trade agreements became effective worldwide. Of all these agreements, there are 136 goods trade agreements, 1 service trade agreement, and 129 goods and services trade agreements, which increased by 2 times more than a decade ago.[4]

(3) The important content of TPP and TTIP is service trade

[1] Zhao Jin: Global Service Trade Reaches Nearly US$10 Trillion While Service Trade Business Opportunities Surge. *People's Daily*, December 20, 2015.

[2] WTO: *2015 International Trade Statistics*, 2015.

[3] Zhao Jin: Global Service Trade Reaches Nearly US$10 Trillion. *People's Daily*, December 20, 2015.

[4] Some Figures on the Regional Trade Agreement Notified to the GATT/WTO and in Force. WTO website, January 18, 2016.

Developed countries led to promote the transfer from market access as the core of the "first-generation" trade rules to regulation integration as the core of the "second-generation" trade rules, of which the most important is service trade talks. By December 15, 2015, the United States concluded 14 free-trade agreements, while accelerating the Trans-Pacific Partnership Agreement (TPP) and Transatlantic Trade and Investment Partnership (TTIP) negotiations.[5] The EU signed free trade agreements with 19 countries while speeding up TTIP negotiations with the U.S.[6]

2 The Second Round of Opening-Up with Service Trade as the Focus

In the last round of globalization, the market opening of China's manufacturing industry and the demand expansion of global goods trade formed a historical intersection, when China managed to grasp the historical opportunity and join the WTO, gradually becoming one of the world's manufacturing powers and trading powers. At present, the two-way opening of China's service market and the global free trade process are once again forming a historical intersection. In this connection, therefore, creating the "second opening" with emphasis on service trade will lay sound foundations for China to grow to be a service-industry power (see Table 1).

2.1 The Opening up of the Industrial Market Has Basically Been Completed

The opening up of the industrial market has played an important role in promoting China's industrialization. The opening pattern of the industrial market has basically been completed.

(1) Great achievements have been scored in opening up the industrial market

[5]Free Trade Agreements: US International Trade Administration Web, December 15, 2015.

[6]Free Trade Agreements: European Commission Web, December 15, 2015.

Table 1 The "first opening" and the "second opening"

	The "first opening"	*The "second opening"*
Staring point	Initial stage of industrialization (*domestic environment*) Manufacturing globalization (international environment)	Mid-and-late industrialization (*domestic environment*) Globalization of service industry (*international environment*)
Objectives	Economic growth One-time transformation Active integration into the system of global division of labor	Sustainable economic development Second-time transformation Active construction of more effective global industrial chains and value chain
Focal points	Goods trade The market opening of manufacturing industry	Service trade The market opening of service industry
Route	Entry into the WTO and global governance mechanism	Full implementation of the strategy of free trade zone
Institution	Building an export-oriented economic system: forming a series of institutional mechanisms that encourage and support the development of export-oriented industries based on the export-oriented strategy	Building a new system of open economy: building a free trade-oriented open institutional mechanism
Role	Recipient, participant and follower of international rules	Reformer, shaper and dominant of international rules

Source The table is prepared by the research group of China (Hainan) Institute for Reform and Development

In the early stage of industrialization, taking the entry into the WTO as the important symbol, China seized the historical opportunities of the demand expansion of global goods trade and the transfer of developed countries' manufacturing industry and promoted the opening of manufacturing industry and direct integration into manufacturing globalization, thereby becoming the world's second largest economy and the world's largest trading nation in goods while making great contributions to the global economic and trade growth. Generally, the opening of the industrial market has made China's industrial "cake" bigger, greatly accelerating China's transition from the early stage of industrialization to the late stage of industrialization and scoring remarkable achievements.

(2) The opening of industrial market plays an important role in promoting China's industrialization

First, the Chinese industry can participate in international division of labor and international competition, forming its own comparative advantage. Second, the liberalization of the industrial market and the introduction of competition have greatly enhanced the efficiency and competitiveness of the manufacturing industry. Third, the process of introducing foreign capital and learning advanced experience is conducive to improving the industrial technology and management. Fourth, opening to the rest of the world has greatly accelerated the process of domestic reform by forcing domestic market reform and government transformation.

(3) The opening of industrial market is basically in place

China has achieved a deep opening to the outside world in many industrial fields, such as automobiles and home appliances. Not only have many products been imported, but many industrial products like color TV sets, refrigerators and high-speed trains have gone overseas.

2.2 China Stands at a New Historical Starting Point of "Second Opening"

At present, in the context of global service economy, the space of the "first opening" with emphasis on the industrial market has been shrinking day by day. It is imperative to turn to the "second opening" with emphasis on service industry.

(1) The 13th FYP period represents the historical window period for opening-up and transformation

It is a period of opening-up and transformation from goods trade to service trade, which has become a gateway for China to move from a manufacturing power to a service power. Whether to raise the proportion of producer service industry to promote the transformation from production-oriented manufacturing to service-oriented manufacturing or to upgrade the service industry's own structure all needs to further expand service trade and further open the service to the outside world, so as to introduce advanced technology, experience and human resources of foreign service industry.

(2) Deepening reform in an all-round way has to be integrated directly with opening-up

① Direct integration should be promoted between the reform of investment system and the opening up of service market. On the basis of the coordinated development of service industry market in opening up the internal and external markets in two directions, a market environment that does not discriminate between domestic capital and foreign capital will gradually take shape.

② Direct integration should be promoted between market regulation and transformation and the reduction and elimination of trade barriers. Besides, reforms of the investment system with a focus on the negative list should be pushed through in order to promote service trade.

③ Direct integration of reforms in the fiscal, taxation and financial system and the "going out" of production capacity should be promoted. At the same time, the fiscal, taxation and financial system should serve as the guiding role in the process of "transferring a certain quantity of production capacity", while actively facilitating international cooperation on production capacity and promoting the "transfer" of excessive capacity.

④ Direct integration should be promoted between the construction of domestic free trade zones and the acceleration of implementation of FTZ strategies. It is to be followed by opening the door to internal and external links so as to speed up bilateral and multilateral free trade.

(3) Efforts shall be made to speed up the "second opening" with service trade as the focus and the full implementation of free trade strategies as the route

Compared with the "first opening" of promoting the globalization of China's manufacturing industry, the historical mission of the "second opening" is to fully implement free trade strategies with service trade as a focal point, create in the opening-up favorable external conditions for economic transformation and upgrading and promote the process of global free trade.

2.3 It Is Important to Form the "Second Opening" Focusing on Service Trade

Currently China's economy is in a critical period of transformation and upgrading. In terms of economic transformation and upgrading, or the acquisition of the right of institutional discourse, or the acceleration of structural reforms, it is all necessary to speed up the formation of China's "second opening" with emphasis on service trade.

(1) Economic transformation and upgrading put forward new requirements for the opening of service industry market

Observed from the historical experience of developed countries, service industry development needs to participate in the international division of labor. Only by participating in the international division of labor can a country's own comparative advantages be formed, can the international market be used to make a big "cake of service industry", and can the quality of service industry development be raised.

From the perspective of domestic situation, it is by actively participating in global service trade that domestic economic transformation and upgrading can better be promoted. First, with China's urban and rural residents' consumption pattern shifting from material orientation to service orientation, its demand for service trade is rising rapidly, so the urgent demand for the two-way opening of service market has been put forward. Second, the accelerated internal and external opening of service market in China and the process of global free trade with emphasis on service trade have formed a historical intersection, driving the open transformation from goods trade to service trade, which has become China's only way from the manufacturing power to the service industry power.

(2) As the world's second biggest economy, China will have to become the important driver of the global service trade before it can acquire the right of institutional discourse.

If it is just an adaptor to international rules in the WTO era, China as the second largest economy in the world should play an important role in the new round of reconstructing international economic rules. The major challenges for China are as follows. First, the world has entered the age of service economy with the service industry's proportion making up more than 70% of the world economy (2012).[7] The total service trade volume accounted for 1/5 of the total world trade volume (2015).[8] Having no say in service trade means not having much say in global economic governance. Second, the mainstream trade agreement is the service trade agreement. Without the important progress in service trade, it is difficult to gain the right of institutional discourse in the construction of the new international economic order. Third, without significant progress in service trade it is hard to share the benefits of the new round of global free trade.

(3) Direct integration between structural reform and opening-up should be promoted

At present, in the complex and severe economic situation both at home and abroad, accelerating the development of service trade can promote the optimization of foreign trade structure, which is crucial to foster new economic drivers and engines. On February 14, 2016, the State Council's executive meeting decided that in two years, ten provinces and cities across the country and five State-level new areas should carry out pilots for service trade innovation and development, the focus of which is to explore the system construction in the eight aspects of service trade to expand open access to service industry in an orderly manner. At present, it is a prominent feature that the structural reform focusing on the opening of service market is directly integrated with the opening to the outside world. This requires the opening of service market to force the opening of social capital, so as to share dividends from the new round of globalization through the opening of service market while making the "cake" of service industry even bigger.

3 Forming Basically a New Pattern for Opening-Up with Service Trade as the Focus

To speed up the formation of a new pattern for opening-up with the focus on service trade and actively promote the internal and external opening of service markets is both the "second opening" that brings

[7] Qiu Hong: Service Industry Makes Up 70% of the Total World Economy. www.people.com.cn, April 26, 2012.

[8] WTO: *2015 World Trade Report*, 2015.

about the focus of market-oriented reform and the key to forming the external environment favorable for economic transformation and upgrading.

3.1 *It Is Imperative that Service Trade Should Make Up 20% of the Total Trade by 2020*

Specifically, it is to accelerate the construction of domestic free trade zones focusing on service trade, to speed up the development of new competitive advantages of service trade, to facilitate the process of bilateral and multilateral free trade, and to further open your trade partners' service market internally and externally, thereby turning service trade into the new engine which drives the transformation and upgrading of domestic economy.

(1) China's service trade needs to "improve its weaker link".

① The proportion of service trade is too low. In 2014, China has become the world's second largest service trading nation, second largest service trade importer and fifth largest service trade exporter, but its service trade has still accounted for a low proportion of the total foreign trade. In 2014, China's service trade volume only made up 12.3% of its total foreign trade volume, which is lower by 8.3 percentage points than the global average, and significantly lower by 19.6, 22.1, and 26.5% than the global average, the United States, and India respectively in 2013. In 2015, China's import and export service trade totaled US$713 billion, less than one-fifth of the goods trade.[9] China's goods trade volume accounts for more than 10% of the total world goods trade, but its service trade volume only makes up 6.2% of the world service trade volume. Among the top ten service trading countries in the world, China's per capita service trade on average is US$448, 12% of that of the US, 6% of that of Germany and 16% of Japan respectively. According to the data calculation from the WTO's *International Trade Statistics*, the key to achieving economic transformation and upgrading and enhancing the competitiveness of China's foreign trade is to increase the proportion of service trade greatly.

[9] *Statistical Bulletin on National Economy and Social Development 2015*. www.statis.gov.cn, February 29, 2016.

② Service trade is still dominated by traditional services. China's service trade export is mainly concentrated in transportation, tourism and other more traditional areas. The structure taken by the relatively small portion of modern service trade like finance, education and medical care has not changed much. In 2014, China's three major traditional service import and export, namely, tourism, transportation services, and construction services, made up 62.6% of the total import and export of service trade, whereas finance, insurance, computer and information consulting services accounted for 0.14, 0.86, 3.51, and 8.89% respectively.[10] All this shows that there is a big gap with developed countries in service trade.

③ The service trade deficit widens year by year. From 1995 to 2014, China's service trade has been in deficit for 20 consecutive years and meanwhile the deficit has been widening yearly. In 2007 it was US$7.6 billion, and in 2014 it reached US$198 billion, 26 times that of 2007.[11] In January-September 2015, China's service trade export and import valued at US$171.6 billion and US$323.7 billion respectively, resulting in the deficit of US$152.1 billion, which registers an increase by 30.9% as compared with the same period of time last year.[12] The competitiveness index of China's service trade is far lower than that of such major service trade exporters as the United Kingdom, the United States, and France. The United States remains the world's largest surplus country in service trade, with a trade surplus of US$231.8 billion,[13] whereas China is the world's largest deficit country in service trade.[14] The comparative competitive advantage of China's service trade mainly lie in resource-intensive and labor-intensive traditional industries, but its knowledge-intensive and technology-intensive industries are obviously in a competitive

[10] Analysis of the Overall Situation of China's Service Trade Development in 2014. *China Business Information*, May 7, 2015.

[11] The State Administration of Foreign Exchange: *China's Service Trade Has a Deficit of 1.2 Trillion Yuan in 2014*. January 27, 2015. Note: 26 times represent a change in nominal value; the influence of exchange rate is not calculated.

[12] Ministry of Commerce: *The Situation of China's Service Trade*. www.mofcom.gov.cn, November 5, 2015.

[13] Trade Data 2015. US Department of Commerce Economic Analysis Bureau Network, January 12, 2012.

[14] WTO International Trade Statistics 2013. www.wto.org, January 12, 2016.

disadvantage. In 2013, China's producer-service trade ran up a deficit of US$66.38 billion, accounting for 56% of the service trade deficit.[15] As the producer-service industry that is an important support of the change from "made in China" to "intelligently made in China" is seriously underdeveloped, China's manufacturing industry has still been in a low-level position in the global industrial chain and value chain.

④ There is uneven development in service trade regions. Although the development gap of China's domestic regional service trade is narrowing, the development of service trade in various regions is still very unbalanced. In 2015, the total import and export of service trade in eleven provinces and cities along the Yangtze River economic belt accounted for 40% of China's total, while the import and export of service trade in the central and western regions accounted for only 15%.[16]

⑤ The openness of China's service trade is significantly lower than that of other countries. At present, the restrictions index (0.366) of the country's service trade is still higher than that of the United Kingdom (0.14), the United States (0.18), Germany (0.18), Japan (0.23), Korea (0.23), France (0.26) and other major developed countries in the world. Compared with other BRICS countries, China's service trade restrictions index is only lower than that of India (0.66), but higher than that of Brazil (0.23), Russia (0.26) and South Africa (0.35). Some industries still have strict restrictions on market access, and others are not yet open. For example, the restrictions index of service trade in express delivery, radio, air transportation, telecommunications, legal, audit, and insurance services, and commercial banks is 0.868, 0.784, 0.591, 0.529, 0.524, 0.5, 0.496 and 0.492 respectively. This shows that China's service trade is applying relatively bigger restrictions, and in a low level of openness.[17]

(2) China needs to set the 20% proportion of service trade in its total foreign trade as the expected target of the 13th FYP.

[15] Data is based on the *National Statistical Yearbook 2014* prepared by the National Bureau of Statistics.

[16] The Double Growth Rate of China's Service Import and Export in 2015 Exceeded 10% for 12 Months Running. www.chinanews.com, February 3, 2016.

[17] Yang Changyong: A Study of China's Strategic Thinking on Expanding the Opening-Up of Service Industry. *Intertrade*, Issue 4, 2015.

Table 2 Predictions for China's GDP, total foreign trade, and total service trade and their respective proportion in 2020 and 2030

Predicative indicators in the 13th FYP	*2014 (base period)*	*2020*	*2030*
China's GDP (growth rate 6.5%) (US$100 million)	103548	151091.3	283619.1
China's GDP (growth rate 7%) (US$100 million)		155397.6	305690.7
Total foreign trade (share of GDP: 45%) (US$100 million)	9058.3	67991.07	127628.6
Total foreign trade (share of GDP: 50%) (US$100 million)		77698.81	152845.3
Total service trade (proportion in the total foreign trade: 20%) (US$100 million)	6043	13598.2 (Situation 1: GDP's growth rate 6.5%; foreign trade proportion: 45%) 15539.8 (Situation 2: GDP's growth rate 7%; foreign trade proportion: 50%)	25525.7 (Situation 1: GDP's growth rate 6.5%; foreign trade proportion: 45%) 30569.1 (Situation 2: GDP's growth rate 7%; foreign trade proportion: 50%)
Service trade average growth rate (base period: 2014)		14.5% 17.0%	9% 11%

Source Data calculation is based on World Bank database and *China National Statistical Yearbook 2015*

So it is important to seize the historical opportunity of the new round of service trade liberalization and increase the proportion of service trade to at least 20% of China's foreign trade by 2020. Judging by the reality, it is possible that service trade will be able to reach 20% (see Table 2).

① It is ascribed to the upgrading of consumption pattern and the promotion of population urbanization. With the acceleration of consumption upgrading and population urbanization, by the end of the 13th FYP period, the proportion of urban residents' service consumption will rise to about 50% from less than present 40%.[18] The rapid growth of service consumption will drive the growth of service trade.

[18]Chi Fulin: The 13th FYP: New Trends, New Structure, and New Driving Force for Economic Transformation. www.chinareform.org.cn, November 14, 2015.

Table 3 The development of China's service trade in 2001–2014 (unit: %)

2001–2014	Average growth rate of China's service trade	17.8
	Average growth rate of China's service trade	17.8
2001–2007 (before the economic crisis)	Average growth rate of China's service trade	23
	Average growth rate of China's service trade	27
2008–2014 (after the economic crisis)	Average growth rate of China's service trade	12.1
	Average growth rate of China's service trade	9.4

Source Calculation is based on *China National Statistical Yearbook 2015*, WTO's *World Trade Report* and *International Trade Statistics*

② It is ascribed to the transformation and upgrading of industrial structure. Both the service orientation of manufacturing industry and the structural optimization of service industry itself will promote the further increase of the proportion of service trade.

③ It is ascribed to the promotion by "the Belt and Road Initiative". The implementation of the major infrastructure connectivity project of "the Belt and Road Initiative" will significantly promote the growth of relevant service trade. As a result, the proportion of service trade during the 13th FYP period will possibly increase by 1.5% annually.

④ It is ascribed to the development of domestic pilot free trade zones. To turn the free trade zones into the "upgraded version" of China's economy, it is necessary to make a major breakthrough in trade facilitation, especially in service trade facilitation which, once tried first, will be conducive to providing a model for copy and follow domestically. This is the right way to improve the environment and level of China's service trade development (see Table 3).

From the realistic perspective, to ensure the growth rate of service trade at 14.5–17% during the 13th FYP period, namely, the growth rate at least slightly higher than that after the financial crisis, the "second opening" with emphasis on service trade can be able to release even larger dividends than the "first opening". Up to 2020, China's total service trade in the total world service trade will increase from 6.2% in 2014 to 10%. Then, the trade structure of balanced development of traditional trade and modern service trade will be formed so as to strive for a new competitive advantage in the telecommunications, information technology, e-commerce, health care, education and other modern service trade areas.

3.2 It Is of Importance to Accelerate the Construction of Domestic Free Trade Zones with the Focus on Service Trade

It is the historical mission of the domestic free trade zones (FTZs) to accelerate the opening of service market and promote the service trade process. To serve the overall domestic situation of economic transformation and upgrading and actively participate in the global service trade process, the domestic FTZs need to play a leading role on a trial basis.

(1) The construction of domestic FTZs needs to focus on the overall situation of the country's opening-up.

① It is urgent to raise the opening level of service industry. At present, the service market has become the largest investment market. In 2000–2014, the proportion of foreign investment actually used in China's service industry increased from 25.7 to 55.4%.[19] In the 13th FYP period, with the constant release of service demand, the potential and space for the introduction of foreign capital into the service industry is still enormous. Some studies show that the contribution of opening-up to China's manufacturing industry's growth is about 28%, whereas the contribution to the growth of China's service industry is only 7%.[20] As the opening-up of China's service industry is seriously lagging, it is difficult for the said industry to make full use of international advanced technology and management experience, thus restricting the effective supply of the service industry while bringing about prominent problems about the consumption outflow of domestic education, health care and other services.

② Domestic FTZs need to focus on the exploration of the market opening of service industry. Since the establishment of the Shanghai FTZ in 2013, the construction of domestic FTZs has developed rapidly from one zone to four zones. The opening-up of service industry is the important content of China's first four major Pilot Free Trade Zones (PFTZs) in Shanghai, Tianjin, Guangdong and Fujian. The opening and testing of

[19]Zhang Fei: Liberalizing Service Industry to Release Market Dividends. *Shanghai Securities News*, April 14, 2015.

[20]Chi Fulin: Transition and Reform: The Megatrend of China's Shift to a Big Service-Oriented Nation in the 13th Five-Year Plan Period. *Journal of Shanghai University (Social Science Edition)*, Vol. 32, No. 1, 2015.

the four PFTZs have boosted the development of service trade to some extent. Take Shanghai for example. Its service trade import and export volume in 2015 was US$196.672 billion, an increase by 14.5% over the last year, which accounted for about 27.6% of the country's service trade volume. The total import and export of Shanghai's service trade kept its proportion growing in the city's total foreign trade, from 27.3% in 2014 to 30.3% in 2015.[21]

Special Citations [4-1]

The Opening-Up of Service Industries in the Four Major Free Trade Zones

In 2013, Shanghai Pilot Free Trade Zone chose to open further in six major fields like financial service, shipping service, business service, professional service, cultural service, and social services, and 18 industries with suspension or cancellation of investor qualification requirements, stock ratio restrictions, business scope restrictions and other access restrictions, thereby creating an environment of equal access to the market conducive to all kinds of investors.[22] The newly established PFTZs in Tianjin, Guangdong and Fujian copied the successful experience of the Shanghai Pilot Free Trade Zone in the mode of "pre-entry national treatment + negative list".

From April 2015 on, the four PFTZs began to share the same negative listing, implement the record system of the establishment and change of foreign-invested enterprises, speed up the reform and innovation in investment management, trade supervision, financial openness and market regulation, and carry out a trial in the decentralized and optimized services.

On April 20, 2015, China published *Special Management Measures (Negative List) for the Access of Foreign Investment in the Pilot Free Trade Zones*, which lists special management measures for the access of foreign investment that are applicable to the four PFTZs in Shanghai, Guangdong, Tianjin, and Fujian but not in conformity with the principle of national treatment. The negative list of PFTZs is divided into 15 categories with 50 items and 122 special management measures according

[21] *Shanghai Statistical Bulletin on National Economic and Social Development 2015*. www.statis-sh.gov.cn, February 29, 2016.

[22] The State Council Announces the Opening List of 18 Industries in the 6 Major Areas of the Shanghai Free Trade Zone. www.china.com.cn, September 27, 2013.

to the *Industrial Classification for National Economic Activities* (GB/T 4754-2011). The special management measures include specific industry measures and level measures applicable to all industries.[23]

Compared with the 2014 edition of the negative list of Shanghai FTZ, the *Negative List of Pilot Free Trade Zones* shared by the four PFTZs, reduced the 3 categories and 17 special management measures, shortening the list by 12.2% and improving the openness and transparency of the FTZs.

The four FTZs are similar in terms of openness with the same goals but different priorities. For example, the main task of Guangdong PFTZ is to promote the economic integration of Guangdong, Hong Kong and Macao, especially in the service sector. In 2015, the liberalization of service trade was basically achieved within the framework of Closer Economic Partnership Arrangement (CEPA) in these three places, while there were 160 service trade departments. Guangdong has 153 departments open to Hong Kong and Macao, which is characteristic of PFTZ in Guangdong.[24]

Source Citations are prepared by the research group of China (Hainan) Institute of Reform and Development.

③ The role of domestic FTZs needs to be further clarified. In response to new trends and new challenges brought about by the change in the global trade patterns and rules, China needs to accelerate the construction of domestic FTZs with the focus on service trade and conduct an earlier trial for a more open institutional mechanism and for the higher standard economic and trade rules and explore the optimal open mode that meets the needs of the economic transformation and upgrading, in order to provide practical basis for China to promote the process of global free trade and participate in making rules of global trade and investment.

(2) It is of importance to break through the restrictions on the opening of service industry market on a larger scale

① The opening of service market is the key to expanding service trade. The opening of service market contains enormous space for trade

[23] A List Shared by Four PFTZs in China. www.yicai.com, March 23, 2015.

[24] The Liberalization of Service Trade Is Basically Achieved in Two Places. *Yangcheng Evening News*, November 28, 2015.

and investment. Judging from the experience of developed countries, the opening of service market has greatly promoted the development of service trade. Firstly, on the premise of effective demand, the more open a sector is, the larger the scale of trade and investment will be. Foreign direct investment (FDI) in service industry is positively correlated with service trade. According to the preliminary estimate, for every additional 1 percentage point from FDI in the service sector, service trade will grow by 0.79%.[25] If the greater openness of service industry were achieved during the 13th FYP period, it would greatly promote the development of China's service trade. Secondly, the opening of service market would enable the domestic service companies in the competitive environment of international market to step up eliminating the inferior while keeping the superior, so as to form the competitiveness of domestic service companies for the benefit of China's service trade both in quality and growth as a whole.

② It is of importance to substantially reduce the number of negative lists. At present, China's four FTZs have achieved remarkable results in implementing the negative list management. However, in promoting the opening of service markets, their goals are not clear and there has been no substantive breakthrough. In the FTZs, for example, there have still been a considerable number of restrictions on openness to service trade. Among the 122 items from the "negative list", namely, *Special Management Measures for the Access of Foreign Investment in the Pilot Free Trade Zones* (published in 2015), there are 80-odd items for service industry.[26] It is suggested that by 2020 the number of service trade items in the negative list of the FTZs should be reduced to 40 items, thus providing important experience that can be duplicated and popularized for other regions in implementing the negative list management.

(3) It is of importance to explore new rules for service trade

① The opening-up of service trade should be sped up on an earlier trial basis. The FTZ can first carry out a daring pilot scheme in the depth

[25] Calculation is based on the data prepared by the research group of China (Hainan) Institute for Reform and Development according to *China Statistical Yearbook 2014* of National Bureau of Statistics.

[26] Chi Fulin: The 13th FYP: Promoting Transformation and Upgrading Through Structural Reform. *Economic Information Daily*, December 16, 2015.

and breadth in important service trade, gradually expand the open experimental content based on the summary of experience, and then while following the service open model and standard of international high-level free trade zones in developed countries, promote the opening of service industry by trying the “negative list” management model. Furthermore, it is by lowering the threshold of entry and lifting restrictions on business scope as well as expanding the open area that overseas investors in services will be attracted to local markets to effectively promote the service competition and improve service levels. In doing so, therefore, China will be able to build open heights in the international service industry competition at a higher level, forming the new international competition advantage.[27]

② New rules of service trade should be proposed on the basis of experiments. It is important to take the domestic FTZ as a platform to explore ways to integrate domestic and foreign rules, accelerate reforms of the foreign-related economic system, and establish both a market-opening and market-operation system and a policy system that are in line with international norms. By 2020, China’s version of the international trade rules, especially the new rules on service trade, will preliminarily be formed. Stress tests and isolation tests are to be carried out on new topics such as anti-dumping rules, global supply chain liberalization, natural person mobility, e-commerce and foreign investment protection. On a pilot basis, the global value chain (GVC), infrastructure connectivity, development assistance, e-commerce and industrial parks will be incorporated into the new bilateral and multilateral free trade agreements.

(4) It is of importance to promote the expansion of domestic FTZs

① Rational distribution should be achieved in coastal, border and inland areas. At present, various provinces and cities in China have been highly active to apply for free trade zones. Guangxi, Chongqing, Hubei, Jiangxi, Shandong, Hainan and more have reported plans for free trade zones. Therefore, on the basis of accelerating the construction of the four FTZs, it is possible and necessary to choose to establish PFTZs with

[27] Zhao Jinping: Essential Features and Innovative Points of Free Trade Zones. www.people.com.cn, June 19, 2015.

different industrial focuses in other coastal, border and inland areas in which the industry is service-oriented or service industry is developing rapidly.

② It is necessary to promote the upgrading of a number of border cooperative zones into FTZs. During the 13th FYP period, a batch of border cooperative zones should be upgraded to FTZs and open innovation models, in which service trade liberalization and service market opening are being strengthened and a distinctive service trade base is being formed, so as to expand service trade with surrounding areas of China in information, finance, insurance, logistics, and transportation, promote emerging service export in culture, traditional Chinese medicine, software and information service, and develop the competitive advantage of service trade, finally forming a new growth point of service trade export.

③ It is necessary to cooperate with major trading partners to build cross-border cooperative trade parks. At present, China's enterprises are investing in 69 projects with characteristics of overseas cooperation zones, which are distributed in 33 countries including various types such as processing and manufacturing, resource utilization, trade logistics, and scientific and technological research and developments.[28] Service trade, especially cross-border financial services, should be taken as an important task in constructing overseas economic cooperation zones so as to set up an overseas platform for Chinese service enterprises to go abroad. In addition, In line with local needs and in consultation with local governments, it is important to implement policies of service trade liberalization and facilitation in overseas cooperative trade zones for the benefit of cross-border investment and financing activities on the part of enterprises. Meanwhile, local currency trading should be facilitated, cooperation between RMB (*Renminbi*) and local currencies be accelerated, and the internationalization of RMB promoted.

3.3 It Is Essential to Speed Up the Two-Way Opening of Service Market Between Countries

The opening of service market is not only the opening of China's service industry to the outside world, but also the opening of other countries,

[28] Jiang Yu: Chinese Enterprises Are Building 69 Overseas Cooperative Economic and Trade Zones in 33 Countries. www.chinanews.com, October 14, 2015.

especially developed countries, to China. Its essence is the two-way opening of market. In other words, China should not only actively promote the opening of domestic service industry to foreign investment, but also strive for the equal opening of service industry in other countries to Chinese enterprises.

(1) It is important to further open China's domestic service industry to the rest of the world in an orderly manner

① The threshold for foreign capital's entry should be lowered. China should accelerate the implementation of the pre-entry national treatment and negative list model and narrow the scope of the negative list. So it is good to implement the registration and filing system for foreign investment in service industry. In general service trade, the examination and approval procedure for the establishment of foreign companies will gradually be changed to the record management. The system of information reporting and sharing will be implemented for the sake of foreign-invested enterprises.

② Key service domains should be opened up in an orderly manner. The opening of such service domains as finance, education, culture, and health care will first be promoted in an orderly way. Then access restrictions on foreign investment will be lifted in childcare and elderly care, architecture design, accounting and auditing, trade logistics, and e-commerce.

③ Preferential access should be opened to FTZ partners. While speeding up the implementation of FTZ strategies, China should give priority to the opening to FTZ partners in its service domains in urgent need of economic transformation and industrial upgrading and in service areas with trading partners having complementary advantages. With reference to the practice of the Mainland's opening service trade to Hong Kong, China will further open the service trade departments to its partners of free trade agreements and give them the national treatment in areas based on the service mode of "commercial presence", accelerating the bilateral opening of service trade.

④ Service outsourcing business should vigorously be developed. Service outsourcing has gradually replaced manufacturing outsourcing as a new trend of globalization. It is suggested to formulate the plan of action to revitalize China's international service outsourcing industry with the focus on developing software and information technology, research and development, design, the Internet, medical care, industry, and energy, to accelerate the development of service outsourcing in education, health care, cultural creativity, finance, transportation and logistics, and scientific and technological services, to improve the value added of service outsourcing, to increase the number of service outsourcing demonstration cities, and to develop a number of demonstration cities able to integrate the supply chains of specific service domains (specific destination countries) and featured areas (specific industries). Considering all these, therefore, related policies should come out ASAP to popularize demonstration cities nationwide in terms of successful experience in creating brand, technology and credit, to promote the standardized and rapid development of service outsourcing market, and to raise the development level of China's service industry by making full use of service outsourcing or BPO (business process outsourcing).

(2) It is important to promote two-way market access with free trade partners

① The establishment of bilateral and regional agreements on service trade should be sped up. It is imperative to break down the barriers of some countries to China's service trade and jointly reduce tariff and non-tariff barriers. The first thing is to make breakthroughs in emerging economies, Europe and other countries and regions, and then to speed up the opening and cooperation with major trading countries in the financial, information, logistics and other service industries, making the opening of service industry and the liberalization of service trade a priority of bilateral and multilateral cooperation.

② It is important to sign agreements on mutual protection and promotion of investment in order to support enterprises' "going global". So, to follow the trend of industrial transfer in China means to speed up the signing of agreements on investment protection and promotion with surrounding countries and provide legal guarantee for the "going global" of China's manufacturing enterprises. To follow the trend of industrial transfer in China means to expedite the signing of agreements on investment protection and investment promotion with countries along the line of "the Belt and the Road" to promote the capacity cooperation and industrial cooperation between Chinese enterprises and enterprises of countries along "the Belt and the Road" line. And to follow the trend of industrial transfer in China means to accelerate the signing of agreements on investment protection and investment promotion with developed countries while urging the United States and the European Union to admit China's market economy status (MES), giving China's enterprises and investment companies and other market economy countries and their investment equal status and treatment without setting up separate technical barriers and national security review system for China's enterprises.

③ It is important to promote the reciprocal opening of the government procurement market. The scale of the government procurement in developed countries generally accounts for about 10% of the annual GDP.[29] The scale of government procurement in emerging markets has been expanding. In 2014, the scale of China's government procurement accounted for 1.7305 trillion yuan (US$0.2884 trillion), which makes up the proportion of national fiscal expenditure and GDP at 11.4 and 2.4% respectively.[30] There must be still much room for further development. During the 13th FYP period, China should actively join the WTO's Government Procurement Agreement (GPA) in promoting the modification and improvement of GPA exception clauses, and reducing the discrimination against Chinese enterprises caused by foreign government procurement. Meanwhile, it will also improve laws and regulations on domestic government procurement, gradually reduce unreasonable restrictions on foreign investment in government procurement, and improve the transparency of government procurement. In the negotiation of bilateral and multilateral trade agreements, it should take the reciprocal and mutually beneficial opening of the government procurement market as an important part of the content so as to gradually expand the opening of China's government procurement market.

(3) Great efforts have to be made to break the developed countries' restrictions on the export of high-tech services to China

Developed countries are in the leading position in electronic technology, aviation, information and communications technology, life science

[29] Cui Ying: Financial Crisis in the Context of Our Country in the Area of Government Procurement Management Countermeasures Commercial Bribery (*sic*). *Journal of Beijing Institute of Technology* (Social Sciences Edition), No. 6, 2009.

[30] The Scale of Government Procurement Reaches 1.7305 Trillion Yuan Last Year. www.gmw.cn, July 31, 2015.

technology, and energy environment, which are not yet open to developing countries. Although the United States, Europe and other developed countries generally adopt the negative listing model, foreign enterprises' products can still be restricted by such means as technological barriers and national security review. For example, the threshold of entry by foreign products and services has been raised and the competitiveness of these products has thus been weakened by the United States' policies like "improving technical standards", "increasing the inspection items" and "changed technical regulations" in its government procurement.[31] While China's service industry market is opening up to developed countries in an orderly way, no efforts will be spared to achieve a new breakthrough through trade negotiations in the opening of developed countries' high-tech service industry to China.

4 Accelerating the Construction of "the Belt and the Road" with the Goal of Expanding FTA Network

In the post-WTO era with service trade as the focus, bilateral and multilateral free trade has become a main trend in the new round of globalization. In the specific context, therefore, "the Belt and the Road Initiative" does not simply mean "going out" of manufacturing industry. The more important is to take the establishment of a bilateral and multilateral free trade network as a goal to pursue, promoting the "bringing in" and "going out" of service industry and forming the heights in the new round of comprehensive opening-up.

1. The construction of "the Belt and the Road" focuses on building a FTA network

The key to the construction of "the Belt and the Road" is, through the FTA strategy, to formulate trade rules that both meet the needs of China's economic transformation and propel the process of global free trade, and to make the Chinese voice heard and inject more Chinese elements in promoting the formation of the new system of international economic and trade rules.

[31] Chen Deming: GPA Negotiation: Be Vigilant Against Unequal Opening. www.prcfe.com, June 21, 2015.

(1) Bilateral, multilateral, regional and global free trade processes ought to be promoted

On December 17, 2015, the State Council issued the *Several Opinions on Accelerating the Implementation of Free Trade Zone Strategy*, which put forward “upholding and promoting the close connection of the joint construction of ‘the Belt and the Road’ and China’s foreign strategy”, “building step by step the globe-oriented high-standard free trade zone network that is based upon neighboring countries and regions, radiating “the Belt and the Road”. The “Belt and Road Initiative” (BRI) is aimed at building a free trade area network and promoting the process of global and regional free trade. In the next five to ten years, more bilateral and multilateral free trade areas should be established with the focus on countries along “the Belt and the Road” line, significantly reducing tariff and non-tariff barriers to trade with major trading partners and accelerating the process of bilateral and multilateral, regional and global free trade.

(2) The free trade thoroughfare ought to be opened up.

Countries and regions along “the Belt and the Road” shall be chosen as strategic nodes, thus opening up the free trade thoroughfare in “BRI”, while promoting regional economic integration with emphasis on the free trade areas, and gradually forming a mutually beneficial large market in Asia and Europe. Then, the combination shall be promoted between the construction of free trade area network under “BRI” and the improvement of the global multilateral trade system, while integrating the trade agreements of the Asia-Pacific region to prevent the fragmentation of the regional trade and the situation of vicious competition.

(3) China’s new international trade rules ought to be formed gradually.

The establishment of China’s own Silk Road Fund and China-led Asian Infrastructure Investment Bank chiefly represents the interests of emerging economies, reflecting the demands of emerging economies and demonstrating to the world the image of China as an open, inclusive and responsible big nation. In this connection, therefore, the BRI should be taken as the focus to combine the further opening-up with striving for voice in global economic governance. Meanwhile, China is supposed to play a leading role in constructing new rules on balanced development, mutually beneficial and win-win trade and investment in accelerating the implementation of free trade area strategies. Particularly, it is better for China to gradually become the guide to new rules on service trade.

2. A network of bilateral and multilateral free trade areas should be optimized and constructed on the basis of neighboring countries and regions

The BRI contains 65 countries, with its greater emphasis on the opening to neighboring countries and emerging economies in Asia. In terms of spatial arrangement, the BRI will be more able to display its comparative advantages, making it easier to achieve substantive results in building bilateral and multilateral free trade network.

(1) It is important to turn the upgraded version of the "10+1" free trade area into "the Belt and Road" model of multilateral free trade area.

① There is an enormous space for cooperation in service industry between China-ASEAN (10+1). Generally, the level of service trade liberalization between China and ASEAN is still lower than that of ASEAN-ROK Free Trade Area, ASEAN-Japan Free Trade Area, and ASEAN-Australia-New Zealand Free Trade Area respectively. In service trade, for example, China has opened over 30 departments to ASEAN, whereas South Korea, Japan, Australia, New Zealand have promised to open 85, 164, 85 and 116 departments respectively.[32] So there is still much room for China and ASEAN to further expand the mutual opening of service trade. Building an upgraded China-ASEAN Free Trade Area is the most important task for China to optimize the layout of FTA construction on the basis of its surrounding countries. During the 13th FYP period, based on the implementation of the CAFTA's upgraded version of the agreement, the liberalization and integration of "10+1" trade and investment should continue to be promoted under the guidance of

[32] FTAAP Will Be Possibly Formed from the Expansion of RCEP. *21st Century Business Herald*, November 7, 2014.

"quasi-EU", bringing about driving and demonstration effect by the "Belt and Road"'s FTA construction.

② An upgraded version of "10+1" will be created in the orientation of "quasi-EU". In the existing framework of "10+1" free trade area will be formed a unified market with the free circulation of goods, services, capital, resources, labor, technology and management, speeding up the construction of international thoroughfare. Dead-end highways and bottleneck roads between China and Burma, Laos, Vietnam, and Thailand will be opened up ASAP, forming the radiation-type and networking traffic layout and promoting the cross-border efficient allocation of various resources and market connection.

③ Construction of an upgraded version of trade liberalization with higher standards should be accelerated by focusing on the opening up of service trade. In one aspect, the liberalization of service trade is gradually getting in line with the liberalization of service trade in Hong Kong and Macao. The commitment to open service trade to Hong Kong and Macao will gradually be introduced into the China-ASEAN Free Trade Agreement. On the basis of shortening the transition period, efforts will be made to enable the proportion of zero tariff items and that of trade volume to reach 95–100%. Issues covered in FTA negotiations will gradually be expanded, with a view to arriving at the consensus in new issues such as e-commerce, competition policy, government procurement and environment and laying a sound foundation for the construction of 2.0 updated versions of liberalized trade and investment. A study of high-standard investment and trade rules will be jointly conducted to promote the upgrading of rules on regional trade and investment.

In another aspect, efforts will have to be made to remove institutional barriers to the development of service trade. Firstly, it is to actively lower the entry threshold. Service markets will be further opened in an orderly manner with the focus on education, healthcare, finance and cultural entertainment. Secondly, it is to actively promote the two-way market opening. Knowledge-intensive information service, financial service, and technical service will gradually be opened, while coordinating the import and export of labor-intensive and knowledge-intensive service and optimizing the internal structure of service trade. Thirdly, it is to promote the reform of the foreign investment management system. The foreign capital management will also be changed ASAP from the current Catalogue of Industries for Guiding Foreign Investment to the "negative list" management mode, with focus on strengthening the construction of financing channels of ASEAN investment enterprises, setting up special funds for investment cooperation, providing credit support, and establishing an information platform with ASEAN economic and trade cooperation.

(2) It is imperative to accelerate the construction of the free trade area between China, Japan, Japan and ASEAN ("10+3")

① Joint efforts are to be made to improve trade and investment facilitation. Negotiations on the 10+3 free trade area will actively be promoted in light of the upgraded CAFTA and CKFTA practices. More free circulation of goods, services, and capital will be promoted in the said FTAs; the cooperation of capacity and equipment manufacturing will be strengthened; and the promotion of East Asia's industrial chain and value chain and the construction of twenty-first century "Maritime Silk Road" will jointly be facilitated.

② Regional financial cooperation in the "10+3" area will be enhanced. It is necessary to further expand the local currency swap and settlement of cross-border trade in local currencies and strengthen the establishment of a clearing mechanism. It is also important to strengthen fiscal and financial cooperation, jointly respond to potential short-term liquidity disturbances in the region, and jointly establish an efficient regulatory coordination mechanism and early warning mechanism.

③ It is essential to promote the cooperation between the Asian Infrastructure Investment Bank and the Asian Development Bank. It is suggested that Infrastructure interconnectivity be taken as the important content of "10+3" Free Trade Agreements or the "package" economic cooperation agreement, so as to strengthen the cooperation between the two in the "10+3" infrastructure interconnectivity and discuss the list of the first batch of jointly constructed projects ASAP.

(3) A free trade area is to be established with the Eurasian economic union

① It is necessary to explore the development of free trade areas in China and central Asia. The establishment of the free trade areas should be taken as the focus of connection and cooperation between the construction of the Silk Road Economic Belt and the construction of the Eurasian economic union. In addition, industrial parks and cross-border economic cooperation areas need to be jointly built. So it is important to accelerate the construction of strategic channels like China-Mongolia-Russia, the new Eurasian Continental Bridge, and the China-Central Asia-West Asia and China-Pakistan Economic Corridor, to accelerate the construction of energy, electric power and information for connectivity, and to accelerate the construction of "big customs clearance" system, improving the level of customs clearance facilitation.

② It is important to promote the progress of the BRICS free trade area. Joint studies should be carried out ASAP to formulate a multilateral free trade agreement on the basis of equality and mutual benefit. It is to be followed by promoting trade and investment facilitation, including technical standards, express customs clearance, inspection and quarantine, trade relief, intellectual property rights, competition policies and market access. Free trade will be taken as the focus to build a framework for closer economic partnership among the BRICS. It is through consultation that the BRICS integrate the rules formed in promoting the establishment of bilateral and multilateral trade framework and reaches a basic consensus on the basis of basic rules, strengthening the resultant force of BRICS that will influence the global trade and investment.

5 Promoting Changes in Global Economic Governance

China's economy has a profound impact on world economy and cannot leave world economy. Since 2014, China has successively established the Silk Road Fund and the Asian Infrastructure Investment Bank. In 2015, the RMB joined the Special Drawing Rights' (SDR) basket of International Monetary Fund (IMF). This is a sign that China continues to provide win-win public goods to the world and has begun to play an important role in pushing the global governance system towards greater equality, justice and win-win cooperation.

5.1 An Important Historical Juncture for Changes in Global Economic Governance

Eight years have passed since the international financial crisis. The global economy is still not out of the shadow of crisis In the next three to five years, the success or otherwise of the economic transformation of emerging economies will determine whether the global economy can truly recover. The world economy is undergoing a complex and profound adjustment in a new round of global rebalancing. A "zero-sum game" or "multiple-win cooperation" between developed countries and emerging economies depends on the change in the global economic governance system.

(1) Emerging economies have not yet acquired a voice commensurate with their economic status and contributions

Emerging economies have become a major force in world economic growth and rebalancing and have made important contributions to the stability and development of the global economy. According to the *Annual Report on the Development of Emerging Economies 2016* released by Boao Forum for Asia on March 22, 2016, in the situation of the overall downturn in the global economy, emerging economies (E11, 11 emerging countries) increased their proportion in the global economy from 29.3% in 2014 to 30.3% in 2015, representing the contribution rate of 52.9% for the global economic growth, which is far more than 22.9% of G7 and 12.2 of the EU.[33] BRICS'GDP and trade volume made up 21.8% of the world's GDP (2014)[34] and 16.4% of the world trade volume (2013)[35] respectively. Given this, however, the new economies represented by BRICS and 11E still have not much say in global governance, which does not match their contributions, and in turn form restrictions on their economic transformation and sustainable growth.

(2) The global economic governance system based on developed countries is not conducive to the transformation of emerging economies

① The transformation of emerging economies has become more dependent on changes in global economic governance. In the past two years, as external demand has continued to shrink and internal economic transformation has lagged behind, economic growth in emerging

[33] China and India Rank First in the Group of 11E That Contributes More Than 50% to Global Economic Growth Last Year. www.cnstock.com, March 22, 2016.

[34] The figure is calculated according to *BRICS Joint Statistical Handbook 2015* prepared by China's National Bureau of Statistics.

[35] The figure is calculated according to WTO's *World Trade Report 2014*.

economies has generally slowed down, while some emerging economies are at risk of a stall in economic growth. According to some projections, if economic transformation in emerging economies were successful, emerging economies and developing countries would enable their proportion in the global economy to rise to 63% by 2030 from the present 38%,[36] making great contributions to the sustained growth of the world economy. In order to meet the needs of the economic transformation of emerging economies, the reform of global economic governance should be accelerated with economic transformation as the orientation.

② The disorder of the global free trade system has brought adverse external environment to the transformation of emerging economies. The multilateral trade framework both dominated by developed countries and represented by TPP, TTIP and TISA, has raised the threshold excessively in the short term. This has made the new trade protectionism more hidden, which is not conducive to emerging economies and developing countries in making use of free trade to accelerate the development of domestic economy transformation, while restricting the release of the potential of global free trade growth.

③ Spillover effects of macro policies in developed countries have increased the external risks of the transformation of emerging economies. Under the current management system, developed countries can export the crisis through a variety of ways, but emerging economies have to face frequent international capital flows, exchange rate fluctuations, deterioration of trade environment, etc.

④ Sharp fluctuations in prices of bulk commodities like energy have added to the difficulties of transformation in emerging economies. The current governance system lacks risk coordination and control for global economic and financial crises. Considerable fluctuations in prices of energy like oil not only increase difficulties of transformation in emerging economies that mainly rely on energy exports, but also bring a lot of uncertainty and risk to emerging economies and developing countries that are now in a critical period of industrialization and have enormous demand for bulk commodities.

(3) The global governance system faces restructuring

[36]The Globe is in the Third Economic "Super Cycle" and Emerging Market Growth is Key. *Southern Daily*, November 11, 2013.

① The traditional economic governance pattern of "three carriages" is facing restructuring. Facing the requirements of world economic transformation and the complex and profound changes of the world economic pattern, what are known as "three carriages" in China—WTO, World Bank and IMF—established after World War II for global economic governance have been lagging in reform and increasingly powerless in maintaining the global economic, financial and security order. Especially in IMF and World Bank there is a congenital defect, namely, an imbalance in the right of discourse between developed countries and emerging economies. This has made it difficult to adapt to the demands of promoting economic transformation and global sustainable growth.

② How to institutionalize the G20 has become the core issue of global economic governance. Since the outbreak of international financial crisis in 2008, the proportion of emerging economies in world economy has further increased. In 2015, emerging economies and the G7 economies were basically equal in terms of economic aggregate. Under this trend, the G20 will gradually replace the G7 as an important platform for global economic governance. However, the current problem is that as the G20 is a kind of informal dialogue mechanism, it still lacks authority and binding force in coordinating with the member states the implementation of the agreement reached at the G20. It is characteristic of "no decision after deliberation, no action even with a decision". To make sure of an effective G20 mechanism is the realistic choice for emerging economies and developing countries to have much say in the future, and also the key to rebalancing the global governance structure, which is of great significance to promote the transformation of emerging economies and the sustainable development of global economy.

5.2 *Playing a Role as a Major Country in Promoting the Establishment of New Rules on Service Trade*

To adapt to the new trend of global free trade, China should take the promotion of the establishment of new service trade rules as the focus when participating in global economic governance. Through active participation in bilateral, multilateral and regional service trade agreements and the acceleration of domestic open test on service trade in FTZs, it should promote the formulation of fair, win-win, inclusive and developing new rues on service.

(1) China should actively participate in the formulation of bilateral, multilateral and regional rules on service trade

① Service trade should be regarded as the focus of negotiations on bilateral and regional free trade agreements. By taking the liberalization of service trade as an important objective of bilateral and regional trade agreements, China must actively participate in and lead the development of rules on service trade, and actively propose new issues that meet the needs of its economic transformation and the development trend of global free trade, such as e-commerce. It should include investment access, intellectual property rights, government procurement and movement of natural persons involved in service trade as the basic contents of negotiations on bilateral free trade agreements and regional trade agreements.

② Bilateral and regional service trade agreements should actively be established. According to the regional distribution of service trade, about 70% of the world's service trade is concentrated in Europe and Asia. To this end, it is proposed to sign bilateral, multilateral and regional service trade agreements with such key countries and regions as emerging Asian economies and developed European countries that are clearly complementary to China's service industries. Therefore, China should speed up the development of open cooperation with major service trading partners in financial, information, logistics and other services, and two-way market opening in generally competitive services. It should speed up negotiations on service trade agreements with major trading partners and the upgrading of existing bilateral and regional free trade areas with the focus on service trade.

③ It is necessary to participate actively and prudently in TISA negotiations. According to the need of its economic transformation and industrial structural adjustment, China must conduct an in-depth study of influences of TISA on its domestic economic transformation and deepening reform in these issues such as pre-entry national treatment and negative list, State-owned enterprises, investor-state dispute settlement mechanism, free flow of cross-border data, financial, tax and compensation standards, intellectual property rights, labor rules, and environmental protection, and give overall consideration to what can be offered to different issues, thus promoting the active and orderly opening of service trade.

(2) The open trial of service trade liberalization in domestic FTZs should be sped up.

It is important to seize the opportunity of the establishment of Shanghai FTZ, speed up the implementation of pressure test and isolation trial-and-error method against the standard clauses in the TISA, and explore the open model of "service-trade negative listing + pre-entry national treatment". To accumulate experience from promoting service trade liberalization, it is advisable to construct the open pilot zone of service industry within the framework of Closer Economic Partnership Arrangement (CEPA) and Economic Cooperation Framework Agreement (ECFA). On the basis of the pilot zone will be formed the timetable for national promotion, so as to reduce the foreign ownership restrictions and other market access conditions, restrictions on personnel flow, other discriminatory measures, and restrictions on regulatory transparency and management requirements while gradually raising the level of service trade openness.

(3) The establishment of a service trade regulatory system in line with international trade rules has to be accelerated.

① Service trade rules in favor of emerging economies need to be formed. At present, when major emerging economies have entered the Late Industrialization, there is an obvious trend for economic service transformation and service trade has become an important driving force for growth of emerging economies. Take China for example. The total output value of its service industry is expected to reach 48 trillion (US$8 trillion) to 53 trillion yuan (US$8.83 trillion) by 2020, which accounts for more than 55% of the GDP, whereas that of producer services industry makes up 30–40% of the GDP. "China service" will bring huge market space, becoming a significant positive for sustainable global growth.

Emerging economies face two major challenges in expanding service trade. First, their own service markets are not open sufficiently. Second, developed countries still have quite a lot of export controls in environmental protection, energy, and science and technology. Accelerating the service market opening of emerging economies and breaking the export control of service trade in developed countries should be a "dual task" in the new stage of global economic governance reform.

② It is imperative to accelerate the legislative process in service trade. *China Service Trade Law* and relevant supporting laws should be formulated and promulgated ASAP, so that provisions are made in legal form concerning the principles of service market access, taxation, investment and preferential conditions of service trade. The study is to be sped up to establish *Regulations on the Administration of Service Import and Export* and *Regulations on the Promotion of Service Trade*, and to establish service trade laws and regulations at different levels and different stages of mutual coordination as well as the practical rules and regulations, promoting China's service trade to the systematization and standardization.

5.3 Changes in Global Governance Need to Be Promoted in the Orientation of Economic Transformation

As a responsible economic power, China needs to be committed to providing public goods for global economic transformation, especially for the transformation of emerging economies. The general idea is, in one aspect, to effect quick changes in global economic governance by taking "the Belt and Road Initiative" as the important mission, the expansion of free trade area network as the goal, the development of service trade as the focus, and infrastructure interconnectivity as the backing. In another aspect, an effective global economic governance system needs to be built to promote the forming of a new global governance structure that features equality, justice, win-win cooperation, inclusiveness and diversification.

(1) The free trade area network will be expanded with "the Belt and Road Initiative" as the central focus

Accelerating the progress of free trade areas (FTAs) will not only promote economic transformation of emerging economies and developing countries, but also promote the process of global investment and trade liberalization. The problem is that it is objectively difficult for emerging economies to adopt the same standards as developed countries when they participate in the construction of the FTA network. Although the continuous improvement of standard of free trade in the process of economic globalization is a general trend, it is not suitable to raise the threshold excessively in a short period of time. It is easy to form new barriers to investment and trade, thus excluding emerging economies in economic globalization.

The important goal of China's "the Belt and Road Initiative" is to establish a FTA network in a larger scope on the premise of reasonably set standards and form a trading system in favor of emerging economies. China should give full play to its unique advantages and highlight the expansion of infrastructure interconnection with emerging economies. The low level of infrastructure interconnectivity and insufficient investment across the world, especially in emerging economies, has become a prominent problem restricting economic transformation. China initiated the establishment of Asia Infrastructure Investment Band, forming a joint effort with existing multilateral development agencies, which can not only break the bottleneck of investments in Asia's infrastructure but also become one of the important platforms for global economic governance. In other words, giving full play to the role of multilateral and regional economic organizations is a major measure to improve global economic governance.

(2) It is important to enhance the collective voice of emerging economies

As the world's largest emerging economy, China needs to do something on behalf of emerging economies. First, it needs to improve the status and voice of emerging economies in existing institutions. It also needs to promote reforms in the governance structure of International Monetary Fund and World Bank, increase the voting power of emerging economies and developing countries, and support more developing countries' equitable participation in the current global economic governance mechanism. Second, it should actively create a new mechanism for equitable participation of emerging economies and developing countries. In recent years, China and other emerging economies have actively participated in global and regional economic governance by building a new multilateral mechanism. For example, it founded a new Development Bank with the other BRICS countries in the 12th FYP period, and established AIIB with the countries located all the way along "the Belt and the Road", which forced the stock reform with the incremental reform. During the 13th FYP period, China should continue to play an active role in creating a new mechanism for global and regional governance and create conditions for improving institutional discourse power.

(3) It is essential to promote cooperation and integration between the old and new mechanisms

① It is important to handle the relationship between the G7 and the G20 well. The key is that the G7 will be able to shoulder the responsibility as big powers within the G20 framework, and to make the emerging economies and developing countries seek a voice that matches the contribution and responsibility on the G20 platform and take an equal part in G20 issues selection and agenda setting, thus promoting the development of international order in the direction of equality, justice, cooperation and multiple win.

② The AIIB and World Bank need to be promoted to jointly establish a multilateral financial cooperation network. China's newly established AIIB and Silk Road Fund should be open and inclusive and need to be organically integrated with the original international financial system for common development.

③ The combination of the WTO multilateral trading system and the FTA network needs to be promoted. China will support the participation of emerging economies and developing countries in WTO negotiations and the establishment and improvement of service trade agreements, information technology agreements, government procurement agreements and investment agreements within the WTO framework.

(4) International coordination of macroeconomic policies needs to be strengthened.

① It is necessary to strengthen the macro-policy dialogue and exchanges among countries. At present, the growth trend of developed countries and emerging economies is diverging. The debt and financial risks of some countries and regions are still rather large, and so there is still the possibility of an international economic crisis. First, the G20, APEC and other regional and sub-regional cooperation mechanisms and platforms should be used to enhance information communication between countries' macro-economy and macro-policy. Second, the transparency and predictability of macroeconomic policies need to be improved.

② Reforms in multilateral coordination mechanisms are called for. It is necessary to carry out reforms in multilateral coordination mechanisms in promoting global open cooperation. It is also necessary to promote reforms in regional and multilateral mechanisms such as APEC, and encourage and urge the members to take practical actions in promoting regional free trade and regional economic integration.

③ China should participate in building international and regional multilateral financial regulatory mechanisms and platforms. Specifically, it is to create financial rules for RMB internationalization, support the implementation of Basel III and other rules on international financial governance, actively promote the construction of the global credit system, and work with other countries to build a multilateral mechanism for crisis assistance and emergency management.

6 Promoting the Process of China-Europe Trade Area

It is of great significance to build a china-EU free trade area. For China, this is the key to winning the largest developed economic union, gradually building a globe-oriented network of free trade areas based on the neighboring countries and radiating "the Belt and the Road". For the EU, this is a historic breakthrough in building a free trade area with the world's largest developing country and winning over 1.3 billion people's markets. In addition, this is a major step for China and the EU to push forward their economic transformation and upgrading and cooperate in global governance. For the world, it will help promote the process of free trade in a wider scale and form an important factor supporting sustainable global growth. A major breakthrough in the China-EU free trade area in 2020 would be of overall, win-win and strategic importance.

6.1 There Is a Huge Demand and Space for Free Trade Between China and the EU

In the next five years, as China's economic transformation and upgrading speed up, the two economies will become significantly more complementary. In this particular context, to accelerate the establishment of the China-EU FTA would form a larger market and larger pattern for deepening China-Eu economic cooperation.

(1) Economic transformation and upgrading imply a great demand for China-EU trade.

China and the EU are the world's two major economies. But, compared with the economic aggregate of both China and the EU that accounts for one-third of the world's economic aggregate, it doesn't match adequately that the bilateral trade volume has made up only 1.5% or so of the global trade volume. Clearly, therefore, there is great room for further development in economic and trade cooperation between China and the EU.[37] In the next few years, by speeding up the process of China-EU FTA and further enhancing investment and trade facilitation, bilateral trade would result in annual growth by about 9%, thereby achieving the goal of US$1 trillion in 2020.

(2) China and Europe are highly complementary in economic structure.

Since the reform and opening-up in 1978, China has accumulated the world's leading technology and experience in some industries, the manufacturing sector and infrastructure, but the current service industry, especially the development of producer services industry, is still the "short board". The EU has entered the post-industrial era in which the characteristics of economy servicizing is very outstanding, and especially such producer services industry as electronic technology, aviation, information and communication technology, life science and technology, energy, environment, and such living services industry as health management hold unique advantages and have advanced technology and mature management experience. The differences and complementarities between the economic structures of China and the EU mean that there is an enormous trade space between China and the EU.

(3) Service trade is the greatest potential of China-EU free trade.

Service trade has become a major growth point in China-EU trade. In recent years, the net import amount of China's service trade has increased rapidly from US$3.22 billion in 1997 to US$198 billion in 2014, which registers growth by 60.5 times, namely, average annual growth by 25.7%.[38]

China's economic transformation and upgrading with service industry as a leading industry will make the potential of 40 trillion to 50 trillion yuan (US$6.67–US$8.33 trillion) of consumer demand be released, becoming an engine of important growth of world economy including

[37] Chi Fulin: Brussels Calls for Progress in China-EU FTA. www.chinanews.com, July 1, 2015.

[38] The data on China's international service trade in 2014 was released by the State Administration of Foreign Exchange.

the European Union. By 2020, if China's total service trade amount reaches US$1.2 trillion, with the proportion of its service trade in the EU growing from 13.2% in 2013 to 20%, the total amount of China-EU service trade will reach 200 billion to 220 billion Euros.[39] The EU's service trade surplus with China in 2013 was 12 billion Euros,[40] while that of 2014 was 9.2 billion euro.[41] China ranks third in the EU's service trade surplus (tying with the U.S.). The European Union enjoys its trade advantage in many services, especially in tourism trade, transportation service, exclusive right use and franchise, and insurance service. So it still has a large space on the service export to China.

6.2 *China-EU Cooperation Should Be Deepened with the Focus on Free Trade*

Facing the new trend of world economic trade patterns and rule changes, China will implement a broader, more proactive FTA strategy, which is the key point of its "the Belt and Road Initiative", so as to form the commanding heights of China's new opening up to the rest of the world and provide a new driving force for the global free trade. In this context, therefore, it is of overall, win-win and strategic significance to deepen China-EU's "the Belt and the Road" cooperation.

(1) China-EU investment cooperation needs to be strengthened.

From the perspective of the trend, the scope of infrastructure investment is rapidly expanding to telecommunications, information, culture and the like. In particular, the demand for infrastructure investment based on service trade is rapidly increasing. If the proportion of China-EU service trade in China's service trade rises to 20%, it will provide impetus for the Juncker Plan and "the Belt and the Road" infrastructure investment cooperation.

(2) Financial and monetary cooperation needs to be strengthened

[39] Launching Seminar on China-EU Reform Forum. *Guangming Daily*, March 16, 2015.

[40] Eurostat: *The EU External Service Trade Surplus Rose to 173 Billion Euros*, June 26, 2014.

[41] Economic and Commercial Counselor's Office of the Mission of the PRC to the EU. *China Is the Third Largest Service Trading Partner of the EU*, June 16, 2015.

China-Eu free trade will bring demands for such financial services as trade settlement, financial insurance, taxation, and financial guarantee requirements, while directly driving China-EU monetary cooperation and creating favorable conditions for the stable development and the internationalization of the *Renminbi*.

(3) Production capacity cooperation and industrial cooperation have to be promoted

There are enormous potential demands from China's residents in elderly service, health service, and education and culture, whereas EU countries have a mature management experience, technology and high-end talents in these services. If free trade is to boost China-EU industrial cooperation, the win-win situation will certainly be created.

(4) Cooperation on technology innovation in green environmental protection needs to be promoted

The EU is one of the global leaders in green energy, low carbon technology, and environmental control technology, whereas China is badly in need of the EU's support in advanced technology and experience as it has the world's largest clean energy market and relatively low manufacture cost. Expanding free trade in these fields will give a strong boost to innovation and cooperation between Chinese and European companies.

6.3 China-EU FTA Feasibility Negotiations Must Be Started ASAP

In the context of the new trend of economic globalization, especially of regional economic cooperation, it is recommended to launch negotiations on China-EU FTA while advancing negotiations on China-EU investment agreement.

(1) It is necessary to promote the synchronous negotiation on China-EU investment agreement and China-EU FTA.

Considering the new trend of economic globalization, especially the actual needs of building a large market in Asia and Europe, it is of great significance for the negotiations to proceed at the same time.

(2) Think tanks should be encouraged to conduct joint feasibility studies

Exchanges and cooperation between the think tanks in China and the EU can provide intellectual support, an atmosphere of public opinion and a foundation of popular support for jointly building the China-EU FTA. It is suggested that the Chinese government and the EU governments commission think tanks to conduct joint studies on the feasibility of China-EU FTA and encourage various think tanks to conduct extensive cooperation and exchanges around the FTA.

6.4 The Key Is to Break Down Barriers to Service Trade

The key to accelerating the process of China-EU service trade cooperation is o break the barriers to service trade. That will form a new driving force for the European economic recovery and growth, expecting the China-EU trade to grow at about 9% per year.

(1) The level of openness in service trade has to be improved.

It is necessary to promote China-EU service trade liberalization and facilitation, break down the barriers to service trade gradually in terms of right to practice, personnel movement and technical service, establish a mutual recognition mechanism of product certification and system certification gradually, achieve a consensus in subsidy reduction, government procurement, technology licensing and environmental standards, and promote the combination of China's huge demand for service market and sufficient human capital in European service industry, production capacity and advanced technology.

(2) China-EU trade parks and industrial cooperation parks have to be developed.

By making full use of PFTZs in Shanghai, Tianjin, Guangdong and Fujian as well as service trade liberalization in Guangdong, Hong Kong and Macao, and comprehensive pilot services in Beijing, the exploration of institutions and mechanisms and related reforms of China-EU trade liberalization needs to be accelerated, the demonstration park of China-EU close cooperation needs to be set up, China-EU industrial park cooperation mechanism needs to be innovated, the system and policy of China-EU free trade needs to be tested, and the connection between the rules and standards of China-EU trade and investment needs to be explored actively.

(3) The two-way opening of service market has to be sped up.

China needs to speed up the relaxation of market access to EU enterprises in the service markets of medical and health care, design and R&D, elderly care and professional education. The EU needs to reduce export controls on China in electronics, aviation, information and communications technology, life science technology, and energy and environment. In this connection, therefore, China-EU cooperation and opening-up in financial services must be deepened, while European financial institutions must be encouraged to actively develop RMB and foreign currency settlement service and other financial services.

CHAPTER 6

Education Calling for Second Reform

In the 13th FYP period, China's transition from demographic dividend to human resource dividend is a major trend. Facing the "dual challenge" of economic transformation and upgrading and economic restructuring, it is increasingly urgent to improve human resources by accelerating education structural reform. During the said period, to deepen education reform needs to promote the orderly opening of education and "de-administration" in universities and boost the adjustment of education structure, initially forming the structure of talent supply that adapts to economic transformation and upgrading.

To speed up reforms in education structure to achieve the transformation from quantitative demographic dividend to human resource dividend is the key to improving the total factor productivity (TFP) and an important prerequisite for facilitating economic transformation and upgrading. Therefore, the 13th FYP needs to launch the second reform of education with the goal of improving human resources. It has become a major task of structural reform to achieve the transformation of education system from being scale-type, test-oriented, closed-type and administrative to being quality-oriented, ability-based, open-type and specialized.

F. Chi, *Winning at the Turning Point*, The Great Transformation of China, https://doi.org/10.1007/978-981-32-9479-0_6

1 A Main Trend from Demographic Dividend to Human Resource Dividend

From the perspective of international experience, transformation from the demographic dividend to HR dividend, improvement of total factor productivity, and upgrading of the quality of economy are an important prerequisite for a country to grow from the middle-income stage up to the high-income one. China is in the critical period of transition from demographic dividend to HR dividend. In this particular stage, reforms in education structure need to be placed in a prominent position.

1.1 China Is at the Historic Juncture of the Transition from Demographic Dividend to HR Dividend

In the next five to ten years, to seize the opportunity for the historical meeting between the new round of scientific and technological revolution and the transformation and upgrading of China's industry, the emphasis is on achieving the transformation from the most populous country to a major country with huge human resources, thereby providing human capital support for China to become a high-income country.

(1) Demographic dividend is gradually diminishing with the decline of total factor productivity.

According to data released by the National Bureau of Statistics, in 2015, working-age population aged 17–59 decreased by 4.87 million as compared with the population by the end of 2014, which accounts for 66.3% of China's total population.[1]

Meanwhile, labor costs are rising fast. In 2003–2014, the real wages of rural migrant workers in cities grew by an average of 10.7%, higher than the growth of GDP in the same period. According to data from the Conference Board, in 2007–2012, China's overall labor productivity grew at the average annual rate of 9.5%, but fell to 7% in 2014. That means that wage growth outpaced productivity growth.[2] In other words, in the beginnings of reform and opening-up, due to the shortage

[1] National Bureau of Statistics: *The National Economy in 2015 Progresses Well and Performs Well in Its Steady Operation*. www.statis.gov.cn, January 19, 2016.

[2] Cai Fang: Some Views on "Demographic Dividend". *Economic Daily*, June 18, 2015.

of capital and technology, abundant, low-cost labor resources formed "demographic dividend", which supported more than 30 years of rapid economic growth in China. But as the share of the working-age population falls rapidly, the traditional low-cost labor dividend is fading fast.

(2) The exploitation of human resource dividend can solve the problem of potential decline in economic growth.

The potential economic growth depends on the structure of human resources and total factor productivity. In 2010–2014, the proportion of population with tertiary education or above in China's total population increased from 8.75 to 11.01%. The proportion of population with high school education (and/or secondary specialized school education) in China's total grew from 13.72% up to 16.35%, which register an increase by 2.26 and 2.63 percentage points respectively. The increase surpassed the decline in the proportion of working-age population.[3] Research shows that during the 13th FYP period, if the average annual growth rate of total factor productivity increases by 1%, the potential average annual economic growth rate can increase by 0.99%.[4] It has become an important driving force for China's medium-to-high growth. Education dividend and human resource dividend will counteract the effects of considerable decrease in demographic dividend. In order to adapt to the trend of economic transformation and upgrading, it is urgent for China to grasp the important historical opportunity of transition towards the "education dividend period", "human resource dividend period" and "talent dividend period".

(3) Only by exploiting human resource dividend can the challenge of aging population be met.

International experience has shown that the transition from an aging society to an advanced age society[5] is the last window period for

[3]Five Years from "Demographic Dividend Period" to "Talent Dividend Period". *Guangming Daily*, December 11, 2015.

[4]Cai Fang: Total Factor Productivity Can Extend the Traditional Demographic Dividend. *Beijing Daily*, November 23, 2015.

[5]An advanced age society refers to a society in which the population aged 60 or above reaches 18% of the total population, or the population aged 65 or above reaches 14% of the total.

addressing the challenges of aging population and the disappearance of "demographic dividend". If the corresponding public policy adjustment and institutional mechanism innovation are both lagging, the probability of economic crisis and social crisis will increase significantly when the advanced age society comes. Currently, improving the productivity, perfecting the supply structure, and achieving the innovation and scientific and technological progress, in order to reduce the risks of aging population and the impact on the economy, lessening the impact of rapid population change, are severe challenges China is facing, while leaving us very limited time and space to take up these challenges.

1.2 Economic Transformation and Upgrading Are Increasingly Urgent to Improving Human Resources

The general trend of China's economic transformation and upgrading has put forward a realistic demand for a diversified, multi-level and innovative talent supply structure. Promoting strategic adjustment of talent supply in the 13th FYP period has become a major task of education structural adjustment.

(1) Improving manufacturing requires advanced skilled workers.

In 2012, China's manufacturing labor productivity was only equivalent to 4.38% of the United States, to 4.37% of Japan, and 5.56% of Germany. According to sixth national census data (2010), the average years of education China's manufacturing workers have received number 9.8, 3.2 years on average less than their U.S. colleagues in 2006 who have received 13 years of education. China's manufacturing workers are mainly composed of junior or senior high school graduates and those with college education or above only make up 9.8% as compared with 32% in the U.S. In the second quarter of 2015, the ratio of job vacancies to job seekers at various technical levels in China was greater than 1. Among them, the ratios of such job vacancies as technicians, senior technicians, senior engineers, and senior workers to their respective job seekers were higher, which represent 2.0, 1.94, 1.81, and 1.77 respectively.[6]

[6]Department of Employment: *Analysis of Market Supply and Demand of Some Urban Public Employment Services in the 2nd Quarter of 2015*. www.mohrss.gov.cn, July 15, 2015.

Due to the lack of innovation and creativity, "made in China" is still at the low end of the international division of labor and the industrial chain. For example, the world's most iPhones are assembled in China, but the profit earned for assembling only accounts of 1.8% of the total profit for the whole phone.[7] During the 13th FYP period, industrial transformation and upgrading urgently call for all kinds of professional and technical talents and innovative talents, providing human capital support for achieving the strategic goal of "made in China 2025".

(2) Population urbanization requires rural migrant population to be better educated.

From the perspective of international experience, education is highly correlated with the level of population urbanization, with the correlation coefficient around 0.7.[8] Research by American economist Micha Gisser shows that for every 10% increase in the education level of rural residents, an additional 6–7% of farmers can be channeled into non-agricultural industries in urban areas.[9] At the same time, it is necessary to adapt to the changes in the demand structure of talents brought about by urbanization transformation and increase the supply of skilled workers needed for living services industry and producer services industry. However, the overall technical skill level of migrant workers is still not high, which makes them less competitive in urban employment. According to *Monitoring and Investigation Report on Rural Migrant Workers 2014*, migrant workers who received skill training accounted for only 34.8% (see Table 1). Transformation of population urbanization is in urgent need of improving the vocational education system for rural migrant workers, especially new-generation migrant workers, letting them both have skills and stable employment and have an opportunity to gain personal ascension.

(3) Industrial reform requires a large number of practical talents.

[7]Liu Shaohua: Upstream of Global Value Chain: Chinese Companies Are Coming. *People's Daily* (Overseas Edition), January 14, 2016.

[8]Zhu Jinsong: Empirical Research on Education Level in China's Rural Areas and Urbanization Rate. *Commercial Times*, Issue 14, 2010.

[9]Chi Fulin: Transformation and Upgrading Need to Deepen Education Reform. *Economic Information Daily*, June 5, 2015.

Table 1 The proportion of migrant workers who received skill training in 2013–2014 (unit: %)

	Those who have received agricultural skill training		*Those who have received non-agricultural vocational skill training*		*Those who have received skill training*	
	2013	*2014*	*2013*	*2014*	*2013*	*2014*
Total	9.3	9.5	29.9	32	32.7	34.8
20 years and below	5	6	29.9	31.4	31	32.6
21–30 years	5.5	6	34.6	37	35.9	38.3
31–40 years	9.1	8.8	31.8	34	34.1	36.1
41–50 years	12.7	12.6	27.8	29.9	32.1	33.7
Above 50 years	12.4	12.7	21.2	24	25.9	28.8

Source *Monitoring and Investigation Report on Rural Migrant Workers in 2014*. http://www.stats.gov.cn/, April 29, 2015

Take health service consumption for example. It is predicted that by 2020 the production of China's health industry (including biological pharmaceutical service, medical equipment and health service) reach 14 trillion to 16 trillion yuan (US$2.33 trillion to US$2.67 trillion), becoming the world's largest health service market.[10] However, due to the lagging development of vocational education of health management, there is a serious shortage of health service personnel, and the gap of subhealth managers and children health managers is close to 20 million.[11] Take Internet finance for example. According to the estimate, since employees in the banking institutions and small loan companies account for 53.76% of the total in the financial industry, the number of Internet financial professionals will amount to 1.04 million in 2019 and reach 4.35 million in 2024. In the next five to ten years, the gap of Internet financial professionals in China will exceed one million.[12] In implementing "the Belt and Road Initiative" and participating actively

[10]Wang Changlin: Supporting 7% of the New Impetus for Industrial Development. *Guangming Daily*, August 7, 2015.

[11]Subhealth Management and Child Health Management Are Expected to Be the Hottest Jobs. *Beijing Morning Post*, August 28, 2014.

[12]Cao Ting: Professionals Become the Bottleneck Restricting the Development of Internet Finance. *Economic Information Daily*, September 17, 2015.

in global economic governance, how to bring up more management professionals, financial professionals, legal professionals, and investment managers with international vision, know-how about the international operation rules and specialized knowledge has become the new subject for improving the level of opening to the rest of the world in the new era. From the perspective of reality, the shortage of international talents has become a prominent bottleneck for China to improve its opening-up. For example, China is the third-largest shareholder in the World Bank and IMF, but it has only 2–3% of the staff and fewer senior executives working in both institutions.[13] Many Chinese enterprises are developing service outsourcing, but their "going global" like this has been restricted by a lack of international talents. For example, the average talent gap in China's service outsourcing industry is 20–30%, and there is a trend of continuous increase in both proportion and absolute number.[14] With the full implementation of "the Belt and Road Initiative" and the establishment and operation of the AIIB, the BRICS bank and Silk Road Fund, China will have an increasing demand for international talents.

1.3 The Structural Contradictions in the Supply of Human Resources Are Prominent

Because the current education structure does not match the development trend of economic transformation and upgrading and the change in employment structure, the human resources that are urgently needed by the society are seriously insufficient, and the phenomena of unqualified personnel training and idle and wasted human resources are rather striking, while the human resources that are not needed by the society are constantly produced.

(1) There is shortage of skilled, practical and professional human resources.

① "Recruitment difficulty" and "employment difficulty" coexist. With the gradual disappearance of demographic dividend, the problem of

[13] Ma Wenpu: "The Belt and Road Initiative" Needs to Train Professional International Talents. *China Enterprise News*, July 27, 2015.

[14] Li Shaowen: High-End Talent Shortage Restrains Service Outsourcing Upgrading. *International Business Daily*, May 30, 2014.

"labor shortage" becomes more and more serious. It is both seasonal and normal. It not only happens in the Pearl River Delta and other developed coastal areas, but also extends to central and western China. At the same time, college students are faced with the dilemma of "the most difficult employment in history". Every year, about 25% of new graduates cannot find suitable jobs before graduation.[15] For some college graduates who have been unemployed for a long time, it is more difficult to find jobs. According to related statistics, however, since 2010, China's overall ratio of job offers to job seekers has been around 1, but 1.09 in the second quarter of 2015, which suggested that the labor market was in short supply.[16] The coexistence of "recruitment difficulty" and "employment difficulty" essentially reflects the increasingly prominent structural contradiction in talent supply and the unreasonable education structure.

② Shortage of skilled personnel and structural unemployment coexist. Data from the Ministry of Human Resources and Social Security show that the number of skilled workers now accounts for only about 20% of China's total workforce, while only 5% are highly skilled workers.[17] In recent years, the ratio of job offers to job seekers for skill workers has been more than 1.5, and that for senior skilled worker has even reached more than 2.[18] For China's unemployment problem, there are more important structural factors than cyclical factors. In the next five to ten years, the adjustment of economic structure and industrial structure will enter a critical period, and the structural unemployment risk will increase significantly. Take the Internet industry for example. According to a report released by McKinsey (an American firm), the Internet revolution will increase productivity and create 46 million new jobs in China by 2025, while 31 million traditional jobs will be eliminated.[19]

[15] China Academy of Social Sciences: Prominent Structural Problems in Employment Under the New Normal. *China Business Economics*, December 25, 2014.

[16] Chi Fulin: Our Education Needs a Second Reform: On the Structural Adjustment and Reform of Education in the "Thirteen Five-Year Plan" Period. *Journal of China Executive Leadership Academy Jinggangshan*, No. 5, 2015.

[17] Yin Weimin: Improving the Treatment of Skilled Workers. *Economic Daily*, December 14, 2015.

[18] Li Lan: It's Urgent to Ease Up the Structural Contradiction in the Employment Market. *Economic Information Daily*, March 5, 2015.

[19] The Internet Will Create 46 Million Jobs in China by 2025. www.cn.chinadaily.com.cn, February 2014.

③ Jobs are not suited to employees' special training and employees' salary is far from being based on their education background. The contradiction between the supply and demand of educated or trained personnel leads to the phenomenon in which "graduates' education does not fit them for their jobs" and "high education but low salary". According to the data, the years 2013–2015 witnessed a year-by-year declining trend for the contracted employment of graduates not relevant to their field of study. The year 2015 saw only 60% of job relevance/suitability, which showed a decrease by 20% over 2014.[20] The relatively low job relevance/suitability of graduates shows on the surface that the direction of graduates' specialty or vocational training supplied by human resources does not match the employment demand of enterprises. In fact, however, school education is not closely combined with the actual demand of personnel needed. In the aspect of salary, the phenomenon began to appear that employees' salary is not based on their education background. *The Employment Report on Chinese College Students 2015* shows that the monthly income of 2014 college graduates six months after graduation was 3487 yuan (US$581).[21] But, skilled workers at the end of their diplomas earned more than 10,000 yuan (US$1667) a month and are in short supply.

(2) The education structure is not rational.

① The contradiction exists between "labor shortage" and the lagging development of education. At present, the educational background only and diploma only employment system is quite common. The social recognition degree of vocational education and vocational school graduates' social status and income level are still relatively low, resulting in the serious lag in the development of vocational education, which is the source of "labor shortage" of enterprises. In 2014, the students of China's vocational higher education institutions made up 39.5% of the country's total college and university students (see Chart 1). But, more than 50% of German high school graduates have received vocational training before going to college, and more than 57% of the U.S. workforce has

[20] 2015 Sees Low Number of China's Graduates Who Want to Work in Beijing, Shanghai, Guangzhou and Shenzhen. *Yangcheng Evening News*, June 12, 2015.

[21] MyCOS Research Institute: *Chinese 4-Year College Students' Employment: Annual Report (2015)*. Social Sciences Academic Press, 2015.

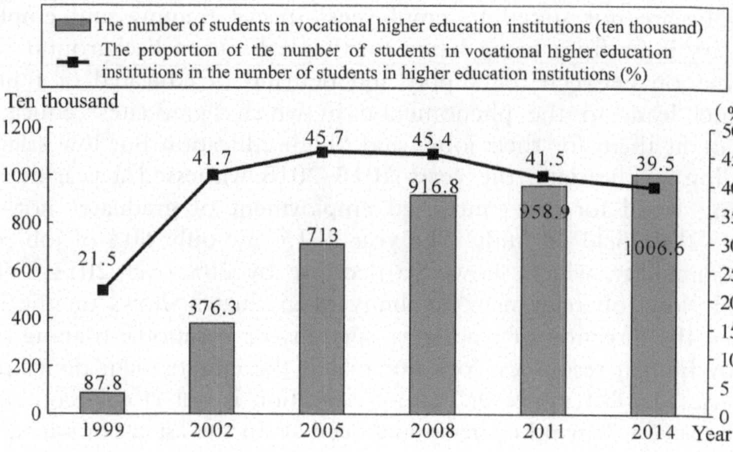

Chart 1 Changes in the number and the proportion of students of China's vocational higher education institutions in 1999–2014 (*Source* The preparation of the chart is based on the educational statistics of the Ministry of Education in 1999–2014)

received vocational training.[22] In western developed countries, especially in major manufacturing powers, the number of highly skilled people accounts for more than 40% of the total number of workers. In 2014, China's skill workers numbered 157 million, including 41.36 million skilled personnel, which only accounted for 26.3% of the total.[23]

② The contradiction exists between the "difficult employment" of college students and the development of "homogenization" in higher education. At present, education in China is highly characterized by "production of students in large numbers" and "one thousand schools with one same face". Since the college enrolment expansion in 1999, China's higher education has undergone highly rapid development with the number of graduates growing from 1.14 million in 2001 to 7.49 million in 2015 (see Chart 2), namely, the average annual growth rate of 14.4%. However, such expansion did not bring about the corresponding

[22]Wang Xueli: Improving the Treatment of China's Skilled Workers and Promoting "Made in China 2025". *China Labor Social Security News*, November 1, 2015.

[23]Yin Weimin: Improving the Treatment of Skilled Workers. *Economic Daily*, December 14, 2015.

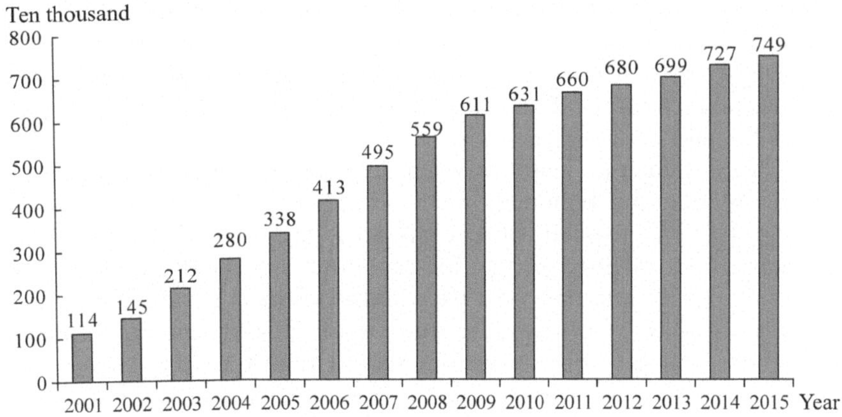

Chart 2 The number of China's college graduates in 2001–2015 (*Source* The preparation of the chart is based on the educational statistics of the Ministry of Education in 2001–2015)

rapid improvement of human capital, while the overall quality of college graduates declined. One popular Chinese saying goes, "It is not difficult to find 100 college students, but it is extremely difficult to find 100 senior bench workers", which partly reflects the maladjustment of education's supply structure and economic development. Quite a number of colleges and universities focus on the pursuit of "large and complete" disciplines with a lack of characteristics, causing the outstanding problem of "homogeneity" in setting up majors or specialties. In order to keep pace with the first-class universities both at home and abroad, many colleges and universities, regardless of their actual level, blindly open new majors, build laboratories and compete to set up master's and doctoral programs. It seems that all universities should change to research-oriented universities. Under the guidance of unclear educational orientation, the goal of personnel training is even vaguer, and the quality of personnel training is declining. As a result, students' professional foundation is not solid and their professional emotion is not strong, which ultimately leads to employment difficulties.[24] In fact, there

[24]Yan Jingyi: Phenomena of Homogenization in Chinese Universities and Countermeasures. *Journal of Dalian Nationalities University*, Issue 4, 2015.

are very few in the world-class universities that cover all disciplines and specialties. According to the Classification of Instructional Programs of US's Department of Education, the discipline coverage of Massachusetts Institute of Technology, Princeton University, and Stanford University is 54.2, 62.5, and 70.8% respectively.[25]

③ The contradiction exists between the change of industrial structure and the lagging and blindness in the adjustment of specialty setup. In one aspect, the adjustment of specialty setup lags behind the change in the demand for talented people for economic and social development. According to *Regulations on the Administration of Undergraduate Specialty Setup in Ordinary Institutions of Higher Learning*, public and private colleges and universities should report to the Ministry of Education for record in terms of specialty setting and adjustment in strict accordance with the requirements of relevant documents. Even those schools that have obtained the right of autonomy can only set up their own specialties based on the Guidance Specialty Catalogue and cannot change their specialties. For colleges and universities to set up any new specialties that have not been included in the specialty catalogue, strict procedures shall be followed to report to the MOE for approval. For private colleges and universities that are most close to the market demand, the curriculum and specialty setup should follow the formal procedures as public colleges and universities, and their characteristics are difficult to be highlighted, which seriously restricts the diversified development of students. In another aspect, many colleges and universities rush headlong into action in setting up specialties, despite the lack of basic teachers and practical hardware facilities. The lagging and blindness in specialty setting adjustment result in the relative surplus or shortage of talent supply, and the problem of disconnection from market demand will become more prominent.

(3) The irrational structure of education reflects lagging in the transformation of educational development mode.

① Higher education is emphasized over basic education. According to *Statistical Bulletin on the Implementation of the National Education Fund 2014*, in education spending at all levels, both students' average

[25] Du Yubo: Higher Education Should Be More Adaptable to the Needs of Economic and Social Development. *China Education Daily*, July 24, 2014.

Table 2 National public expenditure on education at all levels in 2014

	Students' average public budget expenditure on education	*Students' average public budget expenditure on public funds*
Primary schools	7681.02	2241.83
Regular junior high schools	10359.33	3120.81
Regular senior high schools	9024.96	2699.59
Secondary vocational schools	9128.83	3680.83
Regular colleges and universities	16102.72	7637.97

Source Ministry of Education and National Bureau of Statistics. *Ministry of Finance's Statistical Bulletin on the Implementation of the National Education Fund 2014*. www.moe.gov.cn, October 13, 2015

public budget expenditure on education and students' average public budget expenditure on public funds were the highest, 2.1 and 3.4 times more than those for primary school students.[26] (see Table 2) The government's high investment in higher education not only caused the government to interfere too much in the autonomy of higher education, but also produced a certain "crowding-out effect" on non-basic public services such as social capital investment in higher education.

② Public education is heeded rather than private education. Both private education and public education belong to national public welfare undertakings. Private education has changed from a supplementary education to an important part of China's higher education, which has strongly promoted the popularization of higher education. In reality, however, private education is difficult to acquire support from fiscal, taxation, land and other policy resources. For example, in 2013, Shanghai's financial support funds for private higher education was 400 million yuan (US$66.67 million), which only accounted for 2.2% of the city's financial input for education, while the number of private college students made up 18% of the city's total number of college students. Likewise, in 2011–2013, Shenzhen's average annual investment in non-governmental education was 500 million yuan (US$83.33 million) only, making up less than 2% of the city's total input for education, while the number

[26]Ministry of Education and National Bureau of Statistics: *Ministry of Finance's Statistical Bulletin on the Implementation of the National Education Fund 2014*. www.moe.gov.cn, October 13, 2015.

of private school students constituted 38.4% of the city's total number of students.[27] Unequal treatment is also reflected in the students. One related survey shows that the probability for public college students and private college students to acquire student loans is 7.79 and 1.17% respectively, whereas that for them to gain funding scholarships is 56.6 and 11% respectively.[28]

③ Theory is emphasized over practice. The structural contradiction in China's HR supply is also manifested in the knowledge structure in which theory is emphasized over practice, and in poor practical skills. According to *Employment Report on Chinese College Students in 2013*, college graduates from 2008 to 2010, no matter whether they are university undergraduate or vocational college graduates, had a lower level of basic working ability than required by the job upon graduation. In recent years, in order to alleviate the employment pressure, quite a number of college students had to return to the vocational school after graduation.

④ General education is heeded rather than vocational education. In 2005–2013, financial funds on vocational education grew at the average annual rate of 25%. However, judging from the proportion and based on data from *China Educational Statistical Yearbook 2014*, in 2013, the State financial funds on vocational education made up only 10.38% of the State financial funds on education (see Chart 3), which is still significantly lower than that (26.43%) for general education in the same phase.

(4) The scale-type, test-oriented, closed-type and administrative education system is difficult to carry on.

① The education system is of scale-type, test-oriented, and closed-type nature. No matter whether they are teachers or students, the mass production of them is quite a prominent characteristic. The test-oriented ability has been put in the first place. In terms of the human resource evaluation system, it is limited to the self-evaluation within the closed system. For example, the employment difficulties of college graduates are directly related to the structure of the faculty and the evaluation system

[27] Zhu Yongxin: Creating a Fair and Friendly Institutional Environment for Private Education. *Henan Education* (*Basic Education Edition*), Issue 10, 2014.

[28] Zhou Xiaohua: Bringing Private Higher Education Institutions into the Scope of National Financial Security. *Changsha Evening News*, March 8, 2015.

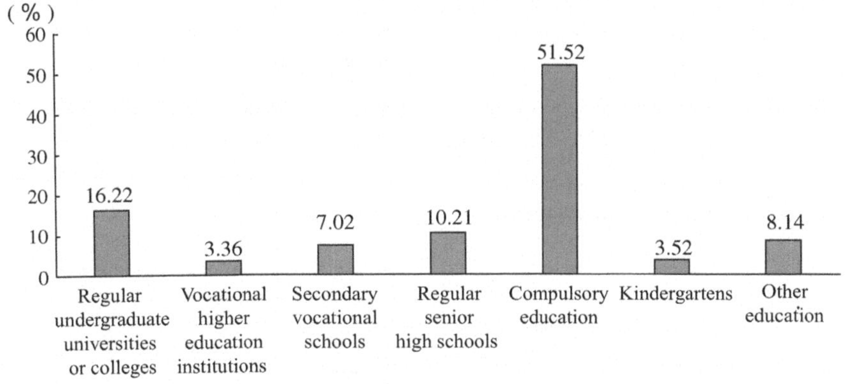

Chart 3 The distribution ratio of State financial education funds at different levels of education in 2013 (*Source* Department of Finance, Ministry of Education & Department of Statistics on Social Science and Technology and Cultural Industry, National Bureau of Statistics. *Statistical Yearbook on China's Education Fund 2014*, China Statistics Press, 2015)

of teacher performance. In Europe and the United States, universities of applied technology generally bring in excellent professional and technical personnel and highly skilled personnel from industrial enterprises. However, the source of college and university teachers in many places of China is relatively single, and the proportion of "double-qualified" teachers is not high, which makes it difficult to meet the needs of skilled professional personnel training (see Table 3). In addition, for a long time, from regular colleges and universities to vocational colleges, "papers only" has become the main assessment index for teachers' professional title evaluation. No matter how good their teaching ability is, only "work points" are recorded for their teaching load. Instead, the number of papers published in China's "core journals" serves as the chief criterion for their professional title assessment. This kind of teacher evaluation system, which focuses on scientific research and pays less attention to teaching, can only turn out students with weak hands-on ability and poor application ability of knowledge, which is difficult to meet the needs of enterprises.

② Much of bureaucracy can be found in college administration. At present, the management of higher education is dominated by administration. So there is still a long way to go before the implementation of

Table 3 Comparison of teachers of Chinese and American vocational education

	China	*The United States*
Admission criteria	Required education background; Teacher Certification (test for pedagogy, educational psychology, and *putonghua*); no test for actual teaching ability	Generally, Bachelor's degree within the scope of teaching; more than one year of practical working experience for the technical course(s)
Teacher structure	Low proportion of "double-qualified" teachers; low quality of some of the "double-qualified" teachers	The majority of part-time teachers have first-line practical experience. For example, the number of part-time teachers in American community colleges accounts for more than 60% of all teachers
Assessment	The assessment of teachers is generally completed in the school, and the assessment effect is not obvious	Annually, in-service teacher qualifications shall be evaluated and identified, which includes teaching, scientific research and service. The service includes service for off-campus groups or participation in social services, such as product development for enterprises
Curriculum	Teachers generally ignore or give up the study and research on the teaching rules of vocational education, which results in the teaching process focusing on theoretical learning and neglecting applied and practical knowledge	Different curriculum systems are set up for different majors, and the curriculum is highly personalized, which plays an important role in improving students' interest and training skills
Term of office	Generally, a life tenure	The system of the set term of office for teachers is practiced in vocational colleges or schools in the U.S. It generally includes the short-term contract system and the application right system for life tenure
Teachers' on-the-job training	The pre-job training and post-job training of teachers have not formed an integrated mechanism, which makes teachers lack the opportunity to conduct training in enterprises and fail to form an effective mechanism for training and using teachers jointly with enterprises	By the mid 1990s, the comprehensive teacher development project had been implemented from teaching-centered to learning-centered. Meanwhile, the synchronous development of managers, teaching staff and teaching assistants had also been heeded. The training of all whole staff is carried out, including training programs from pre-job training to on-the-job training

Source The research group of China (Hainan) Institute for Reform and Development

school autonomy and expert governance. In the of resource allocation of higher education, the allocation dominated by administration is more inclined to regular higher education, while the investment in vocational higher education is insufficient.[29] Despite the rapid development of China's vocational education in recent years, however, the contradiction between vocational education and the process of economic and social transformation is rather prominent from the overall perspective, which is still the "short board" of education in China. In this case, to optimize the development environment of private education, to encourage social sectors to run schools, and to form a new pattern of equal competition and common development between private education and public education, the key is to promote the reform in the "de-administration" of education and form an environment of fair competition system. Therefore, it is necessary to further clarify the functional division of education between the Central government and local governments, and form the governance structure of education that is suitable for improving the quality of education and accelerating the economic and social transformation and upgrading.

③ The opening of education market lags behind. In reality, the openness of China's education market is still not in line with the needs of education development. The entry of social capital and foreign capital into the education domain still faces more policy constraints and complicated procedures for administrative approval. For example, to establish a private vocational college would face various difficulties such as administrative license, capital, land, and personnel system. This is how it has missed development opportunities and greatly restricted the vigor and vitality of education market.

2 Forming Basically Educational Structure for Economic Transformation and Upgrading

Since the reform and opening up, the abundant working-age population has supported the rapid development of China's economy. Nowadays, however, in the real situation of China's aging population and annual declining labor-force population, the numerical population dividend is

[29] Chi Fulin: Our Education Needs a Second Reform: On the Structural Adjustment and Reform of Education in the "Thirteen Five-Year Plan" Period. *Journal of China Executive Leadership Academy Jinggangshan*, No. 5, 2015.

decreasing year by year. It is not until 2020 when the education structure is basically formed in line with the economic transformation and upgrading that China will have the conditions to form a new human resource dividend and form a system guarantee to improve the total factor productivity.

2.1 *It Is Important to Form a Education Structure That Matches the Economic Transformation and Upgrading*

With the focus on the trend for economic transformation and upgrading and based on prominent realistic contradictions, it is highly necessary to speed up the strategic adjustment of education structure and achieve the transformation of education from the scale-type, test-oriented, closed-type and administrative nature to quality-oriented, competency-based, open-type and professional nature. By 2020, education modernization will basically be realized and a learning society will basically be formed, thus ranking China among the human resource powers.

(1) Basic education must be strengthened.

For a country to become a human resource power, basic education is fundamental. Only when basic education is done well, can high-quality vocational education and higher education be developed. Basic education means the fairness and universality of education, so that all students have the equal opportunity to receive education, which is the cornerstone of building a shared society. Specifically, it is to guarantee that citizens shall have the right to receive education, to promote the balanced development of compulsory education, to rationally allocate the education resources, which favor the rural areas, remote and poor areas and ethnic minority areas, to speed up narrowing the gap in education, and by 2020, to popularize high school education and first waive regular high school's tuition and miscellaneous fees for students with financial difficulties in their families for whom special files are established, providing financial assistance to all those financially difficult students. What's more, great efforts will be made to popularize 12-year compulsory education nationwide, enabling the gross enrollment ratio in senior high school to reach more than 90%.

(2) Vocational education must be highlighted.

The development of modern vocational education will be placed in a more prominent position, thus greatly increasing the number of vocational schools, promoting in-depth integration of production and education, implementing the system of free education for secondary vocational education, improving the financial aid policy for students from families with financial difficulties, and developing skilled personnel that meet the actual needs. By 2020, it will be required that the years of education new labor force receive on average should increase from 12.4 to 13.5 years, and those for the main working-age population on average should increase from 9.5 to 11.2 years, basically forming the modern vocational education system that meets the need of economic transformation and upgrading and industrial revolution, and represents the concept of life-long education and the coordinated development of secondary and higher vocational education, thereby satisfying both the needs of people who want to receive vocational education and the economic and social demands for high-quality workers and skilled personnel.

(3) The structure of higher education must be adjusted and optimized.

At present, China has more than 25 million institutions of higher learning with over 30 million students, ranking the first in the world. However, the structure of higher education is not rational, which is mainly reflected in the fact that there are more schools for training theoretical and academic personnel and fewer schools for training technical and skilled personnel. Therefore, it is necessary to establish the status of colleges and universities of applied technology type in the higher education system, increase the funding input to colleges and universities of applied technology, optimize the discipline and its specialty, subject type, level and structure, promote cross-discipline and interdisciplinary integration, and focus on expanding the training scale of applied, compound and skilled students. By 2020, therefore, a number of internationally renowned, distinctive and high-level vocational and technical schools will be established, and a number of universities will reach or approach the level of world-class universities. The international competitiveness of higher education will significantly be enhanced.

2.2 *It Is a Major Task to Adjust the Education Structure*

The 13th FYP period is a key period for education reform.

With the focus on the trend for economic transformation and upgrading and based on prominent realistic contradictions, overall planning should be made to promote the market opening of education and the reform of education system with the emphasis on the adjustment of education structure.

(1) The structure of higher education should be adjusted with vocational education as the focus.

① The construction of diversified higher education system should be promoted. It is suggested to divide institutions of higher learning into three major categories for management, namely, comprehensive universities, research universities, and technology application universities, so as to clarify the development orientation, training objectives and models of different categories of universities, constantly optimize their respective professional structures, highlight their own characteristics, and avoid the "homogeneous" development. Comprehensive universities adopt the general subject training model, pay attention to improve students' comprehensive quality and learning ability, and focus on cultivating learning talents. Academic universities focus on training research-based students. Universities of technology application focus on cultivating high quality technical talents.

② The structure of higher education should be adjusted with the emphasis on increasing proportion of technology-oriented colleges and universities. The ratio of technical and academic student training in developed countries in Europe and America is generally 8–2, but there is a large imbalance in China.[30] During the 13th FYP period, it is necessary to accelerate the transformation of a number of general comprehensive colleges and universities into technology application ones, select a number of vocational colleges and universities to upgrade to those of technology application, and constantly increase the proportion of technology application colleges and universities.

③ The training mechanism for professionals at undergraduate and graduate levels should be innovated. It is necessary to relax restrictions

[30] Wang Zhiying: On Approaches to Transformation of Local Undergraduate Universities to Universities of Application Technology. *Modern Enterprise Education*, Issue 16, 2014.

on graduate programs to be offered by vocational colleges and encourage vocational education colleges to explore ways to train professional degree graduates. It is also necessary to encourage vocational higher education institutions to adapt to market needs, analyze the curriculum needs of different professions, and allow some graduate courses to be transformed into vocational higher education courses. In addition, it is important to explore the credit accumulation system vocational education, in which students can apply for the graduate degree certificate if they meet the conditions.

(2) It is significant to achieve the substantive breakthrough of reforms in higher education system.

① The function of the government in education management should be clarified. The education development pattern under the "monopolizing" government must be changed, so as to clarify the responsibility of the government to guarantee the basic education service supply. The leading position of education administrative departments in education decision-making and their function of policy making and supervision must be strengthened, so as to reduce and eliminate the micro-intervention of education administrative department in various schools.

② Public education institutions need reform in the orientation of "public welfare, professionalism and independence" to form a professional and efficient education implementation system. The "de-administration" of schools will have to be accelerated and the administrative levels of schools be gradually eliminated in order to establish a professionally oriented school governance structure and promote the school governance by experts. To further streamline administration and delegate more power and increase the autonomy of schools in running schools, the point is to comprehensively increase the autonomy of schools in the areas of enrollment scale, innovation in specialty setting and teacher evaluation and recruitment.

③ The division of education responsibilities of the Central government and local governments must be clarified, while increasing the autonomy of local higher education in running schools. So it is important to specify the division of responsibilities between the Central and local governments at each level, and encourage the local governments to actively explore and give priority to education reform.

④ The classified management system of private colleges and universities needs exploration. It is necessary to actively explore the establishment of a classified management system for non-profit and for-profit private schools, giving non-profit private colleges as well as public colleges equal treatment in land use, financial support and teacher training.

(3) Education needs further reform with innovation as the focus.

Low quality and insufficient innovation are the prominent contradictions in education development. Despite the continuous expansion of total education in China, few innovations have been made. For example, in 2011, the overall labor productivity of the U.S. information service was 4.1 times that of China. The lack of innovation leads to low self-sufficiency rate of key technologies in China, and the dependence rate of foreign technologies is more than 50%, while that of developed countries is less than 30% on average, while that of the United States and Japan is only about 5%.[31] In the face of the new global scientific and technological revolution and the general trend of China's economic transformation and upgrading, especially in the era of "Internet plus", the most important thing is to develop people with innovative thinking, critical thinking and innovation ability. Therefore, it is necessary to break the exam-oriented education model, to innovate the education mode, to stimulate students' curiosity and imagination, and to form a new concept of innovation-oriented education.

3 Promoting the Opening-Up of Education Market

China has entered a new stage of development and the demand of vast social members for education tends to be diversified and individualized, but the government still goes it alone in education. Accelerating the opening of education market and forming diversified investing subjects in education have become the fundamental way to resolve the structural contradiction between supply and demand in education.

[31] Chi Fulin: Construction of Education Public Service System in the 12th FYP Period: Prominent Contradictions and Main Tasks. *Comparative Economic & Social Systems*, Issue 2, 2011.

3.1 *The Education Market Is to Be Opened to Meet Diversified and Personalized Demands for Education*

It is not correct to regard the opening of education market simply as education marketization. Meeting the diversified and personalized needs for education is a major measure to improve the country's human resources. The diversification and individualization of education demand have objectively formed a large education market in China. This market should not be suppressed, and its potential should be fully tapped instead.

(1) Education demand in China shows a trend for diversified development at present.

With the development of China's economy and society, education demand has been developing in a diversified way. Education demand not only expands in aggregate, but also presents a trend of diversified demands. Diversified education demands are not only reflected in diploma educational, but also put forward higher requirements for non-diploma education. The idea of quality education and whole-person education is more popular among people. It is shown not only in elementary education and secondary education, but also in tertiary education. In addition, various kinds of education demands such as boarding education, special education, high-quality education and education for children of migrant workers emerge endlessly. For example, the statistical bulletin on China's education development in 2014 shows that among the students in the stage of national compulsory education, children of rural migrant workers amounted to 12.95 million in total, while left-behind children in the rural areas totaled 20.75 million.[32] Their demand for education was so great that their problem of education couldn't be ignored at all.

(2) Restricted education market leads to insufficient education resource supply for social needs.

① There is insufficient supply of education. As diversified, pluralistic and personalized demands for education are increasing constantly, the current supply of education in China appears to be "out of reach", and there is

[32] *Statistical Bulletin on China's Education Development in 2014*. www.moe.gov.cn, July 30, 2015.

even a unique phenomenon of "Chinese-style entry into a higher school". One typical case is "sky-high price of school district housing". In addition, the inequality of distribution of education resources is more prominent. For example, by checking the regional distribution of key universities under the "211 project" and the "985 project", it is clear that they are excessively concentrated in such places as Beijing, Shanghai, Guangzhou, eastern coastal provinces or big cultural provinces in central China like Hunan and Hubei. There is nearly no national key university in western provinces or autonomous regions like Xinjiang, Ningxia, Qinghai, and Tibet.

② There is low quality of supply. With the improvement of people's living standards, the education demand of urban and rural residents, especially those from the middle- and high-income groups, is changing from being able to go to school in the past to being able to go to a good school. However, due to insufficient supply of high-quality education resources in China and low openness in the education domain, a large amount of education consumption go overseas. By now, China has become the world's largest source of international students, who tend to be ever younger. In 2015, the Chinese students going abroad for study totaled 523,700 in number, which is 63,900 more than the figure in 2014, or an increase by 13.9%.[33] The contribution Chinese students make to the US economy and the UK economy each year exceeds US$4.4 billion and reaches about GBP£8 billion respectively.[34] In the past, the majority of Chinese students went abroad for graduate studies. Now the proportion of Chinese students studying for undergraduate programs has been on the increase, which is a 9-fold increase from 2005 to 2012.[35] More and more Chinese students have been seeking better education opportunities abroad than at home.

(3) There is a low degree of openness of education market.

① The development of private education is relatively backward. At present, the proportion of public schools mainly dependent on government financial support is still very high. The proportion of high quality

[33]Chinese Students Going Abroad in 2015 Exceed 500,000. *Beijing Evening News*, March 23, 2015.

[34]Que Mingkun: Promoting the Consumption Upgrading of Private Education Through Supply-Side Reform. *CPPCC News*, December 9, 2015.

[35]The Number of Chinese Studying in the US Continues to Grow and Both Countries Benefit. www.cn.chinadaily.com, September 30, 2014.

private schools and self-supporting and transformed public schools sponsored by social public welfare organizations is too low and these schools are too less developed to meet the education service demand of some people for diversification, distinctiveness and excellent quality. Besides private pre-school education, the proportion of students at other levels of and in other kinds of education is generally lower than the average level of OECD countries. In addition, compared with regular colleges and universities, the gap in public funding between private education and public education is enormous. For example, in 2008, China's regular university students' average public budget funding on education was 7578 yuan (US$1263), whereas the funding for private colleges and universities was only 67 yuan (US$11.17).[36] According to *Statistical Bulletin on China's Education Development in 2014*, the number of children/pupils/students in private schools at all levels and in all kinds of education accounts for 53% of the total children in the Chinese kindergartens, 7% of the total pupils in the Chinese primary schools, 11% of total students in the Chinese junior high schools, 10% in the Chinese senior high schools, 11% in the Chinese secondary vocational education, and 23% in the Chinese higher education respectively.[37]

② The internationalization level of education is on the low side. According to *Data Survey and Statistical Analysis of the Internationalized Development of China's Key Universities*, the proportion of foreign students in the total number of students of each China's key university made up about 3.7% on average, which is still a big gap compared with the average level of 10–20% in Europe and the United States.[38] In addition, the proportion of foreign teachers in China's colleges and universities was on the low side. There were less than 40 full-time foreign teachers on average in each of key universities, which accounted for 2.3% of the total number of full-time teachers. But, the proportion reached 3.4% in Japan, and 9.5% in Germany.[39]

[36] Wu Ni: Current Situation, Characteristics, Problems and Future Trend of China's Private Education Development: Comparative Analysis Based on Statistical Data and Policy Texts. *Educational Science Research*, Issue 2, 2015.

[37] Ministry of Education: *Statistical Bulletin on China's Education Development in 2014*. www.moe.gov.cn, July 30, 2015.

[38] Cheng Ying, Zhang Meiyun and Zu Yuanyuan: Data Survey and Statistical Analysis of the Internationalized Development of China's Key Universities. *Journal of Higher Education*, Issue 8, 2014.

[39] The Value of Academic Degrees and the Mandarin Chinese Are the Biggest Obstacles to Foreigners Studying in China. *Studying Abroad*, Issue 32, 2015.

(4) The opening of education market should be promoted in an orderly manner.

① The education market should be open to social capital. The lagging development of private education has led to difficulty in satisfying the consumption demand of Chinese people for diversified, personalized and characteristic education. After the market-oriented reform since the reform and opening-up, China has liberalized the industrial sector, and social capital has met with many policy constraints and complicated administrative approval when entering the service sector such as education. During the 13th FYP period, it is important to take the encouragement of social capital to enter the education market and the vigorous development of private education as the key task of increasing education service supply and optimizing the education structure.

② The education market should be open to foreign capital. In line with the general trend for education internationalization, it is necessary, through opening the education market in both directions, to integrate overseas high-quality resources, encourage the "bringing in" and "going out" of education, so as to expand the domestic demand for education, attract the return of overseas consumption of education, and improve the internationalization level of education.

3.2 Social Capital Is to Be Made an Important Force for Education Development

Social education should be run with social capital, which is an important way to overcome the problem of the single supply of education and alleviate the contradiction between supply and demand of education. To open the education market to social capital and make social capital an important force for education development is a major task of the second reform in the education domain.

(1) It is crucial to ensure the open channel of social capital for education.

In recent years, some wealthy people in China have donated a lot of money to foreign schools, which has caused much social controversy. In fact, in developed countries, it is quite normal to run education with social donation. If the proportion of social capital is artificially limited and the access of social capital to education is not smooth, the potential of social donation will not be released.

It is suggested to implement negative list management in running education with social capital ASAP. All fields of education will actively be open to attract social forces and private capital, create a fair and orderly competition environment for different participants, and constantly enhance the supply capacity of public goods in education. Various types of school-running entities will be supported for running schools through various forms of cooperation (such as sole proprietorship, joint ventures, shareholding system, etc.). Large and medium-sized enterprises should be encouraged to invest in running schools, mainly vocational schools, while encouraging high-quality public schools to participate in and support the running of private schools in various ways.

(2) The development of social capital holding schools should be allowed.

① The expected target will be set to increase the proportion of social capital in the total investment of education to 5% during the 13th FYP period. Social capital accounts for 5–10% of the total investment in education in terms of the world's average level.[40] In recent years, the total amount of China's social capital investment has been increasing, but the proportion of social capital (which consists of organizers' input and social donation) in the national education funds has been on the decline, which decreases from 1.09% in 2010 to 0.77% in 2013 (see Chart 4). Preferential policies should be adopted during the 13th FYP period to strive to promote the contribution of enterprises, social organizations and other social means to run education. By 2020, the proportion of social capital in education funds will be increased to 5% or so as an important predictor.

② Social capital holding schools in the education domain should not be subject to unreasonable interference by the government as long as they can act in accordance with State laws and regulations. It is suggested to run pilot schools of mixed ownership and allow the development of mixed ownership of private capital holdings and share holding

[40] Chi Fulin: *Historical Challenges for Structural Reform in the 13th FYP*, China Workers Press, 2016.

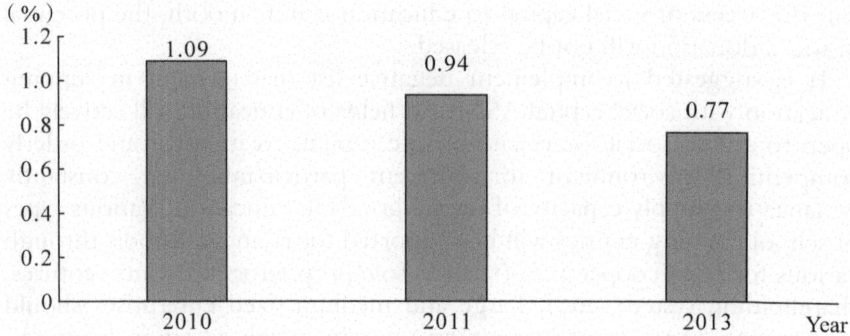

Chart 4 The proportion of social capital in the total education fund. *Note* Social capital—private school organizers' input + social donations (*Source* The calculation is based on the data from *Statistical Yearbook on China Education Fund [2010–2014]*)

in higher education. Such factors as capital, knowledge, technology, and management should be allowed to participate in running schools and enjoy corresponding rights, while encouraging profit-making private education institutions to establish equity incentive mechanisms. The reform of public universities should be promoted by using mixed ownership, while introducing social capital. Listed companies and technology enterprises should be encouraged to invest in founding technical universities, while exploring the establishment of a corporate structure of mixed-ownership schools. At the same time, it is necessary to actively encourage public and private schools to purchase management services, teaching resources, and scientific research results from each other. And it is significant to promote the public-private partnership (PPP) model, encourage social capital to participate in education infrastructure construction and operation management, and provide professional services.

③ The introduction of social enterprise system should be explored. By drawing on the experience of the UK and the US, the social enterprise system can be introduced to profit-making private colleges and universities for exploring the cross-industry combination of public welfare purpose and business model. It is fundamental to implement the stock ownership system for teaching staff, and dividends can be distributed on a limited basis. In terms of taxation, tax reduction and exemption can be enjoyed like new and high technology enterprises.

(3) The government should treat both public education and private education equally.

① Both public and private education enjoy equal treatment in land, financial support and other aspects. It is clear that non-profit private schools enjoy the same policies as public schools in terms of government purchase, financial support and land use. Private schools that use electricity, water, gas and heat implement the same price policy as public schools.

② Both public education and private education enjoy the same tax preference as public schools. All kinds of schools and kindergartens run by enterprises shall be exempted from urban land use tax and property tax for self-use real estate and land. Non-profit-making and profit-making private schools engaged in pre-school education and credential education shall be exempted from business tax in accordance with the current regulations of the state. In accordance with the relevant provisions of the current tax law, less than 12% of the amount of annual profit shall be allowed to be deducted when calculating the taxable income amount of enterprises supporting the cause of education. The public welfare donation expenditures of individuals supporting the cause of education shall be deducted before personal income tax in accordance with relevant regulations.[41] Donations from abroad to non-profit private schools established in accordance with the law in China shall, in accordance with relevant regulations, be reduced or exempted from import duties and VAT in the import links.

③ Teachers and students of private schools shall enjoy the same treatment as those of public schools. Only with equal treatment can private schools retain more good teachers and attract more good students. Therefore, teachers in private schools should have the same rights as teachers in public schools in terms of qualification recognition, job evaluation, training, merit recognition and medical insurance. Students of private schools shall enjoy the same rights as public schools at the same level in terms of awards, appraisal, entry into a higher school, employment and social preferential treatment. Students of all kinds of non-profit private schools and public schools at all levels shall, in accordance with the relevant regulations, equally enjoy State funding policies such as student loans, awards and grants.

[41] Shenzhen Office for the Aged: Overarching Design for Developing Elderly Services and Industries. *China Social Work*, Issue 7, 2013.

3.3 *The Two-Way Opening of Education Market Should Be Promoted*

It is an important way to revitalize the national education cause to overcome the closed education and improve the internationalization level of education. For one, China's education needs to learn the advanced experience of developed countries, which requires the introduction of high-quality education. For another, China's education with its own advantages can "go out" to improve the country's soft power.

(1) It is necessary to emancipate the mind in education market opening to the outside world.

In recent years, it is more and more common for families with better economic conditions to send their children to study abroad. Rather than make Chinese children pay more to study abroad, they would "import" high-quality education resources from developed countries. In the opening up of education market, we need to go beyond traditional thinking and look at problems from the perspective of improving national human resources rather than simply preventing foreign capital from running schools in China.

(2) It is significant to support the introduction of high-quality education resources from developed countries.

① Overseas high-quality education resources are worth introducing. It is an active way to introduce world-renowned universities for the cooperative running of schools, and to allow and support famous universities and vocational education institutions from overseas countries and regions like Hong Kong, Macao and Taiwan to set up joint-venture branch campuses in the Chinese mainland by way of shareholdings and establish wholly owned branches in particular areas. In addition, foreign investors will be encouraged to invest in founding schools for children of foreign nationals, and be supported for investing in setting up education training institutions and projects through Chinese-foreign cooperation, with a view to optimizing the allocation of education resources both at home and abroad to achieve complementary advantages and positive interaction.[42]

[42]Chi Fulin: Our Education Needs a Second Reform: On the Structural Adjustment and Reform of Education in the "Thirteen Five-Year Plan" Period. *Journal of China Executive Leadership Academy Jinggangshan*, No. 5, 2015.

Excellent private schools with distinctive features should be encouraged and supported to introduce quality subjects, courses, teachers and management through brand chain operations and Chinese-foreign cooperative school-running ways, so as to improve the education and teaching quality as a whole. Private schools should also be encouraged to introduce foreign advanced resources and employ qualified foreign teachers with professional qualifications. In addition, it is important to support teacher exchanges, student exchanges, mutual recognition of credits and joint awarding of degrees between Chinese colleges and universities and their overseas counterparts. For excellent education resources imported from abroad, preferential policies shall be implemented in respect of tax, land use and profit retention, allowing profit-making education institutions to make profits.

② More opening policies on education should be allowed for exploration in the FTZ. Bold exploration in the PFTZ should be allowed to establish the education experimental zone for comprehensive reform of international cooperation and exchanges and the international demonstration zone for higher education, and to implement the more opening policy on education. Meanwhile, it is suggested to reduce the restrictive management clauses about education in the negative list, break the numerous restrictions on education opening, and on the basis of scientific supervision, allow the exploration of running direct branch schools outside the mode of Chinese-foreign cooperation.

Special Citations [5-1]

Negative List in the FTZ Education Domain in 2015

Article 93 Foreign education institutions, other organizations or individuals shall not set up schools and other education institutions (excluding non-academic vocational skills training) with Chinese citizens as the main objects of enrollment separately.

Article 94 Foreign education institutions may, in cooperation with Chinese education institutions, run education institutions with Chinese citizens as the main target of enrollment. Chinese and foreign cooperators may, in cooperation, run education institutions of all kinds at all levels, but:

(1) it shall not hold education institutions for the implementation of compulsory education and education institutions for special areas such as military, police, political affairs and party schools;

(2) foreign religious organizations, religious institutions, religious education institutions and clerical personnel shall not conduct cooperative educational activities in China, and Chinese-foreign cooperatively-run schools shall not conduct religious education or religious activities;
(3) regular secondary education institutions, higher education institutions and pre-school education institutions belong to the restricted category and shall be led by the Chinese side. (The principal or chief administrative officers shall have Chinese nationality and reside in China; the number of Chinese members of the council, the board of directors or the joint management committee shall not be less than one half. Education and teaching activities and course materials shall comply with the relevant laws and regulations of China.)

Source Notification of the General Office of the State Council on the Issuance of Special Administrative Measures for Foreign Investment Access to the Pilot Free Trade Zones (*Negative List*) (2015). www.china.com.cn, April 8, 2015.

(3) It is important to encourage China's quality education resources to "go global".

① It is necessary to encourage the allocation of quality teaching resources to be extended overseas. It includes, for example, carrying out Chinese-foreign cooperative education programs abroad and establishing Chinese-foreign cooperative education institutions. In addition, it is important to support leading disciplines in China's universities for participating in and establishing international academic cooperative organizations and international science programs, and joint research and development bases with overseas high-level education and scientific research institutions. Colleges and universities with competent strengths should also get support for running schools overseas and carrying out international cooperation and cross-border educational services.

② It is of importance to establish major education projects for "Silk Road". So, overall international planning must be strengthened in selecting advantageous disciplines and quality vocational education in China, which will "go global" in collaboration with enterprises. To provide intellectual support for China's implementation of "going-out" strategy, full coverage of country-specific and regional research centers along the "One Belt and One Road" must be achieved.

③ Students must be encouraged to study abroad. It is imperative to select the talented people and outstanding students needed by the country and send them to foreign schools, research institutions and international organizations for further study. Also, it is necessary to strengthen services for self-funded overseas students, standardize self-funded overseas study intermediaries, improve the early-warning measures for overseas study, and increase the national scholarship for outstanding self-funded overseas students. In the meantime, it needs to actively carry out government-sponsored overseas programs in western universities while encouraging students from these universities to go overseas, so as to develop the international vision and better serve the construction of West China.[43]

(4) It is necessary to establish a sound education supervision system.

There are fears of chaos in the country as the education market opens up to social capital and foreign investment. In fact, the government can establish the education regulatory system in accordance with national laws and regulations, so as to avoid relying on administrative approval for control. This requires the establishment of the national standard system of education international quality: to improve the school quality assurance system and cultivate the education standard recognized by the world, including the construction of the world's primary and secondary school teacher training base, and the establishment of the education quality index system with the consensus on the cooperative running of schools and coming to study in China; establish the quality standard of overseas study supervision and establish the education international comprehensive monitoring system.

3.4 *Focus Should Be Given on Increasing the Opening of Vocational Education Market*

Developing modern vocational education is not only an education problem, but also an economic problem and a major people's livelihood issue. In the 13th FYP period, the development of modern vocational education should be placed in a more prominent position, with a focus on expanding the market opening of vocational education, promoting

[43]Zhen Xuejun: On Liberalizing Investment in Education and Its Outlook (*sic.*). *China Opening Journal*, No. 2, 2014.

in-depth integration of industry and education, and forming a synergy between the government, enterprises and society to jointly promote the development of modern vocational education.

(1) Social capital needs to be encouraged to enter the field of vocational education.

① The restrictions will be relaxed on running vocational education with social capital. The threshold will be lowered for social capital to enter the field of secondary and higher vocational education, so as to actively support social educational institutions for establishing vocational education through various forms of investment. The approval procedures will be simplified for the establishment of vocational education colleges, while giving private vocational education institutions and public institutions equal status and treatment in land use, financial support, government purchase and personnel training. Large State-owned enterprises and leading enterprises in the industry will be encouraged to set up a vocational education group, explore the personnel training mode for making training plans according to the actual needs of the industry, and promote the in-depth integration of vocational education with industrial development.

② School-enterprise cooperation needs to be deepened. It is necessary to expand the pilot scope of the apprenticeship system and encourage the local governments to carry out the experimental modern apprenticeship system, which ensures that "the recruitment of students means the recruitment of workers; admission into schools means admission into factories; schools and enterprises are both responsible for joint training", while implementing and guaranteeing the enrollment autonomy of the pilot colleges. Furthermore, it is important to encourage vocational schools and cooperative enterprises to conduct in-depth cooperation through the apprenticeship system, commissioned training, and purchase contracts, and provide tax deduction for the investment of enterprises in vocational education and training. On the basis of the in-depth cooperation between the university and enterprises, the integration between the academic certificate and the vocational qualification certificate should be promoted. The certificate of vocational education should represent the high vocational ability. The professional and technical vocational qualification certificate obtained in the enterprise can be used as a certificate for entering a higher vocational education institution.

③ The institutional innovation of introducing social capital needs to be explored by making full use of comprehensive pilot reforms in vocational education. It is necessary to explore ways to develop joint-stock and mixed-ownership vocational colleges and universities, and encourage social capital to enter public vocational education institutions by means of equity transfer, stock cooperation and joint training. Capital, knowledge, technology, management and other factors are allowed to participate in the running of schools and enjoy corresponding rights.

④ Overseas capital is encouraged to enter the field of vocational education. Various vocational colleges and universities will be supported in introducing quality overseas education resources and be encouraged to conduct exchanges between Chinese and foreign vocational education institutions. So it is necessary to carry out Chinese-foreign cooperation in running educational programs for vocational colleges and explore ways to standardize their overseas operations. An effort is also required to promote the development model of vocational education, which is compatible with the "going global" of Chinese enterprises and products, and focus on developing local professionals that meet the needs of Chinese enterprises in overseas production and operation.

(2) The institutional mechanism needs to be innovated to improve the level of vocational education.

① Horizontal connection needs to be promoted between vocational education and general education. It is through transformation, merger, transfer and integration that a number of general undergraduate colleges and universities can be turned into applied technology institutions of higher learning, thus running vocational education at the undergraduate level. In terms of financial allocation, financing conditions, land use and personnel training, general education and vocational education should be treated equally.

② The exploration of mutual connection between secondary vocational education, higher vocational education and general undergraduate education must be accelerated. So it is necessary to speed up the reform of the enrollment system for vocational education, which adopts "registration for admission". Specifically, junior high school graduates may register for admission into secondary vocational schools; secondary vocational school graduates may register for admission into vocational colleges. It is also necessary to accelerate the exploration of the "credit bank" system, promote the credit transfer between general colleges and vocational colleges, and actively explore the mode of training integrated professionals for secondary vocational education, vocational higher education, and undergraduate education. In this context, therefore, the reform of the vocational education system has to be accelerated so that general universities can recruit graduates from vocational colleges and jointly train high-level application-oriented professionals with vocational colleges.

(3) Policy guarantee for vocational education needs to be strengthened.

① Strong financial preference needs to be given to private vocational education. Government purchase service should be increased for non-governmental vocational education. According to the number of qualified graduates trained by private schools in the same year, private vocational schools shall be given awards on an average per student basis, which are not less than the average standard amount of funds for public vocational schools on an average per student basis. Local governments are encouraged to grant subsidies to private vocational colleges in accordance with a certain proportion of the per capita budgetary appropriations of undergraduate universities, and gradually increase the proportion of subsidies.

② Vocational education vouchers need to be promoted. A direct subsidy scheme for individual students will actively be implemented. The combination of the development of private vocational education and the implementation of vocational education vouchers will be promoted so as to perfect subsidy policies aimed at farmers, rural labor transfer, in-service workers, the unemployed, the disabled, and retired soldiers who need to receive vocational education and training, it will be beneficial to students from urban and rural families with financial difficulties and children of rural migrant workers and conducive for private vocational education institutions to improve the quality of private vocational education through fair competition.

4 Accelerating the Change of the Mode of Educational Development

Just before the reform and opening-up (1987), the education system reform marked by the resumption of national college entrance examination broke the ice (late 1977). The educational circles have ever since become one of the earliest fronts for ideological emancipation in China.

After 40 years of development, however, various ills and malpractices in the said circles have emerged, which reflects the deep contradiction of the development mode of traditional education. Therefore, promoting the transformation of education's development mode has become an inevitable major task for "second reform" in education.

4.1 *The Development Mode of Quality-Oriented, Competency-Based, Open-Type and Specialized Education Should Be Form*

The current development mode of China's education is characterized by scale-type, exam-oriented, closed-type and administrative nature, which is the root cause why it is difficult to form the independent innovation ability, giving rise to the imbalance of talent supply. At present, it is necessary to accelerate the transformation to the mode and concept of educational development, which are characterized by quality-oriented, competency-based, open-type and specialized nature, so as to make education fully conform to human development and social development.

(1) It is important to achieve the transformation of education development mode from the scale-type mode to the quality-oriented mode.

The main contradiction of education development in China is no longer a problem with a lack of total scale (see Chart 5), but the low-quality problem in the development of education. The existing mode of education development is characteristic of prominent scale-orientedness. All kinds of education have the phenomenon of pursuing the quantity of production of students and other personnel. In terms of scale alone, the total number of university students, master students and doctoral students produced in China in recent years has topped the world. Reckless expansion of graduate education in some subject areas has also appeared in the mode of "big leap forward", largely ignoring the connotation development and benefit increase of education. As a result, therefore, education resources, competent teachers, and specialty setup can't keep up with the demand of economic and social transformation for talented people, which leads to the fact that the comprehensive quality and skill levels of college graduates fail to adapt to the demand of industrial development demand does not adapt. That is why "difficult employment" is unavoidable. Therefore, it is necessary to accelerate the

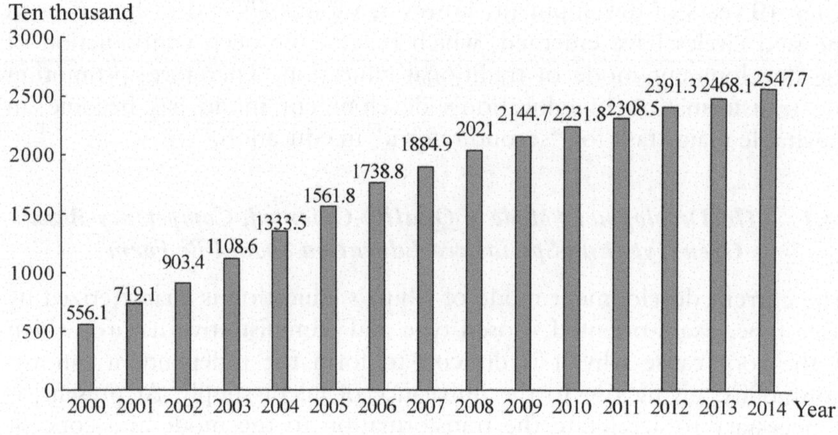

Chart 5 The number of students in undergraduate universities and postsecondary specialized colleges in 2000–2014 (*Source* National Bureau of Statistics. *China Statistical Yearbook 2015*, China Statistics Press, 2015)

transformation of education development mode from the scale expansion mode to the quality-benefit mode. To be specific, ① deepening the reform of the enrollment system, gradually narrowing down the scope of unified national college entrance examination and unified enrollment, and separating some schools and some disciplines from unified examination and unified enrollment; ② adhering to the employment orientation, reform the specialty setup system, ensuring students' mastery of practical application skills, and providing effective human resources for the society; ③ taking teaching as the primary indicator of teacher assessment, changing the current university teacher evaluation system of "emphasizing scientific research rather than teaching", continuously optimizing the teacher structure, introducing highly skilled teachers, and improving the faculty strength.

(2) One of the modes of education development needs to be changed from the exam-oriented mode to the competency-based mode.

As early as June 1999, the CPC Central Committee and the State Council promulgated the *Decision on Deepening the Reform of Education and Pushing Forward the Quality Education in an*

All-Round Way, in which quality education was defined as the long-term policy of education reform and development in China. Over the years, however, exam-oriented education has actually still taken the dominant place, and both "test scores" and "enrollment rates" have still served as the "baton" and "mandatory quotas" for evaluating students and teachers. "As long as you can't learn till death, don't be afraid to learn to death" and "Get one more point, and you will be like killing a thousand candidates"—these are the famous slogans to stimulate national college entrance examination candidates to score the best possible results. But this practice has caused many students' interests and passion for exploring the unknown world to be submerged in exam-oriented education, and teachers and students have been "slaves" to test scores. The phenomena of "classes of poor students", "accompanying villages" (temporary villages for a large number of parents to accompany their children with their study for going to higher schools) and the like are known as the "strange eggs" under the exam-oriented education system. To be specific, the "classes of poor students" are given the worst classrooms and substitute teachers. Near those secondary schools with the city's best education resources have emerged "accompanying villages"... The exam-oriented education concept, education method and evaluation mechanism with "test scores" as the baton and "knowledge indoctrination" as the main function have produced great side effects and distorted the standard of educating people. Unless all these would be changed, it is hard to achieve education for all-round development.

The transformation of education development mode from the exam-oriented mode to the competence-oriented one is a major event that is expected from all aspects of society. Comprehensive measures should be taken ASAP to achieve new breakthroughs in reform. For example, it is necessary to promote the innovation of the school-running mechanism and build a school-enterprise cooperative personnel training mode for vocational development and employment-orientation. Efforts have to be made to strengthen the teaching in practical links and increase the proportion of practice courses according to the requirement of professional ability training, thereby promoting the connection between the curriculum content of vocational education and vocational standards and realizing the power sharing among governments, universities, teachers, students and the market in setting up disciplines and specialties by respecting students' wishes and choices to set up and select disciplines and specialties.[44] In addition, large enterprises, scientific research institutions and trade associations should be encouraged to run special colleges that combine personnel development and staff training, develop production, education, and science and education in an integrated way, and embody professional features.

(3) One of the modes of education development needs to be changed from the closed-type mode to the open-type mode.

The re-training after the graduation of college students reflects the deep-seated problem that the closed-type education mode of colleges and universities has been divorced from the needs of economic and social development for a long time. The closed nature of China's institutions of higher learning is reflected in specialty setting up, curriculum design and setting, teaching mode and more. For example, the construction of specialties in China's colleges and universities is based more on the logical development of disciplines themselves and the needs of schools than on the actual needs of economic and social development. Especially in the trend for accelerated development of service industry, the closed model of specialty setup can hardly adapt to diversified talent demand and change the structural contradiction of talent supply.

To change the serious disconnection between education development and economic and social development in China, the key is to break the closed education model of "ivory tower" type and open up the connecting channels between schools and society, schools and enterprises, governments and schools, and learning and entrepreneurship. It is to remove institutional barriers, delegate power to the market, the society, the local governments, and the colleges and universities, and cause the education model to go from the closed one to the open one. For example, it is advisable to promote the reform experience of teaching and student registration management system in some provinces and cities, and establish a credit accumulation and conversion system for innovation and entrepreneurship. College students who suspend their schooling and start their own business shall be allowed to adjust their academic progress and provided with the opportunity to retain their student status.

[44] Zhao Yingsheng, Zhong Binglin and Hong Yu: An Inevitable Choice to Promote the Scientific Development of China's Education—Also on the Pattern Transition of Educational Development. *Education Research*, No. 1, 2012.

(4) One of the modes of education development needs to be changed from the administrative mode to the professional mode.

Unless education is "de-administrated", it will be difficult to implement the autonomy of running schools. In recent years, the State government has taken it as the focus of education reform to promote "de-administration" in colleges and universities. From the perspective of the actual situation, however, the administrative degree of public education institutions indicates an increasing trend in some aspects, which mainly reflects the control of administrative power over education resource allocation. For example, the standards for professional title assessment are mainly formulated by administrative authorities. The administrativization of public education also extends to private education, which is highlighted by the lack of autonomy of private colleges and universities in running schools. The private colleges and universities' power of enrollment, specialty setting, course offering and fee collection is mostly restricted by the administrative power. Another example about enrolment by private schools. Some local education administrative departments designate the area for enrolling students, the number of enrollees, enrolling standards, and enrolling time. That is how the enrolment of both private schools and public schools is "regulated". All these require straightening out the relationships between the government and schools, between public schools and private schools, and between the school internal administration and academic affairs, accelerating the breaking of de-administration of education, and reforming public education institutions under the guidance of "the public welfare, professionalism and independence", while further promoting decentralization and increasing the school autonomy, thereby forming a professional and efficient education executive system.

4.2 *"De-administration" in Education Has to Be Promoted Quickly*

Replacing and weakening professionalization with administration not only inhibit the development of education itself but also produce the problem of academic corruption. So, to respect the law of education, let the school return to the standard of education, and promote running the school by experts are an important link to deepen the comprehensive reform of education and break the institutional contradictions in the system of educational development.

(1) "De-administration" in education can overcome various malpractices in the domain of education.

① It is significant to implement the running of schools by experts. The administration requires uniform standards and uniform practice, so as to manage schools easily. But this has made nationwide schools stay at a low level and seriously homogenized. Therefore, it is essential to guide education in accordance with the academic rules, to solve the problem that few great masters have been developed, and turn out various talents by every possible means.

② It is important to avoid education corruption. In this connection, therefore, it is imperative to fix problems like some school leaders' embezzlement of public funds, some responsible persons' corruption concerning the school infrastructure, and accepting bribes for enrolment. It is also imperative to prevent some teachers from being less concentrated on their work and earning extra money by moonlighting here and there, and to stop academic corruption and put an end to corrupt style of study.

③ It is of primary importance to increase school leaders' loyalty to their duties and responsibilities. Without the administrative ranking, they will be able to concentrate on their work, take responsibility for their subject, and focus on the cause of education itself, rather than seeking promotion through relationships.

(2) The corporate governance structure within the school calls for improvement.

① It is imperative to cancel the school administrative level. For "de-administration" in education, the key is to abolish the administrative level of the school, the first being to cancel the "official hat" of the head of the school. To be specific, it is to increase the number of pilot local schools for public selection for heads of schools, and remove the administrative rankings of those selected heads. Furthermore, it is to explore the rank system of school heads, and promote the practice of "expert school heads", thus letting educators run education and achieving "professionalization of school heads' position". During the term of office, there will be no administrative rank for appointed heads of schools.

② It is necessary to establish and improve the university council. Specifically, regulate colleges and universities should establish councils and optimize the composition of council members. The establishment of the system of an independent council is worth exploring. By doing so, the school council can play a positive role in strengthening social cooperation, expanding decision-making democracy, securing educational resources and accepting social supervision.

③ It is ensured that the academic committee exercise its functions and powers in a relatively independent way. The academic committee shall be established in accordance with the law, and an academic management system and organizational structure centering on the academic committee shall be gradually formed, and the functions and powers of decision-making, deliberation, evaluation and consultation in academic affairs shall be exercised to achieve the relative separation of administrative power from academic power and ensure the independent exercise of academic power. It is a must to establish and improve the procedures and methods for the identification of academic violations and behaviors against academic norms, and maintain a good academic atmosphere.

④ It is fundamental to establish an open system of school affairs. Specifically, it is to improve all kinds of information disclosure system, especially in such aspects as the enrolling test, financial assets and charges, the faculty and other personnel, teaching quality, student management services, degrees and disciplines, and foreign exchange and cooperation of colleges and universities, to ensure that teachers and staff, students and the general public have the right to know the major issues of the school and the important system, accept the supervision of the relevant stakeholders. In addition, it is necessary to establish a press spokesperson system to respond promptly and accurately to teachers, students and social concerns.

(3) The autonomy of colleges and universities in running schools needs to be expanded.

In the mid-twentieth century, Stanford rose rapidly from a mediocre university to a top research university in the world, a shift that began in 1951 with the decision of Frederick Terman, dean of the Stanford school of engineering, to set up an industrial park on campus and to lease nearly a thousand acres of campus cheaply to start-ups and research institutes. It was such a decision that laid the foundations of Silicon Valley and radically changed the fortunes of Stanford. The case, as it were, a typical one that the university runs independently and by operating their own assets and funds, has managed to reach a deep fusion of academic and educational logic and the logic of enterprise and market. As a result, Stanford University benefits immeasurably in the innovative talent training and high-tech research and development, which has also made the US high-tech development across a big step forward. Drawing on the successful experience of developed countries, it is to expand and implement the right of independent enrollment in colleges and universities, expand the right to set up specialties in colleges and universities, expand the right for management of positions establishment in colleges and universities, and expand the right to manage property and funds in colleges and universities.

(4) The relationship between the government and schools needs to be handled properly.

The government should change the way to manage the schools as its subordinate administrative organs and change the "unified, inclusive and administrative mode". For basic education, the education department of the government should clearly define its main responsibilities: first, to guarantee the investment in schools in accordance with the law, and solve the problems of poor conditions in running school, low quality of teachers and uneven development; second, to supervise schools in running education in accordance with the law, and not to directly interfere in running schools, or not to properly use the administrative power to make evaluations resulting in a waste of labor and money.

For higher education, the main responsibility of the government should be macro management, mainly making relevant laws, regulations and policies and supervising the quality of schools. The government needs to change the mechanism of direct management of colleges and universities, direct allocation of resources, etc. Otherwise, the leadership of schools will only be responsible to their superiors, instead of the students, for obtaining resources.

4.3 Full Play Shall Be Given to the Important Role of the Market in Education Resource Allocation

At present, one of the tasks for reform of the education system is to give full play both to the "invisible hand" of the market and the "visible hand" of the government in building the sound system of the government macro management, running school independently, and social multiple evaluation, and to form the new pattern of education development in which "the government supervises education, schools run education, and society evaluates education".

(1) The market should play an important role in education resource allocation.

Since the founding of New China in 1949 until the 1980s, the government remained the sole entity in allocating education resources in line with the planned economy. For a long time, this highly centralized management system has resulted in insufficient education resource inventory, insufficient increment, low efficiency of use, and the ubiquitous lazy consciousness of schools only "waiting for, relying on and wanting resources to be allocated by the government".

Take two phenomena for example. First, China has relaxed market access to education in recent years, but there are still many administrative controls in education, especially the high-end education market, causing a large number of education consumers to outflow. Nowadays, the trend for studying abroad has grown from universities and high schools to primary schools. Studying abroad at a young age has become a new trend. According to survey results of *Education Consumers' Map of Chinese Families in 2016* jointly published by iResearch Consulting Group with the help of the country's largest community, 45.7% of the parents surveyed wanted to send their children to study abroad.[45] Second, the lagging reform of education has led to difficulties in the development of private education. Excessive control over private education is one of the important causes for the decrease in social investment and the number of schools in private education these years.

(2) The effective supply of education public services should be expanded.

At the Fifth Plenary Session of the 18th Central Committee of the CPC, it was proposed to "innovate the way of providing public services. The government will not directly undertake those services that

[45] Education Consumers' Map of Chinese Families: Studying Abroad at a Young Age Has Gradually Become a Trend. Tencent Education Network, March 11, 2016.

the government can provide by government purchase. The government will attract social capital widely to participate in providing public services, which can be provided by cooperation between the government and social capital." Education is no exception. It should become a key area for the government to purchase public services, so as to promote the transformation of administrative functions of education and expand the effective supply of education public services. Education has certain particularity in resource allocation. On the premise that the government "ensures the bottom line and maintains fairness", market should be fully activated in running schools, so as to acquire diversified providers and modes of supply, and to satisfy diversified and multi-level education consumption demands. In particular, in non-basic public services, such as higher education and vocational education, accelerating market-oriented reform, promoting competition among schools and improving the quality of running schools will not only promote the full employment of graduates, but also encourage students to put their studies to use, enhance their ability to create innovations and release talent dividends.

(3) The government's concept of governing education should be changed.

At present, contradictions and problems appearing in the education domain are directly related to the lagging concept of education. During the 13th FYP period, effective performance of the education management function of government are rendered chiefly in terms of five shifts in education concept: a shift from running education to supervising education, a shift from micro management to macro management, a shift from the focal supervision of colleges and universities to the basic and fair supervision of them, a shift from focal attention to credential education to full attention to national education, and a shift from close attention to management of examination and approval to supervision during and after the matter. Whether emancipating the mind or transforming the education concept will largely determine the prospect of the second reform of education, determine the success or failure of "making the people satisfied with education", and also determine the transformation and upgrading of China from a nation with a large population to a nation full of talented people.

CHAPTER 7

Establishing a Fair and Sustainable Social Security System

In the 13th FYP period, with the advent of an aging population, the demand for social security such as senior citizen care and medical care has increased rapidly. Population urbanization requires the establishment of a unified social security system between urban and rural areas. Expanding domestic demand and boosting consumption depend on a sound social security system. The 13th FYP should focus on the national pooling of basic pensions, speed up the establishment of a fair and sustainable social security system, consolidate the institutional foundation supported by social policies, and provide strong impetus for economic transformation and upgrading.

During the 13th FYP period, economic transformation and upgrading will comprehensively enhance the dependence upon the reform of social security system, while deepening the reform of social security system with the heightened sense of acquisition as the focus. It is conducive to forming the system environment to release domestic demand potential and is one of the key tasks to push forward the reform of supply-side structure.

1 Towards Shared Development as a Major Trend for Social Security Reform

To grasp the general trend of China's entering the new stage of development, to establish a social security system benefiting 1.3 billion people, and to form a more equitable and sustainable social security system

F. Chi, *Winning at the Turning Point*, The Great Transformation of China, https://doi.org/10.1007/978-981-32-9479-0_7

have become a strategic choice for promoting the transformation of the growth model and building a shared society.

1.1 New Background of Social Security System Reform

Since the reform and opening up in 1978, China has entered a new era of mass consumption. The upgrading of consumption pattern has unleashed enormous consumption potential and become a powerful driving force for economic transformation and upgrading. The problem is that China's imperfect social security system has seriously inhibited the potential release of consumer demand, leading to insufficient impetus for economic transformation. By focusing on the trend of upgrading the consumption pattern, accelerating the implementation of the plan for the national insurance, steadily raising the level of social security and effectively narrowing the gap in social security benefits can the consumption expectations of more than 1.3 billion people be boosted, thus providing powerful impetus for China's steady growth and transformational promotion.

(1) The upgrading of consumption pattern has increased the overall dependence on social security.

Since 2010, China's consumption rate has reversed the downward trend, showing a slow rise. Compared with the huge domestic consumer market, however, 51.2% of the consumption level in 2014 was still on the low side. Its root causes are mainly as follows. First, (consumers) "dare not to buy it", because the social security system is not sound, the level of security is not high, and the amount of preventive savings is increased, which limits the purchasing ability of ordinary residents. In 2013, China's savings rate reached 50.2%, ranking third in the world. Many studies have shown that the imperfect social security system is an important reason why consumption is difficult to release and upgrade. Second, (consumers) "can't afford it". Due to the insufficient inclination of primary distribution to labor, the insufficient social equity of secondary distribution and the low level of social security, China's Gini coefficient has been at a high level for a long time, and general residents have insufficient purchasing power. Third, (consumers) "cannot get it", because the service market is not open enough, the service supply is limited, high-quality and affordable social security services are not available. In the next five years, if the social safety net that focuses on the social security system in an all-round way can be improved, the consumption rate of Chinese residents is expected to increase by 10–15 percentage points in the 13th FYP period, reaching about 50%. Therefore, promoting the reform of social security system has become a major task of supply-side structural reform in the 13th FYP.

(2) To promote the transformation of population urbanization is a realistic demand for social security.

A fair and sustainable social security system is not only an important goal of population urbanization, but also an important task and basic guarantee of population urbanization. If the construction of a unified urban and rural social security system in the 13th FYP can't resolve the problem, it will be difficult for China to make substantive progress in population urbanization. In the past 10-odd years, China has successively established the new rural cooperative medical system and the new rural social pension insurance system, which have changed the pattern of absence of rural social security and basically achieved full coverage of the insurance system. The problem is that social security, such as pension insurance, medical insurance, minimum living security system and old-age welfare policy, has obvious segmentation between urban and rural areas. For example, in terms of pension insurance, that for urban workers is compulsory, whereas the new rural social pension insurance is to be taken out voluntarily under the guidance of the government, and there is a huge gap between them in the level of security. In 2013, the monthly basic pension that covers urban workers averages 2054 yuan (US$342) per capita, whereas that for rural residents averages 91 yuan (US$15) per capita. The former pension is 21.6 times more than the latter on average. Although workers' pension insurance and urban and rural residents' pension insurance are subject to institutional arrangements of different nature, the significance of direct comparison between their absolute values is limited, this still reflects the fact that the level gap under different institutional arrangements is too big, especially compared with the standard of guaranteeing the basic right to life of a social member. To emphasize a unified social security system between urban and rural areas, the system should be unified, and there can be a gap at the level, but the gap cannot be too big.

(3) Overall poverty elimination poses an urgent need for social security.

The Fifth Plenary Session of the 18th Central Committee of the CPC clearly stated that by 2020, the rural poor population in China will be lifted out of poverty, and all the poverty-stricken counties will be lifted off their "hats of impoverished counties" to address overall poverty in the region. Overall poverty elimination is a must for building a moderately prosperous society in all aspects, which requires that social security play an important role in targeted poverty elimination. At present, the proportion of China's rural elderly who take pension as the main source of their income remains low, and it accounted for only 6.1% in 2010. But the proportion for the urban elderly was about 10 times higher than the rural elderly.[1] The vast majority of rural elderly people are mainly dependent on their children or other relatives. Studies have shown that the comprehensive influence of the rural social security level on rural poverty reaches −0.608.[2] Therefore, it is necessary to improve the social security system as an important basis for overall poverty elimination in the 13th FYP period.

(4) The aging of the population has a realistic need to improve the social security system.

China has entered the age of population aging, in which the degree of aging is increasing rapidly, and the contradiction between being old before you get rich and being old before you take out insurance is quite prominent. In the next five years, whether or not to be able to accelerate the improvement of social security will have a decisive impact on addressing the challenges of population aging. According to statistics, China had a population of 220 million above 60 years of age in 2015, which accounted for nearly 16.15% of the country's total population, while the population aged above 65 exceeded 140 million, which accounted for 10.47% of the country's total. Then, its senior population

[1] Only over 20% of the Elderly in China Live Mainly on Pension. *Beijing News*, October 23, 2012.

[2] Zheng Xin: *Study on the Relationship Between Rural Poverty and Social Security Level—Based on the Statistics Analysis of 30 Provinces and Cities* (sic.). Shanghai University of Engineering Science, Master Degree Thesis, 2014.

size tops the world. In 2030, according to the United Nations' prediction, China's senior population size will double to nearly 350 million. With the aging of the population, the demand for pension service is increasing. According to the tracking investigation on China's health and elderly care issued by the National School of Development at Peking University (NSD), 23.8% of elderly people had difficulty in daily operation, 54% had high blood pressure, and 40% suffered from depression. According to statistics, among the senile empty nesters in the rural areas, those generally in poor health made up 27.2%, those with chronic diseases accounted for 65.5%, and those suffering illness for years constituted as high as 70–80%. Therefore, in order to adapt to the aging of the population during the 13th FYP period, it is a must to accelerate the improvement of the social security system.

1.2 Prominent Problems Facing the Social Security System

With the all-round development of China's economy and society, the demand of urban and rural residents for equitable social security has increased generally. At the same time, contradictions and problems in China's social security system are increasingly exposed.

(1) The low pooling level of basic pension has become a prominent contradiction.

① The payment ratio of pension insurance is not unified. At present, the social pooling account of China's urban workers' basic pension insurance is borne completely by the enterprises of which they are employees. Twenty percent of the total wage of a worker shall be paid to the account. However, due to the different levels of development in different regions, the pension burden is not balanced, and the proportion of enterprise payment varies widely. In the enterprises in Beijing, Tianjin, Hefei, and Chengdu, the payment ratio is 20% of per capita wage, whereas in the southeast coastal developed areas, due to the influx of young and middle-aged workers that makes the dependency ratio not high, there is a relatively low payment ratio for the enterprises. In Guangzhou and Hangzhou, for example, the payment ratio is only 12 and 14% respectively (see Table 1).

② The pension fund management is not unified. There are two types of management of national pension insurance fund, namely, provincial

Table 1 The payment ratio of enterprises for urban basic pension insurance in 13 cities

Cities	*The payment ratio of enterprises for urban basic pension insurance in 13 cities (%)*
Beijing	20
Shanghai	21
Tianjin	20
Guangzhou	12
Hefei	20
Nanjing	20
Hangzhou	14
Xi'an	20
Taiyuan	20
Ji'nan	20
Fuzhou	18
Changsha	20
Chengdu	20

Source The table is prepared by the research group of China (Hainan) Institute for Reform and Development

unified collection and expenditure and provincial and municipal adjustment management.

③ The pension insurance collection system is not unified. Because provinces choose different collection and management institutions and collection methods, the collection system is not unified, which affects the coordination and efficiency of social security collection and management.

(2) Major disease insurance is most important for improving the social security system.

The 18th National Congress of the CPC proposed that basic public services in urban and rural areas should be equalized by 2020. In the past few years, the Chinese government has intensified its efforts to adjust social policies, increased financial input, basically covered all basic public services, and continuously raised the level of security. In terms of basic medical insurance, China has established the largest insurance network in the world. At the same time, the problem that urban and rural residents are put "in poverty caused by diseases and return to poverty due to diseases" has become rather prominent. Some patients with serious or even critical diseases often cannot discontinue their treatment due to high costs. At the end of October 2015, Premier Li Keqiang pointed out in a speech at the Party School of the CPC Central Committee that "out of nearly 30 million poor families across the country, about 12 million ones have suffered from poverty due to diseases." In other words, about 40% of these families have become poor because of diseases. The construction of the sharing society in the 13th FYP period has called for an urgent need for the comprehensive implementation of major disease insurance.

(3) The "low payment dilemma" restricts the functioning of the sustainable system.

Generally speaking, the pension insurance system should reflect both the fairness of treatment level between different groups and the fair link between the payment and treatment in the same people covered by the same pension insurance. China's pension insurance system has institutional differences in terms of the fairness of treatment, and there are also many loopholes in the link between contribution and treatment. This is an important cause for moral hazard and adverse selection. The first is that the actual rate is lower than the stipulated rate. This is a rare case in any other countries in the world. For example, in developed regions like Guangdong and Zhejiang, the payment rate of enterprises is much lower than that of other regions. The second is that the actual payment base is less than the real payment base. In order to pay less, the vast majority of enterprises and employees have reduced the payment base not by paying as per the real wage level of workers, but by paying as per the local social average wage. By calculating on the basis of the payment ratio of nationwide workers covered by pension insurance, the wage base for payment is only about 60% of real wages, and the contribution income is reduced by at least one-third. This situation, therefore, has affected the sustainability of the pension insurance system seriously.

1.3 The Goal that Meets the Requirement of the Reform of the Social Security System

The 13th FYP period is a key period for China's social security reform and an important node for the establishment of the system. In the next five years, the general idea of China's social security reform is as follows:

objectively grasping the basic trend for the development of the internal and external environment in the country; based on the basic national conditions; taking "the unified system, the fair bottom line, positive incentive, and financial sustainment" as the basic goal; taking full coverage, actuarial balance, moderate burden, perfect system, basic coordination, and value preservation and appreciation as the key link; and setting up a major nation's social security system that adapts to the comprehensive well-off society by 2020.

(1) Establishing a fair and sustainable social security system.

① The system is sustainable and adjustable. Whether the system functions well or not depends on whether the system itself is capable of self-adjusting. A sustainable social security system needs to be compatible with the level of economic and social development and with other social and economic systems. Especially in the three important system parameters that are support rate, replacement rate and payment rate, it adapts to the changes of economic situation, population structure and labor market, realizing self-elastic adjustment to ensure the sustainable system.

② Financial support is sustainable. The normal operation of the social security system requires sustainable financial support. First, it needs to be a stable source of financing. Second, the social security system should be able to cope with the challenges of trends brought by the aging population and diversified interests. Third, in the face of macroeconomic and financial market fluctuations, the social security system has a strong capacity for financial adjustment.

③ Enterprises can afford it. The payment from enterprises and individuals is the most direct source of social security, and such payment forms the direct cost of enterprises. The basic source of sustainability of social security lies in enterprises. This requires the organic combination of enterprise sustainability and social security sustainability to avoid both the "low welfare trap" and the "high welfare trap".

(2) Basic principles of social security system reform.

① It is necessary not only to adhere to the direction and goal of equality and sustainability, but also to boldly explore new ways and approaches. At the Third Plenary Session of the 18th CPC Central Committee, the goal of "establishing a more equitable and sustainable social security system" was put forward, and the direction of social security construction in China in the next several years was quite clear. Objectively speaking, however, many reforms are still in the process of exploration. For example, there is still no clear answer to the question about the cost of transformation, and there are still many challenges to face in integrating the system. Therefore, China's social security reform should not only adhere to the reform direction and objectives proposed by the Central Government, but also boldly explore new paths.

② It is necessary not only to improve the construction of a unified national system, but also to give full consideration to arouse the enthusiasm of all sides. In the process of reforming the social security system, full consideration needs to be given to the initiative of all. The core is to clearly distinguish between the responsibilities of the Central Government and local governments. Under the precondition of making overall plans for basic social security, the Central Government must not take over too many responsibilities. It must not interfere too much in non-basic and regional social security projects and place too much emphasis on unified standards. Full play should be given to the enthusiasm of enterprises and individuals, while leaving more space for free choice to be made by different types of people in the system design.

③ It is necessary not only to see the overall strengthening of time and space constraints, but also to accelerate breakthroughs in major tasks and make clear the priorities. Judging from the development trend of the whole society's demand for social security, both the time and space constraints of social security reform have been strengthened. The 13th FYP period is a key period to move towards a fair and sustainable social security. If China cannot establish the framework of a fair and sustainable social security system by 2020, it not only will aggravate the contradictions and risks in the social security field, but also may spread to the social field, or even to the economic field, and become the incentive for China to fall into the "middle-income trap". Therefore, the overall goal of reform should be realized ASAP in the context of overall strengthening of time and space constraints.

④ It is necessary not only to strengthen the top-level design of reform, but also pay attention to social consensus and participation. Social security reform is one involving the vital interests of all, which requires that the design of social security reform be designed, planned and promoted at the top level of the Central Government. In the process of formulating the reform plan, it is advisable to fully involve the public in the discussion and reduce social differences. All sides attach great importance to social security reform. Some public issues, such as postponing retirement and levying medical insurance premiums for retirees, are likely to become sensitive topics and cause social disputes. Therefore, it is necessary to objectively reflect the challenges and problems of social security to the whole society, to explain to the society the basic considerations of reform and the possible impact on individuals, and to form a broad social consensus.

(3) The overall objective of social security system reform.

In accordance with the spirit of the Third Plenary Session and of the Fifth Plenary Session of the 18th CPC Central Committee, China should speed up the building of a fair and sustainable society security system, and by 2020 initially form a fair and sustainable institutional framework: One is to adhere to the basic pension insurance system that combines social pooling with personal accounts, improve the system of personal accounts and the sound mechanism for more pay more incentive, ensure the rights of the insured, realize the national cooperative basic pension system, and hold to the principle of actuarial balance. Two is to improve the transfer and continuity policy of social insurance relations, expand the coverage of insurance payment, and appropriately reduce the social insurance rate at the right time. Three is to establish the mechanism of separate accounts management preliminarily before achieving the transformation from "the combination of social cooperative accounts and individual accounts, the management of mixed social cooperative accounts and individual accounts, and the operation of empty individual accounts" to "the combination of social cooperative accounts and individual accounts, the management of separate social cooperative accounts from individual accounts, and the operation of real individual accounts". Four is to strengthen the management and supervision of social investment in insurance funds, promote the marketization of funds and the operation of diversified investment, formulate and implement preferential policies such as tax exemption and deferred taxation, accelerate the development of enterprise annuity, occupational annuity and commercial insurance, and build a multi-tiered social security system.

2 Promoting the Equalization of Basic Social Security

To achieve the grand goal of building a moderately prosperous society in an all-round way by 2020, the primary task is to equalize the basic social security. During the 13th FYP period, it is necessary to accelerate the reform of social security system and integrate the "fragmented" social security system, establishing a sound urban-rural integrated and well-connected social security system.

2.1 *Accelerating the National Pooling of Basic Pension*

The Fifth Plenary Session of the 18th Central Committee of CPC has clearly proposed the goal of "realizing the national pooling of basic pension for employees", which requires the reform path of reasonably planning the national pooling of basic pension through top-level design. According to the standards of "unified system, unified management and unified technology", the basic pattern of "double pooling" at the Central and provincial levels should be formed ASAP, giving full play to the final responsible role of the Central Government and taking into account the development differences in different regions.

(1) The national pooling of basic pension is related to the equitable and sustainable development of social security.

① The settlement of the payment gap in some areas depends on the national pooling of basic pension. According to the *Report on China's Pension Development 2012*, in 2010, 15 provinces across the country failed to make up for their expenditures, with a total shortfall of 67.9 billion yuan (US$11.32 billion). Although the provinces that couldn't cover their expenditures were reduced to 14 in 2011, the total revenue gap of these provinces was higher than the total number of 2010, reaching 76.65 billion yuan (SU$12.78 billion). In 2014, after deducting financial subsidies from the basic pension insurance fund of enterprise employees, there were 22 provinces whose current revenue could not be offset. In terms of the cumulative balance, the total balance of the national urban workers' pension insurance fund in 2013 reached 2826.918 billion yuan (US$471.153 billion). The cumulative balance of nine provinces and municipalities including Guangdong, Jiangsu, Zhejiang, Shandong, Sichuan, Beijing, Liaoning, Shanxi and Shanghai exceeded 100 billion yuan (US$16.67 billion), which accounted 64.36% of the national balance. However, many other regions, such as the three northeastern provinces, faced severe challenges in economic growth, while a large population were moving out and the population was aging considerably, making it difficult to achieve the self-balance of pension by relying on the strength of their own regions. The establishment of a nationwide pooling of basic pension can not only build a system bottom line for difficult areas and the difficult masses and solve the problem of the pension payment gap in some areas, but also balance the pension funds at the national level, so as to make the pension more fully used.

② The reduction of social security rate depends on the breakthrough of national pooling of basic pension. The expansion of coverage brought about by the national pooling will expand the funding sources of the pension fund, and bring the high rates borne by some regional enterprises to a lower level. At present, China's urban population burden ratio is 0.16, and the support rate in the pension insurance system is 0.33, which is 2 times the population burden ratio. This means that the burden ratio of the pension insurance system still has room to decrease. The national pooling of basic pension can incline the system burden ratio towards the population burden ratio, make room to lower down the social security rate, and reduce the cost pressure of enterprise transformation and upgrading. At the same time, it can reduce the payment pressure on the insured, strengthen the payment incentive, further increase the coverage of the pension insurance system, and form a sound cycle of "a low rate → an increase in the number of the insured workers → a younger pension insurance system → a lower rate".

③ The transfer and continuation of pension insurance for floating population depends on the national pooling of basic pension. The national pooling can provide convenient employment and insurance conditions for workers, increase their enthusiasm for taking out insurance and labor mobility, and help to build a unified labor market. The main factor restricting the expansion of China's pension insurance coverage at present is the problem about insurance covering rural migrant workers. Through the national pooling of basic pension, the pension rights and interests of the insured in different regions can be effectively guaranteed. This practice provides a safe and stable expectation for the floating employment population, which is the basic condition for expanding the coverage of pension insurance system and building a unified national labor market.

④ The narrowing of regional income gap depends on the national pooling of basic pension. One of the important goals of the national pooling of basic pension is to narrow the income distribution gap between regions. At present, because the basic pension has not yet been ready for the national pooling, each region has still determined the basic pension treatment standard according to the situation of its own development. In 2013, the per capita annual pension fund expenditure of urban retirees in various regions of China was not far behind the per capita disposable income of urban residents. The correlation coefficient between the annual expenditure of pension fund and the disposable income of urban residents is as high as 57.4%. However, the role of pension in narrowing the regional gap of urban workers is not obvious. In 2013, for example, the per capita disposable income ratio of urban residents in Beijing and Jiangxi was 1.84. The per capita fund expenditure ratio of workers' pension insurance in these two places should theoretically be smaller than the average per capita income gap, and actually reached 1.96, which expanded the actual income gap.

Compared with urban workers' pension insurance that has been in operation for many years, the effect of urban and rural residents' pension insurance on the balancing of regional gap is even less obvious: Not only there is a large gap between different provinces, autonomous regions and cities, but there is also a significant gap between the urban and rural areas in the same province, autonomous regions and cities. When it comes to China's urban and rural residents per capita pension funds, the ratio between the highest expenditure of the region (Shanghai) and the lowest expenditure of the region (Hunan) in 2013 was up to 11.11, which was far higher than that of the residents' income gap (2.64) in these two places. Within the same province, in terms of the gap in treatment between the urban workers' pension fund and the urban and rural residents' pension insurance, and even in Shanghai where the urban and rural residents enjoy the best treatment in pension insurance, the per capita expenditure of the urban workers' pension fund is 4.6 times as much as the urban and rural residents' pension insurance. For the poor treatment in Jiangxi, urban workers' pension fund is 25.13 times that of urban and rural residents' pension insurance, which is much higher than the income gap between the local urban and rural residents.

Both the strong correlation between the pension benefits and the residents' income and the too big regional gap between the pension benefits have seriously affected the role of social security in balancing the income distribution among the residents. The regional gap of pension treatment is too big, even far exceeding the income level gap, which means that the pension system has the effect of "robbing the poor to benefit the rich". To realize the national pooling of basic pension ASAP is not only of great importance to reduce regional inequality, but also to realize the equal basic pension in the context of imbalance in regional development.

(2) The top-level design will be carried out for the national pooling of basic pension.

To realize the national pooling of basic pension involves many aspects, but the core is to come up with a reasonable scheme to pay the system transition cost, which cannot be separated from effective top-level design. At present, all parties have put forward a lot of proposals for the national pooling of basic pension, and their goals are the same. The difference is whether to advance the proposals in one step or step by step. Judging by checking the needs of the medium and long-term development of pension security system and international experience, it is necessary to make clear ASAP the nationwide reform path of the national pooling of basic pension in the top-level design, so as to stabilize the expectations of all parties (see Table 2).

(3) Basic requirements for the national pooling of basic pension.

① The unification of the system needs to be achieved. With reference to the current standard of provincial pooling, it is fundamental to uniformly formulate the insurance coverage, the insured, financing methods, payment base and proportion, payment standard determination method and overall planning project for urban employees and urban and rural residents' pension insurance nationwide. The pension insurance system in different regions of the country is unified in standards on basic pension, with a fair bottom line and a transferable relationship.

② The management mode needs to be unified. The first is to establish an integrated vertical management system for pension insurance institutions across the country. The Central competent authority will carry out vertical management of basic pension insurance and change the current management pattern of local division and compartmentalization. The second is to formulate and implement the basic pension insurance fund

Table 2 Major plans of the domestic national pooling of basic pension

Major plans	*System design*	*Concrete measures*
A "three-steps-in-one" way towards the national pooling of basic pension	Bypass the provincial pooling and implement the unified national collection and allocation for the nationwide unified system, unified payment ratio, unified calculation and distribution, and united organization and management	1. Under the separate budget system for basic pension insurance, local governments collect pension insurance premiums in accordance with the annual budget and pay all of them to the Central Government, which shall calculate and pay a certain proportion of the average wage level and the personal indexed contributory wage in different places 2. Separate the old and new financial accounting and follow the incremental reform 3. Form a Central and local vertical management system 4. Make clear the accounting plan of pension insurance equity
Stabilize the provincial pooling and promote the national adjustment of basic pension	Implement the provincial unified collection and allocation of basic pension and establish a national basic pension adjustment fund system	**Provincial pooling**: 1. The subject responsible for budget planning: provincial social insurance agency mechanism 2. Fund revenue and expenditure: provincial unified revenue and expenditure; fund overspending; provincial balance settlement 3. Provincial governments' vertical management of cities and counties **National adjustment of basic pension**: 1. The Central pension insurance institution calculates the proportion of contributions according to the actual situation of each province and makes clear the amount of budgetary contributions, while the province pays the pension insurance fund in full monthly, and deposits it into the special account of basic pension adjustment fund 2. When the Central Government allocates the basic pension adjustment fund, it measures comprehensively the number of the insured, coverage rate, treatment level and overall economic strength in various regions; in allocating the adjustment fund, in order to avoid the occurrence of unreasonable centralized adjustment practice, which results in new unfairness, the Central Government should fully consider the amount of financial subsidies to local pension insurance

(continued)

Table 2 (continued)

Major plans	*System design*	*Concrete measures*
Achieve the national pooling based on the provincial pooling and with the regional pooling as the transition	First, implement provincial unified collection and allocation; then, according to the actual situation, conduct the regional management of pension insurance fund concentrated in the east, central and western regions for the regional pooling; finally, implement the national pooling	Implement the provincial pooling, and then carry out pilot schemes in several provinces with complementary demographic age structures according to the situation; in line with the unified national standard, design the model of smooth transition to the national pooling
	Improve the provincial pooling, conduct a related experiment in several provinces for smooth transition to the national pooling	

Source The research group of China (Hainan) Institute for Reform and Development

budget at the national level, and clarify the budget responsibility of the Central, provincial, municipal and county governments while the government at all levels shall implement and adjust in strict accordance with their budgets. The third is to unify procedures and management systems for the handling of basic old-age insurance services for urban workers and urban and rural residents throughout the country, and implement unified data standards.

③ Unified technical standards need to be achieved. A unified national pension insurance information system should be established as the basic platform for the national pooling management. This is not only the precondition and foundation of the national pooling of basic pension, but also the basic content of the national pooling of basic pension fund.

(4) A pattern of "double pooling" of basic pensions between the Central Government and local governments needs to be formed.

① The comprehensive plan of "double pooling" should be considered. The Central Government should not only play a fundamental role, but also take into account the differences in the level of development in various regions.

First, each provincial government will turn the provincial pension insurance pooling fund over to the Central Government according to a certain proportion. The turned-over fund will be used together with the Central finance to contribute to form the Central-level pooling fund, which is to be transferred by the Central finance between the provinces. In operation, a part of the enterprise's contributory payment is transferred directly to the national pooling fund (10%, for example), the remaining part being transferred to the provincial pooling fund.

Second, the level of settlement and payment of the national pooling fund shall be formulated by the Central Government uniformly, regardless of the differences between provinces, and shall not be affected by the provincial pooling. The part as the national pooling is accessible to all those covered by the pension insurance without differential treatment, no matter what occupations the insured have and no matter where they live on an individual basis.

Third, the remaining part after the provincial government turns over its contribution to the Central pooling fund will be established as the provincial pooling fund. Differential payments will be made after giving due consideration to the level of local economic development and the structure of the population. In terms of labor mobility, the treatment that an employee enjoys in accordance with his/her job in different provinces is calculated by working time segment.

Therefore, the basic pattern of "double pooling" is formed at the Central and provincial levels: the basic pension is divided into national basic pension and local basic pension, while the Central pooling fund and local pooling fund are divided accordingly in terms of fund raising. The Central Government pays the State basic pension and the local governments pay the local basic pension. The Central and local governments will ensure the payment and treatment of two categories of basic pensions.

② "Double pooling" will be completed in three steps.

The first step is to establish a national pooling fund. It needs to be clear that the universality of the national pooling fund means the full coverage of pension insurance for urban and rural residents and urban workers in different regions. All the existing subsidies from the Central Government to the pension insurance are integrated in full into the national pooling fund. All kinds of basic pension insurance shall be divided according to a certain proportion of the revenue of the overall account and be classified into the accounts of the Central and provincial pooling funds. Considering the complexity of pension reform, this stage can adopt the mode of "incremental sharing, full return and subsidy sharing". In other words, the incremental part of pooling account revenue of all kinds of basic pension insurance is to be divided and the divided portion that is put into the national pooling fund will be returned in full. Meanwhile, according to the situation of various kinds of basic pension insurance, the financial subsidy and the returned portion will be granted together. So, it is important to have a comprehensive grasp of basic pension insurance information, on the basis of strengthening local active involvement in the national pooling fund.

The second step is to give full play to the Central coordinating and transferring function. On the basis of the initial completion of the first step, the second step can be considered, that is, to give full play to the national coordination of the transferring function. Based on the basically grasped information about all kinds of local basic pension insurance in various regions, the divisible portion of pension can be transferred for the sake of the national coordination according to the local insurance information. For it is highly necessary to balance the financial resources and guarantee levels of different basic pension insurance in different places, while building and improving the information base of national pension insurance.

The third step is to give full play to the central management function of the Central Government. On the basis of completing the first and second steps, the national pooling fund should be turned from the goal of balancing financial resources and treatment to a unified system, in which according to the insurance information base of the national pension insurance, the unified management of different basic pension insurance in different regions should be implemented. Even if the areas for the insured differ and the types of their pension insurance differ, they can all be kept in the records and management through the unified archives of national pooling fund, which lays a solid foundation for the future reform of pension.

(5) The portion which the Central Government is responsible for as the national pooling will gradually be transformed into the "zero pillar".

① The Central Government shall bear the sole responsibility for the minimum pension security. The responsibility of the Central Government is to ensure that all people, regardless of income, occupation, payment and type of insurance, can enjoy the lowest pension security treatment. From the perspective of international experience, this is the "zero pillar". In the process of reform of the national pooling of basic pension, the Central pooling is taken as the "zero pillar", which can lay an essential foundation for eliminating the problem of low pooling level without changing the institutional framework of "the combined social cooperative accounts and individual accounts". At present, some local governments in China have been experimenting with the minimum pension system. Since October 1, 2013, Dongguan (a city in Guangdong) has raised the minimum pension line for retirees. Among them, the basic pension minimum guarantee line for enterprise retirees was increased from 430 yuan (US$71.67) per person per month to 680 yuan (US$113.33). The minimum pension line for village (community) retirees was raised to 510 yuan (US$85) from 300 yuan (US$50) per person per month.[3] But the pilot city was too small and directly linked

[3] Dongguang's Basic Pension Minimum Guarantee Line Raised. *Southern Daily*, September 12, 2013.

to the local economy. To take this practice up to the Central level is the Central Government's responsibility of the "national pooling". For the Central Government, the key to establishing a minimum old-age security system lies in further expanding the coverage of old-age insurance and realizing the universal coverage. Only when the full coverage is achieved will the effect of the national pooling of basic pension be magnified.

Special Citations [6-1]

Experience in the Arrangement of Minimum Pension System in Some Countries (Zero Pillar)

1. The concept of the three-pillar structure proposed by the World Bank in 1994 is that the first pillar is mandatory and non-cumulative and is a government-managed DB (defined benefit) system; The second pillar is mandatory DC (defined contribution) accumulation by market management. The third pillar is voluntary retirement savings. In 2005, the World Bank proposed five pillars, which expanded two others. The fifth one is the "zero pillar", a basic pillar aimed at eradicating poverty. The fourth is a non-economic pillar, which includes other broader social policies, such as family support, medical services and housing policies.

2. Norway has a minimum pension. Basic pension is the first pillar of Norway's national insurance scheme. According to the regulations, anyone who has taken out the national social welfare insurance for more than three years between the ages of 16 and 66 and has lived in Norway for more than 20 years can receive a basic pension. Basic pension treatment depends on the length of time in which the party concerned is covered by the national social welfare insurance, having nothing to do with the party's income before retiring and paid tax. Those who have been insured for more than 40 years will receive a full basic pension, with the remainder receiving a degressive amount of pension. But for Norwegians with no income and no record of paying taxes, a minimum pension will also be available upon retirement, with the current base level at 160,000 Norwegian kroner per year.

3. In the design of the pension system in Sweden, guaranteed pension is clearly set up. For those with low incomes or no income, the Swedish government has set up a minimum pension line to guarantee a minimum standard of living, providing guaranteed pension to the senior citizens through budget allocations.

4. The Britain in social security reform has also increased the pensioners' minimum income protection, from 68.80 pounds a week in 1997 up to 114 pounds a week nowadays. In addition, there is a minimum pension for the poor and the vulnerable, which is the last line of defense to maintain a minimum standard of living for old-age pensioners (OAP) and prevent them from falling into poverty.

Observed from the system design of various countries, although the specific system design is different, there are corresponding minimum pension security arrangements. The basic starting point of this arrangement is to prevent the social members who cannot afford to take out the pension insurance from falling into poverty in their old age.

Source The research group of China (Hainan) Institute for Reform and Development

② The payment level of the Central pooling (the zero pillar) shall be determined reasonably. In determining the level of "zero pillar", it is reasonable to equate the minimum pension standard with the minimum living allowance standard. By measuring the demand of the minimum pension, the scale demand of the national pooling of basic pension can be derived. The minimum living allowance is a kind of social relief, and its object and scope are mainly determined according to the actual situation of the year. It is temporary and individual in the system. But the minimum pension is long-term and universal. It covers the whole nation, and can be shared by the whole society in the same way. According to preliminary calculations, in November 2015, the per capita subsistence allowance for urban residents was 439 yuan (US$73.17), and that for rural residents was 255 yuan (US$42.5). Based on the calculation by the year of 2015 when people aged over 65 totaled 143.74 million and the urbanization rate was 56.1%, if all the old people were subsidized by subsistence allowance, the total amount of money would be 617.89 billion yuan (US$102.98 billion).[4] In view of the aging population and the

[4]The basic estimate is as follows: by calculating according to the average urbanization rate 56.1%, the subsidy needed for urban senior citizens is 143.74 million × 0.561 × 439 yuan × 12 = 424.80172 billion yuan (US$71.3003 billion); the subsidy needed for rural old-aged residents is 143.74 million × 0.439 × 255 yuan × 12 = 193.09169 billion yuan (US$32.1819 billion), the sum total of which is 617.89 billion yuan (US$102.98 billion). The actual amount of money needed should be smaller than this estimate, since the rural population is more aging and one part of the existing expenditure of subsistence allowance

adjustment of the treatment level, 700 billion yuan (US$116.67 billion) can be taken as the starting point of the Central pooling of basic pension and dynamically adjusted. For one thing, the absolute poverty line should be linked to the subsistence level to reflect the difference in economic development level (local cost of living, etc.). For another, a dynamic adjustment formula should be established to adjust it with economic development and price changes.

③ The Central Government will gradually implement the reform of fees and taxes by pooling the payment sources. At present, there is a big controversy about tax and fees in social security reform. In terms of different pooling levels, the role and positioning of tax and fees are different. Under the "two-level pooling" model, the pooling part responsible for the Central Government is the minimum pension security fund. It is also the experience of Norway and other Nordic countries to consider gradually adopting tax forms and to form a strong financial security. Responsible for the provincial pooling, the existing form of "fees" remains unchanged. After the tax-for-fees reform in the central pooling, the direct payment burden of enterprises can be significantly reduced, thus bringing about the structural tax reduction effect.

(6) The provincial pooling should be accelerated substantively.

① It is necessary to accelerate the provincial pooling substantively. In 2007, the former Ministry of Labor and Security and the Ministry of Finance jointly issued the *Notice on Promoting the Provincial Pooling of Basic Pension Insurance for Enterprise Employees*, which put forward six concrete criteria for achieving the provincial pooling. In reality, there are not many provinces that have truly achieved the provincial pooling, and in most of these provinces the provincial governments are responsible for fund transfer, a quasi-pooling which has not solved the problem of too-low-level pooling, or changed the actual control of local social security funds. However, the six criteria lack the most important one, namely the management criterion of capital revenue and expenditure, which does not stipulate the criterion of unified collection and unified expenditure. So it is difficult to provide guarantee for the provincial pooling. In the "two-level pooling" scheme, the pooling criteria should be clearly

is used as subsistence allowance for the old age. If the part mentioned above is included in the basic pension, there will be no need to add money in this regard.

defined, including the levels of revenue, expenditure, accounting, management and transfer of the fund flow of pension insurance payment. The core criterion should be fund. In other words, the level of management that is responsible for the concentrated funds can show which level of pooling has been achieved.

② It is necessary to clarify the responsibilities of local governments. In the context of the overall planning of the whole country, the executive subject of the overall fund budget should be governments at all levels. This requires that the responsibilities of governments at all levels, especially local governments, should be clarified, which promotes the local governments' active expansion of the coverage of pension insurance and control the abnormal growth of retirees. The gap between revenue and expenditure generated in the fund plan or budget should mainly be filled by fund transfer for coordination but by supplementary fund from local governments. The gap between revenue and expenditure created by abnormal causes should be closed mainly by compensation of local governments but by fund transfer as a supplementary means, or even fully by the local governments (see Table 3).

2.2 *Improving the Urban and Rural Cooperative Basic Medical Care System*

At present, the major disease insurance in China is to be allocated by the government from the medical insurance fund to purchase the major disease insurance from the commercial insurance institutions. For the insured with major diseases, the compliance medical expenses that need to be borne by individuals after the reimbursement of the basic medical insurance will be reimbursed twice. The accumulated medical expenses incurred by insured persons in excess of the maximum payment limit of basic medical insurance during the year may be compensated for in part or in whole through medical insurance for major diseases.

(1) Full coverage of major disease insurance shall be achieved.

Compared with the coverage rate of basic medical insurance for urban and rural residents, the coverage rate of major disease insurance is about 70%. The State Council's *Opinions on the Comprehensive Implementation of Major Disease Insurance for Urban and Rural Residents* clearly put forward that "where conditions permit, local governments shall be

Table 3 The relationship between the Central Government and the local governments after achieving the national pooling of basic pension

	Under the Central Government	*Under the local governments*
Financial responsibilities (*allocated*)	1. To subsidize the current pension gap (including the pension payment effected within the "same payment period as the contribution period" of employees from the enterprises under the Central Government and from the enterprises under the local governments, hereinafter known as "Central enterprises" and "local enterprises") 2. To subsidize the payment of fees for special groups of employees in Central enterprises 3. The Central Government shall transfer payments for establishing local additional pension in underdeveloped areas 4. To grant a certain proportion of personal account funds	1. To subsidize the payment of fees for special groups of employees in local enterprises 2. To make your personal account a real one 3. To establish local additional pension and provide pension service subsidies
Supervisory responsibilities (*allocated*)	1. The Central social insurance agency shall be responsible for the formulation of budget decisions, strategic planning, policies and law, and standards and norms 2. The Central administrative department of social security shall exercise the responsibilities of administrative supervision and fund supervision	1. Provincial social insurance agencies shall be responsible for the preparation and submission of draft budgets of social insurance funds to the Central social insurance agency, and for the investment management of individual account funds 2. Local agencies below the provincial level handle specific social insurance matters

(continued)

Table 3 (continued)

		Under the Central Government	*Under the local governments*
Reform and interaction	Information exchanges	1. The Central administrative department shall lead the establishment of a national information management system and speed up the construction of information network infrastructure and the process of information management 2. The new policy will be publicized timely to local governments, and a platform for information exchange among the regions be built	1. The information of pension fund payment, input, accounting, payment and inquiry into the system shall be input timely in response to the call of the Central Government 2. A local government agency should communicate actively with the Central Government and other local governments on relevant policies
	Consultation and decision	1. The Central, local and social representatives shall form a consultative body to conduct reasonable consultations on their respective interests 2. Consultations shall be held on a regular, procedural and standardized basis with the Central authority as the leadership and collective consultation as the orientation	

Source The table is prepared by the research group of China (Hainan) Institute for Reform and Development

encouraged to explore the establishment of an organic and unified insurance system for major diseases covering workers, urban residents and rural residents". The Central spirit must be implemented so as to strive to basically establish a major disease insurance system covering all people by 2020.

(2) The pooling level of major disease insurance needs to be upgraded.

In terms of the pooling level of medical insurance, it is necessary to consider both the characteristics of medical service itself and the constraints of current conditions. Due to China's vast territory, there are large differences in population structure, disease spectrum and medical treatment habits in different regions, unbalanced distribution of existing medical resources, and lack of effective connection and integration of various medical insurance systems, all of which widens the gap both between the regions and between urban and rural areas in the distribution of medical resources. In 2014, the total balance of national basic medical insurance fund amounted to 1064.48 billion yuan (US$177.413 billion), an increase by 16.8% over last year, but some parts of the countries moved into deficit in medical insurance fund. Therefore, there is an urgent need to improve the pooling level of medical insurance and strengthen the fund's capacity to help each other out.

(3) The connection with different medical insurance systems needs to be accelerated so as to build a three-tier medical security system.

① The connection between the major disease insurance and the basic medical insurance needs to be sped up. China's major disease insurance is based on the basic medical insurance for urban and rural residents, which requires accelerating the connection between the major disease insurance and the basic medical insurance. To promote the connection between urban workers and urban and rural residents through "major disease insurance", a differentiated payment and equitable treatment can be adopted. The step-by-step implementation of the integrated management mode of "major disease insurance and basic medical insurance" would be able to improve the information sharing mechanism and the medical insurance payment system and reduce the unreasonable medical expenses, while promoting the connection between the major disease insurance and the basic medical insurance in practical operation, operation management, and the implementation of a number of systems, and effectively establishing the negotiation mechanism of medical insurance agencies, medical institutions and pharmaceutical suppliers and the payment mechanism of purchasing service.

② The connection between the major disease insurance and the new rural cooperative medical security for major diseases needs to be sped up. There are relations and differences between the new rural cooperative medical security for major diseases and the major disease insurance. The new rural cooperative medical security system provides reimbursement for specific diseases on the basis of limited costs, whereas the major disease insurance of urban and rural residents does not set a limit on specific disease categories. At present, there are only 22 kinds of diseases under the new rural cooperative medical security system. From the practical point of view, the above two systems can be coordinated, while the new rural cooperative medical security system can gradually be integrated into the major disease insurance system.

③ The connection between the major disease insurance and the civil medical assistance system needs to be sped up. If urban and rural residents suffer from serious or even critical diseases, families will have to pay a huge amount of medical expenses even if they have obtained basic medical insurance and major disease insurance, causing "catastrophic medical spending". This needs to accelerate the improvement of the medical assistance system in addition to various kinds of medical insurance, and make an effective connection with medical insurance. For those patients who still have difficulty in paying at their own expense after the major disease insurance covers the stipulated amount of medical expenses, medical and charitable assistance should be provided to reduce the probability of catastrophic medical spending of their families.

(4) The development of commercial medical insurance needs to be encouraged.

Internationally, even developed countries with high levels of social welfare attach great importance to the development of supplementary medical insurance. Through tax incentive policies, the governments encourage enterprises and individuals to buy commercial health insurance, in order to make up for the medical expenses beyond the social

Table 4 The development model of commercial health insurance in the US, Germany, and the UK

Country	*National characteristics*	*Social health insurance*	*Commercial health insurance*	*The current status of insurance*	*Development characteristics of commercial health insurance*
The US	Commercial health insurance takes an important position in the health security system	No national medical insurance; government insurance only available to some people; other medical security entirely solved by the market	Basic medical security of enterprise employees can all be achieved via commercial insurance. The governments provide tax preference support and encourages the robust growth of commercial health insurance	A country with the most developed commercial health insurance; the insurance companies hold a large customer base with buyers' advantage; medical expenses can be controlled through managed care	1. Market-dominance and policy support; 2. Controlled expenses and perfect supervision; 3. Health management and reduced expenditure
Germany	Social health insurance takes an advantageous position with commercial health insurance competing	Social medical insurance occupies a leading position	Those with the income exceeding the set amount are exempt from legal social medical insurance but take out commercial insurance	The insurance company is an important payer, from which citizens receive the high-level supplementary medical services; professional health insurance companies take an advantageous place in the market	1. Strict separated supervision policies and appropriate external environment; 2. Business specialization and refinement, taking general needs and special needs into account; 3. Attention is paid to product and service innovation, while staying highly sensitive to changes in policies and external environment

(continued)

Table 4 (continued)

Country	*National characteristics*	*Social health insurance*	*Commercial health insurance*	*The current status of insurance*	*Development characteristics of commercial health insurance*
The UK	The country is dominated by national health service and supplemented by commercial health insurance	National Health Service (NHS) covers 99% of the total population	The country takes less care of policies on commercial health insurance, which is an effective supplement to NHS	Commercial health insurance provides high-end medical services to high-income people and is also an important payer in the private medical service system; it has established a risk-and- benefit-sharing joint mechanism with medical institutions	1. Accurate positioning and targeted products; 2. Attention is paid to establish the health industry chain and to participate actively in health management; 3. The insurance company shall establish an interest alliance and cooperative mechanism with medical institutions, and actively participate in the reform of medical and health system

Source The table is prepared by the research group of China (Hainan) Institute for Reform and Development

basic medical insurance, and for loss of disease costs and absence of nursing care costs. This can reduce the financial pressure on the country's social medical insurance while satisfying the diversity and the high level of the people's health care needs (see Table 4).

In terms of the system design, commercial insurance companies involved in the major disease insurance program can only "ensure break-even and maintain a small profit" and cannot obtain huge profits from this business. In order to inspire commercial insurance companies, commercial insurance institutions can be encouraged to actively develop commercial medical insurance and provide diversified health insurance products on the basis of undertaking major disease insurance. Through cross-subsidization of business, it not only provides more insurance for urban and rural residents, but also brings profits for commercial insurance companies.

2.3 *Improving the Social Assistance System*

It is essential to further strengthen and improve the urban and rural social assistance system, raise the level and scope of assistance for urban and rural residents who are suffering from difficulties, and effectively resolve problems that are of the greatest concern and the most direct to them.

(1) The minimum living standard must be improved.

It is important to make overall planning for urban and rural subsistence allowances, integrate rural subsistence allowances with urban subsistence allowances, and narrow the income gap between poor urban and rural residents. It is also important to establish a mechanism for synchronizing urban and rural subsistence allowances with economic development, and steadily raise the level of subsistence allowances for urban and rural residents. By increasing re-employment, the subsistence allowance system can be linked effectively with employment and poverty alleviation and development policies. Full play must be given to the system of subsistence allowances for rural residents and the policy of poverty alleviation and development, so as to effectively ensure the basic livelihood of the rural poor, improve their income levels and their ability to develop themselves, and stabilize their food and clothing and achieve poverty eradication and prosperity as a result.

(2) The rural five guarantees system must be improved.

It is necessary to further standardize the management of rural nursing homes for the elderly, strengthen standardization and modernization, and provide a standardized and modernized feeding institution for rural five-guarantee households.[5] It is also necessary to constantly improve the centralized feeding standard of the five guarantee households according to the development level of rural economy and society, and to increase financial input to ensure funding for the maintenance, renovation and equipment upgrading of nursing homes.

(3) The urban and rural medical assistance system must be improved.

"Three-no" elderly,[6] important financially difficult families, and poor families living on minimum social security subsidy from which students/pupils and children come, the disable, low-income family members should all be fully insured with government subsidy. In addition, factory employees with financial difficulties, local migrant workers with financial difficulties, retirees of shutdown or bankrupt enterprises, and laid-off or jobless people should all be covered by urban basic medical insurance. The medical assistance system for major diseases and catastrophic diseases will have to be improved, and constantly expand the scope and level of assistance should constantly be expanded and heightened respectively. Great efforts should be made to strengthen medical assistance to "expenditure-type" poor families, effectively relieve the pressure of poor people to seek medical care, and prevent the occurrence of "poverty caused by disease".

3 Increasing Markedly the Proportion of Social Security Expenditure in Financial Expenditure

In the context of profound changes in internal and external conditions, the time and space constraints of economic transformation and upgrading and structural reform in the 13th FYP period have been

[5] **[The Translator's Notes]** "Rural five-guarantee household" refers to peasants/famers in rural villages with old, weak, orphaned, widowed, ill or handicapped folks who are beneficiaries of the five guarantees of food, clothing, housing, medical care and burial expenses.

[6] **[The Translator's Notes]** "Three-no" elderly refers to those with no children, no ability to provide for themselves, and no source of income.

strengthened comprehensively. To establish a modern public financial system by 2020 that meets the needs of economic transformation and to resolve the structural contradictions of economic transformation have become a major task for deepening reforms in the fiscal and taxation systems.

3.1 *Increase Social Security Spending*

In order to adapt to the increasing demand of the entire society for basic public service, during the 13th FYP period, expanding the expenditure of basic public services should be taken as the focus of optimizing the fiscal expenditure structure, while increase clear the goal of increasing the expenditure of basic public services should be made clear, so as to create favorable conditions for consumption pattern upgrading and consumption release, and provide new driving force for the development of service industry and of small and medium-sized enterprises and entrepreneurial innovation.

(1) The proportion of fiscal expenditure on basic public services needs to be increased.

During the 12th FYP period, expenditure on basic public services such as education, medical care and social security increased constantly, but the growth was relatively slow. During the 13th FYP period, although the growth of financial expenditure will slow down with the slowing of GDP growth, the growth of expenditure on such basic public services as education, medical treatment, and social security should not be slower than that for the 12th FYP period, but faster than that for financial expenditure, to provide favorable conditions for the release of consumer demand and provide financial security for fair and sustainable development. Suggestions are thereby put forward as follows:

① The proportion of State financial expenditure on such four basic public services as education, medical and health care, social security and employment, and government-subsidized housing will reach no less than 40% by 2016 from 35.1% in 2013, as a share of GDP increasing from 8.7% to around 10%. The gap between the levels of State financial expenditure on basic public services for urban and rural individuals will be controlled by less than 40%.

② The proportion of State financial expenditure on the above-mentioned four services will reach no less than 50% by 2020, as a share of

GDP increasing to around 14%. The gap between the levels of State financial expenditure on basic public services for urban and rural individuals will be controlled by less than 30%.

(2) The proportion of basic public service expenditure in GDP should be increased.

① The proportion of education expenditure in GDP needs to be increased. In 2015, China's financial expenditure on education as a share of GDP was only 3.9%. From the international point of view, this proportion is still significantly below the proportion of OECD countries or high-income countries respectively by 5.5% on average in 2009. Efforts have to be made to achieve the fiscal expenditure of around 5% of GDP by 2020.

② The proportion of medical expenditure in GDP needs to be increased. In the 12th FYP period, the proportion of China's fiscal expenditure on health care showed a marginal increase compared with the 11th FYP period. In 2015, the proportion of public expenditure on medical and health care in GDP rose by 1.76%. In order to adapt to the demand for medical and health services due to the fast ageing of population in China, to speed up the medical and health services demand, this proportion should be increased to 2.5% by 2020.

③ The proportion of social security and employment expenditure in GDP needs to be increased. Since 2007, the proportion of spending on China's social security in the State fiscal expenditure has shown a downward trend. It was 10.81% in 2015, which is lower by 0.13 percentage points than in 2007. The figure is not only far lower than that of developed countries by 30–50%, but lower than that of India and Thailand. In 2015, the proportion of China's expenditure on social security and employment in GDP registered 2.8%, and efforts must be made to increase the proportion to around 5% by 2020.

(3) A reasonable growth rate of fiscal expenditure should be maintained.

① The growth rate of fiscal expenditure needs to be controlled. Excessive growth of fiscal expenditure will put pressure on the growth of fiscal revenue, thereby squeezing the space for tax cuts. It is suggested that during the 13th FYP period the growth rate of fiscal spending should not surpass that of GDP by 1.5 percentage points, thus creating more space for tax cuts. It is possible to reach the target, according to the preliminary calculation. Even based on the estimate of the growth rate higher than that of GDP by 1.5 percentage points, China's fiscal spending as a share of GDP will by 2020 continue to increase from 24.7% in 2013 to 27.8%, which amounts to 24 trillion yuan (US$4 trillion), 1.7 times as many as 14 trillion yuan (US$2.33 trillion) in 2013.

② The proportion of economic constructive expenditure and administrative expenditures needs to be reduced. In 2013, the proportion of China's economic constructive expenditure in the public finance expenditure accounted for 39.7%, which is higher than the average level in OECD countries by around 10%, and the proportion of social welfare expenditure accounted for 36.9%, which is lower than the United States, Germany, and Japan by 20–30%.[7] In view of the requirements of economic transformation and upgrading, reducing the proportion of economic constructive expenditure and expenditure on basic government functions can not only provide more space for improving the proportion of basic public service expenditure, but also create space for reducing macro tax burden and force the transformation of government functions. In the 13th FYP period, it is necessary to strive to reduce the proportion of expenditures on basic government functions from about 23% to less than 20% and the proportion of economic constructive spending to less than 30%.

③ More than 30% of the dividends paid by state capital will be used to increase expenditure on basic public services. In recent years, for example, the amount of state capital earnings paid by Central enterprises that are appropriated to the public finance budget for social security and other areas of people's livelihood has increased, from 1 billion yuan (US$166.667 million) in 2010 to 6.5 billion yuan (US$1.083 billion) in 2013. It is proposed to increase the proportion of this expenditure from the current 13% to more than 30% in the 13th FYP period.

3.2 The Responsibility of Central and Local Social Security Expenditure Should Be Clarified

Judging from the actual situation in China, the division of administrative authority and expenditure responsibility of Central and local governments is not clear, reasonable or standard, which restricts the equalization of

[7] Gao Peiyong: *Reform in Fiscal and Taxation System and National Modernization*, China Social Sciences Press, 2014.

basic public services. To this end, to improve the division of administrative power and expenditure responsibility of Central and local governments, the priority is to make clear the responsibility of Central and local governments for social security expenditure (see Table 5).

(1) The division of responsibilities of Central and local governments for social security has to be made clear.

① The responsibilities of Central and local governments for social security has to be defined. From a macroscopic point of view, the responsibilities of the Central government for social security mainly consist of the following six aspects:

First, the overall planning of the national social security system, and the study and formulation of reform plans and policies concerning major social security;

Second, the formulation, promulgation and implementation of the national social security system, especially the laws and regulations on social security projects directly under the management of the Central government;

Third, the formulation, issuance and implementation of national social security policies, especially those under the direct control of the Central government;

Fourth, the construction of social security system and fund supervision system, including administrative supervision, social supervision, legal supervision system and system construction;

Fifth, the formulation and promulgation of laws and regulations on the investment and operation of the national social security fund, the construction of the investment and operation system of the centrally administered social security project, and the formulation and implementation of the policies and regulations on the supervision of investment safety;

Sixth, raising the level of social pooling of social insurance funds, allocating rationally the powers of different social insurance projects to the Central and local governments at all levels, and mobilizing the initiative of governments at all levels to manage social insurance funds.

② The social security responsibilities of local governments has to be clarified (see Table 6). Local governments, mainly as the implementing subjects of social security, assume the following responsibilities:

The first is to improve the local social security planning, policy implementation rules and supervisory methods, and establish a

Table 5 The division of authority over society security in countries with developed market economy

Country	*Government levels*	*Pension insurance*	*Unemployment insurance*	*Medical insurance*	*Public health*	*Social relief and social welfare*
The U.S.	Federal, state, and local governments	Federal responsibility	Federal/states' responsibility; the state is mainly responsible	Policy formulated by the Federal and executed by the states	States and local are mainly responsible; Federal is responsible for subsidy	Federal and states are jointly responsible; states are in charge; Federal is responsible for subsidy
Canada	Federal, provincial and local governments	Federal is responsible	Federal is responsible	Provincial is responsible; Federal is responsible for subsidy	Provincial and local are responsible; Federal is responsible for subsidy	Federal is responsible for pension; provincial is responsible for social welfare; Federal is responsible for subsidy
The U.K.	The Central government formulates unified policies; Central-government-dispatched agencies handle concrete matters; local governments provide supplementary social services					
Germany	Federal, state and city and town	Federal policies; social management	Federal is responsible	Federal policies; local execution	Provided by states, cities and towns	Federal is responsible for pension affairs; states and cities and towns for social relief

(continued)

Table 5 (continued)

Country	*Government levels*	*Pension insurance*	*Unemployment insurance*	*Medical insurance*	*Public health*	*Social relief and social welfare*
France	Central, department, and city and town	The Central government formulates policies; independent institutions are responsible for management	Central is responsible	The Central government formulates policies; independent institutions are responsible for management	Provided by cities and towns	The department governments are responsible for social relief; Central is responsible for establishing minimum living standards and providing social welfare subsidies
Australia	Federal, state and local	The Federal government has chief power; state and local governments provide community and health services				
Japan	Central, prefecture, city, town and village	The Central government is responsible for management and subsidy				Central and local are jointly responsible; cities, towns and villages for concrete affairs

Source The research group, Institute of Fiscal Science, Ministry of Finance. An International Comparative Study of Allocation of Authority in Basic Public Services among Governments. *Review of Economic Research*, Issue 16, 2010

Table 6 Division of social security responsibilities between the Central government and local governments

Items	*Division of responsibilities*			
	Policy and policy making	*Management and implementation*	*Supervision*	*Expenditure responsibility*
Old-age insurance, medical insurance, unemployment insurance, workers' compensation insurance, and birth insurance	The Central government formulates national planning and minimum standards	Provincial governments; city governments; county governments	The Central government; provincial governments	The Central government; provincial governments
Social assistance (the minimum life guarantee, medical assistance, social relief, etc.), basic old-age service subsidies, and special care and placement/resettlement	The Central government; provincial governments		The Central government; provincial governments	The Central government; provincial governments
Social welfare (orphans security, rural five- guarantee households, and funeral subsidies)	Provincial governments; city governments		Provincial governments; city governments	Provincial governments; city governments

Source The research group of China (Hainan) Institute for Reform and Development

macro-management mechanism for social security in line with local conditions.

The second is to implement practically all the functions and powers of the social security project funded by local governments, ensure the availability of all funds and supervise their use.

The third is that local governments shall make workable and carry out the Central government's plans, regulations and policies on social security, and formulate and disseminate detailed rules for the implementation of local plans, policies and regulations in line with local conditions.

The fourth is to assume the executive responsibilities of local governments, mainly including social preferential treatment and resettlement, and social relief and disaster relief. In terms of social welfare, local authorities are responsible for planning, policy implementation and fund raising and use. In public health, local authorities are also responsible for the planning and financing of public health, such as disease control and maternal and child care.

(2) The division of labor between the Central finance and the provincial finance in social security should be clarified.

The Central government's financial input focuses on addressing hidden pension liabilities, improving the minimum old-age security level, favoring lower-middle income earners, and keeping within a reasonable level the regional gap and the urban-rural gap in basic pension benefits. Provincial finance should accelerate the adjustment of expenditure structure, increase the provincial pooling of social security fund revenue and expenditure, and form a social security treatment adjustment mechanism suitable to the level of local economic development. Before the national pooling can be achieved, the provincial budget management should be improved ASAP, so as to achieve the provincial pooling practically.

(3) The social security transfer payment system of the Central and local governments should be improved.

Because the Central government and local governments have different responsibilities for financial resources and spending, local governments will face different levels of funding gaps in performing the relevant spending responsibilities as defined by the Central government's social security program.

The State Council's *Opinion on Reforming and Improving the Central Government's System for Local Transfer Payments* made it clear that the proportion of general transfer payments should gradually be increased to more than 60%. Over the past few years, the proportion of general transfer payments in China has gradually increased. In 2013 the proportion of the Central government's general transfer payments to local governments reached 57.1 and 58.2% in 2014.[8] It is expected to reach the target of 60% around 2016. In view of the need to narrow the financial gap of social security among different regions, the target of general transfer payment should be further raised in the 13th FYP period, and the proportion of general transfer payment should reach no less than 75% by 2020. On the basis of clarifying the social security powers of governments at all levels, a formulized and centralized transfer payment system should be established ASAP.

4 Giving Play to the Strategic Role of State-Owned Capital in Social Security

Establishing a fairer and more sustainable social security system by 2020 needs to give greater play to the strategic role of State-owned capital in social security. As the population ages and the dependency ratio rises, the social security system faces a serious hidden debt problem that cannot be avoided. The focus is to increase the injection of the State capital equity and operating income into social security funds.

4.1 Hidden Social Security Debts Need to Be Dissolved with State-Owned Capital

In the transition from planned economy to market economy, the social security system should also be reformed, but it will bring huge transformation costs. With the population aging and the dependency ratio increasing, the social security system faces a serious hidden debt problem. Based on China's actual situation, while adjusting the parameters of social security system, it is necessary to give play to the strategic role of state-owned capital to "provide against a rainy day" for the implicit debt that may appear in the social security in the medium and long term.

[8] State Council: Increasing the Proportion of General Transfer Payments While Intensifying Local Authority. www.cnr.cn, February 2, 2015.

(1) Social security still faces a huge funding gap.

① The number of provinces with the gap between revenue and expenditure in the short term is rising. In 2015, China's total revenue of social insurance fund was 4466.34 billion yuan (US$744.39 billion) with its total expenditure being 3935.67 billion yuan (US$655.95 billion), resulting in the total annual balance being 530.37 billion yuan (US$88.40 billion) and the year-end balance accumulated 5700.23 billion yuan (US$950.04 billion).[9] According to different data, after eliminating the financial subsidies, the net revenue of national social insurance premiums in 2013 was 1.8 trillion yuan (US$300 billion) while the expenditure was 1.9 trillion yuan (US$317 billion). In other words, the expenditure exceeded the revenue. At the same time, the social security revenue grew by 12.4%, whereas the expenditure grew 17.2%. If the trend continued like this, the social security funding gap would be bigger and bigger.

Judging from the situation of different regions in China, the gap between the eastern and western regions is relatively large. At the end of 2014, the accumulated balance of basic pension insurance funds of such provinces and cities as Guangdong, Shandong, Beijing, Zhejiang and Jiangsu all exceeded 100 billion yuan (US$16.67 billion), which constitutes the main source of the national pension balance. The pension gap of other provinces is covered by the balance of these provinces and cities. In 2014, after deducting financial subsidies from the basic pension insurance fund for enterprise employees, the number of the provinces whose current expenditure could not be covered by the revenue reached 22. Even if the financial subsidies were not excluded, the expenditure and the revenue still failed to balance each other in terms of the pension insurance fund for enterprise employees in Hebei, Heilongjiang and Ningxia (two provinces and one autonomous region).[10]

② The hidden debt of social security in the medium and long term will continue to expand. In terms of the hidden debt of China's

[9] Ministry of Finance. Report on the Implementation of the Central and Local Governments' Budgets in 2015 and on the Draft Budget of the Central and Local Governments in 2016. www.mof.gov.cn, March 18, 2016.

[10] Annual Report on the Development of China's Social Insurance in 2014. *China Labor and Social Security News*, July 1, 2015.

medium-and-long-term pension, many experts have done relevant calculation. For instance, the calculated result of Cao Yuanzheng's team is that the hidden debt of China's pension would be as high as 18.3 trillion yuan (US$3.05 trillion) by 2013.[11] According to the research of Ma Jun's team, if fiscal subsidies are assumed to remain at the same level in 2011, their accumulated balance will be exhausted by 2022, and then they will be in debt, with a cumulative gap of 37 trillion yuan (US$6.17 trillion) from 2013 to 2050.[12] Li Yang's team predicted that if the current pension system were continued, with the aging of the population, the national pension insurance for enterprise employees would be unable to cover the expenditure by 2023, resulting in a funding gap. By 2050, the proportion of the fiscal subsidy in the GDP, which is needed to maintain the working of the pension system, would reach 8.46%, while the proportion in the fiscal expenditure of the same year would reach 34.85%. In other words, more than one-third of the fiscal expenditure would be used to make up for the shortfall of pension insurance.[13] Studies by Zheng Bingwen's team show that in 2012 as a benchmark, the hidden debt of the social pooling account was 83.6 trillion yuan (US$13.93 trillion); the hidden debt of the individual accounts was 2.6 trillion yuan (US$433.33 billion); the hidden debt under the system of the unified account of basic pension insurance for urban workers was 86.2 trillion yuan (US$14.37 trillion), accounting for 166% of the GDP in 2012.[14]

Although the research perspectives and results differ slightly from team to team, the common conclusion reached is that the hidden debt scale of China's pension insurance will continue to increase, forcing the government to take action ASAP. Otherwise, the longer the delay, the greater the cost of future reform.

[11] Cao Yuanzheng et al.: Reshaping the State Capacity for Asset and Liability. *Caijing Magazine*, Issue 15, 2012.

[12] Ma Jun et al.: *A Study of China's National Balance Sheet,* Social Sciences Academic Press (China), 2012.

[13] Li Yang et al.: *China's State's Balance Sheet in 2013: Theory, Methods, and Risk Assessment,* China Social Sciences Press, 2013.

[14] Zheng Bingwen: *China Pension Report 2014—Transformation to the Nominal Account System,* Economy and Management Publishing House, 2014.

(2) Institutional arrangements for State-owned capital to make up for hidden social debts must be made.

① It is a common international practice to use State-owned capital to make up hidden debts of social security. Peru used some of the proceeds of privatization to pay down pension liabilities as it privatized state companies. Bolivia's government earmarked 30% of its shares in State-owned enterprises as the property of the new system's pension fund and into the pension accounts of all citizens over the age of 18. By selling off some of its State assets, Argentina used its revenue to make up for the shortfall in its pension fund. Some eastern European countries in transition also transferred part of their revenues from privatizing state assets into pension funds.

② Large amounts of State-owned capital can play an important strategic role. The empty account in the process of China's system transformation is rooted in the fact that in the past, the labor contribution made by "senior employees" out of enterprise employees was internalized into state-owned capital through low wages and low welfare. Therefore, the cost of transformation should be borne by the government's state-owned capital, not by enterprises and individuals.

China has the condition to solve the huge social security fund gap and the transformation cost, because it has the enormous State-owned asset and the State-owned capital revenue. In 2015 China's State-owned enterprise assets totaled 119.2 trillion yuan (US$19.87 trillion); the total profits of State-owned enterprises were 2302.75 billion yuan (US$383.792 billion), a decrease by 6.7% as compared with the previous figure of last year.[15] State capital can play a bigger role in building a shared society. Take the scheme of delayed retirement age for example. For every one-year delay in retirement age, the pension pooling fund can increase by 4 billion yuan (US$667 million) while reducing expenditure by 16 billion yuan (US$2.67 billion), narrowing the fund gap by 20 billion yuan (US$3.33 billion).[16] However, if the State-owned

[15] Department of Asset Management, Ministry of Finance: The Economic Operation of SOEs and State Holding Enterprises in China from January to December, 2015. www.mof.gov.cn, January 27, 2016.

[16] Feng Biao: The Deferred Retirement Policy to Be Out in the 13th FYP Period. *National Business Daily*, November 4, 2015.

Table 7 The proportion of Central SOEs' budget expenditure and people's livelihood expenditure in 2010–2014

Years	2011	2012	2013	2014
Operation budget expenditure of Central SOEs (billion yuan)	76.954	92.979	97.819	141.912
Social security expenditure (billion yuan)	4.0	7.01	8.429	20.558
Proportion (%)	5.2	7.5	8.6	14.5

Note Social security expenditure includes people's livelihood expenditure and social security fund expenditure supplemented by revenue from reduction of the State-owned shares
Source The outcome prepared by the research group of China (Hainan) Institute for Reform and Development is based on the calculation of data from the implementation of the Central and local governments' budgets and the draft of Central and local governments' budgets

capital gains are taken into consideration, even a supplement of 20 billion yuan(US$3.33 billion) a year to the social security fund would be less than a fraction of the annual profits of SOEs. Observed in many ways, the proportion of the State-owned capital gains used for social security and other livelihood expenditure was seriously low (see Table 7). Observed from the country's overall situation, the revenue from reduction of State-owned shares in 2014 that supplemented the national social security fund was 8.283 billion yuan (US$1.381 billion), which only accounted 0.33% of SOEs' operating profits. Observed from the situation of SOEs under the Central government, the proportion of Central State-owned capital operating budget expenditure in 2014 was 141.912 billion yuan (US$23.652 billion). Among them, the transferred public finance budget for social security and other people's livelihood expenditure was 18.4 billion yuan (US$3.07 billion), and the revenue from reduction of State-owned shares that supplemented the social security fund was 2.158 billion yuan (US$359.667 million), which make up 13 and 1.5% of State-owned capital operating budget expenditure respectively.[17] This means that the remaining 120 billion yuan (US$20 billion) was returned to the Central SOEs through different channels.

[17]Ministry of Finance: Budget Revenue and Expenditure of the Central Government's State Capital Operation in 2014. www.mof.gov.cn, February 5, 2015.

(3) The proportion of State-owned assets and public resources revenue should be increased to supplement the national social security fund.

① More State-owned assets, including State-owned bank assets and State-owned insurance assets need to allocated to social security funds, and the proportion can be increased to 30–50%. The proportion of the operating revenue of the assets not allocated but to be turned over to the public finance shall be increased to 30%, and no less than 30% of the turned-over profits shall be used to supplement the national social security fund.

② The proportion of income turned over by Central SOEs to the national social security fund needs to be increased in particular. According to the 2014 rules of the Ministry of Finance, the proportion collected from Central SOEs' State-owned capital gains shall be increased by 5 percentage points on the existing basis. With the increase of the proportion of State-owned capital operation income to be turned over to public finance and the increase of the proportion of supplementary social security fund, the national social security fund can get more capital injection.

③ The proceeds transferred from public resources need to be allocated to social security fund. China has a huge stock of public resources, which will be traded through the open market as market reforms are advanced. The Central government should form a mandatory mechanism ASAP, stipulating that 30% of the net proceeds from public resource transfers should be allocated to social security funds.

Special Citations [6-2]

The Proportion of Earnings Paid by Foreign State-Owned Enterprises

France: State firms pay about 50% of their after-tax profits to the government. Dividends of State-owned capital are turned over to the state treasury, and all the remaining profits after dividends are left to the enterprise, among which 60–70% are used as reserve funds and development funds, mainly used for reinvestment and compensation for losses and the rest are used for rewards and benefits of employees.

The United States: Because of the large budget deficit in the United States, government-sponsored enterprises (GSE) still take a voluntary approach every year to pay 30–50% of their after-tax dividends to the local state governments for government spending. Some states can also use the proceeds from federal government assets to pay dividends directly to the public.

Singapore: Temasek Holdings provides shareholders with an average annual return of more than 17% and pays an annual dividend of 7% to Singapore's Ministry of Finance. The proportion of dividends paid by State-owned enterprises is generally 35–70% of their profits, and even reaches the maximum of 80–90%.

Italy: 20% of the earnings of State companies are in corporate reserves, 15% in special funds for research and development, and the remaining 65% in the state treasury.

Source Ma Naiyun. Enlightenment to China from the Practice of Management and Earnings Collection of Foreign State-owned Enterprises. *Research of Finance and Accounting*, Issue 17, 2010.

4.2 Social Security Fund Must Be Built up by Transferring State-Owned Capital

The national social security fund is composed of funds allocated from the Central fiscal budget and those raised by other means approved by the State Council, which are used to supplement and adjust the social security expenditure. It is actually the national sovereign fund that plays a strategic supplementary role when a gap appears in the social security system. From the perspective of medium and long-term development trend, the social security fund in China is still relatively small in scale, and it needs to rely on State-owned capital to make a large scale ASAP to improve risk prevention capability.

(1) The contribution of State-owned capital to the national social security fund is insufficient.

① The size of the national social security fund is relatively small. The social security fund has grown over the years. By 2014, its assets totaled 1535.39 billion yuan (US$255.898 billion), but the proportion of pension reserves in the GDP was only about 2.41%, which is considerably

Table 8 The proportion of fiscal subsidies and transferred State-owned shares in the total equity of social insurance fund in 2001–2014

Year	*Total equity of national social insurance fund (billion yuan)*	*Net fiscal allocation (billion yuan)*	*The proportion of net fiscal allocation in the total equity (%)*	*Transferred State-owned shares (billion yuan)*	*The proportion of transferred State-owned shares in the total equity (%)*
2001	80.509	59.526	73.94	12.718	15.8
2002	124.186	41.576	33.48	8.81	7.09
2003	132.501	4.908	3.7	0.408	0.31
2004	165.986	27.854	16.78	4.703	2.83
2005	195.427	22.87	11.7	8.265	4.23
2006	272.416	57.424	21.08	N.A.	N.A.
2007	413.975	30.814	7.44	N.A	N.A.
2008	480.381	162.653	33.86	N.A	N.A.
2009	692.773	177.673	25.65	N.A	N.A.
2010	780.918	230.98	29.58	38.734	4.96
2011	772.765	315.219	40.79	16.101	2.08
2012	893.283	382.849	42.86	7.435	0.83
2013	1192.745	600.026	50.3	7.897	0.66
2014	1457.329	657.298	45.1	8.283	0.57

Source The calculation is based on the data from the National Council for Social Security Fund

smaller than that of developed countries. At present, the largest share of GDP is about 83% in Norway, 25% in Japan and 15% in the United States.[18]

② The contribution of State-owned capital financing is small. The social security fund is mainly fiscal subsidies, and the share of its financing from State-owned capital is very small (see Table 8). In 2014, the total equity of national social security fund was 1457.329 billion yuan (US$242.888 billion), including 657.298 billion yuan (US$109.55 billion) from allocated financial fund (*net*), which accounts for 45.1%, and 8283 million yuan (US$1380.5 million) from fund from reduction and transfer of State-owned shares and shares, which accounts for 0.57%. Since June 2009 when the *Implementing Measures for the Transfer of Some State-Owned Shares from the Domestic Securities Market to the National Social Security Fund* began to be taken, the cumulative transfer of domestic State-owned shares has been 106.574 billion yuan (US$17.762 billion). Since 2005 when the policy was adopted to change the reduction of State-owned shares in foreign countries to the transfer of those shares, the cumulative transfer of the shares amounted to 58.762 billion yuan (US$9.794 billion), and the cumulative transfer of State-owned shares both at home and abroad total 165.336 billion yuan (US$27.556 billion), which makes up 18.5% of the total equity of the current national social security fund.[19]

③ The minimum security amount of the national social security fund should be clarified ASAP. The national social security fund should lock in the potential gap of actuarial pension insurance every year, so as to form the minimum safety limit of the national social security fund and expand the scale of national social security fund ASAP. At the same time, almost all of the country's sovereign pension funds have legislative guarantees that they are tied either to fiscal revenues, or to the sale of state assets, or to GDP growth, or to the growth of foreign exchange reserves. Drawing on international experience, it is suggested to institutionalize and legalize the national social security fund through clear documents and legal forms.

[18]Wang Lei, Wang Likun and Pan Min: Pension Gap: Analysis and Remedy Measures. *Journal for Party and Administrative Cadres*, Issue 3, 2014.

[19]The calculation is based on *Annual Report on Fund of the National Council for Social Security Fund 2012*.

(2) State-owned capital should be taken as the main source of national social security fund.

① It has huge potential to transfer some State-owned capital to replenish social security fund. In 2009, the Ministry of Finance (MOF), State-owned Assets Supervision and Administration Commission (SASAC), China Securities Regulatory Commission (CSRC) and National Council for Social Security Fund (NCSSF) jointly issued the *Implementing Measures for the Transfer of Some State-Owned Shares from the Domestic Securities Market to the National Social Security Fund*, stipulating that "a joint stock limited company with State-owned shares which makes IPO and gets listed in the domestic securities market shall, unless it is otherwise provided for by the State Council, transfer some of its State-owned shares to the NCSSF, namely 10% of the actual number of the IPO stocks. If the number of shares held by the State-owned shareholder is less than the number of shares which should be transferred, the transfer shall be made on the basis of the number of the shares actually held by it." By the end of 2014, financially allocated national social security fund and shares totaled 657.298 billion yuan (US$109.55 billion), of which fund from reduction and transfer of State-held shares and shares amounted to 238.411 billion yuan (US$39.735), which accounted for 36.3%. In 2014, financially allocated national social security fund and shares were 55.264 billion yuan (US$9.211 billion), and fund from reduction and transfer of State-held shares and shares were of 8283 million yuan (US$1380.5 million), which accounted for only 15%.[20] Compared with the earnings of SOEs, their potential in supplementing social security funds is far from being realized.

Special Citations [6-3]

History of Transferring State Capital to Replenish the Social Security Fund

In September 1999, the Fourth Plenum of the 15th Central Committee of the Communist Party of China put forward for the first time in the *Decision on Some Major Issues Concerning the Reform and Development of*

[20] National Council for Social Security Fund. *Annual Fund Report of NCSSF in 2014.* www.ssf.gov.cn, May 29, 2015.

State-Owned Enterprises, "Various measures such as selling off some State assets and readjusting the fiscal spending structure should be taken to expand new fund-raising channels for social security program and replenish the social security funds."

In June 2001, the State Council promulgated the *Interim Measures on the Management of Reducing Held State Shares and Raising Social Security Funds*, stipulating that "Any of the joint stock limited companies (...) with its shares owned by the State shall, when issuing shares to the public investors for the first time or increasing the quantity of shares issued to the public investors, sell the State shares at 10% of the financing amount;... The income from the stock selling of State shares shall be totally turned in to the National Social Security Foundation." As soon as the "*Interim Measures*" was announced, there was an immediate uproar. A large number of investors reacted as "hogging money", so they "voted with their feet" and the stock market plunged in no time. The "*Interim Measures*" was suspended on 22 October 22, 2001 because of poor market performance.

In October 2003, the Third Plenum of the 16th Central Committee of the CPC approved the *Decision on Some Issues concerning the Improvement of the Socialist Market Economy*, which once again put forward "taking various ways, including transferring some state-owned assets according to law to replenish the social security fund". In the past 10 years, the State has transferred 10% of the IPO shares of state-owned enterprises to replenish the social security fund, with a total amount of about 230 billion yuan (US$38.33 billion). The social security foundation has managed and operated the transferred capital, which has increased in value year by year, and gained better investment returns, and thereby it has accumulated rich experience in the management of transferred assets.

In 2013, the Third Plenum of the 18th Central Committee of the CPC clearly proposed in its *Decision on Some Major Issues Concerning Deepening the Reform Comprehensively* that "part of State-owned capital should be transferred to replenish the social security fund". In 2015, the Fifth Plenum of the 18th CPC Central Committee proposed to "institute a fairer and more sustainable social security system, implement the national insurance scheme for all, realize the national pooling of basic pension for employees, transfer part of state-owned capital to replenish the social security fund, and comprehensively implement the major disease insurance system for urban and rural residents". This is a significant deployment to improve social insurance fund reserves and improve China's social security system in the new era.

Source The research group of China (Hainan) Institute for Reform and Development.

② It is important to strive to transfer 3 trillion yuan (US$500 billion) to the social security fund by 2020. According to estimates by China International Capital Corporation (CICC), if 10% of the State-owned equity is to be transferred every five years to the social security fund, which will remain till 40% by 2030, dividends after the discount will be equivalent to 25.2% of the GDP in 2014 (approximately 16 trillion yuan, or US$2.67 trillion), which can basically make up for the transformation cost. It is suggested to strengthen the top-level design of State-owned capital transfer to replenish the social security fund at the national level, and strive to transfer 3 trillion yuan (US$500 billion) of State-owned shares to the social security fund in the 13th FYP period.

Special Citations [6-4]

Estimates for 3 Trillion Yuan of State-Owned Shares to Be Transferred to the Social Security Fund in 2020

According to data from the *Annual Report on a Stock Market Value in 2014*, by the end of 2014, the A stock market value of 2592 listed companies in China's capital market hit the mark of 35 trillion yuan (US$5.83 trillion) for the first time, reaching 37.11 trillion yuan (US$6.185 trillion). In the performance of market value of various forms of ownership, the performance of state-owned enterprises is particularly remarkable. In 2014, the market value of listed SOEs under the Central government reached 15.1644 trillion yuan (US$2.5274 trillion). Over the same period, the total market value of the local SOEs reached 9.97143 trillion yuan (US$1.6619 trillion). According to this calculation, the total market value of China's State-owned enterprises in the A-share market in 2014 was 25.14 trillion yuan (US$4.19 trillion), making up 67.7% of the total market value of A shares.

According to the current accounting system, the State shares transferred to the social security fund are accounted by market value. Based on the net worth enjoyed by State-owned shareholders of holding companies under the Central government, if 3 trillion yuan (US$0.5 trillion) of assets are to be transferred to the social security fund by 2020, namely the transferred equity accounts for about 12% of the market value of State-owned enterprises, the net assets transferred during the 13th FYP period will on average make up only 2.4% of the net assets of the former State-owned shareholders. At present, China's State-owned listed companies have an annual value-added ratio of about 10%, so it is perfectly possible to achieve the goal of transfer during the 13th FYP period.

Source Calculation is done by the research group of China (Hainan) Research Institute for Reform and Development.

(3) Specific measures need to be designed for the direct allocation of State-owned capital to social security funds

① It is necessary to increase the proportion of State-owned shares transferred to the social security fund. When State-owned assets are under IPO, the proportion of funds allocated to the social security fund should be considered to increase from 10% to around 30%.

② It is necessary to transfer State-owned capital in some competitive domains directly to the social security fund. It is also necessary to transfer a portion (more than 51%) of the shares of SOEs (including financial enterprises) with excessive State holdings.

③ It is necessary to transfer earnings from State capital operation to the social security fund. Drawing on the experience of developed countries, the proportion of profits paid to public finance by State-owned capital should be transferred to the social security fund by at least 50%.

4.3 The Management Methods of Social Security Funds Need to Be Improved

To transfer some State-owned capital to the social security fund and more state capital gains to social security has raised new requirements for improving the social security fund management system. Accelerating the innovation of the social security fund management system has become a major task of improving the social security system.

(1) Imperfect management system increases the pressure on value preservation and appreciation in fund.

Although the cumulated balance of social insurance fund is constantly increasing, due to the low level of pooling, the system and mechanism of maintaining and increasing the value of the pension insurance fund used for current payment in various regions are not sound, and the rate of return of investment in pension insurance fund is on the low side. The State Council first formulated the *Measures for the Administration of Investment in Basic Pension Insurance Funds* in August 2015, but much work remains to be done to implement them. Studies have shown that if funds from the individual accounts of basic pension insurance had gone into the market for investment operation since 1998, according to the calculation of investment performance (8% annualized returns) of the National Council for Social Security Fund, as of 2011, there would have been 3.8 trillion yuan (US$633.33 billion) in the cumulative balance after deducting the annual payment. In 2012, however, the pension insurance fund had a cumulative balance of only 24 trillion yuan (US$4 trillion) after the annual deduction. Based on this estimate, the balance of pension fund in the hands of the local government led to an annual loss of investment income, namely more than 100 billion yuan (US$16.67 billion), which results in a total loss of 1.3 trillion yuan (US$216.667 billion). Therefore, it is necessary to reform China's investment system of social security fund ASAP.

(2) The investment field must be broadened and investment management be optimized for national social security fund.

① The investment structure needs to be improved and the proportion of separate or self- operation be reduced (see Table 9). From the practice of the National Council for Social Security Fund in the past few years, the investment yielded better results with the average annual rate of returns being 8.5%. In 2015, the fund equity investment income amounted to 228.704 billion yuan (US$38.117 billion) with the rate of return on investment (ROI) being 15.14%, which hit an all-time high. The key to further improving the management level of social security fund is to adjust the investment structure, reduce the proportion of self-operation and expand the proportion of entrusted investment. It is suggested to further reduce the proportion of self-operation on the basis of selecting excellent investors, and strive to gradually reduce it to about 40% by 2016 and about 20% by 2020. The National Council for Social Security Fund should not focus on self-operation but on, through the clear and reasonable procedures for appointment and removal, appointing or electing the board of trustees or the board of directors, while

Table 9 The proportion of self-operation and entrusted investment in national social security fund in 2003–2014

Year	*Total assets under management (billion yuan)*	*Self-operation (billion yuan)*	*Trusted operation (billion yuan)*	*The proportion of self-operation (%)*
2003	132.5	100.61	31.887	75.93
2004	171.14	109.88	61.267	64.2
2005	211.79	138.76	73.029	65.52
2006	282.77	177.11	105.66	62.63
2007	439.69	232.75	206.94	52.94
2008	562.37	305.79	256.58	54.38
2009	776.62	414.51	362.12	53.37
2010	856.69	497.76	358.93	58.1
2011	868.82	504.11	364.71	58.02
2012	1106.037	650.667	455.37	58.83
2013	1241.564	669.774	571.79	53.95
2014	1535.639	771.812	763.827	50.26

Source *Annual Reports on National Social Security Fund 2003–2014*

supervising asset managers effectively, establishing an effective accountability system, and enhancing the transparency of fund management (see Table 10).

② A competition mechanism needs to be introduced. The investment experience of pension fund in Chile can be used for reference in selecting the client. The first is to establish various fund systems to form competitive markets. The second is to let the government change from restricting investment products to restricting risks and simplifying the restrictive rules on investment in social security funds.

③ The investment field needs to be expanded. In view of the general trend of industrial transformation and upgrading, it is forward-looking to invest in some strategic emerging industries. For example, "green investment" and "low-carbon economy" are becoming a new trend for the strategic adjustment of investment in pension fund after the financial crisis. In 2009, ATP, the Danish social security fund, announced a sustainable "green" strategic investment plan to invest in forests and a new type of asset. In a 2009 report to the parliament, Norway's Ministry of Finance said that the Government Pension Fund-Global (GPF-G) would invest US$33 billion over the next five years in environmental industries in emerging markets as a sustainable asset class. With the continuous

Table 10 Returns of investment of the National Council in 2001–2014

Year	*ROI (billion yuan)*	*ROR (%)*	*Inflation rate (%)*
2001	0.742	1.73	0.7
2002	1.976	2.59	−0.8
2003	4.471	3.56	1.2
2004	3.672	2.61	3.9
2005	7.122	4.16	1.8
2006	61.979	29.01	1.5
2007	145.35	43.19	4.8
2008	−39.372	−6.79	5.9
2009	85.043	16.12	−0.7
2010	32.076	4.23	3.3
2011	7.337	0.84	5.4
2012	64.536	7	2.6
2013	68.587	6.2	2.6
2014	139.0	11.43	2

Source National Council for Social Security Fund

development of China's green industry and other industries, the social insurance fund can carry out an exploration of playing a greater role in the green industry and other strategic industries. In addition, the State government prioritizes the involvement of certain pension funds when arranging large projects such as energy and transportation. Pension funds are permitted and encouraged to take equity stakes as strategic investors in the restructuring and listing of key State-owned enterprises.

④ The separation of government and enterprise investment in national social security fund should be promoted. Take Norway. According to Norway's *Government Pension Fund Act*, the Ministry of Finance, which is responsible for pension funds under the Pension Fund Act, commissions the Norwegian Central Bank to manage the GPF-G, develop investment strategies and conduct risk and return assessments. In 1998, the Norwegian Central Bank established Norges Bank Investment Management to be responsible for the specific operation of pension fund, and based on the investment criteria and investment strategies, to independently select objects and opportunities for investment, and to maximize long-term benefits under moderate risks. It is suggested to use Norway's experience for reference and discuss the way of separating government and enterprise suitable for investment in China's national social security fund.

(3) Local pension funds need to be revitalized on the basis of ensuring safety.

① It is necessary to entrust the national social security fund with investment. At present, China has 2.4-trillion-yuan (US$0.4 trillion) pension funds dispersed in over 2000 pooling units/areas nationwide, with the investment channel remaining narrow. Compared with the CPI, the channel is constantly "shrinking". In August 2015, the State Council promulgated *Measures for the Administration of Investment in Basic Pension Insurance Funds*, which clearly states that after the balance of the pension insurance fund of each province, autonomous region and municipality directly under the Central government is set aside for a certain amount of payment according to the *Measures*, the specific amount for investment can be determined and then entrusted to the agency authorized by the State Council for investment operation.

As the rate of return on investment by the national social security fund is relatively high every year, the fund has a rich experience in investment. Since the establishment of the national social security fund, its annual ROR on investment has been 8.29% on average. When the conditions are not yet ready for investment made by the social security funds at the local level, they can entrust the national social security fund with its way to invest, and the entrusted fund investment operation adopts the operating way of integrating into the united account of the existing social security fund, unifying asset allocation and unifying income calculation, while publishing the principal and earnings regularly and realizing the value preservation and appreciation. In 2012, for example, the Guangdong provincial government commissioned the National Council of Social Security Fund to invest and operate 100 billion yuan (US$16.667 billion) from the balance of basic pension insurance for urban workers in Guangdong, becoming the first province in the mainland to make a trial investment in the stock market with local pension fund.

② It is necessary to purchase special national debt. The Central government/finance issued one-year targeted government bonds to local pension funds at a rate slightly higher than the net return on bank deposits (adjusted for inflation). By buying certain government bonds issued by the State at higher interest rates than bank deposits, the security of the social security fund is guaranteed and its value is maintained. It is suggested that according to the saving of local pension funds, the

Ministry of Finance should issue about 2 trillion yuan (US$0.333 trillion) of special national bonds, and encourage and force the local governments to use the saving social security funds to buy them. The interest rate is between the average investment income of general national debt and national social security fund. Treasury bond funds are injected into the national social security fund which is responsible for investing.

③ It is necessary to explore the establishment of a local social security fund to support the "provincial pooling". For provinces with relatively good local financial resources, the establishment of local councils for social security fund can be explored to inject local State-owned assets into the fund. For example, Shandong province published the *Opinions on Deepening the Reform of Provincial State-Owned Enterprises and Improving the Management System of State-Owned Assets*, transferring some State-owned capital to replenish the provincial social security fund. Meanwhile, the provincial council of social security fund needed to be established to undertake the management of transferred State-owned capital of provincial enterprises, perform the function of the investor, explore and promote the equity diversification of State-owned enterprises and the construction of modern enterprise system. The provincial finance department and the State-owned assets supervision and administration authority perform the supervisory function against the provincial council of social security fund according to law. Specific measures for the transfer, management and use of state capital shall be formulated separately. It is clear that the establishment of a provincial social security fund involves a series of institutional arrangements, including the division of social security rights and responsibilities of the Central and local governments, as well as the ultimate responsibility of local finance and social security. This needs to work out the top level design program ASAP.

Special Citations [6-5]

Shandong Takes the Lead in Launching and Completing the Transfer of State-Owned Assets to the Social Security Fund

On May 18, 2015, the government of Shandong Province held a ceremony to officially transfer 30 percent of the State-owned capital of the three State-owned enterprises under the provincial government, namely Shandong Energy Group Co., Ltd., Shandong Airport Group Co.,

Ltd., and Shandong Province Salt Industry Group Company to replenish the social security fund. More than 3.3 billion yuan of State-owned capital in Shandong were officially transferred to the newly-founded provincial council of social security fund, which not only indicates the key step taken in the reform of State-owned enterprises in Shandong, but also more means that the policy about "transferring State-owned assets to replenish the social security fund" which had appeared in the Central government's file for eleven years is no longer a "theory" only. According to the 2014 annual financial reports and paid-in capital status of the capital-transferring enterprises, after the transfer, the Shandong provincial council for social security fund held the paid-in capital of 3 billion yuan, 240 million yuan and 65 million yuan and 400 million yuan of Shandong Energy Group, Shandong Airport Group and Shandong Salt Industry Group respectively. The total transfer of State-owned capital exceeded more than 3.3 billion yuan (US$550 million).

Ten days later, the second transfer started again. Fifteen SOEs under the provincial government, including Lucion Group, transferred 30% of the total equity and 14.76 billion yuan of the State-owned capital officially to replenish the provincial social security fund. The State-owned Assets Supervision and Administration Commission of the Shandong Government and the provincial council of social security fund council shall exercise the shareholder's rights in accordance with the proportion of 7:3. Among these 15 enterprises, all are Level-1 SOEs under the supervision of the provincial SASAC, including several large enterprise groups with hundred billion yuan of assets, except the one that has not yet completed the company system transformation. So far, 18 enterprises in Shandong under the provincial government have transferred more than 18 billion yuan (US$3 billion) of State-owned capital equity to the social security fund. By now, the SOEs under the Shandong government have completed the transfer of State-owned capital to the social security fund.

Source The research group of China (Hainan) Institute for Reform and Development.

④ It is necessary to set up a specialized pension fund management company.

Judging from the experience of various countries, it is a basic trend to accelerate the diversification, marketization and specialization of investment in social security fund. Internationally, the investment management system of basic pension insurance fund is divided into three modes: the first mode concerns the "government investment operation", such as in the United States, New Zealand, and Ireland. The government will entrust the basic pension insurance fund directly to a specific government agency led by the Ministry of Finance. Pension assets are almost exclusively based on buying national bonds or special government bonds, completely cut off from the market. The second mode is about the "market institution investment and operation". For example, the Chilean government directly hands over the pension insurance fund to several licensed pension companies for investment and operation. The companies are competitive and can be eliminated eventually. These companies also undertake one-stop services such as social insurance premium collection and pension payment. The third one involves the "special agency investment operation", such as in Canada and Japan. The governments of these countries will entrust the basic pension insurance fund to specially founded investment institutions to implement the operation mode of marketization, diversification and internationalization. These specialized institutions are authorized by law and organized by the governments, and have modern corporate governance structure.

Judging from China's actual situation, to achieve the diversification, marketization and specialization of pension investment, it is urgent to set up specialized pension fund management companies. This could be the second or the third mode to be adopted. The pension fund management companies have professional investment institutions responsible for the investment and operation of the pension fund. The pension management institutions establish the investment management framework and set up departments according to the requirements of financial market business, while hiring professional talents to set up investment teams.

CHAPTER 8

Promoting Government Reform with a Focus on Regulatory Changes

In the 13th FYP period, market regulation has a strong particularity. For one thing, with the upgrading of consumption pattern, the release of domestic demand potential is directly dependent on the effectiveness of market regulation. For another, the lagging transformation of market regulation has become the "biggest short board" in further promoting the reform of streamlining administration and decentralization. In this context, both further streamlining and decentralization, and upgrading the consumption pattern and releasing the potential of domestic demand directly depend on the effectiveness of market regulation.

The important basis and precondition for stimulating market vitality and the vitality of enterprises are the forming of effective market governance. Accelerating regulatory transformation with the goal of forming an effective market governance system has become a major task of structural reform. In general, the regulatory reform affects the overall reform of the government. It involves not only the change of government regulatory mode, but also the adjustment of deep administrative power structure and the change of government concept. This will be a profound "self-revolution" of the government.

F. Chi, *Winning at the Turning Point*, The Great Transformation of China, https://doi.org/10.1007/978-981-32-9479-0_8

1 Regulatory Transformation as a Main Trend for Decentralization Reform

The reform of streamlining administration and delegating power since the second half of 2014 was quite different from that in the past. It put forward a new idea of "combining the decentralization and control", which requires all departments to take strong measures to strengthen and improve supervision while delegating power. In the new situation, the important goal of regulatory reform is to move from market regulation to market governance.

1.1 The Decisive Role of Market Is Subject to the Lagging Regulatory Transformation

Government reform focusing on streamlining administration and delegating power is the biggest highlight of this government, which has played an important role in unleashing market vitality, promoting economic transformation and addressing downward pressure on the economy. However, from the frequent occurrence of food and drug regulation problems in recent years and the abnormal fluctuations of the stock market in 2015, it could be seen that the regulatory transformation lags behind the reform process of streamlining administration and delegating power, which is significantly different from the actual demand of expanding domestic demand and stimulating consumption and the expectations of social members. In general, the lagging regulatory transformation has become the "the largest short board" in the in-depth development of decentralization.[1]

(1) The lag of regulatory philosophy is universal.

Under the modern regulatory model, administrative examination and approval is separated from supervision, which is mainly a case of in-process supervision and *ex post facto* supervision. Prior administrative examination and approval can be abolished as much as possible, so as to maximize the vitality of the market. In the third party assessment survey under the State Council in 2015, the research group of China (Hainan)

[1]Chi Fulin: Regulatory Transformation is the Key to Deepening Decentralization Reform. *Administration Reform*, Issue 9, 2015.

Institute for Reform and Development found that in terms of the concept many administrative departments still regard both administrative examination and approval and supervision as one and the same thing, emphasizing "whoever approves supervise". In reality, it often evolves into "administrative examination and approval departments are equivalent to supervisory departments" and "less approval, less supervision; no approval, no supervision", etc. Practice has proved that this is not conducive to the reform of the administrative examination and approval system, nor to the improvement of the supervision system in and after the matter.

(2) Supervision methods are old-fashioned and social participation in supervision is seriously inadequate.

① Regulatory technology is backward. Many departments are accustomed to the traditional methods of "large inspection, open inspection and secret inspection, cross inspection, tour-like inspection and spot inspection". Although in 2015 the State Council issued *Several Opinions on Using Big Data to Strengthen Service for and Supervision of Market Players*, the current big data application has not been popular; such business systems as industry and commerce, taxation, local tax, quality control and more as well as the administrative examination and approval work platform at the provincial level in many provinces have not yet achieved information exchange and resource sharing. So it is difficult to form a big data cooperative supervision. Since 2015, there have been safety accidents occurring quite often in various places, like the sinking of SS Oriental Star, the explosion in the Tianjin seaside new area, and the landslide at Shenzhen, which are directly related to backward regulatory technology.

② Supervision lacks a social credit base. Under the modern supervisory mode, the supervision needs to be based on the social credit of enterprises. Under the current supervisory mode in China, however, the social credit system has not been established yet, and some enterprises do not get due punishment for violating the integrity, manufacturing and selling fake products. For example, under the condition of prior administrative approval, the bank is more confident of government approval documents than of the enterprise's credibility when the latter approaches the bank for loan. This makes it difficult for the current supervisory mode to get rid of the dependence on administrative approval, while weakening the effectiveness of supervision.

③ The supervision of social participation is seriously inadequate. "Business has its ways, and trade its rules" This is China's ancient rules. Trade associations and chambers of commerce have played an irreplaceable role in promoting corporate integrity and self-discipline. Under the current system, however, trade associations and chambers of commerce tend to be more administrative. In terms of supervision, the government's "one-man show" is relatively common, while trade associations and chambers of commerce are seriously short of credibility and lacking in self-discipline, which makes it difficult for them to play the leading role of traditional "trade association" effectively.

(3) Substantial breakthroughs have yet to be made in the reform of the supervisory system.

① The system of "integration of administrative approval and supervision" has not been completely broken yet. "Administrative examination and approval" and "supervision" mean administrative powers of different nature. Only strict separation from each other can ensure their own effectiveness. Despite the establishment of various supervisory institutions in China, the institutional arrangement still has the prominent feature of "integration of administrative approval and supervision". For example, some institutions have the power of approval, price regulation and monopoly industry supervision. China Securities Regulatory Commission, China Banking Regulatory Commission and China Insurance Regulatory Commission are not only the examination and approval agencies of market access, but also professional supervisory agencies. This makes it difficult for the regulators themselves to keep their interests detached and exercise their supervisory powers independently.

② The situation that supervisory institutions are too many to make a concerted effort has not been completely changed. In recent years, local governments have carried out an experiment on the integration of supervisory institutions. Shenzhen, Shanghai, Zhejiang, and Tianjin have set up a market supervisory administration (commission) of their own by integrating the related departments in industry and commerce, quality supervision, and food and drug, but the Central government has failed to keep up in establishing an integrated supervisory institution, which has made the local experiments function without being able to go beyond the local limitations. The structural streamlining of the State

Council in 2013 only integrated the supervisory functions of food and drug with many supervisory functions still scattered in other related departments. For example, the Ministry of Agriculture is responsible for supervising the quality of edible agricultural products; the National Health and Family Planning Commission is responsible for the formulation of food safety standards and risk assessment; and supervision of food and drug advertisements is undertaken by the industrial and commercial administration.

③ The professional construction of supervisory departments lags behind seriously. This is reflected not only in the lagging professional construction of the supervisory team, but also in the lack of supervisory standards, which are far lower than those in developed countries. Because of the low regulatory standards, domestic consumers are often discriminated against. In 2015, for example, the media reported, "The cakes produced and sold by Starbucks in China contain raw material for soles". Starbucks responded, "The substance is indeed added to the cake product, but the dosage is in accordance with relevant regulations in China."

(4) Regulatory legislation lags behind.

Observed from the experience of developed countries, statutory regulatory functions, statutory procedures and statutory organizations are important safeguards to ensure the independence, authority and specialization of supervision, as well as to standardize supervision. Since the reform and opening-up in 1978, the regulatory legislation in China has been seriously lagging behind, and the foundation of legal supervision is still relatively weak. For example, the content of anti-administrative monopoly is not included in the *Anti-Monopoly Law*. As the *Securities Law* has not been amended, the registration system reform that originally planned to be launched in the second half of 2015 is inevitably constrained. The *Urban Comprehensive Management Law* has not come out for a long time, and the urban management law enforcement based on administrative regulations has become increasingly passive.

1.2 The Market Can Be Stimulated and Enterprises Be Freed up Through Regulatory Transformation

Economic transformation and upgrading depend on a dynamic market, fair competition and the breaking of the policy and institutional constraints faced by entrepreneurship and innovation of enterprises. At present, in the context of accelerating economic restructuring, especially increasing downward pressure on the economy, what is needed is to increase the intensity of decentralization, to stimulate market vitality and to strictly prevent "putting the market in the cage of power".

(1) It is important to implement the enterprise independent registration system.

① The reform of business registration system has promoted the rapid growth of market players. In the last two years, governments at all levels have sped up the pace of the enterprise industrial and commercial registration system reform, fully implementing a series of measures to lower down the threshold of market access, like changing from the subscription system of registered capital to the paid-in system, from "applying for an administrative permit before acquiring the business license" to "acquiring a business license before processing the administrative permit", and from the enterprise annual inspection system to the enterprise annual reporting system. Specifically, it has highly simplified the procedures of enterprise registration, improved the relationship between the government and the market, and inspired the vitality of market players effectively. For instance, from processing the permit and license in various departments to issuing the permit and license at the same time, further from changing the business license with three respective numbers to the business license with one code. According to statistics, in 2015, the national new market players totaled 1479.8 million, an increase by 14.5% over the same period of 2014. Their registered capital (money) amounted to 30.6 trillion yuan (US$5.1 trillion), an increase by 48.2% over the same period of 2014. Both figures have hit an all-time high.[2]

② There is still a great need for reform of the business registration system. Since October 2015, the registration mode of "three-in-one license" and "one code and one license" has been comprehensively promoted across the country. After the reform, the business license loaded with the unified social credit code that is issued by the industry and commerce administration department is the license from which

[2] National Market Players' Development, Market Competition Environment and Market Consumption Environment in 2015. *China Industry and Commerce News*, January 14, 2016.

the organization code and tax are both canceled. The cycle of business establishment is thus shortened. Local data show that in the past it took a maximum of 48 legal days to complete the business registration, but now a maximum of 3 days only.[3] Even so, there is still a lot of room for reform in the commercial system. First, compared with developed countries or regions, the registration of Chinese enterprises is still not simple enough. For example, business registration in Singapore takes just three hours to complete online. Hong Kong set up a one-stop service called "Easy to Register" in 2011, which allows businesses to register within as short as an hour. Second, after the implementation of the registration system of "three-in-one license" and "one code and one license", due to insufficient policy coordination between departments, individual businesses have been "rejected" by relevant public administrative departments in handling the organization code certificate. Third, the enterprise registration is easy, but enterprise cancellation change is even more difficult. Enterprise deregistration still has to needs the audit by such departments as national tax, local tax, industry and commerce, bank, and quality supervision, each of which has an auditing cycle.

Special Citations [7-1]

Individual Businesses Have Been "Ignored" by the Relevant Administration After the Implementation of "Three-in-One License"

Since October 1, 2015, the registration system of "three-in-one license" and "one code and one license" has begun to be implemented in all parts of the country. While the new system, in which the business license, organization code certificate and tax registration certificate are integrated into one certificate while one license bears one code only, is in full swing, individual businesses have been caught in a dilemma when dealing with the organization code certificate.

Due to business needs, Ms. Huang, who is in urgent need of replacing the organization code certificate to unlock the public account, has been twice denied of the request for such a replacement by the relevant administrative department, which has been no longer responsible for serving individual businesses after the implementation of the new system.

[3] Hubei Issues the First Business License with One Code Only, Fully Implementing the Reform of "3-in-1 License" Registration System. www.people.com.cn, September 11, 2015.

That is why Ms. Huang has twice been on the wrong side of the door while individual businesses have been ignored.

The reporter noted that such encounters, like Ms. Huang's, are now widespread across the country. On the message board of the website of the national organization code management center, many individual businesses have left comments asking for solutions to related problems. They've received the same answer from the center: The center is fulfilling the relevant documents of the State Council and related requirements of the State administration of quality supervision, inspection and quarantine.

After the inquiry, the reporter found that in August 2015, the six departments including the State Administration for Industry and Commerce (SAIC) and General Administration of Quality Supervision, Inspection and Quarantine (GAQSIQ) jointly issued *Opinions of the General Office of the State Council on Accelerating the Progress of the "Three-in-One License" Registration System Reform*, which clearly points out that from October 1 on, the nationwide industrial and commercial administrative departments at all levels are ready to issue and load business licenses with the unified code for the new enterprises and enterprise change, making no mention of individual businesses.

The other day, however, the GAQSIQ issued the *Notice on Implementing the Registration System Reform of "Three-in-One License" and "One Code and One License"*, which clearly indicates that individual businesses are included in the *Notice*. It says that starting from October 1, 2015, the organization code management agencies at all levels will no longer issue and replace the organization code certificates to enterprises, farmers' professional cooperatives and individual businesses. The code certification window should make corresponding announcements and explanations according to the *Notice*.

"Now there is a fast knot. We have been informed by the GAQSIQ that all operations should be suspended, but the industrial and commercial department hasn't taken over the job yet." Explaining the issue to *Workers' Daily* on October 27, a staff member from the administration of quality supervision, inspection and quarantine in Zhengzhou, said the policy among the various functional departments has not been coordinated in the final analysis. Referring to the plight of individual businesses, the staff member said that there was no solution yet. It was not possible to tell when. We had to wait and see what the State governmental departments would say. According to the reporter, the SAIC is coordinating with the GAQSIQ, which are expected to solve the problem and come out with next measures and schemes ASAP.

Source Yu Jiaxi and Min Yaping. Individual Businesses Are Ignored after the Implementation of "3-in-1 License". *Workers' Daily*, November 2, 2015.

③ The enterprise independent registration system shall be fully implemented. When entering the era of "Internet plus", the technical conditions and opportunities are ripe for enterprises to register independently. It is suggested that the experience of Singapore and Hong Kong be used to fully implement the enterprise independent registration system starting from "the 13th FYP period". First, on the basis of implementing the one-stop enterprise registration in the four PFTZs, it is important to establish a nationwide unified enterprise independent registration network platform ASAP in line with international standards on enterprise registration time. Second, policy coordination should be strengthened among the departments to incorporate individual businesses into the implementation of the registration system of "three-in-one license" and "one code and one license" ASAP. Third, the reform should be accelerated to promote the easy cancellation system for enterprises. On the basis of the current pilot program, the easy cancellation procedures should be implemented soonest for individual businesses, enterprises that have not started business, and enterprises with no creditor's rights and liabilities.

(2) It is necessary to cancel the filing system of general investment projects.

① It is an important breakthrough from the investment approval system to the filing system. Before 2004, both government investment projects and enterprise investment projects were subject to the approval system, which played an important role in the industrial layout at the initial stage of China's economic takeoff. However, with China's accession to the WTO, such an examination and approval system is more and more difficult to adapt to the development of domestic and foreign markets, and its disadvantages are being increasingly exposed, which hinders the free flow of elements and is not conducive to activating the market. In 2004, the State Council issued the *Decision on the Reform of the Investment System*, which clearly stipulated that "all projects which enterprises do not use government investment for constructing will no longer be subject to the examination and approval system. The approval system or filing system shall be applied to different cases".

Since the international financial crisis in 2008, China's economy has been under increasing downward pressure due to the dual influence of the domestic and foreign markets. However, the investment environment of domestic enterprises has not been improved to a greater extent, the domestic market potential is difficult to be effectively released, and economic growth is sluggish. During the national "two sessions"[4] in 2013, a member of the CPPCC pointed out that "108 stamps are still a must for investing in a project". This has not only affected the efficiency of enterprise investment, but also not been conducive to stimulating market vitality. From the perspective of preliminary practice, in the past two years, governments at all levels, from top to bottom, have strengthened the reform of the administrative examination and approval system, which focuses on streamlining administration and delegating power, and fully implemented the filing system of corporate investment projects, thus playing an important role in further relaxing control of enterprises' investment.

② Investments that are only necessary for official records system still, in practice, have to be examined and approved in an otherwise way. The original intention of implementing the investment record system is to reduce the administrative examination and approval links as much as possible, shorten the time enterprises spent in handling the procedures with the relevant government departments, and improve the efficiency of the government. Observed from the international experience, the main significance of enterprise investment filing is to report for official records or to notify. The main purpose is to make the government convenient to grasp the investment information of enterprises, and monitor and analyze the investment operation, thereby guiding the social investment. Theoretically, the filing system should be a relatively convenient way, which is conducive to enterprise investment facilitation. In practice, however, filing in some places is generally given the significance of examination and approval, and even takes more time than examination and approval, which is criticized by all kinds of market players. Some departments still adopt the process standard of approval system, and they implement the filing system nominally, which is replaced from time to

[4] **[The Translator's notes]** "The two sessions" refer to the annual sessions of the National People's Congress (the NPC) and the Chinese People's Political Consultative Conference (the CPPCC).

time by examination and approval in a hidden way. This has reduced the effect of the filing system tremendously. For example, some local governments have adopted the policy allocation of public resources by setting up financial support projects and scientific and technological innovation projects, which has factually become a disguised examination and approval. Objectively speaking, the filing system of enterprise investment projects still belongs to the preset administrative control, which cannot effectively reduce the unfair competition and illegal behaviors of enterprises, and may become a disguised examination and approval. Therefore, it is highly necessary to carry out further reforms in the administrative examination and approval system, focusing on streamlining administration and delegating power to lower-level governments.

③ It is necessary to cancel the filing system of general investment projects. Under the condition of market economy, under the premise of the government's strict management of urban and rural planning, land use, environmental protection, and production safety, the general investment project of an enterprise shall be decided by the enterprise according to laws and regulations, and no longer needs to be put on the official records of the administrative department. Currently, starting from the actual effect of strengthening the administrative examination and approval system reform, in order to promote rapidly the CPC spirit of removing the blockage in innovation and development, overcoming the pains affecting business and entrepreneurship, and eliminating blind spots in market regulation, the status of corporate investors needs to be established, so as to timely cancel the filing system for enterprises' general investment projects and return the decision-making power of investment completely to the enterprises.

(3) It is essential to replace industrial policy with fair competition policy.

① Certain industrial policies have promoted overcapacity. During the international financial crisis in 2008, China introduced some industrial revitalization plans, which played an important role in expanding the scale of investment and maintaining steady economic growth. Objectively speaking, however, in recent years, overcapacity is directly related to the inappropriate industrial policies of the government to a large extent. In order to attract investment, some development zones and industrial parks have introduced industrial policies such as "zero land price" and "tax refund", which further aggravates the vicious competition among local governments, increases the tendency of local protectionism, affects the efficiency of resource allocation and violates the market principle of fair competition.

② Generalized industrial policies would be easy to distort the investment behavior of market players. Under the conditions of modern market economy, some specific industries, such as agriculture, have protection policies in all countries, but not all industries can implement preferential industrial policies, which can easily discourage market fair competition, cause the imbalance of supply and demand relations artificially, and hinder the use of market mechanisms to automatically adjust the supply and demand relations and absorb excess capacity. In recent years, the imbalance between the government and the market is largely related to the government's industrial policy, which leads to the market players' excessive dependence on the industrial policy. Observed from the actual situation, the preferential degree of local industrial policies is different, which urges some enterprises to decide the investment behavior by comparing local industrial policies. In this way, it intensifies the vicious competition among local governments, leads to blind investment and repeated construction in some regions, and leads to serious industrial isomorphism. In addition, enterprises' excessive dependence on industrial policy will cause the enterprises to become so weak as not to be able to cope with the market risk. Some enterprises are not focused on exploiting the market and improving the operation and management, but ever ready to find a way to take advantage of the loopholes in the industrial policy, to obtain the government subsidies even through improper means, and to seek government support, once the market volatility. If things go on like this, it will form a "vicious circle". As a large number of industrial funds are scattered in different sectors, some enterprises, driven by interests, repeatedly apply for financial support to different sectors after "packaging" the same investment project in different ways, which is not conducive to the rational allocation of industrial funds. Some industrial policies are well intended to support innovation, but they are also hard to achieve. For example, in order to obtain a large amount of research and development funds, some enterprises do not focus on research and development, but on the effort to obtain financial funds.

③ Industrial policies are not to be used at all or used as little as possible. In the *Decision on Some Major Issues Concerning Comprehensively Deepening Reform*, the Third Plenum of the 18th Central Committee of the CPC proposed "letting the market play a decisive role in the allocation of resources and giving play to the better role of the government".

This is to make a clear definition of the boundary of the government and the market, to speed up the government's decentralization to the market, and to give full play to the institutional role of market in resource allocation, while limiting the government's main responsibilities in public service. In practice, the growth of a large number of innovative enterprises such as Huawei and Alibaba is not the result of government industrial policies. On the contrary, some companies have long relied on government policy support and have not been far along in innovation. Under the conditions of market economy, one of the main responsibilities of the government is to create a good market environment, to use industrial policies as little as possible to intervene in enterprises' investment behaviors, so that all kinds of market players can decide their investment behaviors according to market changes. For this reason, it is necessary to change the practice of direct allocation of resources through government selection, government subsidies and administrative guidance, to clean up and abolish all kinds of preferential policies and government subsidies to guide industrial development ASAP, and to change the situation that the government artificially distorts market signals and unfair competition.

1.3 An Effective Regulatory Framework Should Be Formed

In the 13th FYP period, the key to transforming the traditional market regulation mode into the innovation of market governance is to transform the concept of government regulation and initially form a multi-governance pattern under the joint supervision of government and social forces.

(1) The forming of effective market governance needs to be promoted through regulatory transformation.

① It is essential to make the transition from prior approval to in-process supervision and ex post facto supervision. Observed from the experience of developed countries, modern supervision simplifies the process as much as possible in advance supervision and implements the negative list system, which can lower the threshold of market access for enterprises and maximize the vitality of enterprises and the market. However, the liberalization of the entry threshold for enterprises does not mean that the government remains blindly laissez-faire, which requires the adoption of more stringent regulation for in-process and post-event supervision.

During the 13th FYP period, the government's micro-economic management mode is moving towards negative list management as the number of items subject to prior administrative approval is greatly reduced. In this specific context, during the 13th FYP period, the primary task of China's regulatory transformation is to transform from prior approval to in-process and post-event supervision.

② It is important to make the transition from decentralized supervision to unified supervision. The supervision mode formed in China at present has the outstanding characteristic of decentralized supervision. In practice, decentralized supervision has done more harm than good and is not sustainable. In 2015, for example, it involved both banking industry and securities industry, and it was difficult to distinguish between the responsibilities of China Banking Regulatory Commission and those of China Securities Regulatory Commission. Similar phenomena like "regulatory vacuum" were too many to count, which fully demonstrated that the traditional model of decentralized supervision has been unable to adapt to the new situation. The Third Plenary Session of the 18th CPC Central Committee clearly pointed out that unified market regulation should be implemented. In other words, the transition from decentralized supervision to unified supervision should be realized ASAP during the 13th FYP period, which has become one of the important tasks of supervision transformation.

③ It is significant to make the transition from administrative supervision to law-based supervision. Under the current system, the regulatory institutions mainly exercise their functions and powers according to administrative levels, unable to gain independence and difficult to form a professional team. With the implementation of the "Belt and Road Initiative" and the PFTZ strategy, building an international business environment has become a strategic choice to stabilize economic growth expectations and promote economic transformation and upgrading. In this specific background, it is both realistic and urgent to promote the transformation of market supervision from administrative type to legal type.

(2) A multi-market governance system will basically be formed by 2020.

① It is necessary to develop innovation in market supervision system and mechanism. In line with the management of negative list and based on the principle of strict separation of market supervision from administrative examination and approval, it is advisable to comprehensively sort out the matters that need to be supervised by all departments, and to speed up the establishment of a sound supervision system for consumer market, a financial market supervision system and a monopolistic industry supervision system, establishing a relatively complete in-process and post-event supervision system by 2020.

② It is necessary to establish the information sharing mechanism of supervisory departments. Local governments need to basically realize the barrier-free exchange of information between industrial and commercial departments, examination and approval departments, industry authorities and other departments.

③ It is necessary to initially establish a unified market supervision model. In the principle of reducing the administrative level, integrating the supervisory teams and improving the efficiency of supervision, a unified market supervision team must be set up to form the joint force of supervision. Furthermore, it is advisable to improve the interdepartmental response mechanism and punishment mechanism for breach of trust, and form a joint punishment mechanism for any person who will be restricted everywhere once s/he violates the law somewhere.

④ It is necessary to form a diversified market governance system basically. While emphasizing the main responsibility of the government, full play should be given to the self-disciplinary role of industry organizations, and the supervisory role of professional market service organizations, the public and public opinion, so as to promote the self-restraint and honest management of market players, and effectively play the unique role of social forces in market supervision. By 2020, the government will be the main body, with the general public, social organizations, and news media forming a joint force that participates in market supervision, basically creating a diversified market governance system.

(3) A regulatory framework for the rule of law will preliminarily be established by 2020.

① It is necessary to achieve legal supervisory responsibilities. The supervisory legal system will be preliminarily improved, and every right of supervision and the setting of every supervisory body will be legally justified and accountable.

② It is necessary to realize legal supervision procedures. Important breakthroughs will be made in restricting the discretion of the supervisory authorities through legal procedures, while strictly regulating the exercise of supervision and law enforcement power.

③ It is necessary to realize the legal establishment of supervisory agencies. In accordance with the law, the establishment of supervisory agencies should be standardized reasonably, and the establishment of supervisory agencies be inclined to grassroots law enforcement teams, so as to form a strong institutional guarantee for the professionalization of supervisory teams.

2 Accelerating the Transformation of Market Supervision System

The deep-seated problem of lagging supervisory transformation lies in the lagging reform of supervisory system. In practice, without an in-depth reform of the supervisory system, no substantial breakthroughs would be made in the transformation of consumer market supervision, monopoly industry supervision and supervisory approach. Accelerating the innovation of the supervisory system will become an inevitable major issue for the supervisory transformation in the 13th FYP period.

2.1 No Separation of Examination and Approval from Supervision Is a Prominent Contradiction in Supervisory Transformation

At present, market supervision still maintains the prominent feature of "integration of administrative examination and approval and market supervision", and the contradiction of replacing supervision with administrative examination and approval is more prominent. Excessive preset examination not only inhibits market vitality, but also fails to guarantee the effectiveness of ex post facto supervision. To truly establish a fair and just market order, it is proper to rely on market supervision instead of administrative examination and approval, which requires strict separation of administrative examination and approval from market supervision.

(1) Administrative approval and market supervision belong to different management functions.

① The emphasis of administrative examination and approval and that of market supervision are different. Administrative examination and approval is a means for administrative organs to check in advance, chiefly for the purpose of restricting acts detrimental to public interests and preventing citizens and legal persons from abusing their rights and freedoms, which has certain discretion, mainly including dozens of specific means like examination and approval, confirmation, approval, identification, registration, recognition, recording, inspection, and annual check. Market supervision is the behavior of restricting and limiting market operation activities, including such functions as standardization, supervision, and investigation and prosecution. Therefore, administrative examination and approval and market supervision have essential differences in scope and degree. Under the condition of modern market economy, administrative examination and approval and market supervision are two matters of different nature: prior examination and approval is the administrative power of the government, and the power list should be defined according to law, whereas effective market supervision is mainly a matter of in-process and post-event supervision, rather than a preset examination and approval. As far as possible, therefore, the less the preset approval may be, the better the result will be. In-process supervision and ex post facto supervision really need to be strengthened.

② Market supervision based on administrative approval is not sustainable. Under the traditional system, the market supervision is dominated by the preset administrative examination and approval, which is to check at all administrative levels for enterprises, severely inhibiting the market vitality. Meanwhile, however, the institutional arrangements for in-process and ex post facto supervision are relatively weak. Under the condition of modern market economy, administrative examination and approval and market supervision are different powers, both of which need legal evidence. With the full implementation of the negative list management in the 13th FYP period, both the consumer market and the anti-monopoly field are facing the problem of reconstructing the existing market supervision system while slashing the administrative approval items.

(2) The function of administrative approval and that of market supervision have to be separated.

① The strict separation of the function of administrative approval from that of market supervision is imperative. For many years, the system of non-separation of administrative examination and approval from market supervision has not only led to the problems of laying stress on examination and approval while giving less heed to supervision, but also led to the problem of rent-seeking corruption. Since the second half of 2013, several current or former officials in administrative approval departments across the country have reportedly been removed from their positions for corruption. The important institutional root cause behind these officials' removal lies in the fact that administrative examination and approval are not strictly separated from market supervision and that officials have too much power of examination and approval. In the 13th FYP period, the establishment of a fair competitive market order puts forward various reform demands for the strict separation of the functions between administrative examination and approval and market supervision. Only by the strict separation of both functions can the respective chief responsibilities of administrative examination and approval and market supervision be carried out. Likewise, only by the strict separation of the two can the reform in market supervision institutions be pushed through. The same is true of the closed supervision mode which can possibly be overcome, so as to move towards the open and transparent market supervision, and effectively stamp out power rent-seeking and corruption.

② The strict separation of functions between administrative approval and market supervision must be separated. Currently, the negative list management model has begun to be explored in multiple areas. Take the securities market for example. The goal of the next reform is to realize the registration system of IPO, which means that the securities market will bid a final farewell to the era of access to administrative examination and approval. Therefore, it is necessary to strengthen the supervisory function of the securities market on the basis of the strict separation of functions between administrative examination and approval and market supervision. In the next two to three years, with the implementation of the negative list management model in the domains of finance, energy, infrastructure and public services, it is necessary to achieve the strict separation of administrative approval from market supervision, and strengthen the function of market supervision.

(3) The administrative approval must be separated from market supervision.

① The separation between the examination and approval authority and the supervision authority must be realized. Although China has introduced a lot of laws and regulations on market supervision in recent years, the implementation effect is not quite good. An important cause is that the right to examine and approve and the right to supervise have not been separated for a long time. For this reason, some departments that need to retain the examination and approval items should be scientific, standardized and efficient. Administrative examination and approval and market supervision should be strictly separated from each other.

② Comprehensive and authoritative market supervisory institutions must be founded. Due to the unreasonable allocation of supervisory function and supervisory power structure, the supervision of the same matter is often dispersed in multiple departments. Although some institutions have been adjusted at present, they are far from being in place in terms of consumer market supervision, monopolistic industry supervision and other aspects. They still have a long way to go from the effective supervision system under the condition of modern market economy. Therefore, it is necessary to integrate the supervisory institutions at the national level and establish comprehensive and authoritative institutions of market supervisory ASAP.

③ The independence and professionalism of market supervision institutions must be realized. Under the conditions of modern market economy, the authority of market supervision is realized mainly by the independence and professionalism of supervisory agencies, rather than simply by the will of department leaders. If the market supervision department is frequently interfered with by the superior leaders, it is difficult to exercise the supervisory power impartially and independently. It is suggested that the market supervision institutions be given the quasi-legislative authority and administrative discretion to formulate administrative regulations or normative documents, which are enjoyed by the government or administrative departments at the same level, so as to accelerate the de-administration of the market supervision institutions.

2.2 Supervisory Transformation in Key Fields Needs to Be Promoted

In the 13th FYP period, it is necessary to grasp the overall situation and highlight the key points, focusing on releasing the domestic demand potential to achieve supervisory transformation, while striving to make important breakthroughs in the transformation of financial supervision, consumer market supervision, and monopoly industry supervision.

(1) The transformation of financial supervision needs to be accelerated.

① The transformation of financial supervision is at an important juncture. Both to boost confidence in economic development and to speed up economic transformation and upgrading depend on a healthy and stable capital market. Despite the implementation of the "circuit breaker mechanism" for a period of time, the stock market was still unable to stop its volatility and forced to suspend. The problem is that the root cause of the frequent occurrence of financial risks caused by a supervisory vacuum has not been eradicated. The financial industry has entered the large-scale operation mixed with banking, securities, and insurance. For example, the Ping'an Insurance (Group) Company of China, Ltd. owns banking, insurance, securities, trust and other financial services. In addition, the Internet and traditional finance began to infiltrate each other, and Internet companies such as Tencent and Alibaba began to set foot in payment business, and continued to move into securities, trust and other fields. Under such circumstances, the system of separate financial supervision has been seriously unadapted to the needs of mixed operation, facing the historical challenge of transformation.

② The transformation from separate financial supervision to mixed financial supervision must be achieved. Under the system of separate supervision, each supervision department usually only focuses on its own jurisdiction. In the abnormal fluctuations of the stock market in 2015, some insurance funds frequently raised their cards to listed companies, which became the focus of social attention. At present, the stability of the capital market is not only confined to the securities industry, but also needs the supervisory departments related to banking and insurance industries for full cooperation. Although the State Council issued the document in 2013 asking the Central Bank to organize the System of Interdepartmental Joint Meeting on Financial Supervision and Coordination, it has not been able to effectively prevent the risks due to multiple stock market volatility. Therefore, it is imperative to establish a unified financial supervision system ASAP. Furthermore, it is necessary to learn about the practice of mixed supervision that changed from separate supervision in the European and American countries, to speed up the perfection of the coordination mechanism of the People's Bank of China, China Securities Regulatory Commission, China Banking Regulatory Commission and China Insurance Regulatory Commission, and to form

Table 1 American, British, Japanese, and German modes of financial operation and models of supervision

Countries	*Operation modes*	*Supervision models*
The U.S.A.	Mixed operation	Umbrella functional supervision
The U.K.	Mixed operation	Uniform supervision
Japan	Mixed operation	Uniform supervision
Germany	Mixed operation	Uniform supervision

Source The table is prepared by the research group of China (Hainan) Institute for Reform and Development

the institutional arrangements of mixed financial supervision ASAP (see Table 1).

③ A capital market supervision system oriented to protecting investors' rights and interests must be established. It is a persistent disease in China's capital market in which more attention is paid to financing function than investor protection function. The key to the supervisory transformation of the capital market in the new stage is to change the traditional supervisory ideas and methods of capital market supervision, which focus on financing rather than on investor protection, forming the institutional constraint that listed companies are responsible to investors.

First, it is necessary to establish a mandatory dividend mechanism to form a delisting mechanism for long-term non-profit-sharing listed companies. A listed company is required to pay dividends within a certain period of time. If no dividend is distributed after a certain period, the company will be delisted automatically.

Second, it is necessary to learn from the American experience and establish the class-action lawsuit system ASAP to protect the interests of small and medium-sized investors.

Third, it is necessary to increase the intensity of penalties for criminal offenses in the securities industry, support investors in filing civil claims in accordance with the law, and hold accountable those who are responsible for their criminal liability, so as to form a long-term mechanism for guiding value investment and curbing excessive speculation.

Fourth, it is necessary to form a strong capital market emergency mechanism. It is also necessary to establish a linkage mechanism between fiscal and monetary policies and form a synergy among various departments, including supervisory departments, to stabilize capital markets.

Special Citations [7-2]

"Capital Market Policy-Backed" Lifeboat Package Should Come Out ASAP

At present, many policies have been issued on the basis of "capital market policy support", but they still need to be further improved and institutionalized.

1. The bottom line of capital market intervention is determined. For example, supervisory agencies shall make the promise of strong intervention when the index is below a certain point, giving the market stable expectations.
2. The introduction of major reform schemes shall be sped up to boost confidence in capital market. These schemes concern, for example, the opening up of the service sector market, structural tax cuts, and the reform of mixed ownership of State-owned enterprises, which will provide substantial benefits to the formation of the capital market.
3. An institutionalized financing mechanism shall be formed by taking the China Securities Finance Corporation Limited (CSF) as the main body. The CSF has played an important role in stabilizing the stock market, but has not been professional enough in crisis response. It is suggested to form a national capital market stabilization fund which is nonprofit, specialized and standardized.

Source China (Hainan) Institute for Reform and Development. Deepening Reform to Streamline Administration and Delegate Power with the Focus on Supervisory Transformation (24 Suggestions), *Economic Information Daily*, September 11, 2015.

(2) The potential of domestic demand shall be unleashed by transforming the consumer market.

① It is necessary to accelerate the supervisory transformation of consumer market with the focus on the establishment of traceability system. Since the 1990s, the United States, the European Union, and Japan have gradually introduced the traceability system for the whole process of identification of consumer goods, emphasizing the supervision of the whole process of production, harvest, processing, packaging, transportation and sales to avoid product safety accidents caused by omissions in any link. At present, the traceability technology of domestic products has been implemented in the fields of food, medicine, cosmetics, health care products and agricultural products. However, the standards for product traceability are uneven, and are mainly dominated by enterprises, so it is difficult to truly gain consumers' trust. It is suggested that the quality supervision department should take the lead to establish a third-party consumer product traceability platform authoritative at the national level, form a unified standard, realize whole-process traceability, guarantee the authenticity and integrity of traceability data information, and establish the traceability and recall system of problematic products on this basis.

② It is a must to crack down on the production and sale of fake commodities in the consumer market with severe punishment and severe law. Fake and inferior commodities have become an important factor to restrain consumption. Both the traditional consumption market and the network consumption market are full of fake and inferior commodities. According to the spot checks by the State Administration for Industry and Commerce in the second half of 2014 on key commodities from such main e-commerce platforms as Taobao, Tmall, Jingdong, and YHD, of the 92 different batches of samples for inspection, only 54 batches of samples were quality goods, with the rate of standard products being 58.7% and the rate of nonstandard ones reaching 41.3%.[5] Whether to stimulate consumption or to create a safe and healthy consumption environment, it is necessary to strengthen the fight against counterfeiting in the consumer market. For this reason, it is suggested that first, the penalties for counterfeiting activities should be increased, and the illegal cost of counterfeiting activities should be greatly increased. Second, public security departments need to be requested to work together to combat counterfeiting, while those criminals will be referred to judicial organs. Third, administrative enforcement of intellectual property rights and judicial protection should be strengthened, so as to create a favorable legal and market environment for IPR protection. Fourth, inter-regional coordination needs to be strengthened to establish cross-regional supervisory agencies and thoroughly break down local protectionism.

[5] More than 60% of the Goods Inspected on Taobao Are Unqualified. *Beijing Daily*, January 24, 2015.

③ It is important to accelerate the formation of the institutional framework for comprehensive supervision of consumer market. From the perspective of international experience, the implementation of the Central-level vertical management is an important means by which the world's developed countries overcome the failure of consumer market regulation. From the practice of China's consumer market supervision, it is learned that market supervision functions are scattered in industry and commerce, food and drug administration, and quality supervision bureaux. In the past two years, all parts of the country have begun to explore a unified and comprehensive market supervision system, thoroughly breaking the past pattern of "each department responsible for its own area" and realizing unified supervision of the consumer market. The problem is that this reform still stays at the city and county levels, whereas the reform at the Central and provincial levels has not yet been carried out, resulting in an awkward situation of "one area under the jurisdiction of three departments". Whether to transform government functions or to straighten out the relationship between the Central government and local governments, it is necessary to speed up the reform of the Central and provincial supervision systems in the 13th FYP period, so as to form a unified supervision system for consumer markets from the Central government to local governments and achieve the vertical management from the Central to local.

Special Citations [7-3]

Developed Countries Generally Adopt the Vertical Management Model of Consumer Market Regulation

Developed countries generally adopt the practice of layout of key regions for supervision, coordinate the division of supervisory powers between the Central government and local governments, and effectively mobilize the initiative of all levels. Across countries, there are three general patterns.

First, it is the geographical distribution pattern represented by the United States. Federal regulators set up several agencies according to the geographical region. The Food and Drug Administration has a vast number of field offices, including five regional offices in the central, northeast, southeast, southwest and Pacific regions, 20 regional offices and nearly 200 surveillance checkpoints.

Second, it is the administrative classification model represented by Japan, whose two-level supervision system includes the Central government and local autonomous prefectures such as *to* (metropolis/capital), *do* (circuit), *fu* and *ken*. At the Central level, Japan has set up agencies such as the department of consumer safety and the food and drug administration, which are responsible for transnational regulatory affairs and guide the local authorities to do a good job in supervision. Most administrative permits and daily supervision are handled by local authorities.

Third, it is the model of single regulation represented by Germany. Its federal consumer protection and food safety authority, for example, uniformly regulate markets.

Source The research group of China (Hainan) Institute for Reform and Development.

(3) Regulatory transformation focusing on the elimination of administrative monopoly in the service sector must be achieved.

① An administrative monopoly examination mechanism needs to be established. For many years, it has been difficult to liberalize social capital in the service industry. The key problem is that administrative monopoly in the service industry has not been truly included in the scope of anti-monopoly. Since 2013, China has stepped up anti-monopoly investigations in domestic and foreign enterprises. Transnational enterprises such as GSK (GlaxoSmithKline), Merck, Microsoft, Chrysler and Audi have been investigated. Especially in 2014, China imposed a fine of 1.8 billion yuan (US$3 million) on domestic and foreign-funded enterprises, setting a historical record.[6] With the expansion of service market, anti-monopoly is very necessary to ensure the healthy development of the service industry.

First, anti-monopoly should be normalized and institutionalized, with equal supervision over domestic and foreign-funded enterprises. Whoever monopolizes will be investigated. It is not allowed at all to engage in selective law enforcement, and take sides.

Second, for addressing many current administrative monopolistic activities, there are administrative documents, such as regulations, rules or opinions. Relevant industrial policies and guidance documents that need to be issued by the administrative departments should be filed with

[6] Experts on Anti-Monopoly Fines: Whoever Monopolizes Will Be Investigated. www.zaobao.com, January 3, 2015.

the anti-monopoly committee, and an anti-monopoly examination mechanism should be established.

Third, it is necessary to carry out systematic anti-monopoly examination of the current administrative regulations ASAP, and abolish all kinds of administrative regulations leading to administrative monopoly.

②The supervision standard system of service market needs to be improved. Observed from the international experience, excessive regulation in the service sector will hinder innovation, and inadequate regulation will lead to Gresham's law, or "bad money drives out good" in terms of enterprises. The key problem is that the regulation should have scientific standards. For example, the U.S. government's regulation of the service industry focuses on maintaining market competition order and social public interests, restricting excessive or unfair competition, preventing social risks, and actively promoting the signing of documents such as Trade in Service Agreement, Agreement on Financial Services, and Agreement on Basic Telecommunications. It is suggested to establish regulatory standards in the service industry, which is developing rapidly, innovating quickly and prone to problems. In the producer services industry, focus will be given on accelerating the construction of regulatory standards for Internet finance, e-commerce, research and development, and design.

③ Negative list management of market access in the service sector needs to be realized. It should be recognized that under the conditions of market economy, "everything which is not forbidden is allowed" should be a basic principle. Currently, the service industry still carries out strict administrative approval procedures, which largely restricts the development of service industry. Observed from the national situation, the 16th meeting of the Central Leading Group for Comprehensively Deepening Reforms discussed and adopted the *Opinions on Implementing the Negative List System on Market Access.* Hereby it is suggested:

first, to promote the negative list of market access ASAP, and constantly reduce the length of negative list according to the actual operation;

second, in coordination with the negative list, to speed up the issuance of a list of powers of governments at all levels, so as to truly lock power into the cage of the system;

third, to introduce ASAP a list of responsibilities for governments at all levels, with a focus on market regulation and public services, so as to create a new situation that will force market regulation and reform of the public service system.

2.3 The Reform of the Supervisory Power Structure Should Be Advanced

Supervisory transformation is not a simple technical problem, and it touches on the adjustment of the deep administrative power structure. In view of the overall enhancement in reality and urgency of the supervisory transformation in the 13th FYP period, with the goal of strengthening unity, professionalism and authority, the market supervisory agencies shall be adjusted and optimized ASAP, so as to form institutional guarantee for the effectiveness of consumer market supervision, monopoly industry supervision and financial supervision.

(1) A unified national financial supervisory institution needs to be established.

① Conditions are ripe for the establishment of a unified financial supervision system. Observed from all aspects of the current situation, it is more urgent to adjust the financial power structure. In addition to the need to strengthen the overall planning with coordination between financial supervisory agencies in order to stabilize the capital market, as the innovation of "Internet + finance" continues to emerge and the trend of mutual penetration and intercrossing among banking, securities, insurance and other financial institutions increases, it poses a practical challenge to the separate business supervision model.

② The State administration of financial supervision needs to be established. Strengthening the unity and coordination of capital market supervision is crucial for effectively preventing financial risks. Judging from the abnormal fluctuations of the stock market since 2015, it is urgent to integrate the functions of China Banking Regulatory Commission, China Insurance Regulatory Commission, and China Securities Regulatory Commission and establish the state administration of financial supervision, forming a financial supervision system with "unified leadership, hierarchical responsibility, and integration of departments at different levels". China Banking Regulatory Commission, China Insurance Regulatory Commission, and China Securities Regulatory Commission shall be the executive agencies of the State Administration of Financial Supervision in accordance with the principle of "mutual restriction and coordination of decision-making power, enforcement power and supervision power".

(2) A unified national consumer market supervisory agency needs to be established.

① The time is basically ripe for the establishment of a unified consumer market supervisory agency. Observed from the national level, it is basically mature to establish a unified consumer market supervisory agency. In particular, the era of "Internet plus" has provided important conditions for the establishment of a supervisory system covering the whole process of production, circulation and consumption. At present, many local governments have established comprehensive market supervision bureaux and achieved good results. The 13th FYP period needs to push this reform further and deeper ASAP.

② The national consumer market supervision commission needs to be established. Entering the 13th FYP period, to strengthen the supervision of national consumer goods needs to establish a nationwide unified supervision system for the consumer market and improve the authority, independence and professionalism of market supervisory agencies. Therefore, it is suggested to integrate ASAP the functions of China Food and Drug Administration, General Administration of Quality supervision, Inspection and Quarantine and State Administration of Industry and Commerce in the aspects of consumer product safety supervision. These three institutions serve as the executive bureau of the state market supervision administration, making them independent and professional consumer product safety supervision agencies.

Special Citations [7-4]

The US's CPSC Functions as a Reference

The Consumer Product Safety Committee (CPSC), is a federal agency. Its chief responsibility is to establish standards and regulations for the safety of consumer products and supervise their implementation. It manages over 15,000 products, mainly household appliances, children's toys, fireworks and other consumer goods used in homes, sports, entertainment and schools. However, such products as vehicles, tires, ships, weapons, alcohol, tobacco, food, medicines, cosmetics, pesticides and medical instruments shall not be subject to its jurisdiction.

Take children's toys for example. The inspection items include flame retardancy, disassembly, etc., and the existing or potential danger and harmfulness of children's toys are assessed to prevent children from being damaged. This kind of examination is not to be difficult for enterprises, but to be responsible for consumers. It is not the production quality of the enterprise that is checked, but the safety in the use of the product.

The standards and regulations set by the CPSC are meticulous. For example, the safe use of refrigerator takes into account whether children can get out safely if they climb in. The safe use of lighters takes into account whether children under 5 years of age can light or burn themselves. Other specialized agencies are responsible for safety issues such as motor vehicles and supplies for the disabled, which are not under the CPSC's management.

The management means of CPSC are mainly: (1) fine; (2) exposure of TV media; (3) recall of problem products if necessary; (4) solving problems through legal procedures.

Source The material is prepared by the research group of China (Hainan) Institute for Reform and Development.

(3) A unified national anti-monopoly agency must be established.

① It is necessary to unify anti-monopoly functions. Since the promulgation of the *Anti-Monopoly Law* in 2007, anti-monopoly law enforcement work under the leadership of the Anti-Monopoly Committee of the State Council has been administered respectively by the anti-monopoly bureau of the Ministry of Commerce, the price supervision and inspection bureau of the National Development and Reform Commission and the anti-monopoly and anti-unfair competition law Enforcement bureau of the State Administration for Industry and Commerce. From the perspective of anti-monopoly law enforcement practice, it is difficult to coordinate the investigation and punishment of the three anti-monopoly agencies, and the effect of anti-monopoly is greatly reduced. It is imperative to unify anti-monopoly functions.

② It is necessary to establish a unified national anti-monopoly bureau. To integrate the anti-monopoly legal enforcement powers of the anti-monopoly bureau of the Ministry of Commerce, the price supervision and inspection bureau of the National Development and Reform Commission and the State Administration for Industry and Commerce, and to establish a unified national anti-monopoly bureau as the direct executive body of the State Council.

③ It is necessary to implement a unified anti-monopoly system. The first is to implement unified market supervision standards and rules for enterprises of different ownership to substantially increase the effectiveness of anti-monopoly. The second is to consider the reform of administrative examination and approval departments as a whole, and transfer the personnel of the preset examination and approval institutions to the anti-monopoly law enforcement agencies as much as possible. The third is to gradually establish a legalized and standardized anti-monopoly system applicable to both domestic and foreign capital in line with international practices.

Special Citations [7-5]

Comparison of Plans for Establishing a Unified National Anti-Monopoly Enforcement Agency

Drawing on the establishment of anti-monopoly executive agencies in various countries in the world and taking into account the actual situation of anti-monopoly in China, there are two options available:

Plan 1: The national anti-monopoly bureau directly under the State Council shall be established. It is fully empowered to conduct anti-monopoly professional affairs and fully supervise monopoly phenomena in all economic fields. To prevent local protectionism, an independent supervision could be considered to be under the vertical management of the Central government.

Plan 2: The anti-monopoly law enforcement powers scattered in the three departments of the Ministry of Commerce, National Development and Reform Commission and State Administration for Industry and Commerce shall be integrated into the Ministry of Commerce, so as to establish the vertical management system of anti-monopoly institutions, and unify the supervision of domestic and foreign capital.

Source It is designed by the research group of China (Hainan) Institute of Reform and Development.

3 Creating a New Method for Market Supervision with Big Data as the Focus

Maintaining market order is the common responsibility of the whole society, which needs to form the joint force of the whole nation. While emphasizing the leading role of government market regulation, it is necessary to guide the autonomy of all kinds of market players, promote the self-discipline and good faith management of market players, give full play to the self-disciplinary role of trade organizations and the supervisory role of public opinion and social public, and gradually form a unified open, competitive and orderly market environment, initial setting up the market management system to adapt to the development of market economy.

3.1 *A Big Data Supervision System Needs to Be Established*

Enterprise information is the primary prerequisite and foundation for implementing big data supervision. To strengthen and improve market supervision by using big data, it is necessary to establish a national unified market supervision information platform ASAP.

(1) The "isolated island of information" should be broken and inter-departmental information be co-constructed and shared.

The national unified credit information system should be established ASAP on the basis of the national population basic information bank, information resource base of legal entity and enterprise credit information public system. In this connection, therefore, it is necessary to break the regional blockage and departmental division of information, integrate the credit information of banking, industry and commerce, taxation, traffic management, production safety, quality supervision, statistics and other departments, realize the sharing of credit information of various regions and departments, thus eliminating information barriers among departments. Unless otherwise stipulated by laws and regulations, any information breaking the law or the trust of enterprises shall be disclosed on the Internet to improve the transparency of market supervision and the public credibility of the government.

(2) The full coverage of supervisory matters needs to be promoted while establishing a real-time supervisory mechanism.

By taking advantage of the rapid development of the Internet, the model of "Internet + supervision" is established to promote "intelligent" supervision and realize omnidirectional and real-time supervision of matters. Full use of the Internet technology is made to realize online real-time supervision and strengthen the regulation of off-site enforcement, while through large data bringing enterprise market access, quality supervision, market supervision, consumer rights protection, and food safety into the regulatory system, which records the whole process of the market supervision completely. By doing so, the goal will be realized that supervisory information can be queried, traced and used, thereby increasing the supervision of market efficiency.

(3) The disclosure of enterprise credit information needs to be realized.

Specifically, it is to speed up the construction of market players' credit information publicity system, to make known the basic credit information of enterprise registration, administrative licensing, administrative punishment in accordance with the law, enterprise annual reports, a list of enterprises of abnormal operations and a list of enterprises that constitute a grave breach of trust and/or a serious violation of law, to improve market transparency, and to make a connection with organic exchange and information sharing with the national unified credit information sharing platform. Meanwhile, the *Interim Regulations on Enterprise Information Publicity* needs to be enforced, so as to speed up the implementation of the listing system for enterprises of abnormal operations and the listing system for enterprises that constitute a grave breach of trust and/or a serious violation of law. More efforts have to be made to encourage and guide enterprises to voluntarily disclose more relevant information, to support the development of social credit information publicity services, and to facilitate the public understanding of the credit status of market players.

(4) Big data supervision needs to be implemented fully. In January 2015, the State Administration for Industry and Commerce officially launched the big data pilot work and cooperated with Inspur Co., Ltd. and six other data companies for first pilot projects in ten countries (cities and districts) in Beijing, Shanghai, Jiangsu, Shandong, Henan, Zhejiang, and Guangdong. Through the pilot project, the supervision department has comprehensively mastered the relevant data of market players and the relevant data of the whole network, and filled up the supervision loopholes, providing strong support for strengthening the supervision during and after the event. In this context, it is suggested to comprehensively promote the supervision of big data. First, a big data

supervision system should be established. The supervision department should assess the credit rating of enterprises and set the supervision level according to "normal", "yellow alert", "orange alert" and "red alert". Second, different supervision policies should be implemented to focally supervise enterprises with "yellow warning", "orange warning" and "red warning", forming the coordinated supervision of multiple departments. Thirdly, the expected management of supervisory data and of enterprises with large number of complaints and reports should be carries out, while issuing consumption warning.

Special Citations [7-6]

Big Data Supervision System

1. **The enterprise credit information system**. Information resources are shared among industry and commerce, public security, safety supervision, courts, banks, taxation, enterprises, non-governmental organizations and the general public, forming big data warehouses such as enterprises' production and operations, bank credit, tax payment, illegal situation, personal credit record and business record.
2. **The enterprise credit rating system**. It is necessary to explore the correlation between data in the historical data warehouse and the enterprise's breach of trust and violation of law, etc., and find out the evaluation index system and scientific methods for accurately assessing the enterprise's and individual integrity and predicting the enterprise's occurrence of illegal operation probability.
3. **The information platform for social participation in supervision**. An online complaint/suggestion box, an information feedback window, BBS, etc., are available to get more feedback information about the enterprise in time and discover the abnormal behavior of the enterprise.
4. **The online early warning system platform**. A warning will be given to enterprises that are committing a breach of trust and/or a violation of law. The government will deal with these enterprises according to the content of the warning and the adjustment of enterprises.
5. **The big data supervision and law enforcement system**. Based on the enterprise rating classification model, the enterprises with

low integrity will be sampled and investigated to implement grid management.

6. **The technical support system for big data supervision**. Powerful third-party institutions, such as Alibaba, Tencent and other professional teams, will be introduced to assist the government in establishing technology platforms and seeking solutions to difficult problems.

Source The provided information is prepared by the research group of China (Hainan) Institute for Reform and Development.

3.2 The Self-Disciplinary Role of Trade Organizations Should Be Given Play to

Observed from the experience of developed countries, trade associations play an important regulatory role in terms of industry access, standard setting and industry norms, and their status even exceeds the judicial and administrative law enforcement departments to some extent, creating favorable conditions for them to play a regulatory role independently and fairly. In the 13th FYP period, the de-administration of trade organizations should be realized ASAP, and the basic system of self-discipline of trade associations and chambers of commerce should be formed.

(1) The phenomena of government officials' intermediary must be cleared up to promote the de-administration of trade organizations.

① Trade organizations cannot be attached to government institutions. Since the reform and opening up, although a large number of intermediary organizations have been formed in all walks of life, most of them are attached to the administrative organs and lack their due independence, thus making their role very limited in maintaining the market competition order.[7] In recent years, cross-boundary integration triggered by the

[7]Chi Fulin: Promoting the Transition of Market Supervision to the Rule of Law. *Economic Information Daily*, June 27, 2014.

Internet has produced many new industries. For example, WeChat business, financial P2P and more all need to strengthen industry self-discipline and social supervision. It is suggested to establish trade associations and chambers of commerce in these areas mainly by non-governmental organizations, avoid the old way of administration and push forward the incremental reform of trade associations and chambers of commerce.

② Some trade associations limit competition. Some trade associations, by manipulating prices and crowding out competition, have become important sources of disruption of market order. At present, trade associations, chambers of commerce and the like can hardly play an effective role in the construction of market integrity system. Take food and drug incidents for example. The industry's lack of bottom-line self-discipline is beyond people's imagination. For another example, the stock market is rife with speculation, and the interests of small and medium-sized investors are often not effectively protected.

③ The de-administration of social organizations needs to be accelerated. In line with the reform of streamlining administration and delegating power to the lower level, it is suggested that third-party institutions should be engaged to take part in the investigation, and social forces be mobilized to take part in the supervision, so as to get to the bottom of government officials' intermediary and clean up the government officials' intermediary comprehensively. The existing trade associations' separation from the government and de-administration must be promoted ASAP. And it is imperative to achieve the real separation of administrative organs from trade associations and chambers of commerce in personnel, financial assets, functions and offices, and to form a new funding mechanism to avoid over-reliance on administrative departments by trade associations and chambers of commerce. For market intermediary organizations engaged in intermediary services for preset administrative examination and approval, they must get rid of their relationship with administrative organs or affiliated public institutions in terms of personnel, financial and material aspects, so as to avoid improper intervention of administrative examination and approval by leaders of the administrative departments.

(2) "One trade with multiple associations" should be promoted to support the voluntary establishment of associations by private enterprises in various trades.

Drawing on the experience of developed countries, we support private enterprises in various industries should be supported in jointly establish various chambers of commerce and trade associations on a voluntary basis, so that they can play an important role in industry self-discipline and social supervision. At the same time, the implementation of "one trade with multiple associations" needs to be promoted to accelerate the formation of an effective competition mechanism, so that more social organizations have the ability to undertake government delegated management matters. A framework of intermediary organizations covering all walks of life also needs to be formed by 2020. To this end, here are the suggestion: first, to strengthen the functions of industry self-discipline and enterprise self-discipline of trade associations and chambers of commerce, and to make an essential step in promoting the construction of good faith system; second, to encourage and support small and medium-sized enterprises in establishing "grassroots" trade associations and chambers of commerce on their own initiative, making new breakthroughs in addressing industry barriers, financing difficulties and overcoming arbitrary government charges; third, to give free rein to rural development and support farmers in setting up various types of related cooperatives for rural land, agricultural product distribution and centralized purchase of means of production, so as to make new breakthroughs in improving agricultural organization and specialization and developing large-scale agriculture; and fourth, to develop various "grassroots" consumers' associations and investor rights and interests protection associations, and substantially improve the consumption and investment environment.

(3) The important role of trade organizations should be given play to in the formulation of regulatory standards and supervision of enterprise self-discipline.

① Trade associations and chambers of commerce should be encouraged and supported in establishing industry standards. Trade associations and chambers of commerce should be encouraged to formulate and publish standards for products and services, and participate in the formulation of national standards, industry planning and policies and regulations. Relevant organizations need to be supported in bringing public interest litigation and conducting professional mediation. Meanwhile, it is important to strengthen the construction of trade associations and chambers of commerce and strengthen their ability to participate in market regulation.[8]

② The role of professional institutions needs to be played in market supervision. It is necessary to establish and improve the supervision system of market professional service institutions. For example, law firms, accounting firms, tax firms, judicial expertise institutions, and credit services are encouraged to provide professional services.

③ The corporate governance structure of social organizations needs to be improved. The professional, independent and governance framework of trade organizations should be standardized, so as to form their own social responsibility by establishing a perfect corporate governance structure.

Special Citations [7-7]

The Shanghai FTZ Has Set Up a Social Participation Committee to Guide Social Forces to Participate in Market Supervision

The establishment of the "social participation committee" is an innovative task proposed in the overall plan of Shanghai Pilot Free Trade Zone, which actively encourages social forces to participate in market supervision. The system in which social forces participate in market supervision as one of the six institutional innovations in the PFTZ integrates effectively the administrative management of government departments, the self-discipline of the enterprise's operation and the participation of the public in supervision, which will constitute a complete market management and supervision system.

At present, there are the first group of 42 standing members of "social participation committee", covering four areas of the PFTZ, and gathering enterprises of different natures, including State-owned capital, private capital, foreign capital and joint venture. Among these enterprises, there are not only traditional financial, trade, shipping, processing, manufacturing and warehousing and logistics enterprises, but also new-type enterprises in new business forms and new modes represented by cross-border communication, cloud computing and more. In addition, there are both local trade associations in the pilot area and

[8] *Opinions of the State Council on Promoting Fair Market Competition and Maintaining the Normal Market Order*. www.gov.cn, June 4, 2014.

municipal chambers of commerce and trade organizations, which are widely representative.

After its establishment, the "social participation committee" will take an active part in the policy and system innovation of the PFTZ, promote the improvement of enterprise integrity system and the market autonomy and self-discipline system, and form a comprehensive management and supervision system of administrative supervision, social supervision, industry self-discipline and public participation in the PFTZ.

Specifically, the participation committee will guide the enterprises and related organizations to express their interests and concerns, participate in the pilot policy evaluation and market supervision, support trade associations and chambers of commerce in joining in the FTZ construction, promote the formulation of industry management standards and industry conventions by trade associations and chambers of commerce, and maintain the integrity and the law-abiding, fair and open market order. Meanwhile, the committee will promote and assist social forces in setting up various undertakings conducive to the construction of PFTZs. It will also put forward opinions and suggestions to the administrative organs and their staff, while promoting the transformation of administrative functions to improve work efficiency.

Source Song Ninghua: The FTZ's "Social Participation Committee" is Inaugurated Today. *Xinmin Evening News*, September 29, 2014.

3.3 Social Participation in Supervision Should Be Encouraged

Under the current system, it is difficult to comprehensively solve the contradictions and problems in supervision even if a large amount of additional funds and staffing are given to the supervision departments. The solution lies in mobilizing various forces, especially social forces, to form a joint force of supervision of the whole society and build a diversified supervision system.

(1) The enterprise credit information disclosure system must be established and perfected.

① It is a must to timely release enterprise credit information and accept public supervision. All types of market players shall submit the report of the previous year to the market regulatory authorities through the credit information publicity system on a regular basis every year and make it public to the society.

② It is necessary to establish the list of abnormal enterprises and the list of seriously illegal enterprises. For those enterprises which are included in the list of abnormal enterprises and/or the list of seriously illegal enterprises, the market supervision department shall make them public to the society through the enterprise credit information system, issue an early warning, and transfer the serious cases to the judicial organs for handling.

③ It is important to establish and perfect the credit repair mechanism. Enterprises that have been included in the list of seriously illegal enterprises should be given a chance to make correction and can apply for removal after certain conditions are met.

(2) The supervision mechanism of public opinion must be perfected.

① The media must be encouraged to expose the illegal behaviors of enterprises. The media should be encouraged to monitor the illegal behaviors of enterprises through news, investigation, comments and other means to deter the illegal behaviors and create a good atmosphere for the whole society to participate in market supervision. The supervision departments should promptly investigate and deal with the illegal activities exposed by the news media while supervising how correction is made. If the regulatory authorities muddle through, the relevant leaders should be held accountable.

② Press legislation must be strengthened. In the form of laws, it clearly stipulates public opinion's right of supervision, criticism, and tort liability, improves the punishment mechanism of false publicity and malicious reporting, and severely punishes the behaviors of maliciously vilifying enterprises and consumers by means of paid news.

(3) The social reporting system must be perfected.

① A complaint/reporting hotline platform needs to be established. It is important, on the basis of the hotline 12315, to integrate and optimize the complaint/reporting platform functions of all functional departments, establish a connecting mechanism, achieve information sharing, and gradually build a platform for connectivity, for unified, convenient and efficient consumer complaints, and for economic violation reporting and administrative efficiency complaints.

② Internet supervision needs to be utilized and regulated. It is significant to support the general public in using new media such as WeChat to supervise market players and provide more convenient, unobstructed and effective channels for the public to complain and/or report illegal acts. That is another significant step taken to improve laws and regulations and promote the legalization and standardization of Internet supervision.

③ The reward reporting system needs to be established and perfected. Full play should be given to the general public's role of supervision, so as to establish and improve the incentive mechanism for the public to participate in supervision, perfect the reward reporting system, make arrangements for special personnel to handle complaints and reporting from the public, and keep the reporters confidential according to law. The information involved in the report should be verified ASAP, to be followed by a thorough investigation and legal treatment.

3.4 Innovative Supervision Is Carried Out with Big Data as the Focus

Making full use of big data technology to innovate supervision methods during the 13th FYP period has become a major task to reduce human and material costs and improve the efficiency of supervision. This will not only improve the pertinence and effectiveness of regulation, but also help achieve the "combination of both regulation and deregulation" and give play to the role of the general public in supervising market players.

(1) The standardization, specialization and technicalization of market supervision will be promoted.

Observed from the practice of developed countries, standardization and specialization of supervision are a basic experience. For example, Japan has established a complete legal system for product quality supervision through the implementation of standardization. Laws and regulations such as the *Industrial Standard Law* and the *Basic Law of Consumer Protection* impose strict restrictions on product production standards, and those who violate the regulations will be subject to corresponding sanctions. As China enters the era of "Internet plus", the precondition for standardization and specialization of supervision is informatization, which requires corresponding data to be supported, and the extensive application of big data will provide important conditions for this. To this end, here are the suggestions: first, to actively introduce international standards for the implementation of supervision, draw on the practices of the United States, establish strict technical standards for food and drug, promote the implementation of ISO 22000 standards for food safety identification, severely punish enterprises that do not meet the relevant technical standards, and thoroughly solve the safety problems in China's food and drug field; second, to encourage enterprises to establish business standards that are higher than national, industrial or local standards and that are internationally competitive; and third, to accelerate the revision of the *Standardization Law*, promote the reform of the mandatory standards system, and strengthen the administration of national mandatory standards. Mandatory standards are strictly limited to the scope of safeguarding personal health, life and property safety, national security and ecological environment safety, and market players must strictly enforce the mandatory standards.

(2) Full use of new technologies will be made to strengthen market supervision.

In the process of research and development of market regulation system and policies, the new-generation information technologies, such as big data, Internet of things and cloud computing, are fully used to monitor the regulatory objects, while timely proposing disposal plans, and improving the ability of market supervision. Meanwhile, it is important to make available to the public in a timely manner relevant market regulatory data, statutory inspection and monitoring data, illegal or dishonest data, complaints and reports, and data that should be made public according to laws and regulations by enterprises, so as to strengthen the supervision of enterprises during and after the event. Platforms for information sharing between regulatory departments and public security, judicial and financial departments should be established to enhance joint law enforcement capacity. Supervision and management of e-commerce platforms should also be strengthened to popularize and apply credible signs on websites, and create a safe and satisfied online shopping environment for consumers.

(3) Big data will be used to jointly take disciplinary action against dishonest behaviors and non-standard operations.

It is necessary to improve the credit information sharing mechanism and the joint punishment mechanism for dishonest acts, to make full use of big data collection, analysis and enterprise credit data, to establish an early warning system for a breach of trust by the enterprise, to give full play to integrated regulation efficiency in the industrial and commercial administration and in legal, financial and other fields, to establish cross-functional linkage response and faithless constraint mechanism in market access, administrative examination and approval, government procurement, bank credit, tendering and bidding, social security contributions, food and drug safety, etc., to legally restrict or ban the market access by those that commit a violation of law or a breach of faith, to realize the basic pattern in which "market players are praised for their trust or punished for their dishonesty, and restricted everywhere once they break the law", causing the dishonest people to pay a heavy price and high costs.

(4) Fine supervision needs to be implemented and cooperation among the supervision departments be strengthened.

① It is necessary to implement digital supervision. The supervision and law enforcement personnel make the maximum use of information technology and big data technology to fully implement digital supervision and realize the transformation from traditional subjective judgment and qualitative analysis to data statistics and quantitative analysis management.

② It is necessary to strengthen cooperation between the regulatory departments. On the basis of data and information sharing by the regulatory authorities, a mechanism will have to be established for the regulatory authorities to jointly crack down on the acts of discredited enterprises and encourage the departments of industry and commerce, quality supervision, food and drug supervision, taxation, environmental protection, public security and justice to jointly combat the above-mentioned acts.

③ It is necessary to connect market supervision and law enforcement with justice. If the market supervision department discovers that the illegal act is suspected of involving a crime, it shall transfer the case to the public security organ and copy it to the procuratorial organ at the same level according to law, and shall not substitute punishment for sentence

4 Promoting the Legalization of Market Regulation

The rule of law is the most important guarantee to overcome the subjectivity and arbitrariness of regulation and to form a modern regulatory model that features standardization, specialization and technicalization. It is necessary to guarantee the rule of law whether to consolidate the original reform achievements or to push forward the reform of the regulatory system in the new stage. To promote the transformation of regulation during the 13th FYP period needs to take the legislation-first approach as far as possible and insist that the regulatory reform is based on the law.

4.1 The Legal System of Market Supervision Must Be Perfected

It is important to accelerate the revision of regulatory legislation in key areas such as the consumer market and antimonopoly, and provide a legal basis for regulatory transformation in these areas.

(1) A law on comprehensive market regulation needs to be studied and promulgated.

To adapt to the general trend for the release of consumer demand during the 13th FYP period while transforming the regulation system to unleash the potential of domestic demand, the research and promulgation of a comprehensive *Law on Market Regulation* have to be accelerated. Only by strengthening consumer market legislation and establishing the legal status of market regulatory agencies, can strict sanctions be imposed on the law-breaking behavior of those of market supervision, and strict penalties on the improper supervision by market regulators be stipulated. Therefore, it is a good way to strictly regulate the market supervision procedures, restrict the power of supervision by law, and provide a basis for the comprehensive implementation of negative list management.

(2) Anti-administrative monopoly needs to be incorporated into the *Anti-monopoly Law*.

① There are a variety of advantages for incorporating anti-administrative monopoly into the *Anti-monopoly Law*. First, it is conducive to promoting the reform of the administrative examination and approval system. It can clearly define the unreasonable barriers installed by each administrative department to the non-public economy, and promote the abolition of these administrative approval rights. Second, it is conducive to strengthening the function of government regulation. It can clearly distinguish the boundary between the functions of administrative approval and market supervision, and change the situation of replacing supervision with approval. Third, it is conducive to facilitating the transformation of local government functions. It can clearly define and change the unreasonable setting of trade barriers by local governments and maintain the unified domestic market.

② Anti-administrative monopoly needs to be highlighted in the General Provisions of the *Anti-monopoly Law*. Firstly, it is to add a conduct of "relying on administrative power to form market dominant position" to the definition of monopolistic conducts in Article 3 of General Rules. Secondly, it is often difficult to define accurately in practical implementation the part of Article 7, namely "...the industries controlled by the State-owned economy and concerning the lifeline of national economy and national security...". In addition, it is objectively not conducive to opposing administrative monopoly if such statement is too general as "the State protects the lawful business operations conducted by the business operators therein." It is suggested to modify according to the requirements of the Third Plenary Session of the 18th CCP the said statement is as "the natural monopoly industries which State-owned capital continues to control and operate shall carry out the reform that features such main contents as separation of government function from enterprise management, separation of government administrative function from the responsibility of the government as the owner of State-owned assets management, franchising, and government regulation; that implements the operation separating natural monopoly industries from competitive industries and liberalizes competitive business according to the different characteristics of different industries, thus promoting the marketization of public resource allocation".

③ Some related contents concerning anti-administrative monopoly need to be added to the *Anti-monopoly Law*. It is necessary, therefore, to define administrative monopoly in railway, electric power, telecommunications, petroleum, civil aviation, postal service and other monopolized industries, to define the administrative monopoly of urban public utilities, and to define the administrative monopoly in the competitive link of public services such as education, medical care and culture. Through the above definition, the anti-monopoly can reflect the spirit of market deciding resource allocation.

4.2 A List of Powers and Responsibilities for Supervision Needs to Be Prepared and Published by Governments at All Levels

In line with the list of powers and responsibilities issued by governments at all levels, in accordance with the requirements of statutory functions, efficiency, convenience and equal rights and responsibilities, governments at all levels should highlight the openness and transparency of the list of powers and responsibilities for supervision, truly realizing that "one cannot do anything without lawful authorization", while placing the power of supervision in the cage of the rule of law.

(1) The list of powers and responsibilities of the regulatory departments must be made public according to law.

In practice, Guangdong, Zhejiang and other places have accumulated some experience in promoting the listing of powers and responsibilities. By formulating the list of powers and responsibilities of the government, they further clarify the boundary of powers and responsibilities between the government and the market, the government and society, and the government departments, and promote the standardization, normalization and rule of law of market regulation. As one of the main functions of the government, market regulation needs to define the power and responsibility of the regulation department in accordance with the law. While entrusting its power, it needs to clarify corresponding responsibilities and achieve the consistency of power and responsibility. For this reason, it is suggested that a list of powers and responsibilities for government regulation at all levels should be issued ASAP within one to two years, so that each regulatory item can be implemented to specific regulation departments; that the issuance of a list of powers and responsibilities of regulatory departments should be sped up to promote regulation by regulatory departments in accordance with the law through openness and transparency, and standardize regulatory procedures.

(2) New market illegal phenomena must be brought into the regulatory scope in a timely manner while regulatory authorities be clarified.

With the rapid development of Internet and information technology, the new consumption mode, management mode and transaction mode have undergone historic changes. For example, online shopping, third-party payment platforms and crowdfunding pose severe challenges to traditional regulatory approaches. It is suggested that the regulatory departments should pay close attention to new situations and problems in the development of the market, timely include various emerging market violations against the law and rules into the regulatory scope, and prevent the emergence of "regulatory vacuum" or "regulatory loopholes".

(3) Supervisory departments without legal basis must be eliminated to prevent excessive supervision.

While preventing a "vacuum" of regulation, it is also necessary to prevent excessive regulation from stifling innovation. Take financial regulation for example. The rapid development of Internet finance is a trend. While regulating the development and cracking down on illegal behaviors in financial markets, the regulatory departments should also prevent excessive regulation and curbing financial innovation. Therefore, it is necessary to speed up the clean-up of regulatory activities without legal basis, eliminate all regulatory departments without legal basis, and prevent excessive regulation from increasing the burden on enterprises and inhibiting market vitality, truly achieving the state in which "supervisors cannot do anything without lawful authorization".

4.3 *The Legalization of Market Regulators Must Be Promoted*

In line with the general trend of building a government under the rule of law, it is important to speed up the formulation of legislation and promote the legalization of market regulatory agencies, while insisting on the use of the system to control power, conduct affairs and manage people, and let the people oversee power and make the exercise of power completely transparent.

(1) The inclination of the institutional establishment to the market supervision agencies needs to be realized according to law.

From the practical point of view, as it gets down to the grassroots level, the supervisory power will become weaker, and supervisory tasks will become heavier. At present, some areas have achieved certain results by integrating market supervisory forces. For example, without any increase in institutional establishment and the number of leadership positions, Guangdong managed to promote resources from the posts of original administrative examination and approval, and the micro management to the regulatory and other business sections. Through the reform, the comprehensive institutions like the provincial industrial and commercial bureau and supervision bureau were reduced from six to four, while the institutions engaged in supervision increased from seven to nine, with the regulatory people accounting for more than 60%. It is suggested that the importance of market regulators should be fully taken into account in the formulation of the *Law on the Establishment of National Institutions*. The focus of the establishment should be shifted to market regulatory agencies, especially to local regulatory agencies.

(2) Market regulatory agencies shall become a legal professional body.

Observed from the international experience, the construction of legal professional institutions is a common practice. For example, South Korea has 45 independent enforcement agencies, the United Kingdom has 127 such agencies, and the United States has more than 60 ones.[9] These statutory bodies all have a special law, which clearly stipulates the establishment of institutions, responsibilities and others. It is suggested to refer to

[9] Cao Quanlai: Theory, Legislation and Reference of Foreign Legal Institutions. www.gx-law.gov.cn, April 27, 2015.

the advanced practices of foreign countries to promote the "de-administration" of the regulatory agencies and establish legal professional institutions, so that the regulatory agencies have the authority independent of the administrative organs and avoid the interference of administrative power on the regulatory activities.

Special Citations [7-8]

Characteristics of Public Service Statutory Bodies in Western Developed Countries

Institutional legislation. A statutory body is a body established according to special institutional laws. Each statutory body has a special law, which stipulates the establishment, functions and sources of funds of the body. That is to say, all statutory bodies are established under individual ordinances and are regulated by the relevant body ordinances

Government funding. The activity funds of legal institutions are either fully funded by the government or funded by the government and operated in accordance with the principle of commercialization, but the fees shall be strictly calculated in accordance with the cost.

Operating independently. The legalization of institutions ensures the relative stability and independence of institutions, which is less affected by human factors. As a semi-independent and semi-official organization, it has relatively greater autonomy in management, personnel recruitment and finance compared with government departments. It handles relevant business independently according to law, assumes legal responsibilities independently and is free from interference by State organs and other institutions.

Enterprise management. The legal bodies in Singapore adopt the form of enterprise organization and implement the enterprise management method, and operate within the organization structure of the board of directors (or executive council)—President—staff, hire employees independently, and control the management cost according to the principle of being responsible for their own profits and losses.

Be open and transparent. Institutions and their services are more transparent as their responsibilities, operations and oversight are clearly defined by law. The statutory bodies must hold themselves accountable to the outside world, and conduct of business in accordance with the law shall be open to the public and subject to social supervision.

Exercising social and public powers. The statutory body is an important part of the government structure and is the body that performs public affairs and services outside the civil service system. Generally speaking, statutory bodies are those that are separated from the administrative management system but do not enter the market. They exercise social and public powers beyond the government power, and they are those that affect the field of public interests.

Source The material is prepared by the research group of China (Hainan) Institute for Reform and Development.

CHAPTER 9

Structural Reform with Economic Transformation and Upgrading as the Main Line

The 13th FYP period is an important historical node for China to cross the middle-income trap. In this particular context, structural reform should take economic transformation and upgrading as the main line, and cope with five major relationships. One is the relationship between speed and structure; two is the relationship between the short term and the long term; three is the relationship between policy and system; four is the relationship between the government and the market; and five is the relationship between the top-level design and grassroots innovation.

Compared with the initial stage of its reform and opening-up, China has been in the late stage of industrialization with the characteristics of transformation and development becoming more prominent. In terms of structural reform, to reduce capacity, stock and leverage is important, but the fundamental goal is to blaze a new tail in transformation and development to overcome the middle-income trap. Therefore, this needs to take the transformation and upgrading as the main line to advance supply-side structural reform, and handle the relationships in all aspects.

1 Crossing the Middle-Income Trap by Way of Structural Reform

The 13th FYP period is an important historical node for China to cross the middle-income trap. It is a major challenge for structural reform to overcome the middle-income trap and lay a decisive institutional

F. Chi, *Winning at the Turning Point*, The Great Transformation of China, https://doi.org/10.1007/978-981-32-9479-0_9

foundation for China to enter the rank of high-income countries. Therefore, this requires focusing on economic transformation and upgrading and plan structural reform.

1.1 Structural Reform Faces the Challenge of Overcoming the Middle-Income Trap

In recent years, the issue of the middle-income trap has sparked discussion on all sides. It should be clearly seen that as China has entered the later stage of industrialization, the characteristics of China's transformation and development in the 13th FYP period are very prominent. If the transformation and development do not go smoothly, there is an objective risk of falling into the middle-income trap. To this end, it is necessary to consider crossing the middle-income trap as an important consideration for laying out the structural reform.

(1) China has reached an important historical period to cross the middle-income trap.

Whether a country can successfully realize the transition from the upper-and-middle-income stage to the higher-income stage depends on whether it can adapt to the objective trend in the change of development stage and realize economic transformation and upgrading. Observed from international experience, the decade or so after per capita GDP exceeds US$4000 is the most critical period for a country to overcome the middle-income trap. In 2010, China's per capita GDP exceeded US$4000, reaching US$4382, and it has truly entered the internationally recognized stage of "middle-income" development. From the perspective of world economic history, after per capita GDP reaches more than US$4000, any country that can adapt to the development needs in stages and achieve economic transformation and upgrading can cross the high-income country's standard of US$11,000 relatively quickly. This process took the U.K. 13 years (1974–1987), the U.S. 14 years (1965–1979), Singapore 11 years (1979–1990) and South Korea only seven years (1988–1995).[1] On the contrary, however, if countries without

[1] China Has Entered the Upper-Middle-Income Stage While Experts Analyze How to Avoid Falling into the Middle-Income Trap. www.people.com.cn, June 29, 2012.

substantial breakthroughs in economic transformation and upgrading fail to seize historical opportunities to improve themselves in the most critical five to ten years of economic transformation, as like most Latin American countries, they will fall into the middle-income trap. These countries would find it difficult to have better historical opportunities again to re-enter the rank of high-income countries in terms of the international or domestic environment.

(2) The risk of middle-income trap exists objectively in China.

① The risk is incurred at the low-end of industrial structure. China mainly relies on low-end industries to make per capita income reach the medium level. The policy and institutional environment for the transformation and upgrading of most low-end industries have not yet been formed. As labor costs rise and the demographic dividend fades, other emerging economies' cost advantages appear clearly, making it difficult for even low-end industries to maintain their original size. With the rapid rise of resource cost, environment cost and human cost, China's manufacturing enterprises remain in an unprecedented predicament. Take human cost for example. "Survey and Evaluation Report on National Enterprise Burden 2015" showed that 79% of enterprises reflected the rapid increase of labor cost, which increased by 10 percentage points over the previous year, further increasing the difficulties faced by manufacturing enterprises.[2] In 2007 before the international financial crisis, the growth rate of China's secondary industry was 15%. After the international financial crisis, the said growth rate gradually decreased to 7.3% in 2014. It further decreased to 6.0% in the first three quarters of 2015.

② The income distribution gap is still at a record high. In recent years, the income distribution gap has become a common concern. In the mid-1980s, China's Gini coefficient is only 0.16, but rose to 0.44 in 2008 and 0.491 in 2008. Although the gap eased over the past two years, the Gini coefficient was still higher. It reached 0.469 in 2014 (see Table 1).

Although the income distribution gap between the urban and rural areas is narrowing, the said gap both within the urban areas and within the rural areas is expanding. Within the cities the gap between

[2]China Center for Promotion of SME Development and China International Cooperation Association of Small and Medium Enterprises: Survey and Evaluation Report on National Enterprise Burden. *China Small & Medium Enterprises*, Issue 11, 2015.

Table 1 Change of Gini coefficient from 2003 to 2014

Year	2003	2004	2005	2006	2007	2008
Gini coefficient	0.479	0.473	0.485	0.487	0.484	0.491
Year	2009	2010	2011	2012	2013	2014
Gini coefficient	0.49	0.481	0.477	0.474	0.473	0.469

Source The data are prepared and published by the National Bureau of Statistics

Table 2 The income gap between the urban areas and between the rural areas in China from 2000 to 2014

Year	*Income gap between the rural areas (times)*	*Income gap between the urban areas (times)*
2000	6.47	3.61
2001	6.77	3.81
2002	6.89	5.1
2003	7.33	5.3
2004	6.88	5.52
2005	7.26	5.7
2006	7.17	5.56
2007	7.27	5.5
2008	7.53	5.71
2009	7.95	5.75
2010	7.51	5.41
2011	8.39	5.35
2012	8.21	4.97
2013	10.78	5.84
2014	10.84	5.49

Note The income gap within the rural areas and that between the urban areas refer to the times between the highest 20% per capita income and the lowest 20% per capita income in the rural areas and the urban areas respectively

Source The data from 2000 to 2012 are from *China Statistical Abstract 2015*; the data from 2013 to 2014 are from *China Statistical Yearbook 2015*

the highest 20% per capita income and the lowest 20% per capita income widened from 3.61 times in 2000 to 5.49 times in 2014. The figure of the rural areas became from 6.47 times in 2000 to 10.84 times in 2014 (see Table 2).

③ The contradiction of "getting old before getting rich" appears.

At present, China has entered a period of accelerated aging of its population, and the contradiction of "getting old before getting rich" is prominent. According to statistics, China's population aged 60 years of age or above accounted for more than 16.1% in 2015, and its GDP per capita was about US$7924. In Denmark, the aged population accounted for 14.9% in 2012 and the per capita GDP reached US$56,000. In South Korea the senior population made up 15.98% in 2011, but the per capita GDP reached US$24,000. According to data from more than 130 countries around the world, compared with other countries with similar per capita income levels, the proportion of elderly population in China is higher than the average level.

④ There is a large gap in population urbanization between China and high-income countries. The population urbanization rate in the developed countries are generally more than 80%, whereas China's population urbanization rate in 2015 was only 39.9%. If the urban-rural dual system were not broken and the urbanization rate were less than 50% by 2020, it would be difficult for China to enter the rank of high-income countries.

⑤ The contradiction of low welfare trap is prominent. In social security, for example, compared with high-income countries, the proportion of China's social security expenditure lags far behind the developed countries and even far behind some developing countries (see Table 3). Due to the too low level of welfare, China's consumption rate is relatively low compared with other countries with the same per capita income, and in the actual living standard and welfare level of the members of the society there is still much room for improvement.

Table 3 International comparison of the proportion of social security expenditure

Country	*Social insurance expenditure/ GDP (%)*	*Country*	*Social insurance expenditure/ Fiscal expenditure (%)*
Hungary	24.0	Germany	46.2
Poland	17.8	Sweden	41.4
The Czech	12.4	The U.K.	39.5
Turkey	11.9	France	38.6
Russia	10.4	Italy	38.4
Mexico	7.6	Japan	34
Iran	7.4	China	23.1
Chile	6.1		
China	4.9		
India	3.9		

Source The table is prepared by the research group of China (Hainan) Institute for Reform and Development

(3) Transformational development will help crossing the middle-income trap.

① Transformation and development in Late Industrialization have outstanding features. There is a big difference between the Late Industrialization and the stage of economic takeoff. Development is no longer a simple expansion process of total quantity, but to improve the quality of economic growth through a multi-dimensional structural transformation. From the perspective of industrial structure, urbanization structure, consumption pattern, or foreign trade structure, it has the distinct characteristics of transformational development. To grasp the characteristics of the stage of transformational development is the prerequisite for the smooth progress of supply-side structural reform.

② The total expansion model is not sustainable. The industrial development model, which is dominated by industry and characterized by production-oriented manufacturing and scale expansion, cannot be sustained. From the perspective of international experience, industrial transformation and upgrading are an important feature of Late Industrialization. China has been in the stage of Late Industrialization. Whether in the field of traditional heavy chemical industry or in the field of strategic emerging industries, industrial positioning is still dominated by processing and equipment. The mode of commercial competition mainly relies on low cost price competition. The profitability of research & development, design, finance and other links is obviously insufficient, and the business model innovation of service concept is lacking. The problems of big but not strong industry, core technology being controlled by others, and lack of global famous brand are very prominent. The advantage of low cost has gradually lost. Especially in recent years, industrial capacity has been overall excessive and corporate profitability has generally declined. All these problems indicate that manufacturing, which is mainly characterized by simple processing and manufacturing and scale expansion, has been hard to carry on.

③ Scale urbanization is hardly sustainable. In Late Industrialization, urbanization should have become an important power source for supporting economic growth. In recent years, however, 27 million migrant workers have found themselves hard to settle in cities and towns, whereas houses have been long in stock. These phenomena have become a prominent structural contradiction in the process of urbanization. This shows that the traditional mode of scale urbanization has come to an end.

④ The investment-led model is hard to continue. In Later Industrialization, the consumption pattern that has undergone a historic change should have become an important driving force for economic growth. However, the reality is that in 2014–2015, the contribution of consumption to economic growth increased from 51.6 to 66.4%, while the economic growth continued to decline. The chief problem is that under the traditional investment-led model, the investment structure does not match the consumption pattern, which not only makes it difficult to fully release the potential of the consumption-driven economic growth, but also leads to ineffective investment and low efficient investment. Overcapacity, high real estate stocks and local debts are all directly related to the investment-led model. In other words, it is advisable to find out causes from investment transformation, rather than to attribute the cause for the economic downturn to consumption. In fact, therefore, without the contribution of consumption, the downward pressure on the economy would certainly be much greater than it is today.

⑤ The mode of opening to the outside world, which focuses on the opening of industrial market, is hard to sustain. The rapid rise of service trade has become a new trend of global free trade. However, China's opening-up has still been dominated by manufacturing, and the development of service trade has been seriously inadequate. No change of this pattern would not only make it difficult for China to use opening-up to develop modern service industry, but also make it difficult for China to gain institutional discourse power in the construction of the new international economic order.

(4) A consensus needs to be reached concerning the general trend of economic transformation and upgrading.

① Economic transformation and upgrading call for a consensus. At present, various sides are short of confidence in China's economic growth, with more pessimistic forecasts and fewer optimistic ones. The important reason is that there is a lack of consensus on economic transformation and upgrading. Specifically, short-term problems are to be solved merely in the short run, and the symptoms are to be only alleviated for the illness—there is a lack of policy means to seek both temporary and permanent solutions. Only when a consensus is achieved ASAP on the general trend of economic transformation and effective measures are taken, can a way be truly found to address both the symptoms and root causes, thus resolving the contradictions completely.

② A consensus on service-led industrial reform needs to be reached. At present, some experts believe that industry is China's greater strength, and that moving towards service industry domination will make China lose the advantage of development. Industry is more important than service industry. In fact, the development of service industry is not to abandon industry at all, but to develop more quality and efficient industry. To adapt to the new round of industrial revolution in the world, to develop the producer services industry led by design and research and development and to achieve the transformation and upgrading from manufacturing to service manufacturing can truly improve the international competitiveness of the entire industry, enable China to acquire higher industrial added value and to gradually move towards a high-income country. On the contrary, however, it is difficult to realize industrial transformation and upgrading if the traditional simple processing and manufacturing are maintained.

③ A consensus needs to be reached concerning the transformation from the urban-rural dual household registration system to the residence permit system. Although urbanization is an important area for China to strengthen the new momentum of development in Late Industrialization and the potential of domestic demand contained in urbanization has been recognized in many aspects, it has still been questioned. The main problem is that in reality urbanization has ignored the all-round development of human beings and merely become a "city building movement", which has become a major factor of high real estate inventory and debt risk. In this context, therefore, the key to releasing urbanization dividend is to achieve the transformation from scale urbanization to population urbanization, from the urban-rural dual household registration system to the residence permit system, and to blaze a trail in human urbanization. This is the fundamental solution to the lagging development of population urbanization and an important means to solve practical problems such as urban labor shortage, diminishing demographic dividend and real estate destocking. To this end, the full implementation of the residence permit system will release new reform dividends and create new space for development.

④ A consensus on consumption-led structural reform needs to be reached. Although there is a consensus on the upgrading of China's consumption pattern, there are still many doubts about whether consumption can drive economic growth. If some people think that consumption is pure wealth to consume, not creating value, the motive force that boosts economic growth is investment. The reality is that investment away from consumption often leads to excess capacity, which gives rise to supply without demand. In fact, the upgrading of consumption pattern and the expansion of the consumption scale of over 1.3 billion people are an advantage that no country could match. It can accommodate industrial innovation in any form in China and is a "trump card" for China's long-term economic growth and industrial transformation. The transition from investment-led one to consumption-led is not to avoid investment, but to adapt investment to the general trend of the reform of consumption pattern, and truly upgrade the consumption pattern to become the endogenous power driving economic growth. At the same time, only by changing the traditional mode of development, which emphasizes production over consumption, can economic growth be promoted to reflect the national welfare and create a path of shared development.

⑤ A consensus on the development of service trade needs to be reached. At present, many people have doubts about speeding up the two-way opening of service industry market and developing service trade. Their main concern is that the service industry is not China's strength, and service trade will have a huge impact on China. In fact, some had similar concerns when China joined the WTO at that time. However, the practice shows that participation in international competition will not weaken China's industry, but make China the world's largest manufacturing country. It is hard to imagine that China could go for the service industry power under the closed and monopolistic condition. The development of China's service industry needs to draw on and absorb advanced experience of developed countries in both technology and management.

(5) The "final window period" of China's transformational development.

① The key to adjusting the structure and transferring the mode is 2020. In 2007, the 17th National Congress of the CPC proposed changing the mode of economic development. Today, however, it seems that the mode has not yet been changed in place. At present, the prominent contradictions in economic operation are directly related to the lag of adjusting the structure and transferring the mode. In the next five years, if the structural adjustment and transformation fail to be in place, it will not only be difficult to solve the short-term downward pressure on the economy, but also bring greater difficulties to the medium- and long-term economic growth.

② The key node of achieving the overall well-off society and crossing the middle-income trap is in 2020. Without economic transformation and upgrading, it is difficult for the national income level to be substantially improved. There is a common law between the development of service industry and that of industry. Without competition, there will be no improvement and it will be difficult to form effective supplies of high quality and low price. Whether a new path can be taken of shared development through transformation and to achieve the strategic goal of building a moderately prosperous society in all respects depends on whether decisive results in economic transformation and upgrading can be achieved by 2020.

③ The window period for comprehensively deepening reform with structural reform as the focus is 2020. At present, economic transformation and upgrading are at the historical juncture of overcoming the obstacle and the demand for structural reform is increasing across the board. In reality, however, the process of structural reform is not ideal. Breakthrough progress in structural reform with economic transformation and upgrading as the main line of the 13th FYP has a decisive impact on the fair and sustainable development of China's economy in the next ten and twenty years.

1.2 Growth, Transformation and Reform Are Highly Integrated

Compared with the past 38 years, the reform in the era of establishing the market economy system is very different, and the background of the current reform has undergone profound changes. Today's reform is hardly a single one, but highly integrated with growth, transformation and reform. To grasp the historic features of structural reform, it is necessary to objectively understand the characteristics of the stage that growth, transformation and reform are highly integrated.

(1) The issues of growth, transformation and reform are intertwined.

① The problem of growth is also the problem of transformation. In the case of overcapacity in the steel industry, the future is not that steel is no longer needed, but that high-technology steel is needed. If the steel enterprise itself does not transform, it will find itself hard to continue to grow. In this sense, therefore, just capacity reduction can only solve part of the problem, not the inherent problem. If economic growth could be stimulated through fiscal and monetary policies during the 12th FYP period, it would be difficult, judging from the current situation, to promote economic growth by adopting a flood of stimulus policies again.

② The issue of transformation depends on substantive breakthroughs in reform. The lag of mode transformation in economic development has not been solved for many years, mainly due to the serious lag of related reforms. Take the development of service industry for example. Without institutional innovation, it is difficult for the service industry to develop automatically. The traditional mode of economic development is supported by strong institutional inertia. Without substantive breakthroughs in reform, it is difficult to solve the problems in the transformation of economic development mode.

③ The trinity of growth, transformation and reform is necessary. The current reality is that growth cannot be talked about in terms of growth, nor can transformation out of reform. Growth, transformation and reform are interconnected and inseparable. This requires mastering the internal logic between growth, transformation and reform and enhancing the understanding of structural reform.

(2) Growth depends on transformation.

① Growth is not without room, and the potential for growth is still great. China is still a growing economy. From the perspective of industry, urbanization and consumption, there is huge room for growth, which constitutes the supporting factor for the medium-high growth of China's economy and becomes an important factor for the medium and long-term improvement of the fundamentals of China's economic growth.

② Growth is highly dependent on transformation. For example, the industrial growth rate decreases due to overcapacity, but it does not mean that the manufacturing industry lacks development space. The outlet of the manufacturing industry growth lies in promoting the transformation from manufacturing to service manufacturing. From the perspective of overall economic growth, the potential of the development of service industry is still far from being released while the industrial production capacity is being reduced. In particular, the development of producer services industry is lagging behind. Therefore, it is necessary to realize the transformation from industry-led one to service-led one ASAP.

③ Growth and transformation depend on reform. Growth and transformation mainly depend on whether the initiative of reform can be grasped: the transformation from industry-led one to service-led depends on whether the opening of service market can be taken as the strategic focus of market reform. The transition from scale urbanization to population urbanization depends on whether the comprehensive implementation of the residence permit system can be taken as the key point to break the urban-rural dual system structure and accelerate related supporting reforms such as equalization of basic public services in urban and rural areas. The transformation from material-oriented consumption to service-oriented consumption mainly depends on the acceleration of investment system reform and the return of investment rights to enterprises. Under this premise, diversified investors will be formed. The opening-up and transformation, which focuses on the full implementation of the free trade strategy, depends on whether the two-way opening of service market can be highlighted in the implementation of the "Belt and Road Initiative".

1.3 The Purpose of Structural Reform Is to Provide a Favorable Institutional Environment for Transformational Development

There are different views on structural reform among domestic experts. Different countries in the world have different contents and characteristics of structural reform. Observed from the reality of China, the structural institutional contradictions in the transformation and development are the particular background for structural reform. It is the specific connotation of China's current structural reform to take the problems of transformation and development as the orientation to solve structural institutional contradictions and form an institutional environment conducive to transformation and development.

(1) Transformation and development are subject to structural institutional contradictions.

To adapt to the new situation of economic development, to promote structural reform and form a reasonable institutional structure is the key for a country to form a new driving force for economic growth and ensure sustainable economic development. A country tends to form a specific institutional structure at a specific stage of development, which is compatible with the requirements of a specific stage of development. However, when the development enters a new stage, the old system structure is obviously not adaptable at all, which not only makes it difficult to ensure economic growth, but also brings various new contradictions and even crisis factors. In such circumstances, it is often difficult to solve new problems in the process of economic development by policy adjustments alone, and therefore it calls for structural reforms. Structural reform often has different meanings in different countries, but one common feature is that the problem of the old system structure's inadaptability to the new situation of development needs to be solved, and cannot be solved purely by a single policy adjustment. The whole set of system structure formed since China's reform and opening-up meets the requirements of large economic aggregate in the early stage of industrialization, but it is not adapted to the adjustment of economic structure in the later stage of industrialization. First, great progress has been made in opening the industrial market, whereas the service market lags behind seriously. Second, scale urbanization has been encouraged, whereas the institutional structure adaptable to population urbanization is far from being formed. Third, the existing system structure features emphasis on investment and restraint on consumption. Fourth, the relevant institutional arrangements of opening to the outside world are prominently featured by more attention to goods trade than to service trade.

(2) Major problems of transformation and development cannot be solved by a single reform.

"The basic reform should be turned to the structural reform", which was proposed as early as 2001 when China made great progress in the establishment of market mechanism and the common development of diversified ownership economy, while the structural contradictions of the system became increasingly prominent: ① The structural contradictions within the economic system were quite serious, which are actually reflected in the structural contradictions between the government, the State-owned commercial banks and the State-owned enterprises. ② There was an obvious contradiction between the introduction of certain macroeconomic policies and the process of market reform. ③ The contradiction and problem of the urban-rural dual system structure became more and more prominent, which had a serious impact on economic and social life. ④ The reform of social system lagged behind the process of market reform. Whether and to what extent the reform can be pushed forward depend pivotally on whether the structural reform with government transformation as the focus can be judged clearly and advanced comprehensively.

Today, the situation facing structural reform has undergone new changes. At present, China is confronted with major problems of transformation and development, which cannot be solved by a single institutional reform, and which requires structural institutional reform. In terms of the formation of a service-oriented economic structure, for example, it is necessary not only to open up the service market, but also to form a fiscal, taxation, financial and regulatory system that is conducive to the development of service industry. Take the consumption-oriented economic transformation for example. It is not only necessary to reform the investment system, but also to adjust the income distribution structure and improve social security. Take population urbanization for example. It is necessary to break the urban-rural dual household registration system, realize the balanced allocation of public resources in large and small towns, and form the institutional arrangement of equalization of basic public services.

(3) Structural reform is a comprehensive reform based on the problems of transformation and development and coordinated by a number of institutional reforms.

The general judgment is: at present, the situation of China's transformational development has taken an initial shape, but the institutional environment of transformational development is far from being formed. Supply-side structural reform focuses on creating the institutional environment for transformation and development. Structural reform cannot be simply understood as supply-demand reform, let alone equating structural reform with structural adjustment. Structural reform should urgently resolve major practical problems in the course of transformation and development and form a comprehensive reform plan.

2 Structural Reform with Economic Transformation and Upgrading as the Main Line

The disconnection between reform and economic transformation and upgrading is the most urgent problem at the current stage. To advance the structural reform based on the problem of transformation and development is to promote multi-faceted institutional innovation with economic transformation and upgrading as the main line. This requires both supply-side reform and demand-side reform, highlighting the opening of service market, and focusing on promoting government transformation and reform through power structure adjustment.

2.1 Equal Attention Should Be Paid to Both Supply-Side Reform and Demand-Side Reform

Structural contradictions are both supply-sided and demand-sided. After China entered the Late Industrialization, there have been contradictions of insufficient effective supply and insufficient effective demand. Therefore, supply-side reform is very important, and so is demand-side reform.

(1) The shortage of effective supply and effective demand coexist.

① The problem of insufficient effective supply is prominent. Currently, service consumption is growing rapidly across the board, but the problem of effective supply shortage in the service sector is quite prominent. Therefore, it is urgent to speed up the process of economic service while reducing production capacity and inventory.

② The problem of insufficient effective demand is also prominent. The potential of domestic demand of over 1.3 billion people is far from being fully unleashed and has not yet been converted into new drivers of economic transformation and upgrading. The main cause lies in the lagging development of population urbanization and the inhibition of consumption demand caused by the imperfect social security system. For example, at present, the consumption scale of three farmers is equivalent to that of one urban resident, and rural residents have not become important service-oriented consumers.

③ Supply-side reform and demand-side reform cannot be offset. If the problems of supply-side reform are not solved, it will be difficult to solve the problems of economic structure transformation and upgrading and industrial transformation. At the same time, however, it should be noted that if the problem of demand-side reform is not solved, it will be hard to bring into play the advantages of consumption pattern upgrading and population urbanization, and the medium- and long-term development will be insufficient.

(2) Major breakthroughs should be made in freeing the consumption demand of over 1.3 billion people.

① Good use needs to be made of the prominent advantages of consumption pattern transformation and upgrading. China's supply-side structural reform in the new stage should not be separated from the transformation and upgrading of consumption pattern, but should be based on the exertion of this biggest advantage and find a reform path that solves the shortage of effective demand and that of effective supply in an organically combined way.

② The practice of supply-side school in developed countries cannot be copied. The school of supply in developed countries emerged in the post-industrial era. The problem then was not the shortage of effective demand, but the shortage of effective supply. Consumption demand in developed countries was quite strong, mainly due to the lack of power on the supply side. At that time, the adjustment was mainly made for short-term policies aimed at solving the shortage of effective demand by Keynesianism, and more measures such as tax cuts were used to increase medium- and long-term supply capacity. These can be referred to for China's current supply-side structural reform, but it should also be noted that, as a growing economy, the problem of insufficient effective demand has been alleviated, but it has existed for a long time and has not been truly solved yet.

③ Consumption needs to be taken as the leading trend to move toward shared development. The emergence of a large number of middle-income groups in Later Industrialization will lead to the formation of a consumption-oriented society, which is an important sign of the improvement in the quality of economic development and of social progress. A moderately prosperous society in all respects is not a society that values production over consumption. The realization of consumption-orientation is not only that consumption demand is the endogenous driving force of economic growth, but also that people's own development is truly taken as the fundamental goal of development, thus realizing equitable and sustainable development.

(3) New supply needs to be led by consumption demand.

① A consumer market environment needs to be created actively. Demand-side structural reform is not nothing to do, but much to do. For example, the phenomenon of Chinese residents buying toilets in Japan in recent years reflects the prominent problems of low quality of domestic products and poor consumption environment in their domestic market. It is highly necessary to take improving the consumer environment as an important task of structural reform and adopt a package of reforms, such as strengthening the supervision of the consumer market, reducing logistics costs and advancing the reform of consumption tax so as to create a favorable consumer market environment.

② Service-oriented consumption needs to be cultivated. Reforms to boost domestic demand are not out of date. When a country enters the stage of middle and high income, the middle-income group is the main body of service consumption, but the proportion of middle-income group is obviously low in China. This needs to speed up the adjustment of income distribution structure and cultivate the middle-income group. To this end, it is needed to highlight the equalization of basic public services such as social security, highlight institutional innovation related to population urbanization, and form an institutional environment that supports the release of service-oriented consumption potential.

③ New supply needs to be led by service-oriented consumption. While the downward pressure on the economy is increasing, the development of health, education, old-age care, culture and other fields is gaining momentum. If it is possible to follow the trend and accelerate the formation of a service-oriented consumption supply capacity, it is entirely possible to form a number of new pillar industries and sunrise industries in the service sector to achieve economic transformation and upgrading.

(4) Supply-side reform and demand-side reform promote each other.

Under the particular background of China's transformation and development, supply-side reform and demand-side reform are complementary and mutually conditional. First, China's market reform has not been completed yet. There are both restrained consumer market and supply shortage caused by insufficient competition. Second, demand-side reform aims to unleash development potential and create a large domestic market, while supply-side reform aims to improve production efficiency and improve total factor productivity. Third, supply-side reform should play the decisive role of the market in resource allocation, while demand-side reform should play the effective role of the government. They are complementary, coordinative and supportive to each other, which cannot be neglected.

2.2 *Opening up the Service Sector Is a Major Focus*

The low level of service market openness is a prominent contradiction in China's economic transformation and upgrading. To fully liberalize the service sector during the 13th FYP period is not only an important measure to ease downward pressure on the economy, but also a key step in structural reform.

(1) The opening of service market affects both the demand side and the supply side.

① The key to unleashing new demand is the opening of service sector market. Whether service-oriented consumption demand can become a new driving force for domestic economic growth depends on the degree of service market opening. Currently, the main area where there is demand but no supply is the service sector, and the limited capacity of service-oriented consumption supply is due to the administrative control of the service sector. Therefore, only the opening of the service sector can release new demand.

② The focus of creating new supply is to open up the service market. Adapting to the new trend of the overall rapid growth of service-oriented consumer demand, increasing investment in the service sector and creating new supply in the service sector are the fundamental way to achieve the dynamic balance of investment and consumption under the condition of industrial overcapacity and change the distorted relationship between supply and demand.

③ Both demand-side reform and supply-side reform should highlight the opening of the service market. China's service sector is a big market, but the problem lies in the serious lag of market opening in the service sector. Therefore, to accelerate the opening of the service market is to form a new normal of flourishing supply and demand in the service sector.

(2) The opening of the service industry market is of overall significance for economic transformation and upgrading.

① The opening of the service industry market determines the success or failure of industrial transformation and upgrading. It is of decisive significance to promote the market opening of producer services industry and to realize the transformation from manufacturing to service manufacturing, so as to grasp the new opportunities of the new round of industrial revolution in the world and promote the effective implementation of "made in China 2025".

② The opening of service market affects the process of population urbanization. Promoting the opening up of the living services market is an important basis for improving the development level of health, education, old-age care and culture as well as that of population urbanization.

③ The opening of service industry market is the key to forming a new pattern dominated by consumption. The opening of service industry market will strongly promote the transformation and upgrading from material consumption to service consumption and achieve the rapid expansion of the total domestic consumption.

(3) The opening of service industry market can lead to breakthroughs in the whole structural reform.

① The opening of service industry market will bring about new breakthroughs in market reform. The opening of the service industry market shifts the focus of market resource allocation from the industrial sector to the service sector, thus forming a new pattern in which the market decides the allocation of resources.

② The opening of service market leads to a new breakthrough in China's opening-up. The opening of service market will greatly accelerate China's participation in the global free trade process, provide a new engine for the construction of "One Belt and One Road", and effectively enhance China's institutional discourse power in the opening-up.

③ The opening of service market leads to institutional innovation in finance, taxation, finance, education, social security and other fields. After three to five years of efforts, the entire institutional structure will be adapted to the economic transformation and upgrading, which lays an important institutional foundation for China to become a high-income country.

(4) The opening up of service market is a profound revolution.

In recent years, the Central Government has issued a number of guidelines on the development of service industry, and made special implementation opinions on both producer services industry and consumer services industry. However, as there is no new breakthrough in the opening of service industry market, quite a number of measures are difficult to be implemented. In the case of the four PFTZs in China, the negative list is mainly targeted at the service sector, which mainly limits the market opening of the service sector. A considerable number of service industries are monopolistic in nature. Although the opening of service market satisfies diversified service consumption, it is a profound change to touch existing vested interests. In the opening up of the service market, it is not only necessary to emancipate the mind, but also to break the deadlock of entrenched interests.

2.3 Attention Should Be Paid to Promote Government Transformation and Reform Through Power Structure Adjustment

In economic transformation and upgrading the market is needed to play a decisive role in the allocation of resources and an effective government at the same time. Since the 18th National Congress of the CPC, the reform of administrative system with emphasis on simplification of administration and decentralization of powers has made important progress, especially in the implementation of negative lists, lists of power, responsibility lists, listing of fiscal expenditure and so on. All these reflect focally the economic transformation and upgrading of demand, and important results in handling the relationship between government and market and in promoting the opening of service industry market. But the problem is that the deepening of structural reform has begun to touch on the deep administrative power structure reform. Only when it is determined to reform the unreasonable administrative power structure can new breakthroughs in structural reform be achieved.

(1) National medium- and long-term strategic functions must be strengthened.

The transformation of the mode of economic development, which has been proposed many years before, has still failed to make substantive breakthroughs, largely reflecting the absence of medium- and long-term strategic functions of the country. To achieve economic transformation and upgrading, the government's medium- and long-term strategic functions are crucial. The problem is that due to the unreasonable administrative power structure, the general economic management functions of the government are relatively strong, while the medium- and long-term strategic functions are relatively weak. Some departments that are supposed to focus on macro management and strategic management will concentrate on micro management with administrative examination and approval as the focus, and their medium- and long-term strategic functions are relatively weak. Some strategic planning is lack of foresight, and some planning implementation is lack of rigid constraints. The coordination of planning in different fields is insufficient, and the "connection and integration of all planning at one level of government" has not been fully implemented. The national medium- and long-term planning and decision-making functions are not separate from the implementation function. The disconnection between the local planning and the Central planning and the deficiency of Central planning have caused acute problems. Therefore, it is necessary to make overall consideration of the implementation of administrative examination and approval reform and strengthen the synchronous promotion of medium- and long-term strategic functions of the country, to adjust the institutional setup of the National Development and Reform Commission so that its functions will shift from micro-management and approval management to macro-management and strategic management.

(2) The function of public finance must be strengthened.

High macro tax burden and weak public service capacity are prominent contradictions that restrict economic transformation and upgrading. Both the deterioration of the investment environment and the lagging development of population urbanization make it difficult for consumer demand to be fully released, which are directly related to the public nature of finance. China has entered the Late Industrialization, and the public finance function of the government is an important foundation for the modernization of national governance system and governance capacity. The *Decision of the CCCPC on Some Major Issues Concerning Comprehensively Deepening the Reform*, which was adopted at the Second Plenary Session of the 18th CCP in 2013, emphasizes, "Finance is the foundation and an important pillar of State governance. Good fiscal and taxation systems are the institutional guarantee for optimizing resources allocation, maintaining market unity, promoting social equity, and realizing enduring peace and stability." At present, to build an engine of mass entrepreneurship and innovation, it is necessary to implement structural tax cuts. To build the engine of public goods and services, it is necessary to put the function of public finance in a prominent position.

Due to the unreasonable power structure of the fiscal and taxation departments, the government has relatively weak control over the entire fiscal and taxation. Putting the fiscal budgeting and budget implementation in one department, it is difficult to ensure the scientific nature of the fiscal budgeting and improve the efficiency of the fiscal budget implementation. The separate establishment of Central and local taxation departments would cause the collecting of national tax and local tax at two different levels to increase to extremely high tax cost and reduce the space of structural tax cutting. The separate establishment of fiscal and tax departments would reduce the capacity of the Ministry of Finance as the macro-control department to unify the fiscal and tax policies. Therefore, it is necessary to adjust the establishment of fiscal and taxation departments and strengthen the national fiscal and taxation control capacity. In one respect, it is advisable to strengthen the State Council's capacity to manage and control the national budget, establish a new institutional framework for the entire national budget management, and create conditions for improving the efficiency of budget management and institutionalizing the reporting of the budget to the National People's Congress. In the other respect, the Ministry of finance, as the macro-control authority, should be strengthened to control the entire fiscal and tax policies, highlighting the unity of fiscal and tax policies. It is suggested that a national budget bureau be set up, which is specialized in financial budget, to promote the consolidation of national and local taxes and gradually realize the unified management of finance and taxation by the Ministry of Finance.

(3) The functions of owners of State-owned assets should be performed properly.

The correct government performance of the State-owned asset owners is an important prerequisite for the reform of SOEs to reduce capacity. At present, SOEs mainly adopt administrative measures to eliminate production capacity, which reflects the structural defects of State-owned asset owners' functions over the years. Some SOEs have made excessive profits during the economic boom, but paid little rent and dividends to the government and did not consider their own transformation and upgrading. When it comes to the time of the recession, the State finds them too big to afford their bankruptcy, which has created a financial burden, and their debts have to be paid by the State. At present, to get these SOEs to reduce their production capacity and turn their debts into equity is only to be able to alleviate their current difficulties but not to be able to solve the problem fundamentally. To solve the problem fundamentally, it is also necessary to correctly perform the function of the owner of State-owned assets and form the reform plan of the optimized distribution of State-owned capital.

In addition, the distribution of state economy is still too wide and too scattered. The public welfare of State-owned capital is seriously inadequate. For the scope of "important industries and key fields related to national security and the lifeline of national economy", there is no clear catalogue and standard, which makes it difficult to adjust the strategic layout of State-owned capital. It is difficult to make an overall plan for the structure of State-owned economy from the overall perspective. This requires promoting the separation of the three functions and institutions of State-owned assets management in macro management, capital operation, and supervision and evaluation, straightening out the relationship between the Ministry of Finance, State-owned Assets Supervision and Administration Commission (SASAC), and State-owned capital investment and operating companies, and forming a new State-owned assets management system with the focus on managing capital.

(4) External economic functions should be improved.

Since 2015, with the establishment of Asian Infrastructure Investment Bank and Silk Road fund and the entry of RMB into the basket, China's foreign economic functions have been further strengthened. However, from the perspective of the whole economic function, the pattern of stronger internal economic function and weaker external economic function has not been fundamentally changed. With the in-depth implementation of the "Belt and Road Initiative" and the increasingly prominent strategic importance of economic diplomacy, how to highlight economic diplomacy in the establishment of administrative institutions has become a major task of administrative power structure reform. Take foreign aid for example. The scale of foreign aid continues to grow, but foreign aid is scattered in the Ministry of Commerce, Ministry of Foreign Affairs and Ministry of Finance. How to integrate various kinds of scattered foreign economic functions and form a strong diplomatic function, it is more necessary to start with adjusting the administrative power structure and greatly strengthen the foreign economic functions of the government.

(5) Social functions centering on public services should be strengthened.

The opening up of the service industry market requires the government to purchase public services, and the urbanization of population requires the government to take the equalization of basic public services as a basic function, and the release of consumer demand requires the government to strengthen the social security function and create favorable consumption expectations. That is to say, strengthening the social functions centering on public services is an important area for the government to achieve greatly in economic transformation and upgrading. At the same time, it can be seen that strong economic functions and relatively weak social functions are structural defects of prominent government functions. On the premise of strengthening the ultimate responsibility of governments at all levels, making full use of market mechanism and social mechanism to make the "cake" of public service bigger is an important sign of modern government governance. The new Central government has made a major step in implementing government purchase of public services, the PPP mode and the new mechanism. However, as the problems about no separation between the government administrative function and public institution function, between the government administration and social organizations, and the regulatory function and the executive function remain unsolved in terms of administrative power structure, the reform in public institutions have really been difficult to achieve a breakthrough for years, and the role of public welfare social organizations has been far from being fully played. Therefore, it is necessary to accelerate the de-administration of public institutions, clarify the legal-person status of public welfare social organizations in terms of laws and regulations, promote the community micro power to become an important carrier and platform for grassroots public services, and form diversified suppliers of public service.

(6) Public service-oriented relations between the Central government and the local governments should be established.

Over the years, local governments have taken GDP as the central behavior pattern, which makes them take attracting investment and operating cities as important functions. This has not only led to the distortion of the relationship between the government and business, the distortion of the relationship between the government and the market, but also caused a lot of local debt risks. From a practical perspective, the root cause of the growth doctrine of local governments is that the fiscal and taxation relationship between the Central government and the local governments is oriented by economic aggregate rather than public services. So, it would be difficult to fundamentally solve the problem of local debts without changing the institutional pattern.

To change the trend of local growthism and return local governments to the role of public service providers are actually to put forward new requirements for the reform of the Central and local fiscal and taxation relations. Due to the lagging reform of fiscal and taxation relations between the Central government and the local governments and the mismatch between the public service authority and the financial power, the system of division of public responsibilities between the Central government and the local governments has not been established yet. It is better that some public functions, such as environmental protection and market regulation, are managed vertically from the Central government, but they remain local. The practice in recent years shows that it would be difficult to make substantial progress in transforming government functions or in optimizing the structure and operation mechanism of administrative power without adjusting the relationship between the Central and local governments. For this reason, it is suggested to divide the responsibilities among the Central government and local governments according to the three-level governmental framework of the Central, provincial and county (city) governments, and gradually make the public service responsibilities of the Central and local governments explicit, legalized and accountable. It is also suggested to adjust administrative divisions in line with the trend of population urbanization and achieve the balanced allocation of public resources between urban and rural areas. Therefore, effective local governance should be taken as the basic goal to straighten out the fiscal and taxation relations between the Central and local governments in the new era, so as to redefine the taxation power of governments at all levels in accordance with the framework of three-level governments, while focally inclining the allocation of financial power and financial resources towards the counties (cities), giving them a stable tax source.

3 Structural Reform Needing to Cope with Five Major Relationships

To push forward the structural reform in the context of highly integrated growth, transformation and reform need to keep economic growth within a reasonable range. What is more important, however, is to achieve a major breakthrough in transferring the mode and adjusting the structure. This requires us to cope with five major relationships: speed and structure, short term and medium- and long-term, policy and system, government and market, top-level design and grassroots innovation.

3.1 *The Relationship Between Speed and Structure Needs to Be Handled Properly*

From the perspective of practice, in the period of economic transformation, it is easy to strengthen the old structure in the pursuit of excessively high economic growth rate, which is not conducive to the formation of new structure. Especially in the context of capacity reduction, inventory reduction and deleveraging, it is not realistic to pursue an excessively high economic growth rate. This requires a moderate pace of economic growth to give way to economic quality and structural adjustment, subject to the overall situation of economic transformation and upgrading.

(1) It is necessary to focus more on structure than on speed.

① Focus needs to be on improving economic quality through structural adjustment. The continuation of economic growth under the original structure is not sustainable, and structural adjustment cannot be sacrificed by temporary economic growth. Therefore, the current economic growth rate should give way to the economic quality, and more attention should be paid to the improvement of consumption, the proportion of service industry in economic growth, and the industrial transformation and upgrading.

② Economic growth should reserve space for structural adjustment. While maintaining moderate economic growth, it needs to take structural adjustment as the key point of macro-control. The growing downward pressure on the economy is caused by both the growth cycle and the mode of development. Objectively, these contradictions and problems are directly related to the lag of economic restructuring.

③ Long-term goals of transformation and structural adjustment should not be ignored due to the increasing downward pressure on the economy in the short term. Macroeconomic policies should not be swayed by the speed of economic growth, nor should the timing of economic restructuring be delayed. Reducing capacity, destocking and deleveraging must be carried through. At the same time, a favorable policy and institutional environment need to be created and no effort will be spared to cultivate new economic growth points.

④ The GDP growth should be maintained at the rate of 6–7%. All sides' capacity to adapt to the economic growth rate should be considered. So long as the consumer price rise is kept around 3%, new employment in cities and towns amounts to more than 10 million people, the registered urban unemployment rate is controlled within 4.5%, energy consumption per unit of GDP falls by more than 3.4%, and economic growth won't be stimulated as much as possible by taking monetary expansion and other means, it is likely for China to maintain the GDP growth at the rate of 6–7%.

(2) The focus of structural adjustment is to accelerate the development of modern service industry.

① Intermediate-speed growth is based on the rapid development of modern service industry. In recent years, for every one percentage point increase in China's service industry, the GDP growth will be increased by about 0.4%. If the service industry grows at an average annual rate of 10% in the 13th FYP period, the economy will grow by 4 percentage points. In this premise, the economy can form the bottom line of high-speed growth.

② Full employment needs to be maintained. At present, the service industry can create about one million new jobs for every one percentage point of its growth. If the service industry grows at an average annual rate of 10%, about 10 million new jobs will be created every year in the next five years, becoming a major source of employment and creating a huge market space for innovation and entrepreneurship. Even if the reduction of production capacity and inventory leads to greater economic fluctuations, the unemployment phenomenon brought about by economic restructuring can be digested.

③ New growth points need to be sought in developing service-oriented manufacturing. So it is necessary to focus on developing producer services that focus on research and development, to transform traditional industries, to implement the "Internet + producer services" program, and to promote the rapid development of service-oriented manufacturing. Under this premise, it is possible not only to find a new way to reduce production capacity and inventory, but also to form a new pattern of green development. If the service sector accounts for 55% by 2020, energy consumption will fall by about 14% and the emissions of sulphur dioxide will be reduced by about 18%.

(3) It is important to strive for an annual growth rate of 9–10% in service industry.

① The annual growth rate of service industry in the 13th FYP period should not be lower than that of the past 10 years. In 2001–2013 the service industry grew at an average annual rate of 10.6% in the real sense. During the 13th FYP period, under the condition of the overall rapid growth of service consumption, the service industry will enter a period of rapid development.

② There is a huge space for investment in service industry. The service industry faces administrative monopoly and market monopoly. Once the service industry market is opened to the outside world, huge growth potential will be released. For example, the demand for services such as education and medical care is far from being met. To achieve the overall equalization of basic public services by 2020, an additional investment of at least several hundred million yuan is needed.

③ There are practical needs of industrial reform. In 2015, the value added of service industry as a share of GDP reached 50.5%, and the proportion of service industry will reach 58% by 2020, which will basically constitute the industrial structure with the service industry as the main body, while the value added of service industry is required to maintain an average annual growth at the rate of no less than 9–10%. Under the condition of gradually releasing the potential of producer services industry and living services industry, the annual increase of the value added of service industry can be realized by 9–10%.

3.2 *The Relationship Between the Short Term and the Long Term Needs to Be Handled Properly*

Economic transformation and upgrading are a grand strategy, which cannot be seen as a too short time-span strategy. If one focuses too much on short-term fluctuations, one will lose medium- and long-term opportunities. To master the historical juncture of 2020 and promote the structural reform, it is necessary to focus on the medium term, digest the short term and win the medium and long term.

(1) It should go from focusing on the short term to planning the medium and long term. According to China's GDP by 2020 and the goal that doubles the income of urban and rural residents in 2010, and based on the average exchange rates of 2015, per capita GDP will reach US$11,000 by 2020, and China will basically cross the middle-income stage into the high-income countries. In this sense, 2020 is an important node for China to become a high-income country. Even if it does not reach the standard of high-income countries by 2020, it is relatively certain to enter the rank of high-income countries if the industrial base is available.

(2) The medium term development should be given due attention while easing the short-term economic pressure.

① It is important to objectively understand the short-term pressure brought about by economic transformation. Both excess capacity and overstocked real estate inventory are the result of lagging economic transformation. If the industrial and real estate sectors had successfully transformed over the past five years, this would have not been the case today. In general, the economic transformation and upgrading of the industrial and real estate industries brook no delay. Capacity reduction, inventory reduction and deleveraging can solve short-term problems in economic growth. In the medium and long term, however, structural reform is more important to highlight transformation and development. If the transformational development is done well, the capacity, inventory and leverage can be eliminated by the method of transformational development. Only in this way can short-term problems be digested and the initiatives of medium- and long-term development be won.

② If short-term problems are to be solved from the perspective of the short term, it will not only be difficult to solve problems, but also be possible to bring greater hidden dangers. It is not good to treat the short term problems as in the short run, leaving the contradictions and hidden dangers in the future. To solve short-term problems, it is advisable to start with economic transformation and upgrading to address the symptoms and root causes of the problems. Capacity reduction, inventory reduction and deleveraging are all important. What is more important is that the economy needs new industries, new forms of business and new growth points. Only in this way can the economy avoid a hard landing under the conditions of capacity reduction, inventory reduction and deleveraging.

③ Short-terms problems need to be dealt with based on the medium term of 2020. By making clear the goal of economic transformation and upgrading by 2020 and solving short-term problems from the perspective of the medium term, it will be possible not only to ease the downward pressure on the short-term economy, but also to strengthen the impetus to transform the growth model and adjust the economic structure, and lay a solid foundation for sustainable development in the next ten to twenty years.

(4) The historical node of economic transformation and upgrading must be grasped.

① The key is to overcome obstacles for economic transformation. Just like the price that needed to make a breakthrough during the early period of the reform of market economy system, today's economic transformation is also at an important historical node. It is suggested that an action plan for economic transformation should be formed ASAP to ensure that the foundation of economic transformation can be laid in one to two years, that results can be seen in two to three years and that decisive results can be achieved in five years.

② The years 2016–2017 represent a small "pit", which is somewhat easier to cross. The growth target for these two years could be set slightly lower to ensure smooth structural adjustment. If there is a breakthrough in cultivating new economic growth points in these two years, there will be better growth momentum in 2018–2020. In these two years, the opening of service industry market needs to achieve substantial breakthroughs, so as to ensure that the rapid development of service industry can absorb the huge pressure from capacity reduction and inventory reduction.

③ The year 2020 is a big "pit", which is not so easy to cross. If a substantive breakthrough is made in the opening of service industry, and the service industry accounts for nearly 60% of GDP, the pit can be crossed, which will lay a good foundation for the achievement of economic growth of 6–7% in the next ten years.

3.3 The Relationship Between Policy and System Needs to Be Handled Properly

In the current economic situation, the short-term policy stimulus plays a supporting role. But to eliminate the downturn pressure on the economy, it does not depend mainly on policy stimulus. The key is to adapt to the trend of development, properly handle the relationship between the government and the market, give full play to the decisive role of the market in resource allocation and better play to the role of the government, and give play to the amplifying effect of policies in institutional innovation. At the same time, policies should be compatible with institutional innovation and serve institutional innovation.

(1) It should go from relying on policy stimulus to focusing on institutional innovation.

As long as economic growth is within a reasonable range and without a hard landing, policy stimulus should be avoided; especially a flood of policy stimulus will no longer be applied to maintain growth. At present, the careful use of more leverage in the real estate market and stock market in particular has led to a temporary boom. In terms of real estate leverage, the housing price in first-tier cities is rising rapidly, which increases the pressure on destocking in second- and third-tier cities that really need destocking. In terms of stock market, all kinds of funds are encouraged to enter the market with leverage, which will eventually lead to an irrational boom of the virtual economy, and make it more difficult for the real economy to get the funds needed for economic transformation and upgrading. Therefore, short-term policies should give way to institutional innovation, serve institutional innovation, focus on institutional innovation, and insist on the formation of internal driving force for economic growth and new economic growth points through institutional innovation.

(2) The key is to form the institutional arrangement for opening the service market in two directions.

① Let the market play a decisive role in service industry. The opening of service industry market is not only the key to economic restructuring, but also the strategic focus of market reform. It is suggested that a plan of action for the two-way opening of service industry market be formed ASAP.

② The service industry is fully open to domestic social capital. It is important to further emancipate the mind, fully implement negative list management in service industry, and truly enable social capital to enter the service industry that is not prohibited by law.

③ The service industry is open to foreign investment in an orderly manner. Service domains that can be opened to foreign investment are to be systematically sorted out. A positive list of opening to foreign investment can be formed in the four FTZs in China ASAP, and the opening-up can be realized within a deadline. At the same time, it is proposed to set up a comprehensive reform pilot zone for the opening-up of service industry market, which will play an important role in expanding the opening-up of service industry.

(3) Policies and institutions for the development of service industry should be matched.

In recent years, although the country has allowed many service domains to be open to social capital, it is still very difficult for social capital to enter some service domains due to the unmatched policies concerning price, taxation, land and talent. Under such circumstances, it is necessary to advance the policy equality between the industry and the service industry, and systematically change the traditional policies of stimulating industrial development and restraining the development of service industry. In the modern service industry that the society urgently needs to develop, various preferential policies should be implemented to create favorable policy conditions for the opening of service market (see Table 4).

Table 4 Timetable for structural reform in the 13th Five-Year Plan period

	2018	*2020*
Opening of service market	To open up first to social capital in education, medical care and pension	To break initially administrative monopoly and market monopoly in the service sector; To form a new pattern of two-way market opening in the service sector
Reform of household registration system	To implement the residence permit system fully	Migrant workers withdraw from history; registered population urbanization rate reaches 50%
Reform of investment system	To realize the dynamic balance of investment and consumption; an significant increase in the proportion of fixed asset investment in the service sector	To form a service-led investment structure basically
Acceleration of the 2nd round of opening	To open up the service sector to the outside world in an orderly manner	The service sector gives equal treatment to both foreign and domestic capital; initially developed a foreign trade structure that focuses on service trade
Reform of fiscal and taxation system	Comprehensive completion of BT to BAT reform in 2016; to launch GST reform; to clean up administrative charges comprehensively	To explore property tax, environmental tax, etc.; to initiate consolidation of national and local taxes
Reform of financial system	To promoted the opening up of the financial sector in an orderly way; to encourage the development of all types of private banks; to introduce the reform of the securities market registration system	To establish the framework of modern financial supervision initially; a pattern of financial support for the real economy takes shape
Reform of education structure	Education de-administration makes initial progress	Vocational education grows rapidly

(continued)

Table 4 (continued)

	2018	*2020*
Reform of social security system	The social security system is initially unified in urban and rural areas	The gap between the urban and rural levels of social security narrows considerably
Reform of regulatory system	Initial separation of administrative approval from market supervision functions and institutions; full application of big-data supervision	The supervision system of consumer market and monopoly industries is basically put in order

3.4 The Relationship Between the Government and the Market Needs to Be Handled Properly

How to form an effective government in economic transformation and upgrading while invigorating the market and enterprises is a major challenge for pushing forward structural reform effectively. In practice, many structural distortions in the field of economic life are caused by the distortion of the relationship between the government and the market that results from too much administrative intervention. In the process of capacity reduction, inventory reduction and leverage reduction, however, administrative measures are often applied unconsciously. Therefore, how to deal with the relationship between the government and the market is always a big problem of structural reform.

(1) Structural reforms should prevent the government from replacing the market.

① In the field of economic life, a considerable amount of structural distortion is caused by the distortion of the relationship between the government and the market. The imbalance of investment and consumption, the lag of population urbanization behind scale urbanization, and the unreasonable administrative control in the service sector are all directly related to the distortion of the relationship between the government and the market that results from the government-led model.

② The focus should be on changing the government-led mode of economic growth. For example: first, investment rights need to be returned to enterprises, proceeding from the real demand to resolve the imbalance between investment and consumption. Second, it is essential to change the mode of administration-led urbanization, change the allocation of public resources according to the administrative level, and create conditions for the comprehensive implementation of the residence permit system. Third, the list management should be fully implemented in the service sector, so as to remove unreasonable administrative controls in the service sector.

③ Administrative measures should be avoided as much as possible to reduce capacity, inventory and leverage. Under the conditions of market economy, enterprises should be the main players in capacity reduction, inventory reduction and leverage reduction, whereas the government should not overstep its authority and carry out the functions of enterprises. Unless the government has to do it under special circumstances, it can't normalize it at all.

(2) The key roles of supply-side structural reform are enterprises and entrepreneurs.

① Enterprises and entrepreneurs discover new demand and create new supply. Over the years, both excess production capacity and excess real estate inventory represent an important factor behind government intervention. In fact, enterprises and entrepreneurs are most sensitive to market reactions, and the consequences of their own decisions are borne by themselves. There is no need for government intervention.

② Structural reform cannot simply be viewed as an increase in effective government supply. According to the practice over the years, the technical route of industrial development predicted by the government instead of market players is not successful at all. The government should not set a technical route for enterprise restructuring and innovation subjectively.

③ Enterprises and entrepreneurs are innovators and importance needs to be attached to the entrepreneurship in industrial transformation. Entrepreneurship is the most important factor to promote industrial innovation and industrial reform. The major issues that need to be solved for structural reform before everything else are to give priority to improving the environment for enterprise development, energizing enterprises and promoting entrepreneurship. The vitality of the non-public economy should be encouraged, and private property rights of entrepreneurs and intellectual property rights be protected. In the process of reforming SOEs in reducing production capacity, it is also necessary to pay attention to the display of entrepreneurial spirit. In the process of industrial restructuring, the government should try its best not to play the role of "arbitrary arrangement or forced merger".

(3) The government should become the subject of creating institutional environment.

① The standardization of political and commercial relations must be promoted. In the mode of government-led economic growth, the boundary between local governments and entrepreneurs is often unclear, and the political and commercial relations remain blurred, which not only makes enterprises spend too much time dealing with government officials while playing down the innovation of enterprises, but also leads to too much institutional corruption.

② The government is the institutional supplier, while enterprises are profit pursuer. The government is both the rule maker and the referee that cannot play football in person. The government should treat all enterprises equally and not take sides on any one.

③ The government focuses on optimizing the institutional environment of enterprise transformation and reform. At present, every possible means should be done to reduce the excessive institutional costs of enterprises. While deepening the reform of streamlining administration and decentralization, and cracking down on the collusion between government officials and business people, the starting point will be the comprehensive implementation of the "replacing business tax with value-added tax" in the service sector, carry out a massive tax cut plan, appropriately reduce the cost of five kinds of social insurance[3] and one housing fund for enterprises, and promote the internationalization of business environment.

④ Local governments should become public service providers. Today, with the rapid development of population urbanization, the competition among local governments will gradually shift from focusing on GDP to focusing on providing good public services, improving the quality of cities and attracting population inflow. If the public services in some

[3] **[The Translator's Notes]** Five kinds of insurance for the enterprise refer to insurance for pension, medical care, unemployment, work-related injury and birth.

areas are poor and the population is net outflow, the power of economic development will be exhausted, let alone economic transformation and upgrading.

3.5 *The Relationship Between the Top-Level Design and the Grassroots Innovation Needs to Be Handled Properly*

Judging from the actual progress of the reform in the past two years, some areas have made rapid progress and substantial breakthroughs, but others have lagged behind, and the reform has slipped and idled. At present, the reform has entered the "deep water zone" and the environment and conditions for reform have undergone significant changes, and the difficulty and complexity of reform have increased greatly. This requires the organic combination of top-level design and grassroots exploration and innovation.

(1) The top-level design of structural reform is important, as is grassroots innovation.

① Structural reform is inseparable from grassroots innovation. For example, the understanding of the opening of service market is not unified, but local experiments are worth carrying out, and if successful, they can be implemented nationwide. From the reform experience of the past 38 years, reform and innovation are a process of exploration, and cannot do especially without local exploration practice. The pilot reform program → expanding the pilot program → nationwide popularization of the program has become a practical and effective path for multiple institutional innovations.

② The local situation in a big country like China varies tremendously, and many reforms cannot be carried out at the same time. For example, the situation in Guangdong and that in Northeast China are quite different, so are the situation and task they face in economic transformation and upgrading. If they adopt the same approach to reform, it will be difficult to achieve the same desired effect.

③ Reform needs to give play to two advantages: top-level promotion and grassroots innovation. Structural reform involves the relationship between the Central government and local governments, and involves the interests of departments and industries. So, the gap tends to be rather big between the implementation of reform and the expectations.

This will call for greater coordination and promotion of reform at the top, with greater determination and boldness to break through vested interests. At the same time, it is important to properly arrange reform trials in accordance with the requirements of economic transformation and upgrading, encourage local governments to combine practice with exploration and innovation, and bring into play the initiative at the grassroots level. Local governments should be encouraged to make unified arrangements in accordance with the Central government's plan, and give priority to pilot reform in line with local practice. Local pilot reform should be promoted so as to create an overall environment for social reform.

(2) The organic combination of top-level design and grassroots exploration and innovation needs to be achieved.

① It is necessary to grasp the characteristics of structural reform and optimize the mode of propelling the reform. But the reform task is considerably heavy in implementing the spirit of the Third, Fourth and Fifth plenums of the 18th CPC Central Committee concerning deepening reforms in all respects. From a practical perspective, it is necessary to distinguish which tasks are suitable for implementation by passing on the Central government's documents, and which ones require innovation and active pilot projects at grassroots. Therefore, it is necessary to adopt the optimized reform mode according to the characteristics of reform.

② The construction of infrastructure system needs to highlight the top-level design. Although the specific forms of institutional arrangements can vary, a country's large basic institutional framework can only be completed through the top-level design. In the construction of such basic systems as SOEs, taxation, finance and opening-up, it should be like a national game of chess. The top-level design should be strengthened and promoted from the Central level to the local level.

③ Local pilot projects should be advocated for specific institutional and institutional innovations in economic transformation and upgrading. On the premise of not violating the big principle, considering the specific situation of different provinces and cities, local governments can be allowed to make bold attempts.

(3) An incentive mechanism needs to be established to encourage reform.

① In the specific context of economic transformation and breakthroughs, local governments should be given greater reform autonomy. For example, based on the actual demand of economic transformation and upgrading, it is advisable to set up pilot areas for comprehensive reforms in opening the service market and developing producer services, so that more places can have more room for reform and innovation.

② Concrete measures to encourage reformers need to be formed. Economic transformation and breakthroughs call for the change of the mediocre government, lazy government and negligence. In forming a specific incentive mechanism for promoting those who are bent on reforms, bold and resolute, and capable, the objective is to form a favorable atmosphere for structural reform.

③ A performance assessment mechanism for local governments needs to be established to adapt to economic transformation and upgrading. It is necessary to take the service industry, population urbanization, consumption and basic public services as key indicators for local government performance appraisal and form a new mechanism compatible with structural reform incentives ASAP.

Afterword

The 13th Five-Year Plan period is endowed with the extremely prominent historical features of China's economic transformation. Growth, transformation and reform are highly integrated. Economic transformation and upgrading contain enormous development potential and market space. But, the contradictions and risk factors facing economic transformation are increasing day by day. In this particular context, not only structural adjustment is called for, but also structural reform is. Not only demand-side structural reform is called for, but also supply-side structural reform. Therefore, the 13th Five-Year Plan needs to take strongly promoting supply-side structural reform as a major option for economic transformation and upgrading.

The 38 years of reform and opening up have shown that, whether a region or an enterprise, it often wins not at the starting point but at the turning point. At present, facing the structural contradictions of economic transformation, we need to make breakthroughs in the structural reform with greater determination and boldness and blaze a trail in resolve them through structural reform. To adapt to the trend of economic transformation to promote the structural reform during the 13th Five-Year Plan period, the key is to properly handle the relationship between the market, the enterprise and the government, to more liberally allow the market to play a decisive role in the allocation of resources, to further stimulate the enterprise's vitality, to increase more effective

F. Chi, *Winning at the Turning Point*, The Great Transformation of China, https://doi.org/10.1007/978-981-32-9479-0

system supply, in order to achieve a crucial breakthrough in economic transformation.

This book is based on my public speaking at home and abroad and my in-depth thinking in the past year or two. The completion of the book was assisted by my colleagues Fang Shuanxi, Zhang Fei, Tan Huaiyu, Li Xuka, Yang Tianying, Chen Wei, etc. Zhejiang University Press has given great support to the editing and publishing of the book, and hereby I would like to express my gratitude.

Bibliography

Cai, Fang. A Few Viewpoints on Demographic Dividend. *Economic Daily*, 18 June 2015.

Cai, Fang. Total Factor Productivity Can Extend the Traditional Demographic Dividend. *Beijing Daily*, 23 November 2015.

Cao, Ting. Professionals Become the Bottleneck Restricting the Development of Internet Finance. *Economic Information Daily*, 17 September 2015.

Cao, Yuanzheng et al. Reshaping the State Capacity for Asset and Liability. *Caijing Magazine*, 2012(15).

Chen, Qingsong. Rigorous Financial Test of New Urbanization. *China Enterprise News*, 1 April 2014.

Chen, Yu. The Consumption Potential of China's Elderly Population Reaches About 106 Trillion Yuan by 2050. *Economic Daily*, 3 December 2014.

Chen, Xian, Yin Feng and Cheng Dazhong. *China Service Economy Report 2009*. Shanghai: Shanghai University Press, 2010.

Cheng, Ying, Zhang Meiyun and Zu Yuanyuan. Data Survey and Statistical Analysis of the Internationalized Development of China's Key Universities. *Journal of Higher Education*, 2014(8).

Chi, Fulin. Construction of Education Public Service System in the 12th FYP Period: Prominent Contradictions and Main Tasks. *Comparative Economic & Social Systems*, 2011(2).

Chi, Fulin. Urbanization Should Take a Fair and Sustainable Road. *People's Daily*, 23 January 2013.

Chi, Fulin. The Development of Small and Medium-Sized Towns with the Emphasis on Equalization of Public Resources Allocation. *China Economic Times*, 21 December 2013.

F. Chi, *Winning at the Turning Point*, The Great Transformation of China, https://doi.org/10.1007/978-981-32-9479-0

Chi, Fulin. The Development of Small and Medium-Sized Towns with the Emphasis on Equalization of Public Resources Allocation. *China Economic Times*, 6 January 2014.

Chi, Fulin. Promoting the Transition of Market Supervision to the Rule of Law. *Economic Information Daily*, 27 January 2014.

Chi, Fulin. Transformation and Upgrading Need to Deepen Education Reform. *Economic Information Daily*, 5 June 2015.

Chi, Fulin. Forming a Service-Dominated Industrial Structure. *People's Daily*, 26 August 2015.

Chi, Fulin. Reform in "the 13th FYP Period Should Focus on the Service Sector. *Economic Information Daily*, 29 October 2015.

Chi, Fulin. The 13th FYP: Promoting Transformation and Upgrading Through Structural Reform. *Economic Information Daily*, 16 December 2015.

Chi, Fulin. *The Choice of Transformation for 2020—Trend and Challenge for China's Economic Transformation and Upgrading*. Beijing: China Economic Publishing House, 2015.

Chi, Fulin. Transition and Reform: The Megatrend of China's Shift to a Big Service-Oriented Nation in the 13th Five-Year Plan Period. *Journal of Shanghai University (Social Science Edition)*, 2015(1).

Chi, Fulin. Our Education Needs a Second Reform: On the Structural Adjustment and Reform of Education in the "Thirteen Five-Year Plan" Period. *Journal of China Executive Leadership Academy Jinggangshan*, 2015(5).

Chi, Fulin. Regulatory Transformation Is the Key to Deepening Decentralization Reform. *Administration Reform*, 2015(9).

Chi, Fulin. *Restructuring and Breaking the Blockade—"The 13th Five-Year Plan": Historical Challenges from Structural Reform*. Beijing: China Workers Press, 2016.

Chi, Fulin. New Trends and New Drivers of Economic Transformation. *China Finance*, 2016(1).

China Center for Promotion of SME Development and China International Cooperation Association of Small and Medium Enterprises. Survey and Evaluation Report on National Enterprise Burden. *China Small & Medium Enterprises*, 2015(11).

Cui, Ying. Financial Crisis in the Context of Our Country in the Area of Government Procurement Management Countermeasures Commercial Bribery (*sic*). *Journal of Beijing Institute of Technology (Social Sciences Edition)*, 2009(6).

Du, Yubo. Higher Education Should Be More Adaptable to the Needs of Economic and Social Development. *China Education Daily*, 24 July 2014.

Gao, Peiyong. *Reform of Fiscal and Taxation System and National Modernization*. Beijing: China Social Sciences Press, 2014.

Guidance Reader for the CPC Central Committee's Proposal on Formulating the Thirteenth Five-Year Plan (2016–2020) for National Economic and Social Development. Beijing: People's Publishing House, 2015.

In 2014 Chinese Students Studying Abroad Number 460,000 While Returned Students over 360,000. *Xinmin Evening News*, 10 March 2015.

Ji, Xuejiao. 25 Housing Enterprises' Sales in November Increase by a Big Margin. *Finance and Investment*, 25 December 2015.

Jia, Kang. The Proportional Imbalance of Direct and Indirect Taxation Hinder Economic Transformation. *People's Daily*, 10 October 2012.

Launching Seminar on China-EU Reform Forum. *Guangming Daily*, 16 March 2015.

Li, Keqiang. 1 Percentage Point Growth in GDP Can Promote Employment of 1.5 Million People. *Workers' Daily*, 5 November 2013.

Li, Song. The Investigation Shows the Impulsive Grabbing of Land by Small Towns, Highlighting Illegal Problems. *China Comment*, 2013(13).

Li, Shaowen. High-End Talent Shortage Restrains Service Outsourcing Upgrading. *International Business Daily*, 30 May 2014.

Li, Lan. It's Urgent to Ease up the Structural Contradiction in the Employment Market. *Economic Information Daily*, 5 March 2015.

Li, Hongpeng and Wen Rujun. The Central Government's Pricing Catalogue Reduces the Pricing Range to 7 Categories and 20 Items. *Legal Evening News*, 21 October 2015.

Li, Yang et al. *China's State's Balance Sheet in 2013: Theory, Methods, and Risk Assessment*. Beijing: China Social Sciences Press, 2013.

Liang, Da. Enormous Domestic Demand Potential Can Be Released via Population Urbanization. *Shanghai Securities News*, 9 January 2013.

Lin, Huocan. Establishing a Long-Term Mechanism to Reduce the Overcapacity. *Economic Daily*, 18 November 2014.

Liu, Zhicai. Problems of China's Property Tax System and Improvement Suggestions. *Modern Finance & Economics*, 2006(1).

Liu, Guoyan et al. The Proportional Relation Between Direct Tax and Indirect Tax in China from International Comparison. *Public Finance Research*, 2015(4).

Liu, Shaohua. Upstream of Global Value Chain: Chinese Companies Are Coming. *People's Daily (Overseas Edition)*, 14 January 2016.

Luo, Zheng. Listed Housing Enterprises Seek Transformation Due to Corporate Debt Differentiation. *Economic Information Daily*, 10 September 2015.

Luo, Zheng. Housing Enterprises' Debt Differentiation in the First Half of the Year Leads Some Listed Companies to Seek Transformation. *Economic Information Daily*, 10 September 2015.

Ma, Jun et al. *A Study of China's National Balance Sheet*. Beijing: Social Sciences Academic Press (China), 2012.

Ma, Wenpu. "The Belt and Road Initiative" Needs to Train Professional International Talents. *China Enterprise News*, 27 July 2015.

Miao, Shubin and Fang Shuanxi. It Is a Big Strategy to Expand the Middle-Income Group. *Guangming Daily*, 23 April 2013.

National Market Players' Development, Market Competition Environment and Market Consumption Environment in 2015. *China Industry and Commerce News*, 14 January 2016.

Qi, Bin, Zha Xiangyang et al. Direct Financing and Indirect Financing: An International Comparison. *New Finance Review*, 2013(6).

Qiu, Yue. Farewell to 2015: The Sustainable Growth of Cultural Consumption. *Guangming Daily*, 14 January 2016.

Que, Mingkun. Promoting the Consumption Upgrading of Private Education Through Supply-Side Reform. *CPPCC News*, 9 December 2015.

Shenzhen Office for the Aged. Overarching Design for Developing Elderly Services and Industries. *China Social Work*, 2013(7).

Song, Ninghua. The FTZ's "Social Participation Committee" Is Inaugurated Today. *Xinmin Evening News*, 29 September 2014.

The Globe Is in the Third Economic "Super Cycle" and Emerging Market Growth Is Key. *Southern Daily*, 11 November 2013.

The Report Says Beijing Should Reduce the Household Registration Benefits While Clarifying the Qualifications for Non-native Population. *Guangming Daily*, 27 May 2014.

The Chinese Academy of Social Sciences Estimates China's Elderly Care Market Will Reach 13 Trillion Yuan by 2030. *International Financial News*, 30 November 2015.

Wang, Huimian. A Big Strategy to Expand the Middle-Income Group. *Shenzhen Economic Daily*, 11 March 2014.

Wang, Lei, Wang Likun and Pan Min. Pension Gap: Analysis and Remedy Measures. *Journal for Party and Administrative Cadres*, 2014(3).

Wang, Zhiying. On Approaches to Transformation of Local Undergraduate Universities to Universities of Application Technology. *Modern Enterprise Education*, 2014(16).

Wang, Changlin. Supporting 7% of the New Impetus for Industrial Development. *Guangming Daily*, 7 August 2015.

Wang, Xueli. Improving the Treatment of China's Skilled Workers and Promoting "Made in China 2025". *China Labor Social Security News*, 1 November 2015.

Wei, Houkai et al. *The Way of China's Urbanization to Harmony and Prosperity.* Beijing: China Social Sciences Academic Press, 2014.

Wolf, Martin. China Should No Longer Delay Reform and Adjustment. *Financial Times*, 12 April 2014.

Wu, Chu. We Are Not for the Support Policies That "Appear Attractive but Not Practical" to Micro, Small and Medium-Sized Enterprises. *China Youth Daily*, 8 March 2015.

Wu, Ni. Current Situation, Characteristics, Problems and Future Trend of China's Private Education Development: Comparative Analysis Based on Statistical Data and Policy Texts. *Educational Science Research*, 2015(2).

Xu, Sheng. The Current Situation of Tax Burden of Enterprises: Investigation and Suggestions for Policy. *Study Times*, 26 August 2013.

Yao, Xuanjie. Spillover-Effect Investment in Broadband Infrastructure to Be Launched: Big Potential in Small and Medium-Sized Towns. *China Securities Journal*, 8 August 2013.

Yan, Jingyi. Phenomena of Homogenization in Chinese Universities and Countermeasures. *Journal of Dalian Nationalities University*, 2015(4).

Yang, Changyong. A Study of China's Strategic Thinking on Expanding the Opening-Up of Service Industry. *Intertrade*, 2015(4).

Yin, Weimin. Improving the Treatment of Skilled Workers. *Economic Daily*, 14 December 2015.

Zhang, Rui. Overcapacity Weighs Down All China's Manufacturing. *China Economic Herald*, 27 September 2012.

Zhang, Bin. Health Industry Would Reach 10 Trillion Yuan by 2020 While CSE Actively Distributes the Health Industry. *Economic Information Daily*, 12 April 2013.

Zhang, Bin. Logic of the Downturn Trend of China's Economy. *21st Century Business Herald*, 14 October 2013.

Zhang, Fei. Liberalizing Service Industry to Release Market Dividends. *Shanghai Securities News*, 14 April 2015.

Zhao, Zheng. Mobile Education: Subversion of Traditional K12 Auxiliary Market. *China Business Journal*, 19 July 2014.

Zhao, Jin. Global Service Trade Reaches Nearly US$10 Trillion While Service Trade Business Opportunities Surge. *People's Daily*, 20 December 2015.

Zhao, Yingsheng, Zhong Binglin and Hong Yu. An Inevitable Choice to Promote the Scientific Development of China's Education—Also on the Pattern Transition of Educational Development (*sic*). *Education Research*, 2012(1).

Zhen, Xuejun. On Liberalizing Investment in Education and Its Outlook (*sic.*). *China Opening Journal*, 2014(2).

Zheng, Bingwen. *China Pension Development Report 2014—Transformation to the Nominal Account System*. Beijing: Economy and Management Publishing House, 2014.

Zhou, Zixun. New Urbanization Could Become China's Economic Growth Momentum. *China Economic Times*, 22 December 2014.

Zhou, Xiaohua. Bringing Private Higher Education Institutions into the Scope of National Financial Security. *Changsha Evening News*, 8 March 2015.

Zhou, Di. Aging Population Is Troubling China. *Democracy and Law Times*, 24 November 2015.

Zhu, Jinsong. Empirical Research on Education Level in China's Rural Areas and Urbanization Rate. *Commercial Times*, 2010(14).

Zhu, Min. How to Give Better Play to Urbanization's Role to Boost Consumption. *China Economic Times*, 13 May 2013.

Zhu, Yongxin. Creating a Fair and Friendly Institutional Environment for Private Education. *Henan Education* (*Basic Education Edition*), 2014(10).

The manufacturer's authorised representative in the EU is Springer Nature Customer Service Centre GmbH, Europaplatz 3, 69115 Heidelberg, Germany. If you have any concerns regarding our products, please contact ProductSafety@springernature.com

Printed and bound by CPI Group (UK) Ltd, Croydon, CR0 4YY
25/09/2026
02222881-0008